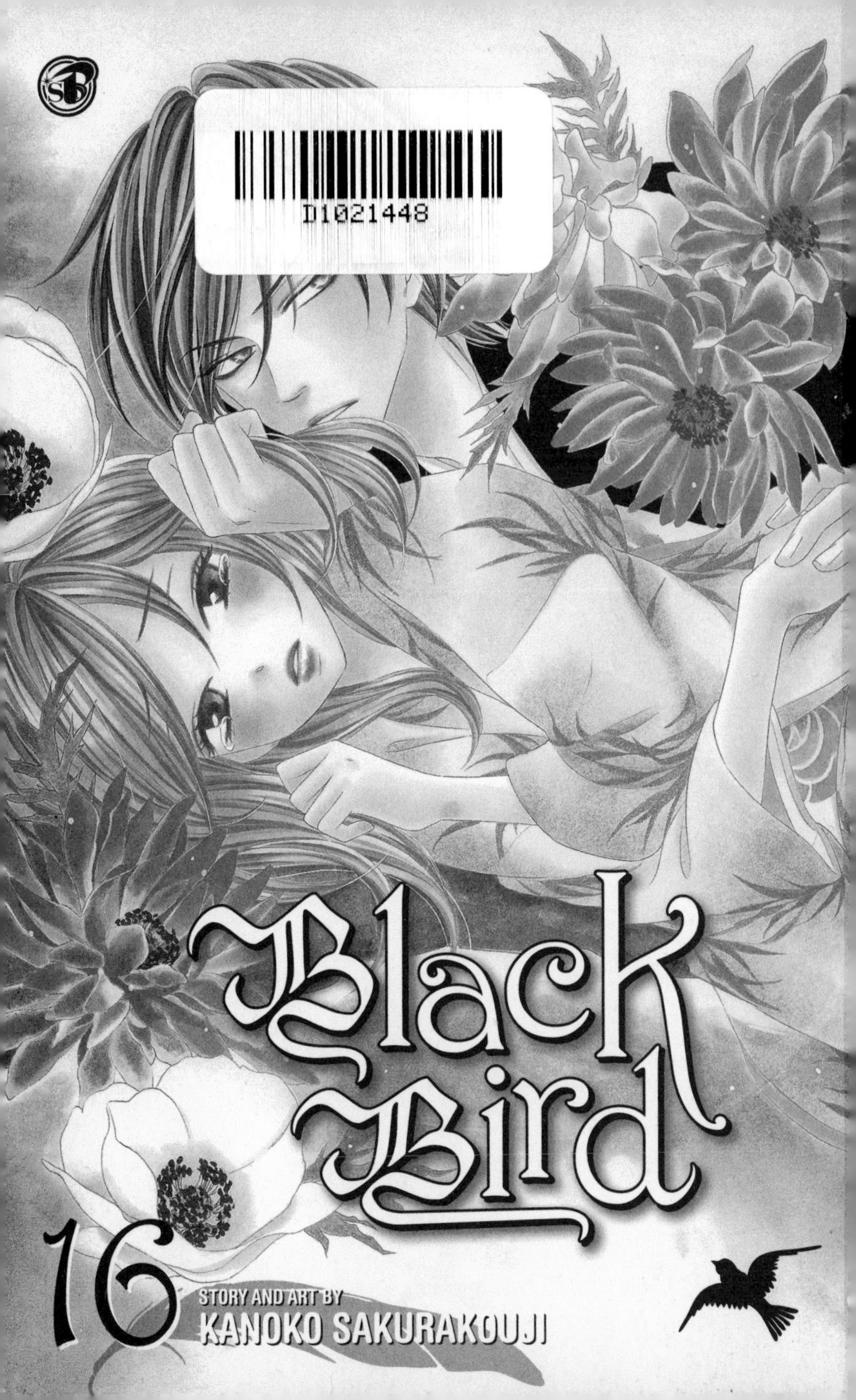

Black Bird
16
STORY AND ART BY
KANOKO SAKURAKOUJI

Black Bird

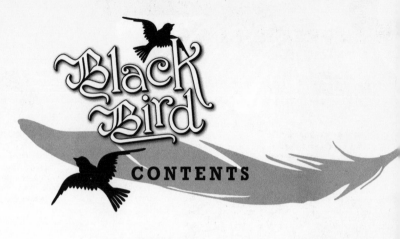

CONTENTS

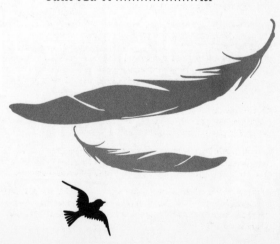

CHARACTERS

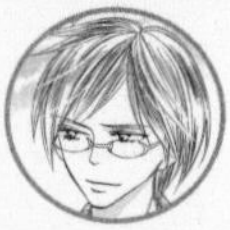

TADANOBU KUZUNOHA
Close childhood friend of Kyo's. Current leader of Kitsune clan.

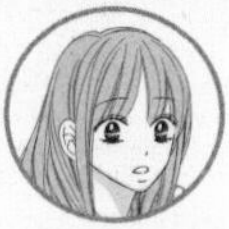

AYAME
Wife of Sagami, Member of the Eight Daitengu.

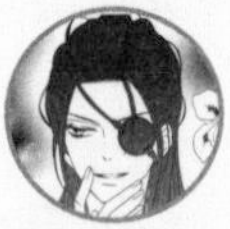

SHO USUI
Kyo's older brother and ex-member of the Eigh Daitengu. He is also kno as Sojo. His attempted cc failed and he later died a duel against Kyo.

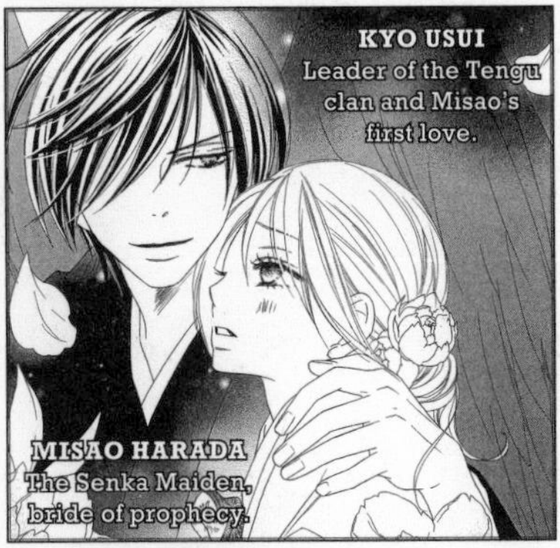
KYO USUI
Leader of the Tengu clan and Misao's first love.
MISAO HARADA
The Senka Maiden, bride of prophecy.

THE EIGHT DAITENGU
Kyo's bodyguards. Their names designate their official posts.

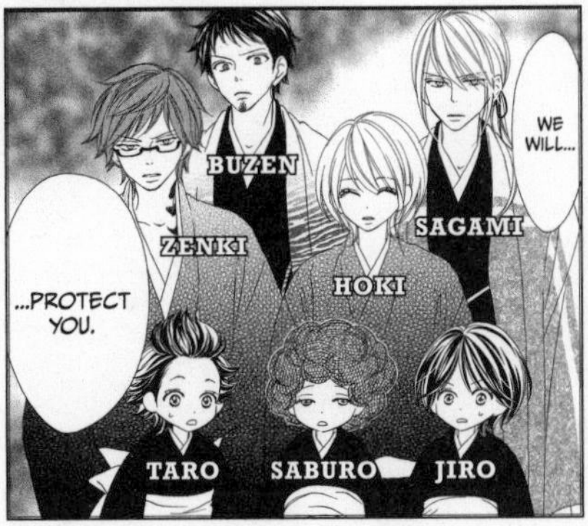
WE WILL...
...PROTECT YOU.
BUZEN
SAGAMI
ZENKI
HOKI
TARO
SABURO
JIRO

STORY THUS FAR

Misao can see spirits and demons, and her childhood sweetheart Kyo has been protecting her since she was little.

"Someday, I'll come for you, I promise." Kyo reappears the day before Misao's 16th birthday to tell her, "Your 16th birthday marks 'open season' on you." She is the Senka Maiden, and if a demon drinks her blood, he is granted a long life. If he eats her flesh, he gains eternal youth. And if he makes her his bride, his clan will prosper…And Kyo is a *tengu*, a crow demon, with his sights firmly set on her.

Kyo avoided sleeping with Misao because he knew that sex with a demon is somehow dangerous for the Senka Maiden, but when poison nearly killed him, he finally gave in and took Misao.

Now that Kyo's powers have no equal, his older brother Sho, presumed dead, reappears. After a brutal battle, Kyo finally defeats Sho. With his last breath, Sho ominously predicts that Kyo will end up killing Misao.

Not long after, Misao's pregnancy comes to light. The Senka Roku, record of the fate of the previous Senka Maiden, is still missing. But a surviving Nue clan member tells them that "…the Senka Maiden will die the instant her baby is born"!

KYO
hand-
riding
size ♥

Black Bird

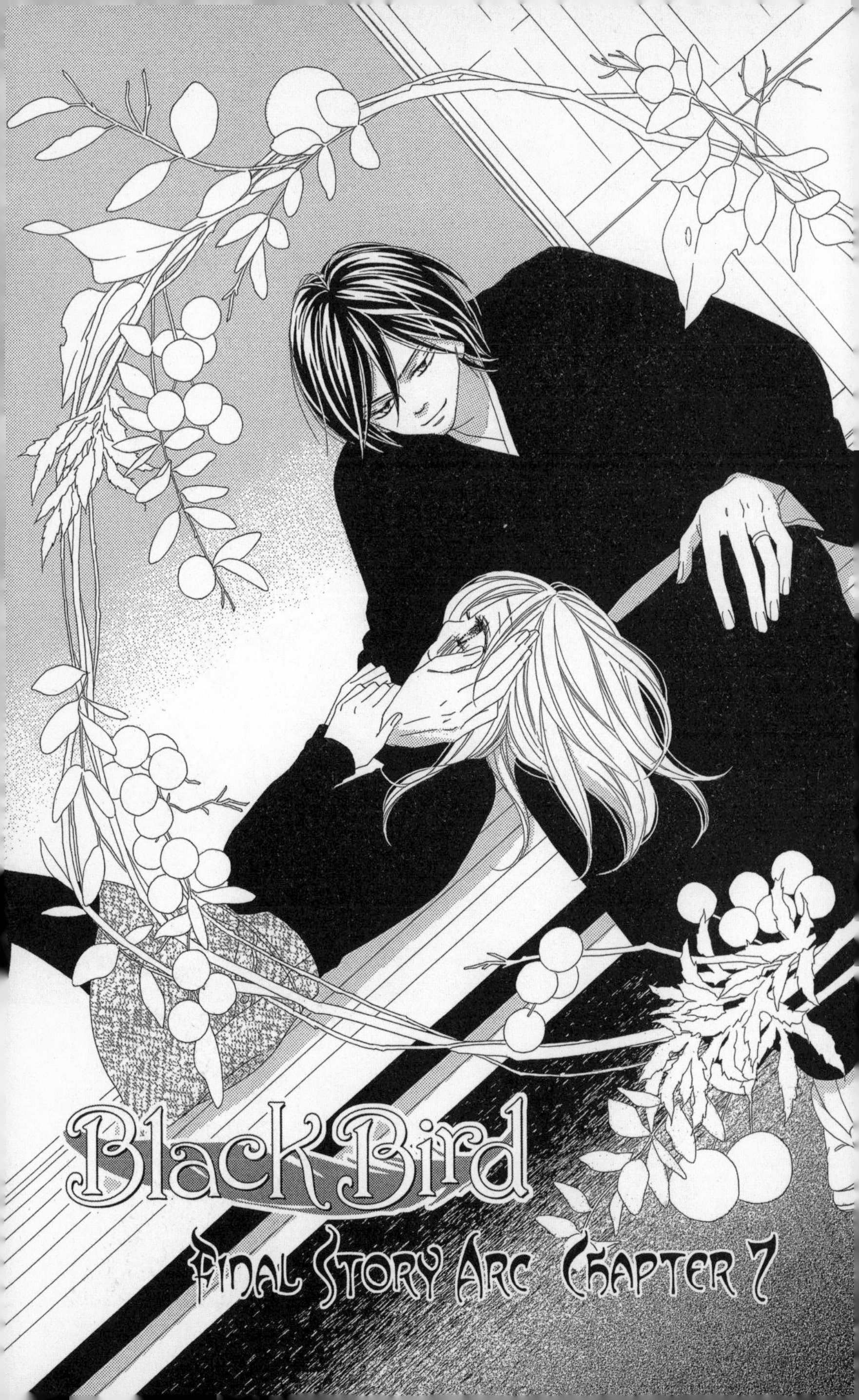
Black Bird
Final Story Arc Chapter 7

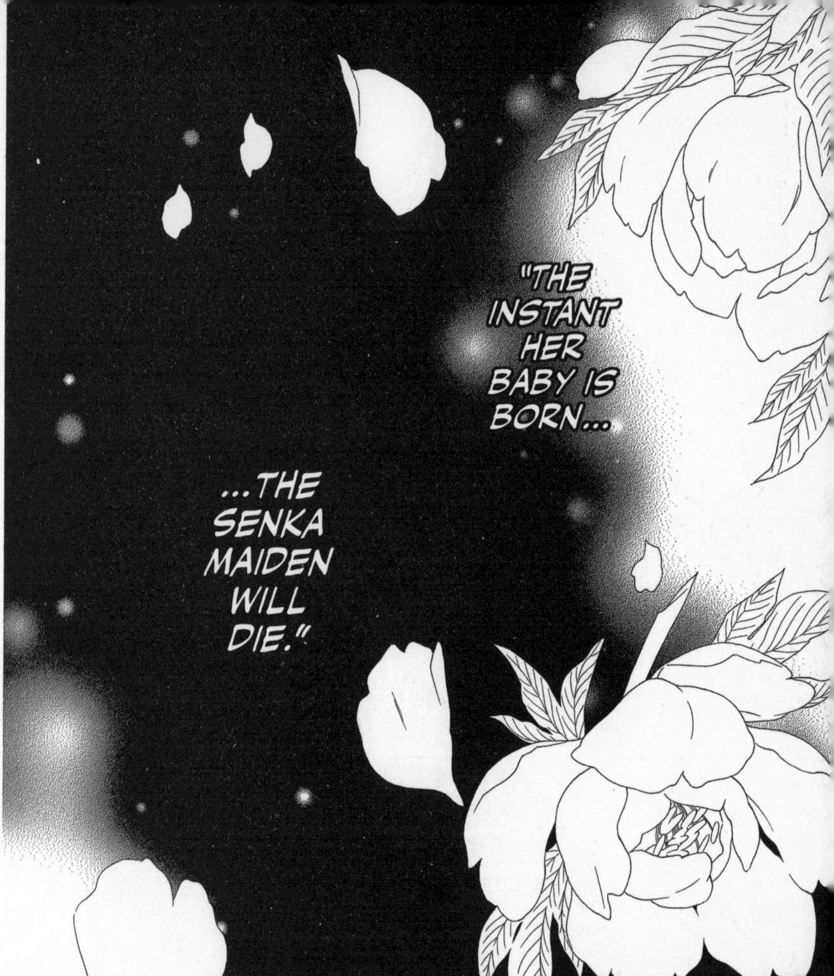
"THE INSTANT HER BABY IS BORN...
...THE SENKA MAIDEN WILL DIE."

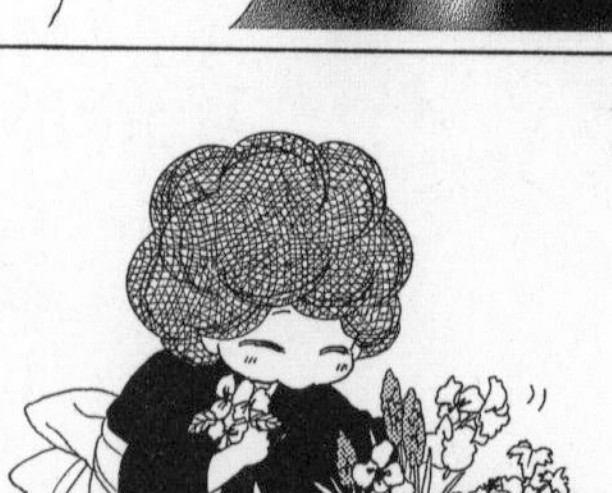

Hello, Sakurakouji here.
Thank you very much for
picking up volume 16!

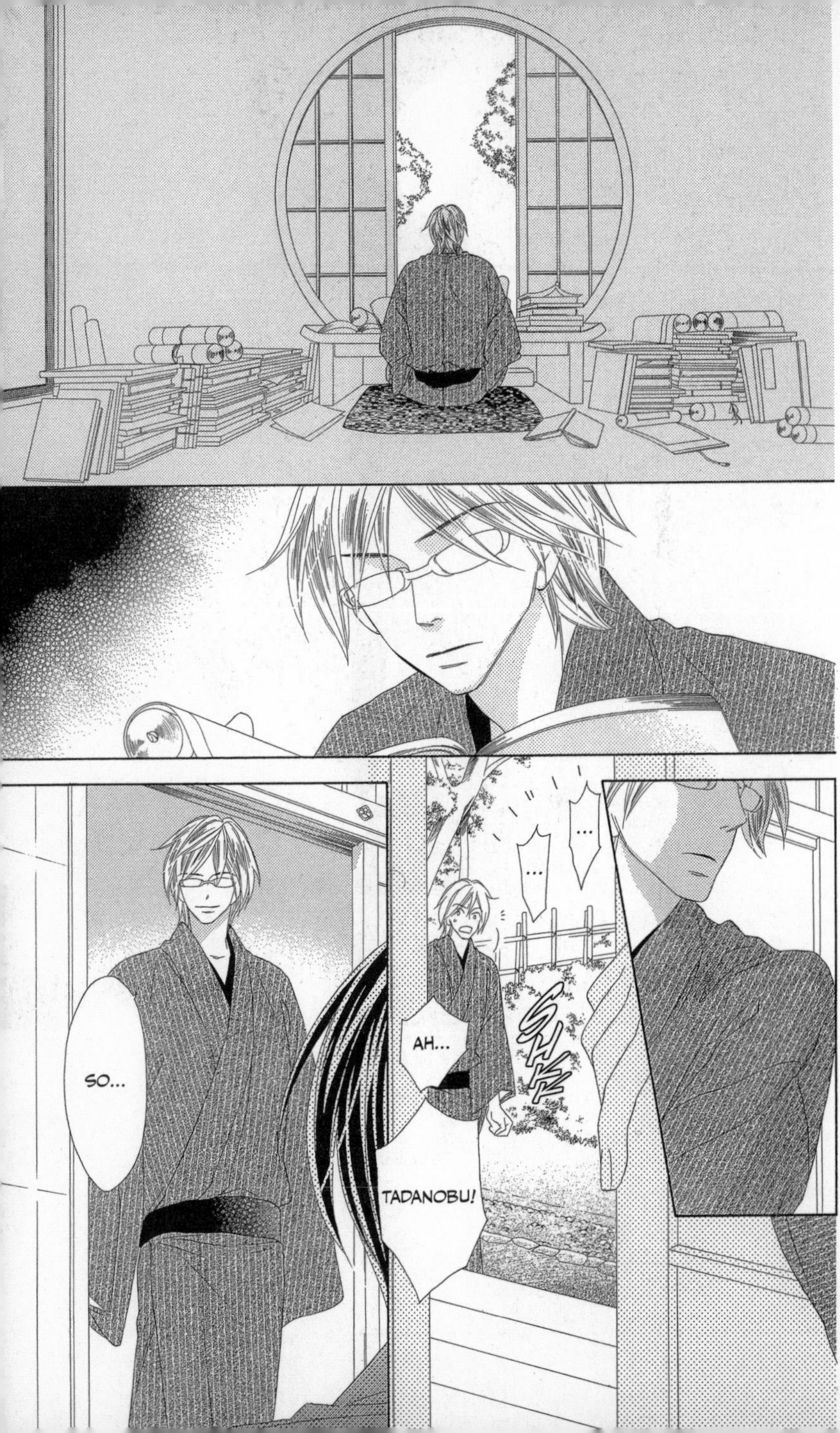
...
...
SHKK
AH...
TADANOBU!
SO...

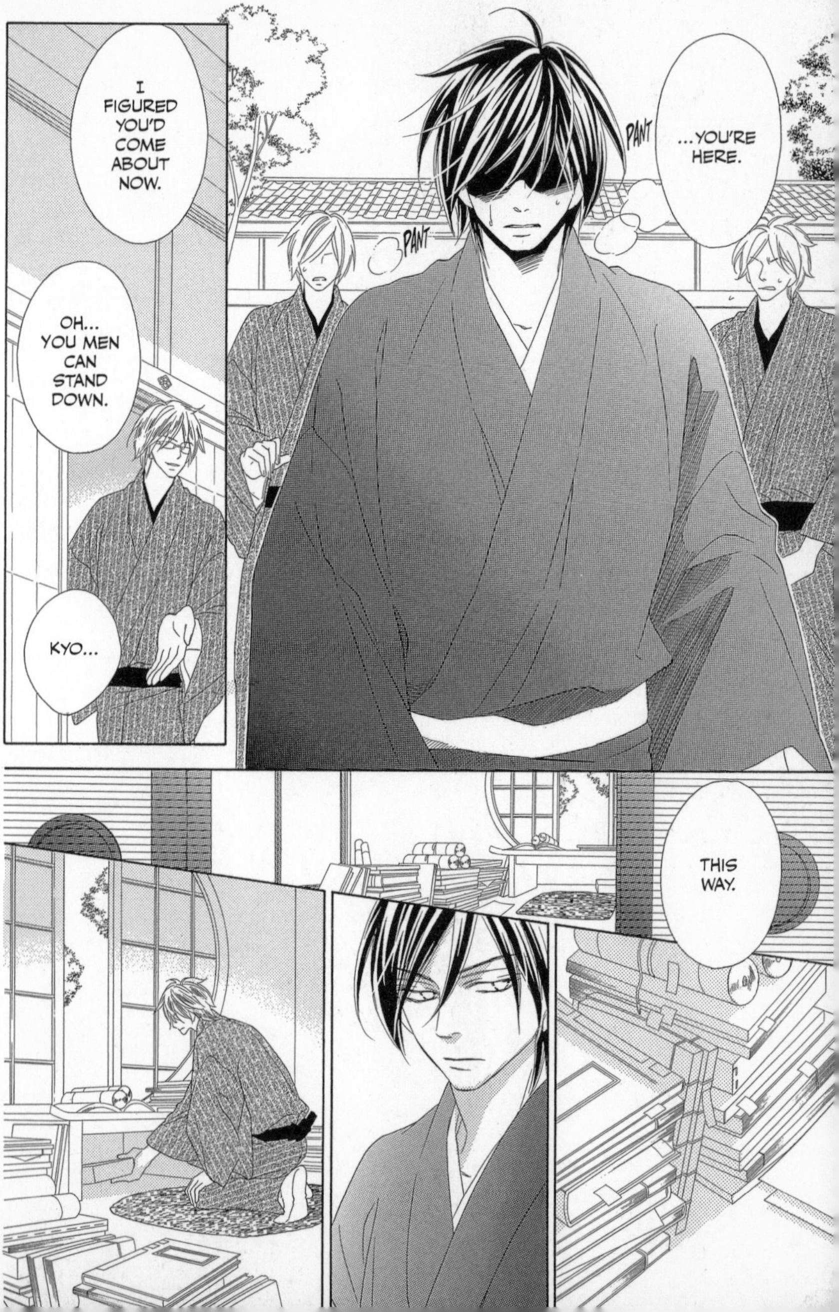
...YOU'RE HERE.
PANT
PANT
I FIGURED YOU'D COME ABOUT NOW.
OH... YOU MEN CAN STAND DOWN.
KYO...
THIS WAY.

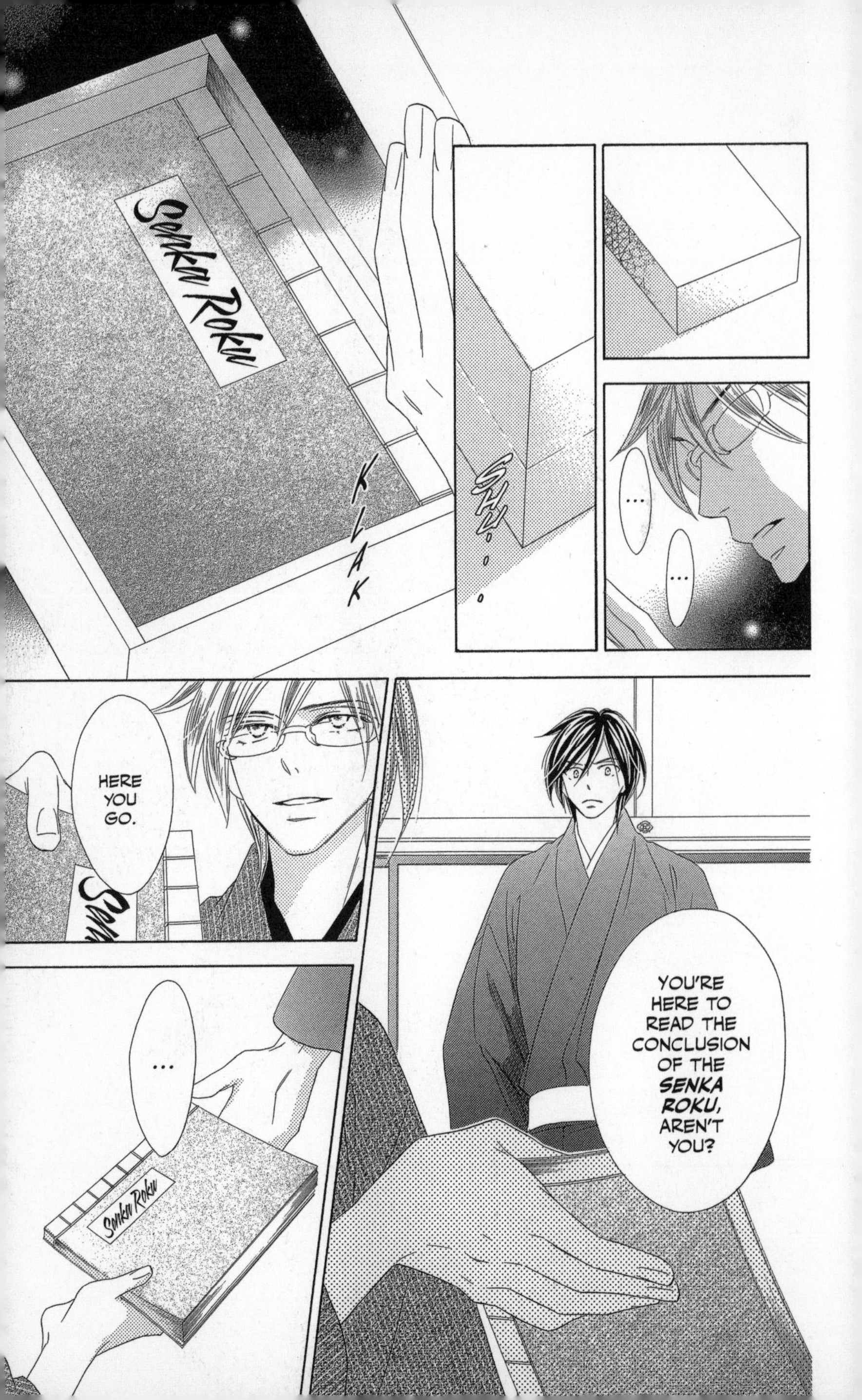
...
...
SHU...
KLAK
Senku Roku
YOU'RE HERE TO READ THE CONCLUSION OF THE SENKA ROKU, AREN'T YOU?
HERE YOU GO.
...
Senku Roku

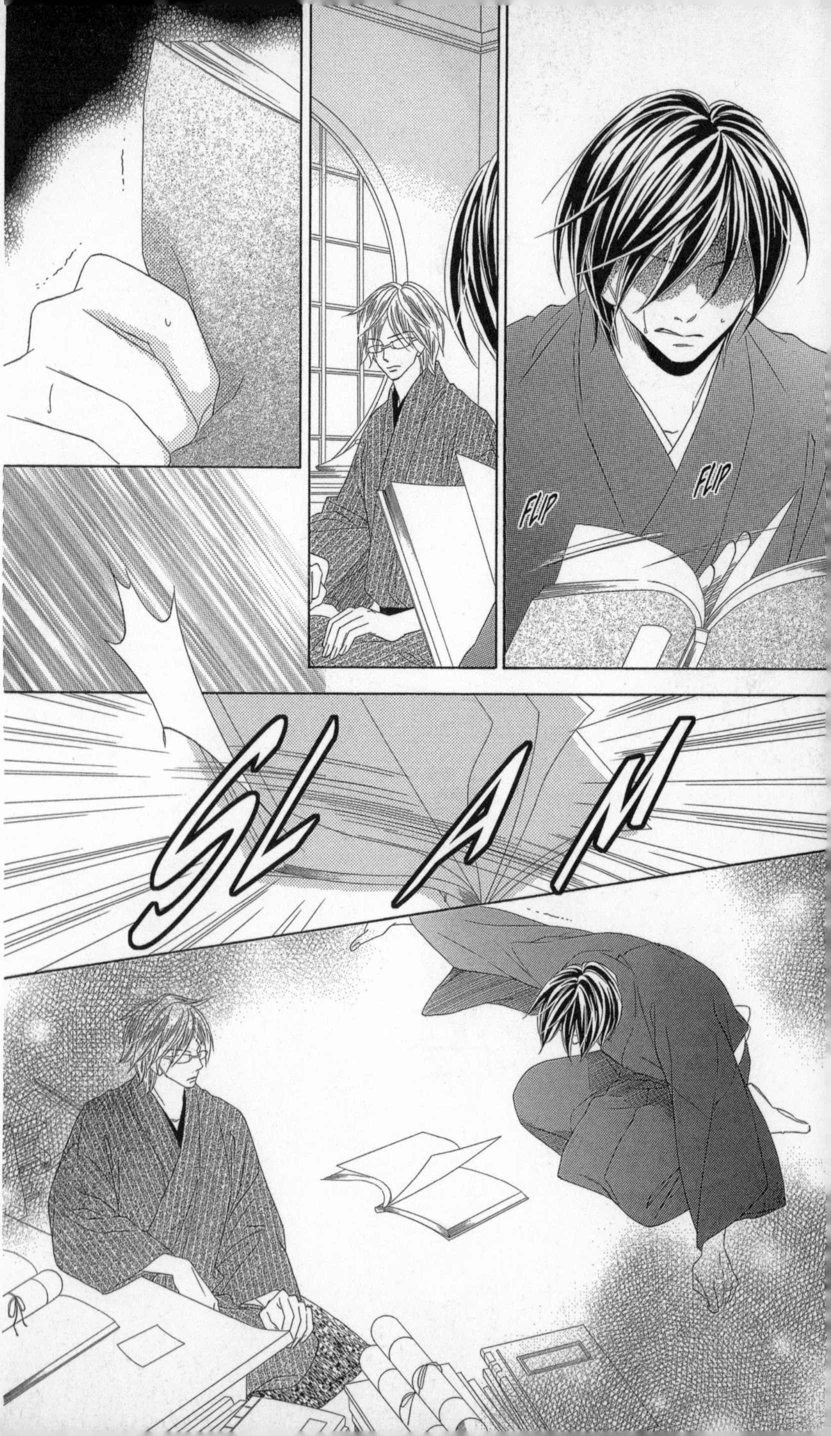
FLIP
FLIP
SLAM

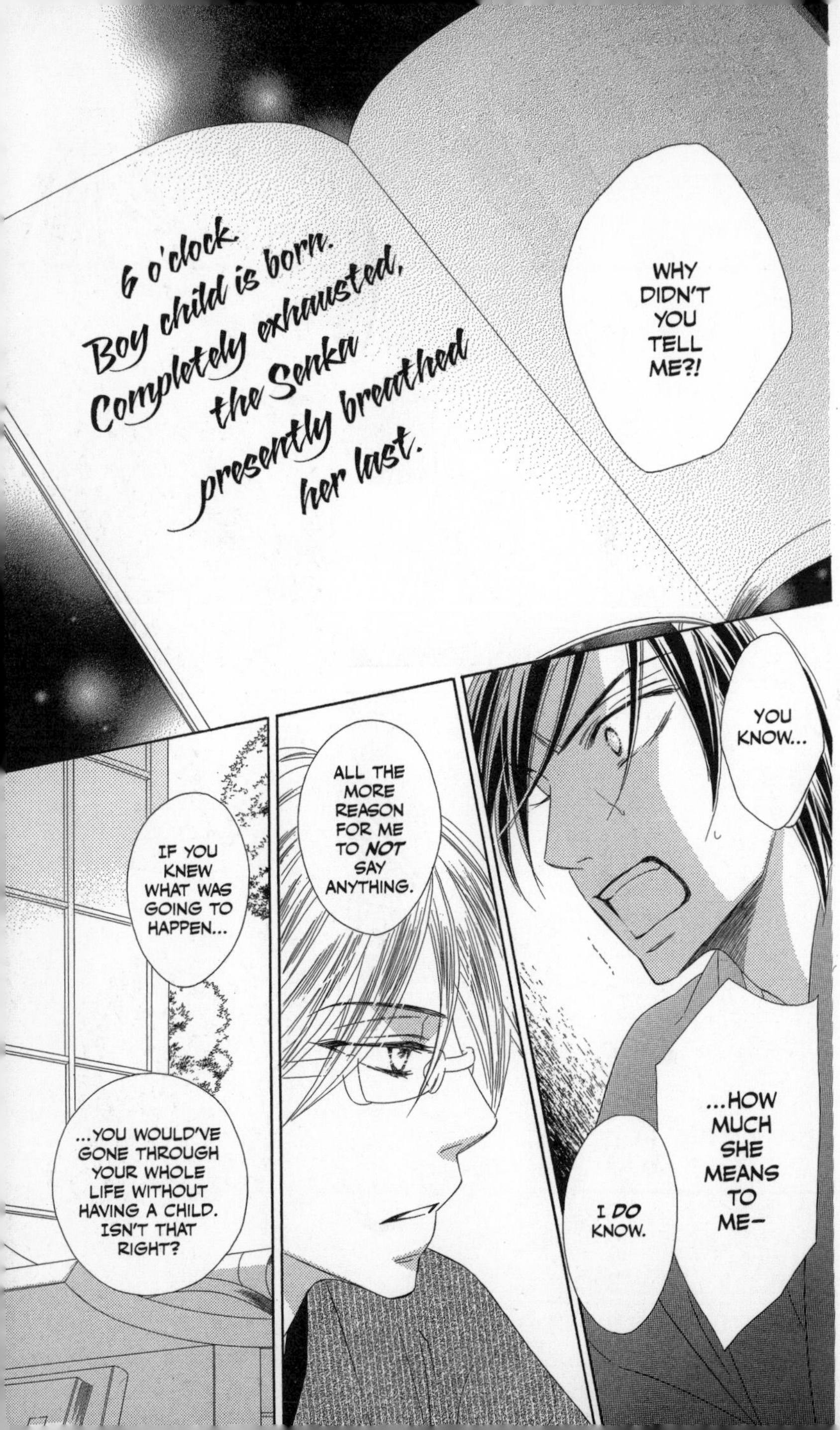
WHY DIDN'T YOU TELL ME?!
6 o'clock. Boy child is born. Completely exhausted, the Senka presently breathed her last.
YOU KNOW...
...HOW MUCH SHE MEANS TO ME—
I *DO* KNOW.
ALL THE MORE REASON FOR ME TO *NOT* SAY ANYTHING.
IF YOU KNEW WHAT WAS GOING TO HAPPEN...
...YOU WOULD'VE GONE THROUGH YOUR WHOLE LIFE WITHOUT HAVING A CHILD. ISN'T THAT RIGHT?

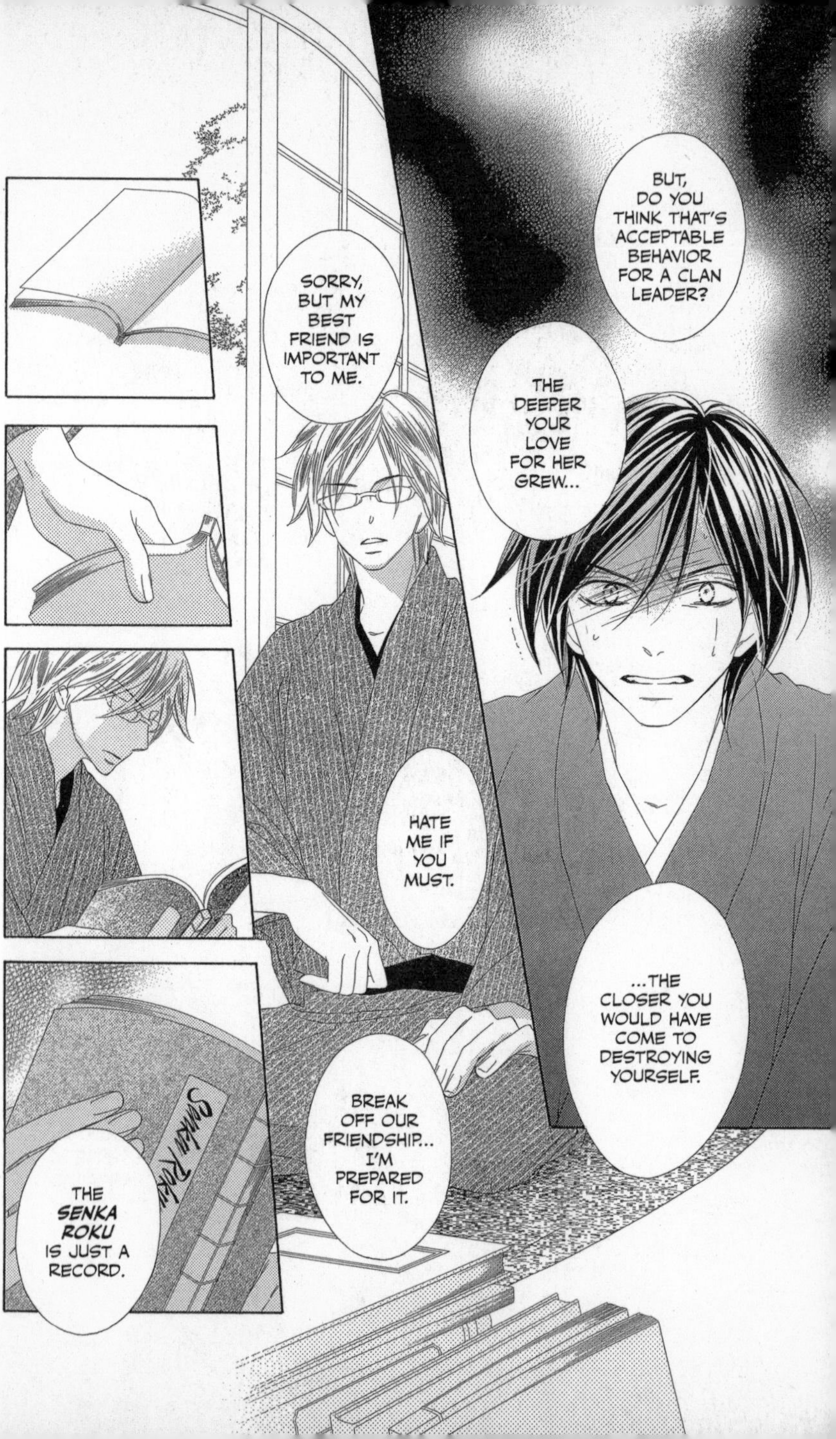
BUT, DO YOU THINK THAT'S ACCEPTABLE BEHAVIOR FOR A CLAN LEADER?
THE DEEPER YOUR LOVE FOR HER GREW...
...THE CLOSER YOU WOULD HAVE COME TO DESTROYING YOURSELF.
SORRY, BUT MY BEST FRIEND IS IMPORTANT TO ME.
HATE ME IF YOU MUST.
BREAK OFF OUR FRIENDSHIP... I'M PREPARED FOR IT.
Senka Roku
THE SENKA ROKU IS JUST A RECORD.

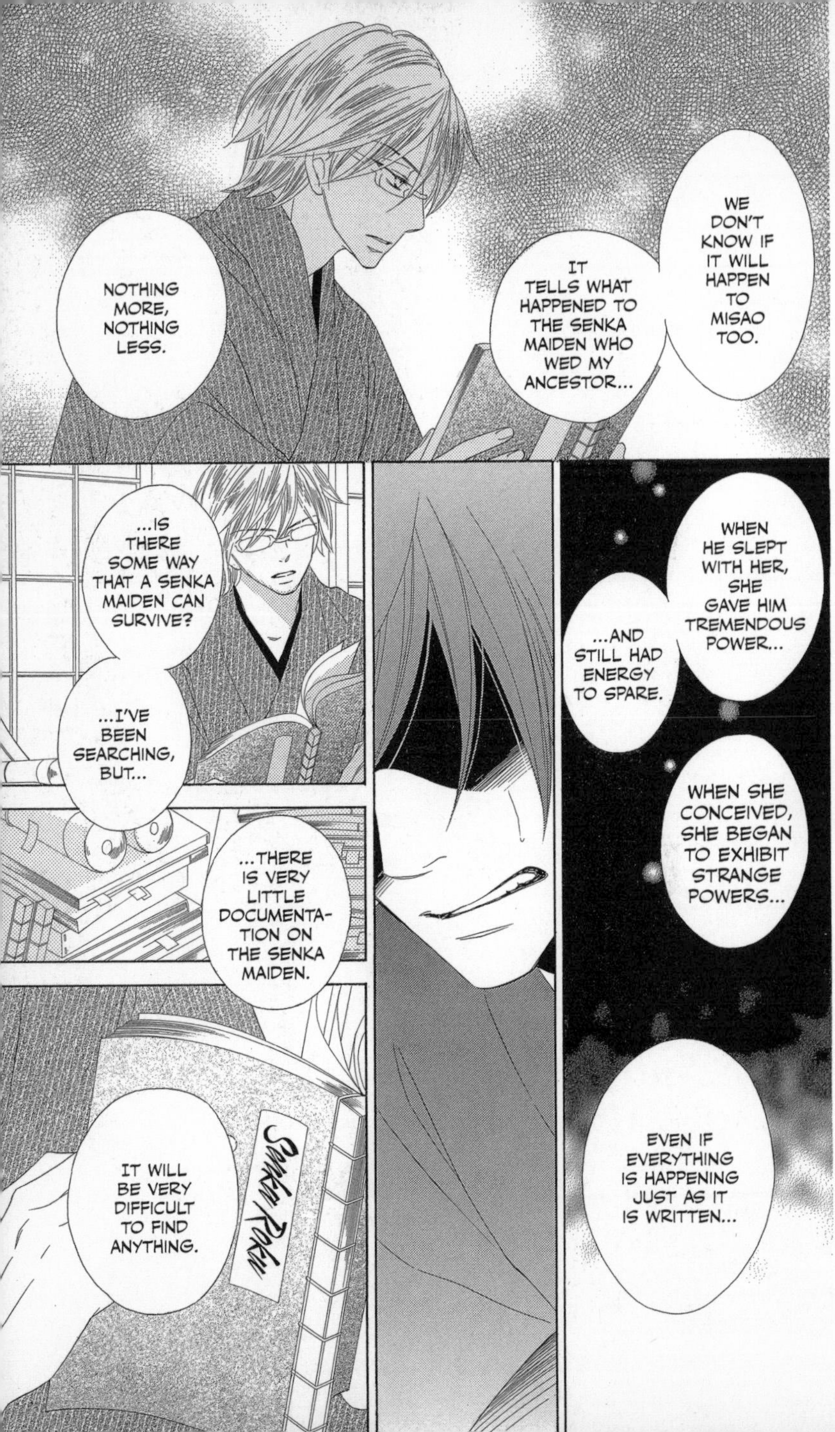
WE DON'T KNOW IF IT WILL HAPPEN TO MISAO TOO.
IT TELLS WHAT HAPPENED TO THE SENKA MAIDEN WHO WED MY ANCESTOR...
NOTHING MORE, NOTHING LESS.
WHEN HE SLEPT WITH HER, SHE GAVE HIM TREMENDOUS POWER...
...AND STILL HAD ENERGY TO SPARE.
WHEN SHE CONCEIVED, SHE BEGAN TO EXHIBIT STRANGE POWERS...
EVEN IF EVERYTHING IS HAPPENING JUST AS IT IS WRITTEN...
...IS THERE SOME WAY THAT A SENKA MAIDEN CAN SURVIVE?
...I'VE BEEN SEARCHING, BUT...
...THERE IS VERY LITTLE DOCUMENTATION ON THE SENKA MAIDEN.
IT WILL BE VERY DIFFICULT TO FIND ANYTHING.
Senka Roku

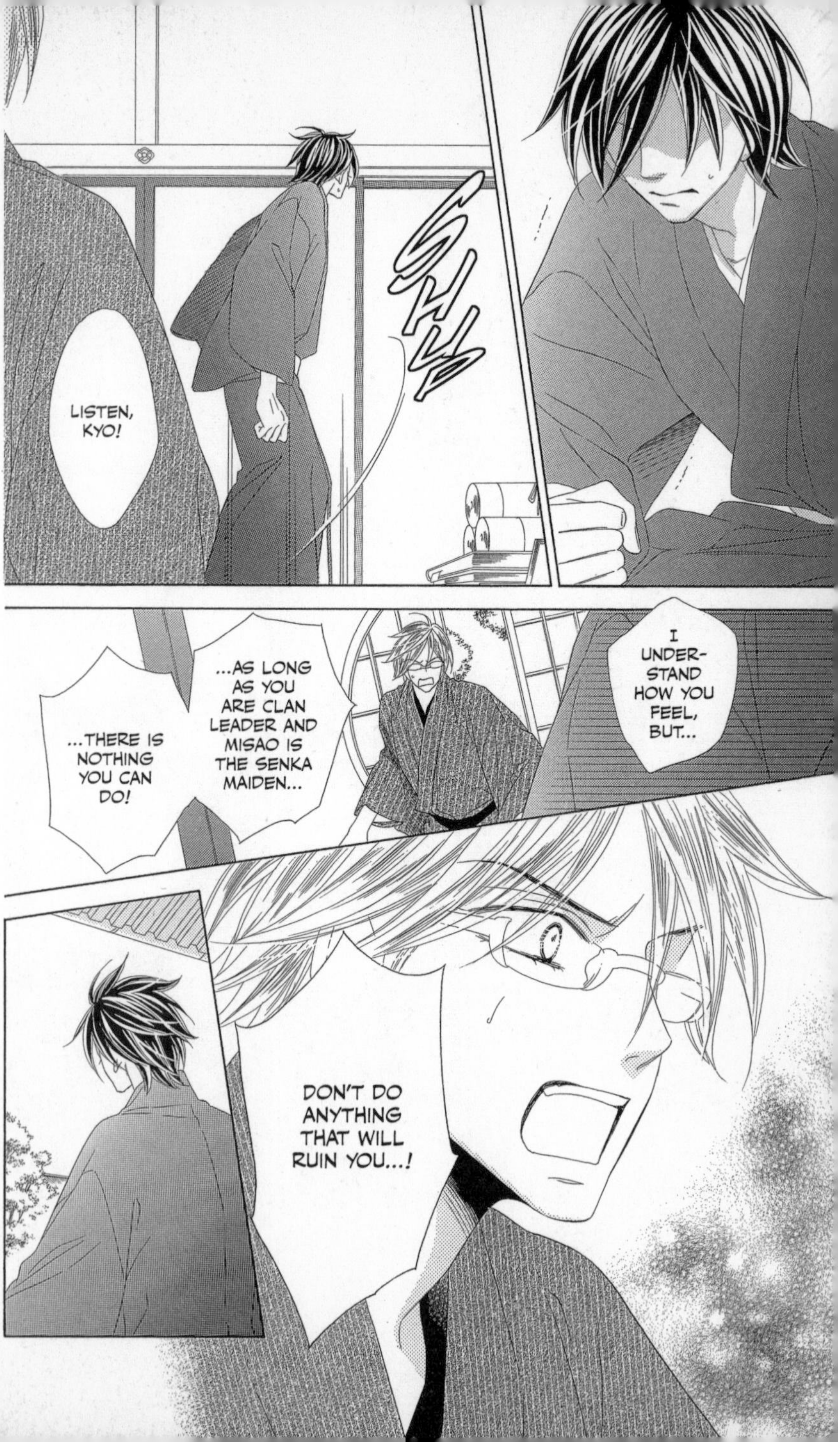

GSHH
LISTEN, KYO!
I UNDER-STAND HOW YOU FEEL, BUT...
...AS LONG AS YOU ARE CLAN LEADER AND MISAO IS THE SENKA MAIDEN...
...THERE IS NOTHING YOU CAN DO!
DON'T DO ANYTHING THAT WILL RUIN YOU...!

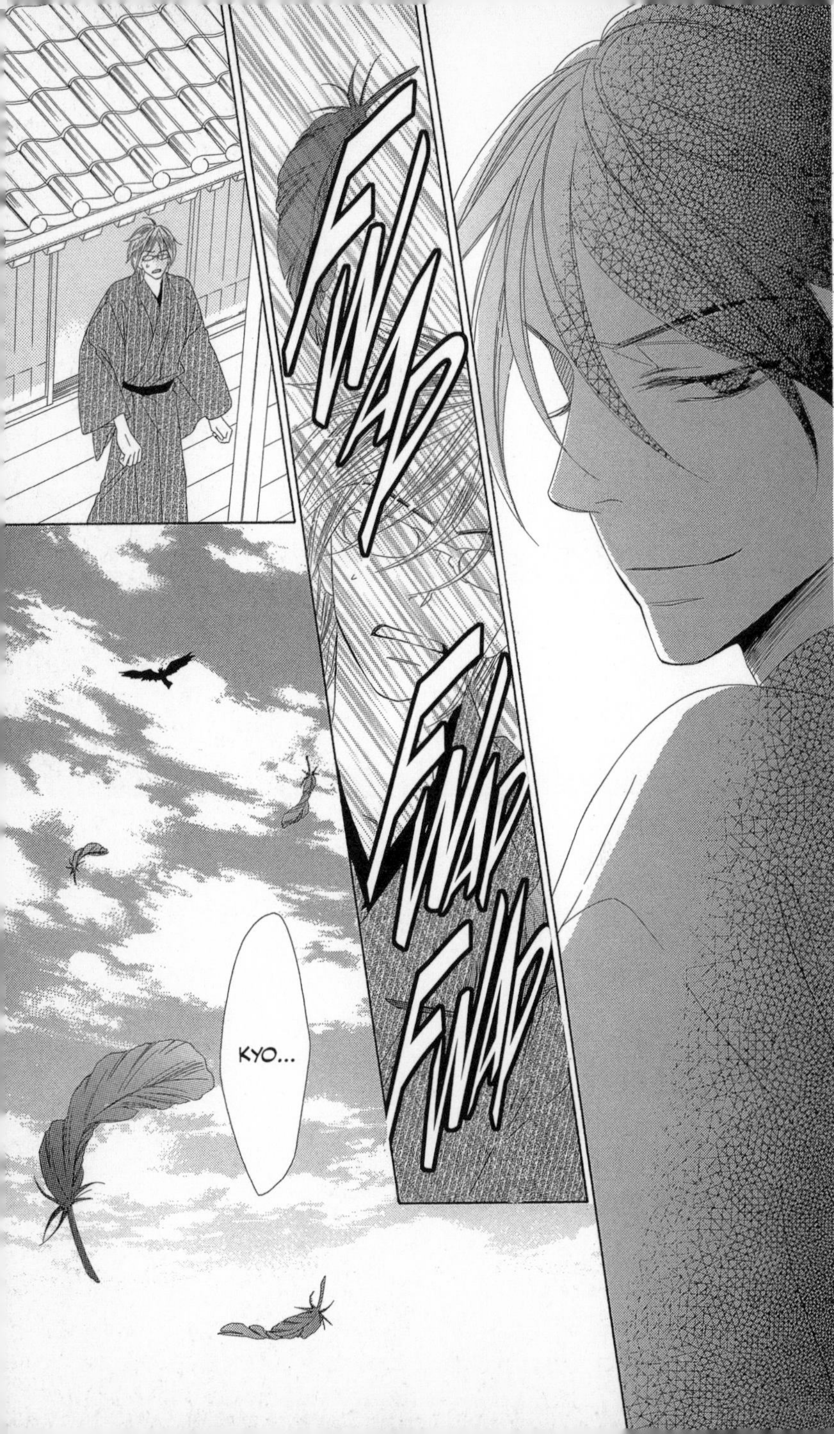
FWAP
FWAP FWAP
KYO...

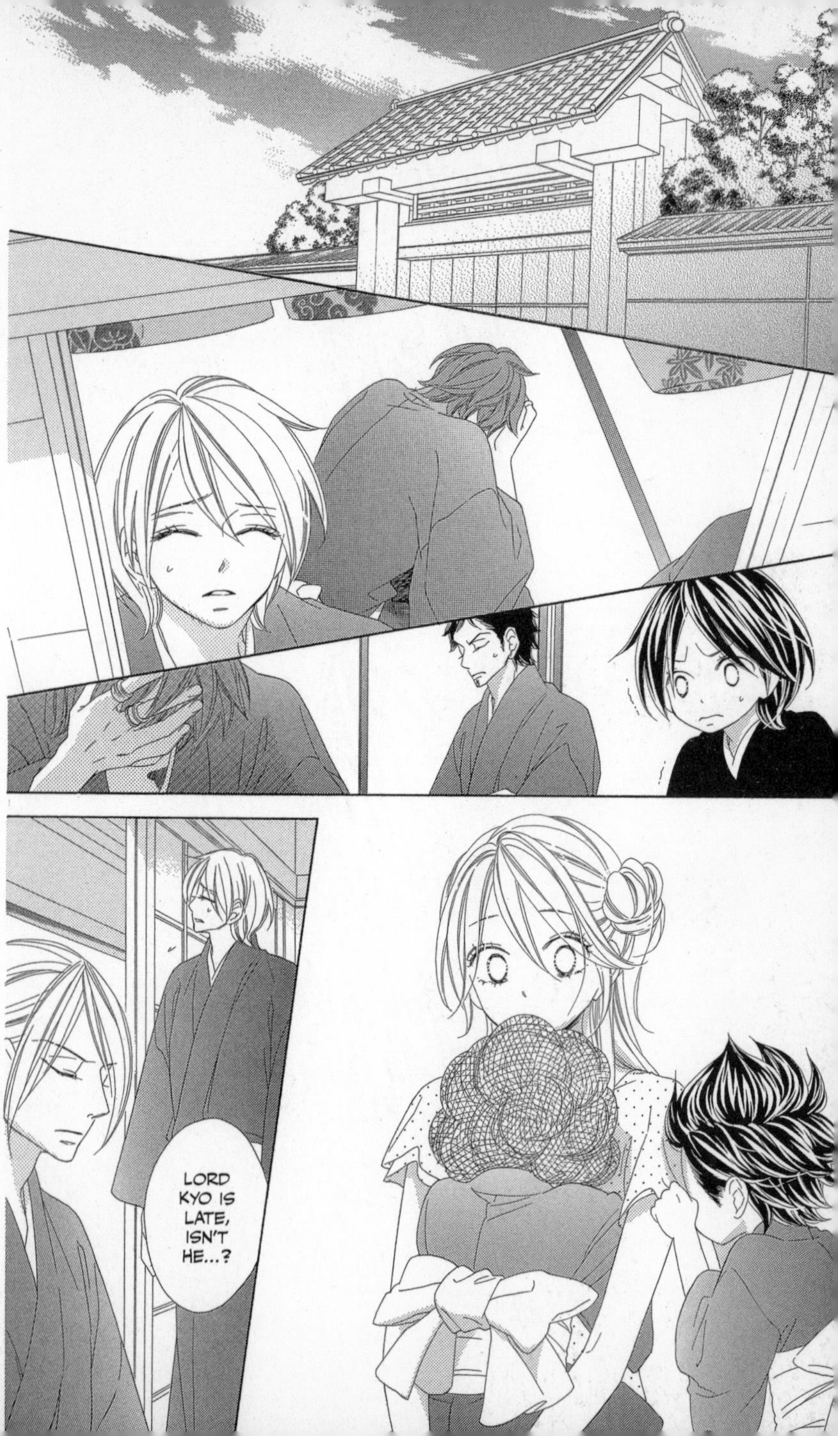
LORD KYO IS LATE, ISN'T HE...?

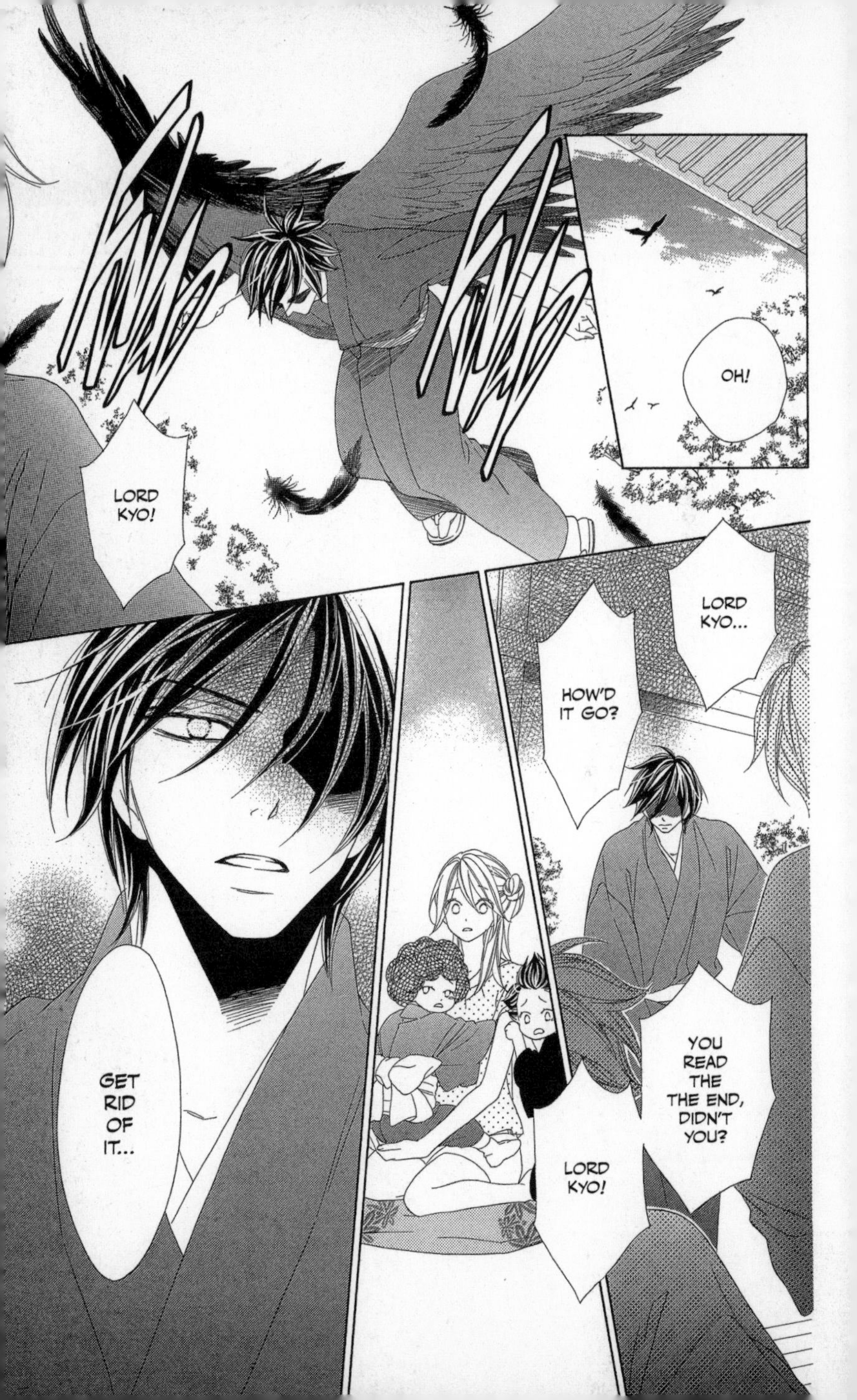
OH!
LORD KYO!
LORD KYO...
HOW'D IT GO?
YOU READ THE THE END, DIDN'T YOU?
LORD KYO!
GET RID OF IT...

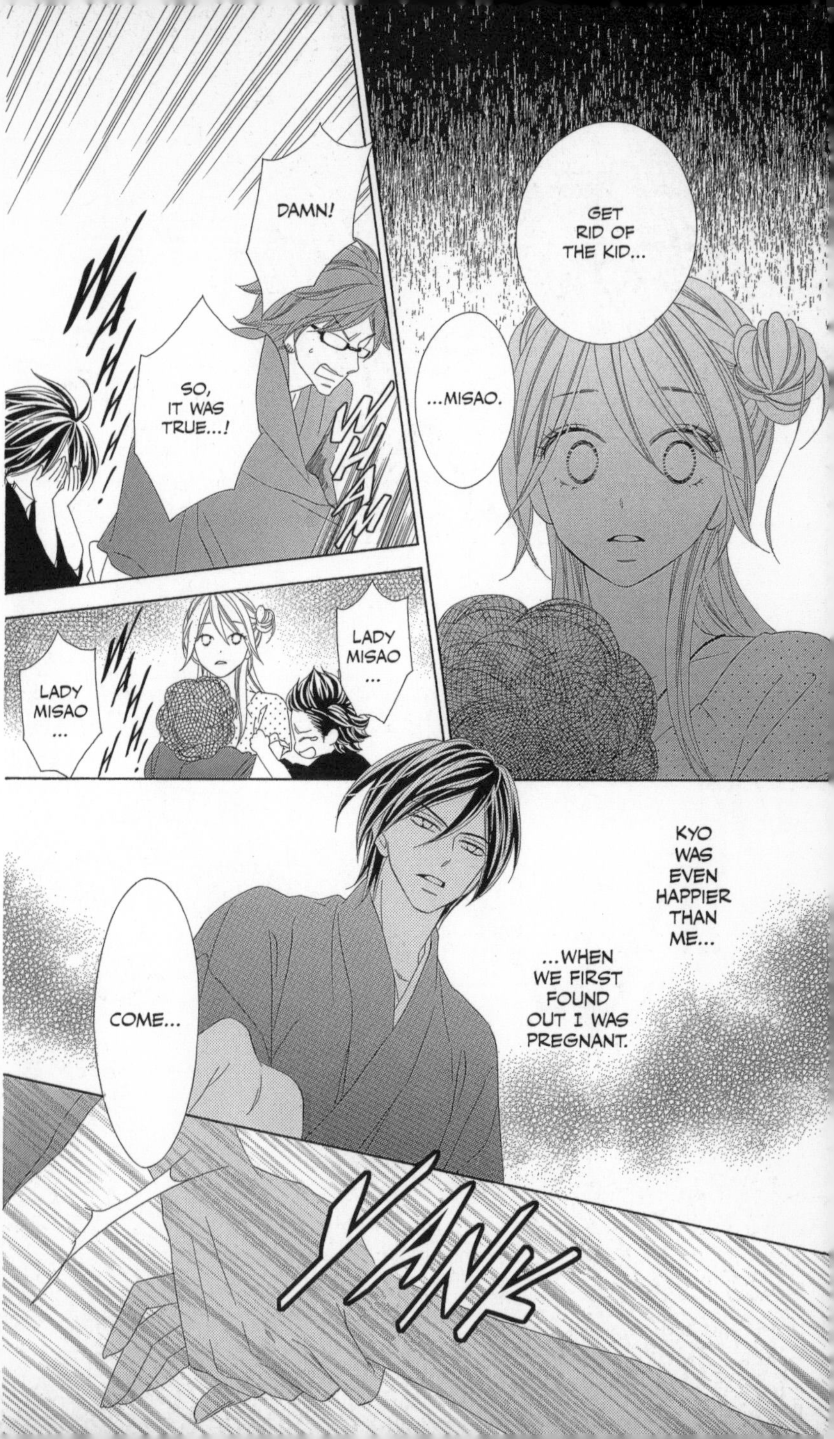
GET RID OF THE KID...
...MISAO.
DAMN!
SO, IT WAS TRUE...!
WAHHHH!
WHAM
LADY MISAO...
LADY MISAO...
WAHH!
KYO WAS EVEN HAPPIER THAN ME...
...WHEN WE FIRST FOUND OUT I WAS PREGNANT.
COME...
YANK

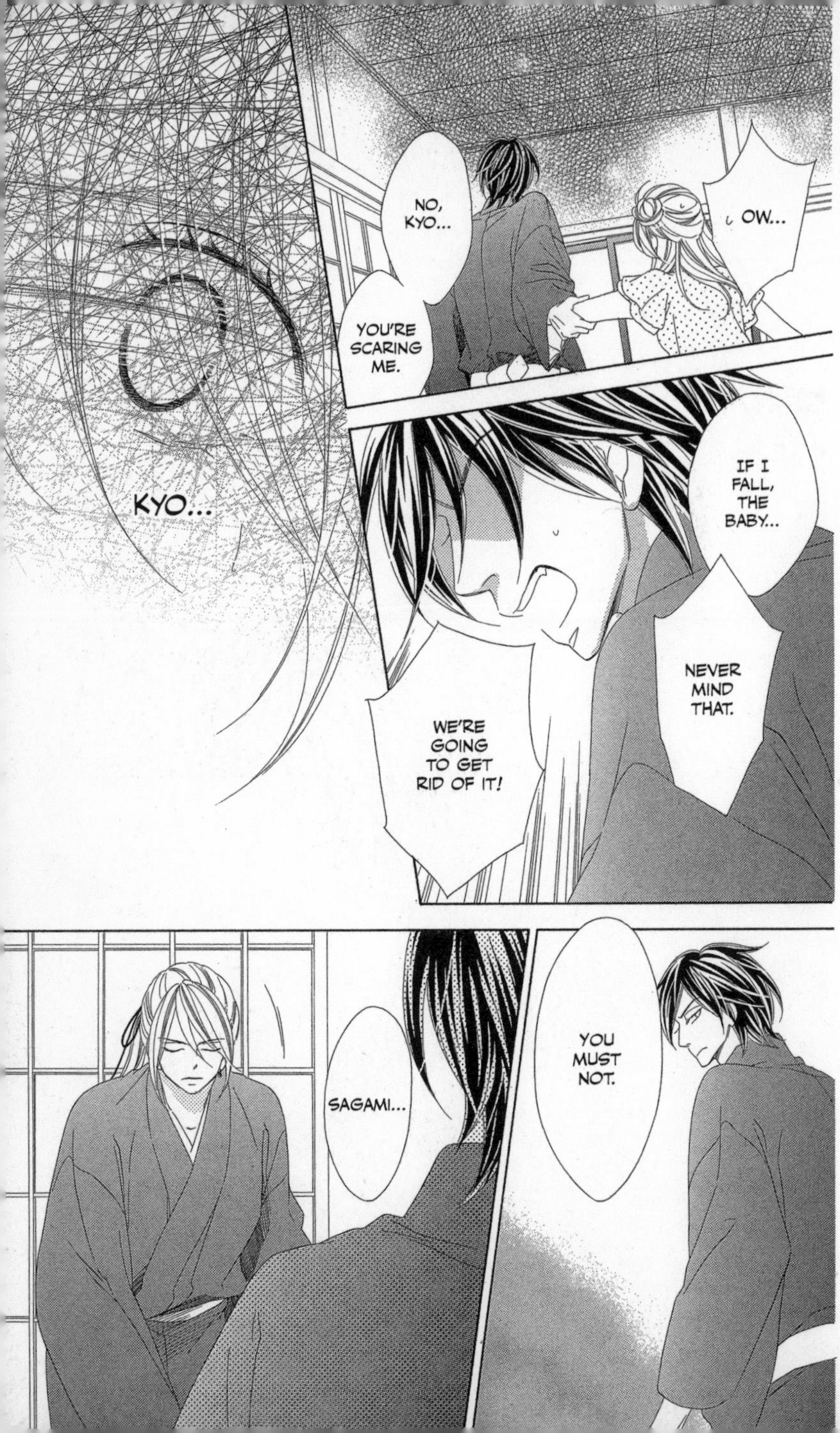
OW...
NO, KYO...
YOU'RE SCARING ME.
IF I FALL, THE BABY...
NEVER MIND THAT.
WE'RE GOING TO GET RID OF IT!
KYO...
YOU MUST NOT.
SAGAMI...

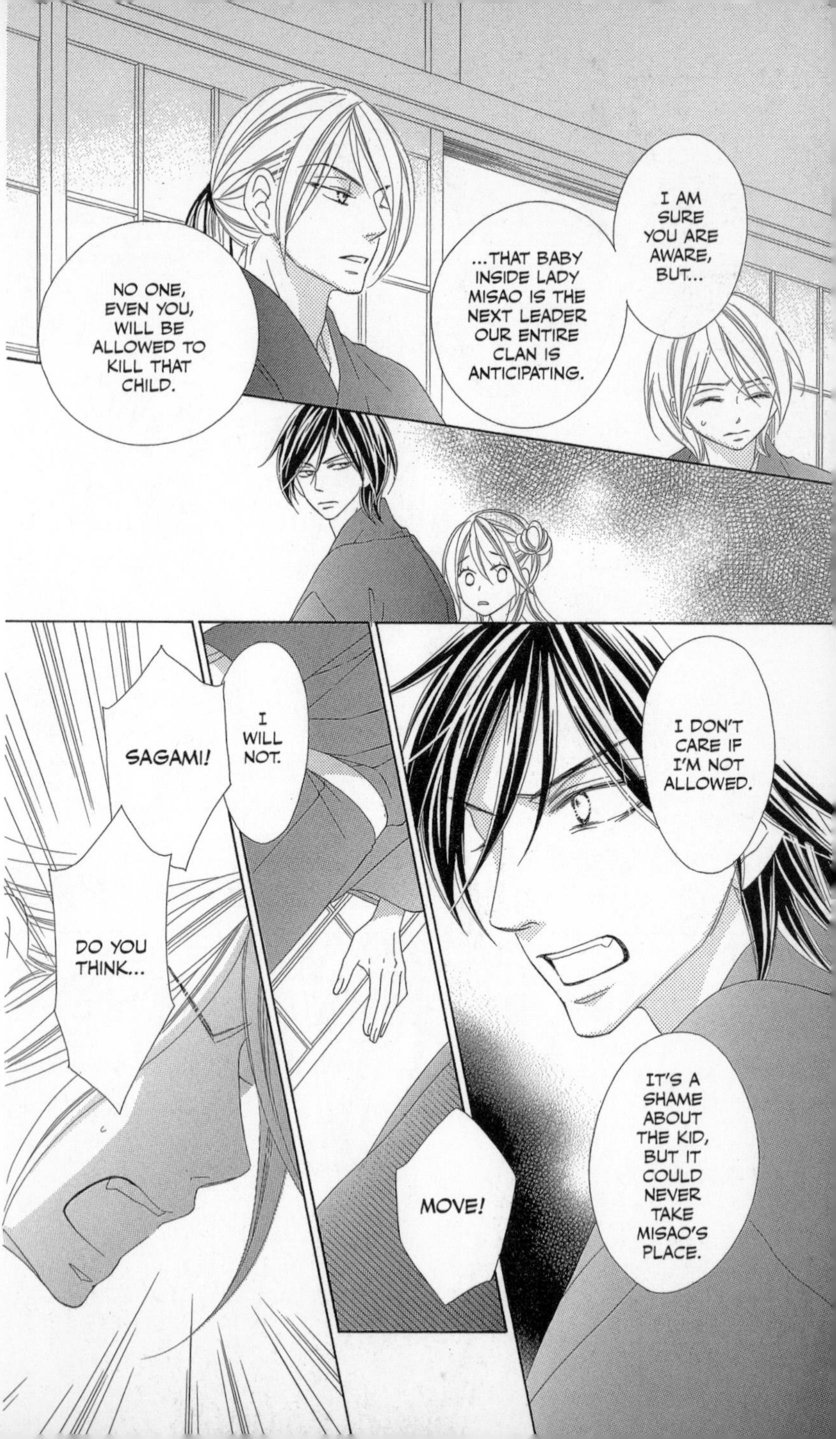
I AM SURE YOU ARE AWARE, BUT...
...THAT BABY INSIDE LADY MISAO IS THE NEXT LEADER OUR ENTIRE CLAN IS ANTICIPATING.
NO ONE, EVEN YOU, WILL BE ALLOWED TO KILL THAT CHILD.
I DON'T CARE IF I'M NOT ALLOWED.
IT'S A SHAME ABOUT THE KID, BUT IT COULD NEVER TAKE MISAO'S PLACE.
MOVE!
I WILL NOT.
SAGAMI!
DO YOU THINK...

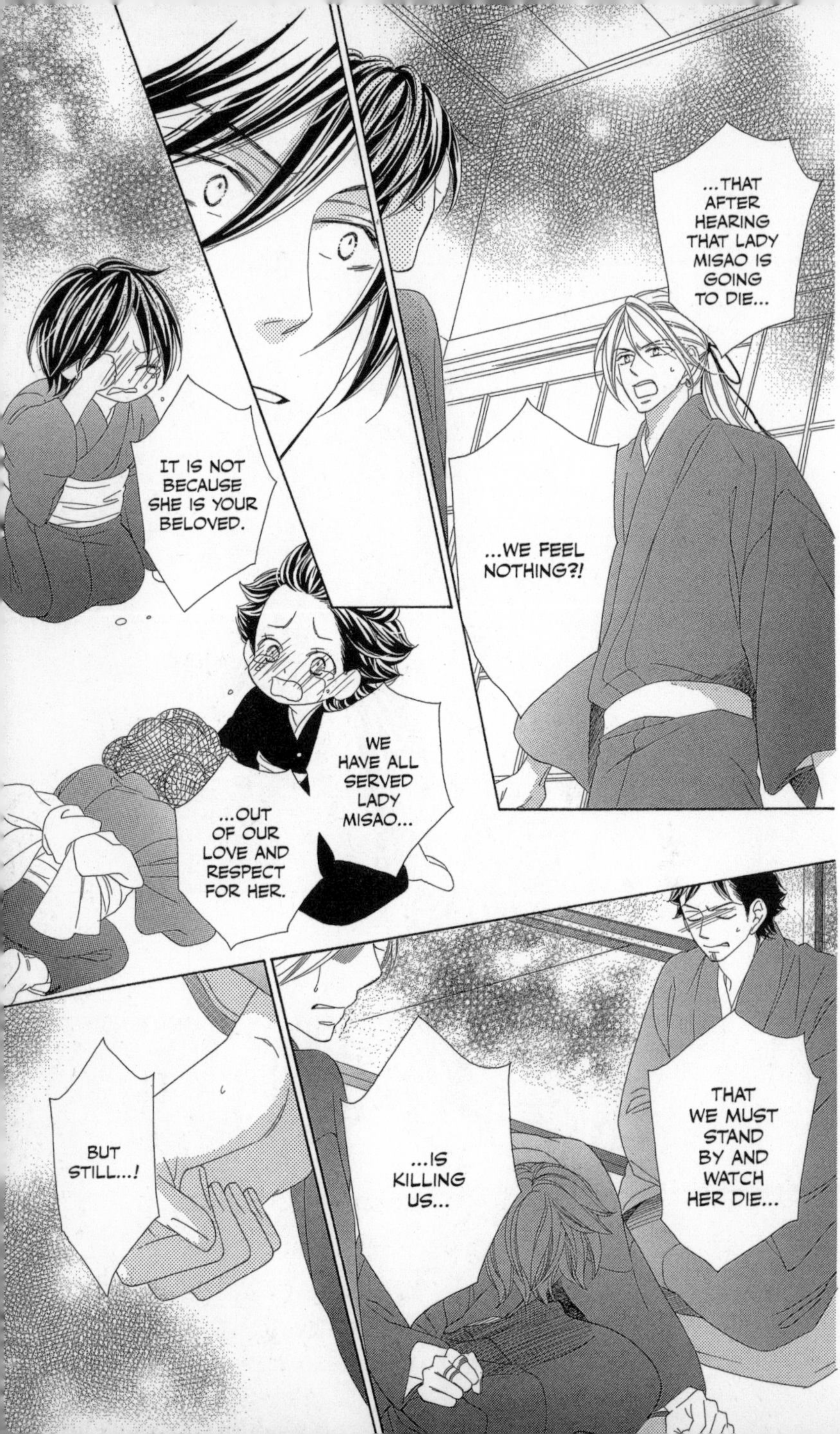
...THAT AFTER HEARING THAT LADY MISAO IS GOING TO DIE...
...WE FEEL NOTHING?!
IT IS NOT BECAUSE SHE IS YOUR BELOVED.
WE HAVE ALL SERVED LADY MISAO...
...OUT OF OUR LOVE AND RESPECT FOR HER.
THAT WE MUST STAND BY AND WATCH HER DIE...
...IS KILLING US...
BUT STILL...!

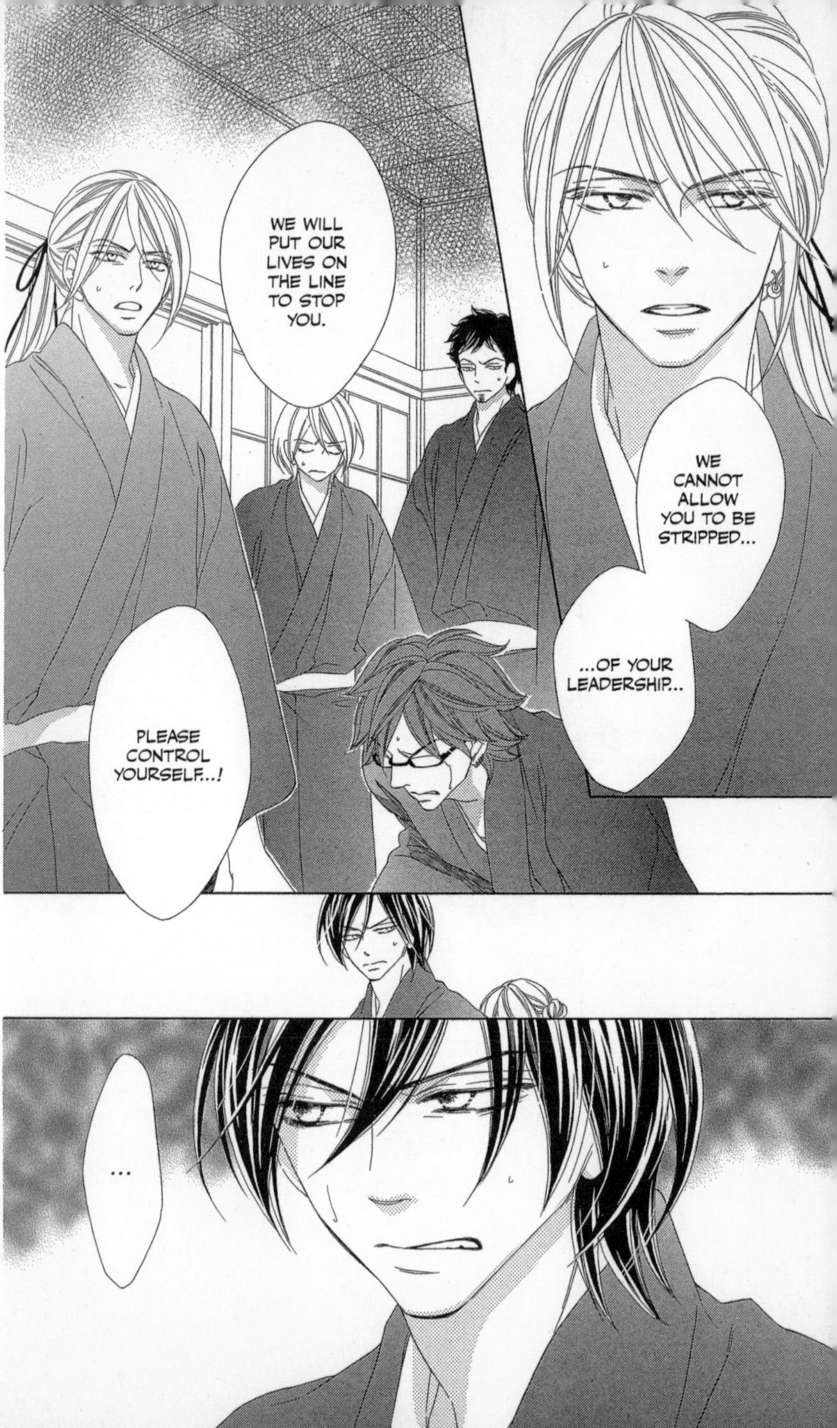
WE CANNOT ALLOW YOU TO BE STRIPPED...
...OF YOUR LEADERSHIP...
WE WILL PUT OUR LIVES ON THE LINE TO STOP YOU.
PLEASE CONTROL YOURSELF...!
...

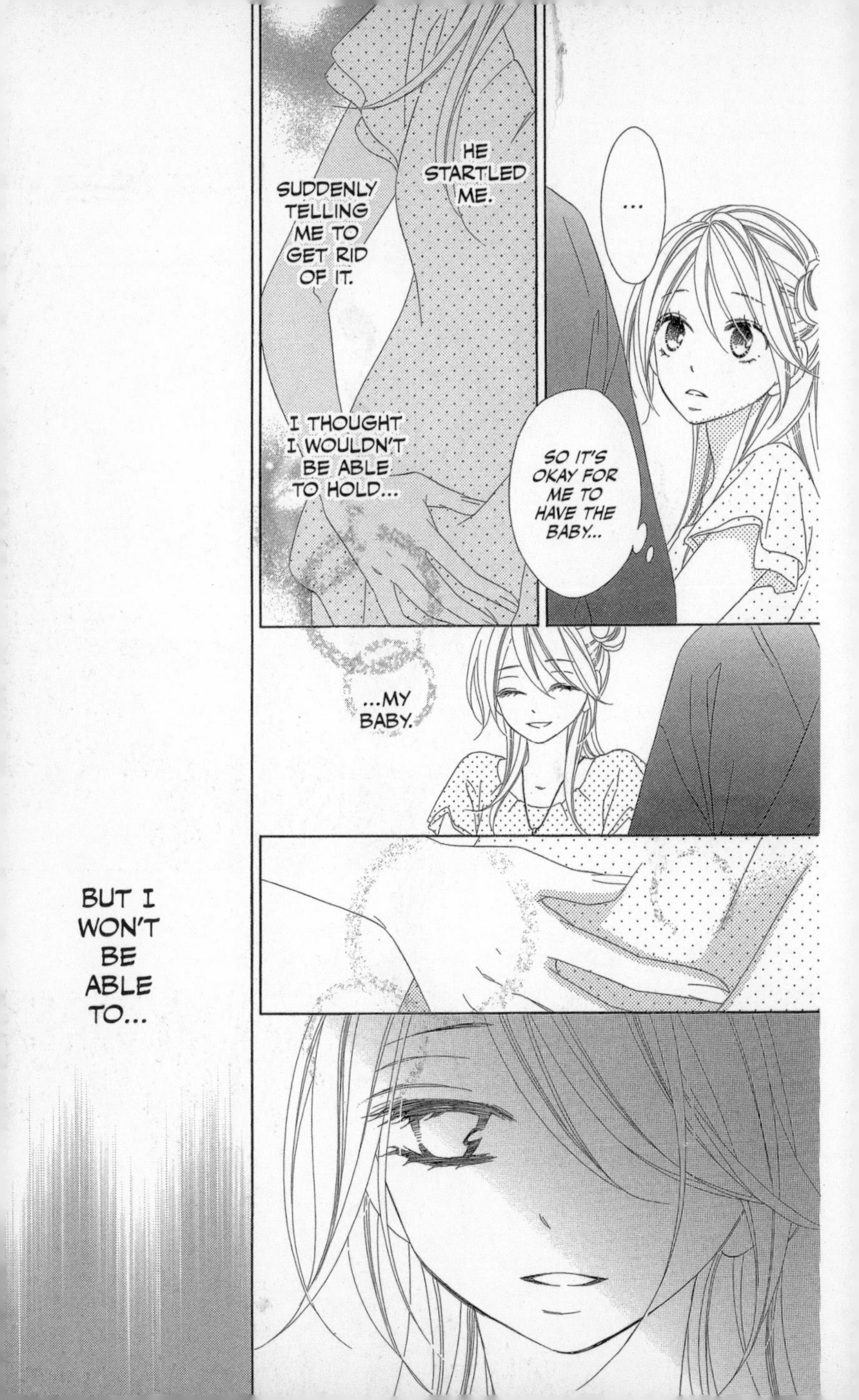
...
SO IT'S OKAY FOR ME TO HAVE THE BABY...
HE STARTLED ME.
SUDDENLY TELLING ME TO GET RID OF IT.
I THOUGHT I WOULDN'T BE ABLE TO HOLD...
...MY BABY.
BUT I WON'T BE ABLE TO...

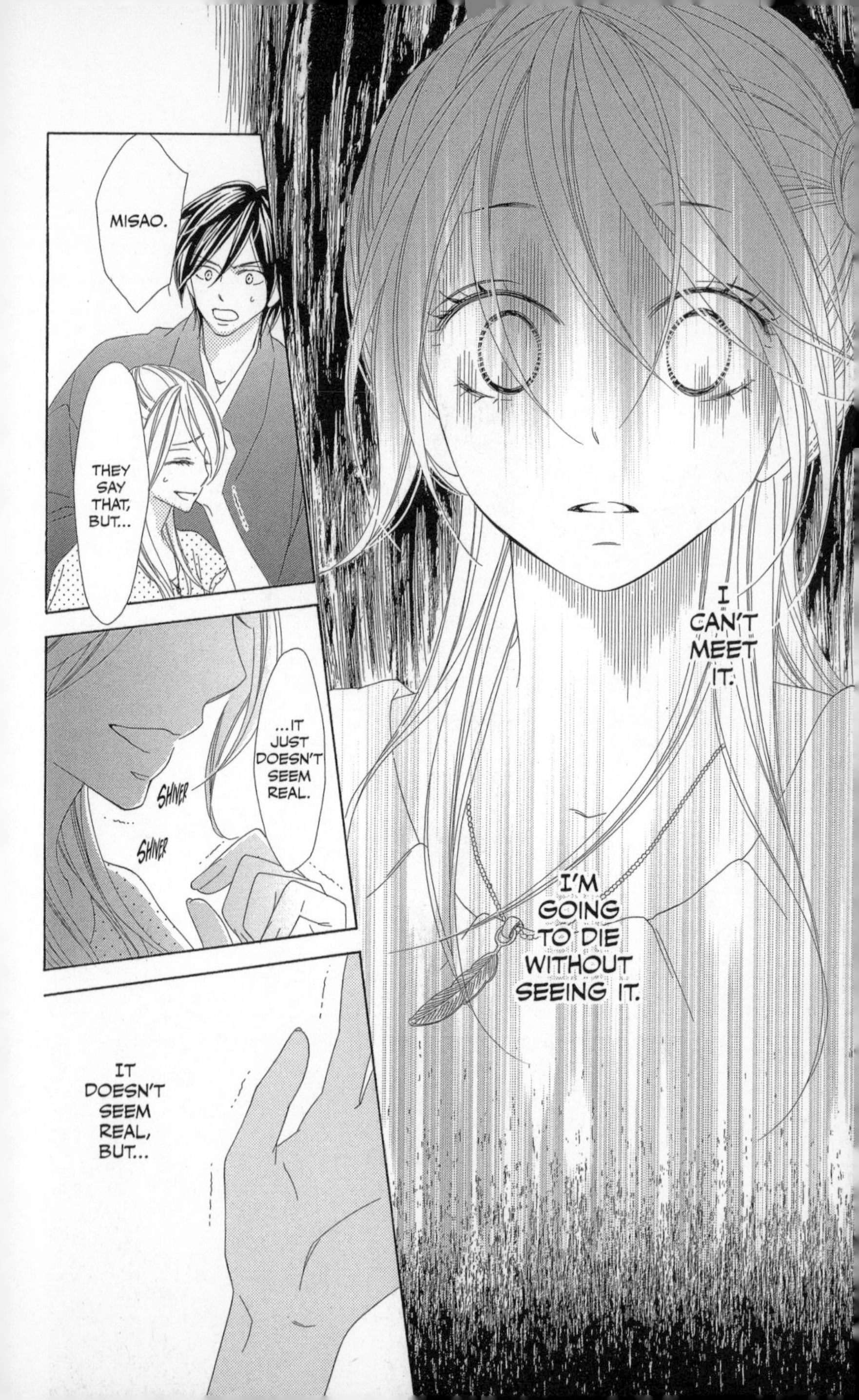
MISAO.
THEY SAY THAT, BUT...
...IT JUST DOESN'T SEEM REAL.
SHIVER
SHIVER
IT DOESN'T SEEM REAL, BUT...
I CAN'T MEET IT.
I'M GOING TO DIE WITHOUT SEEING IT.

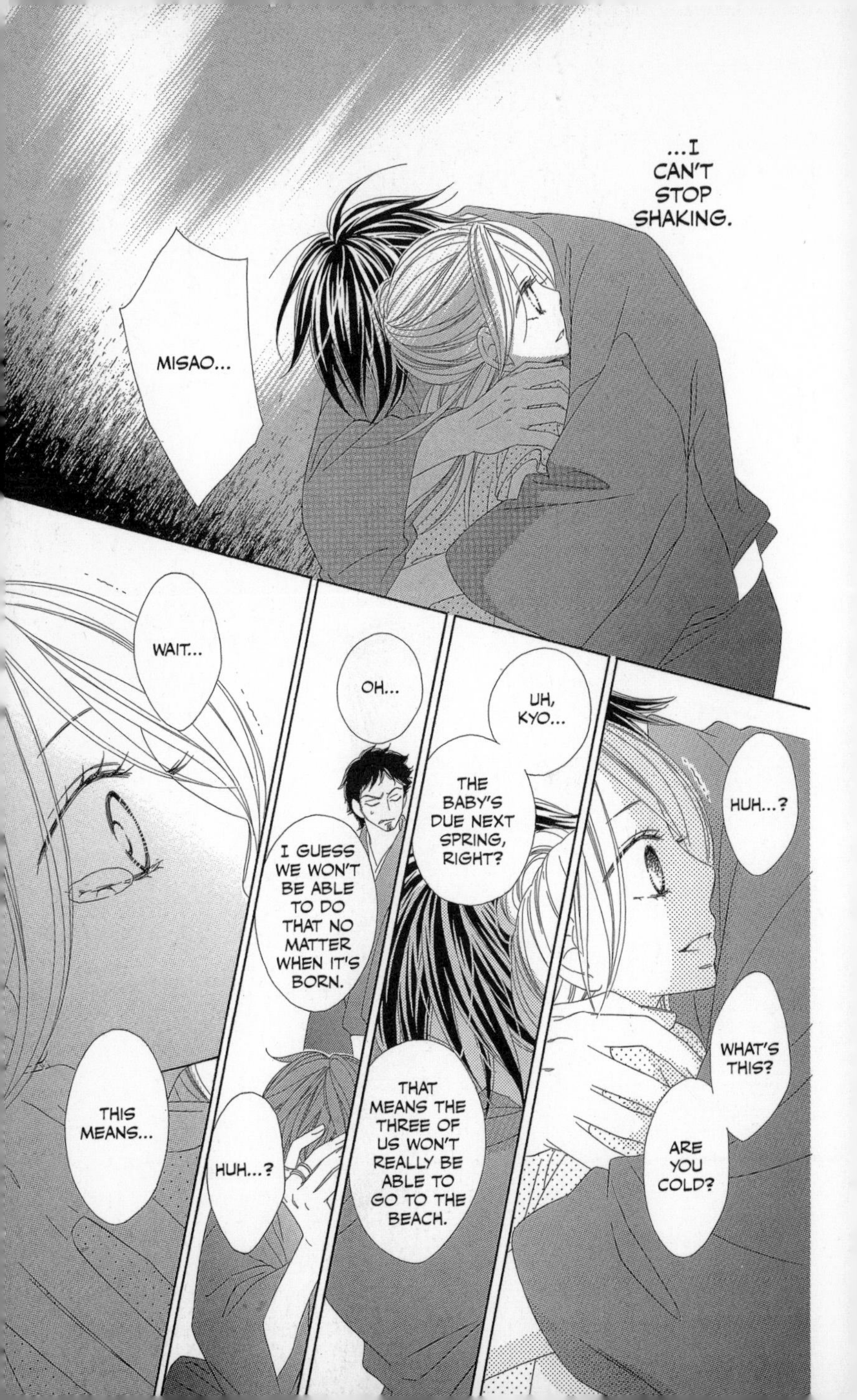
...I CAN'T STOP SHAKING.
MISAO...
HUH...?
WHAT'S THIS?
ARE YOU COLD?
UH, KYO...
THE BABY'S DUE NEXT SPRING, RIGHT?
THAT MEANS THE THREE OF US WON'T REALLY BE ABLE TO GO TO THE BEACH.
OH...
I GUESS WE WON'T BE ABLE TO DO THAT NO MATTER WHEN IT'S BORN.
HUH...?
WAIT...
THIS MEANS...

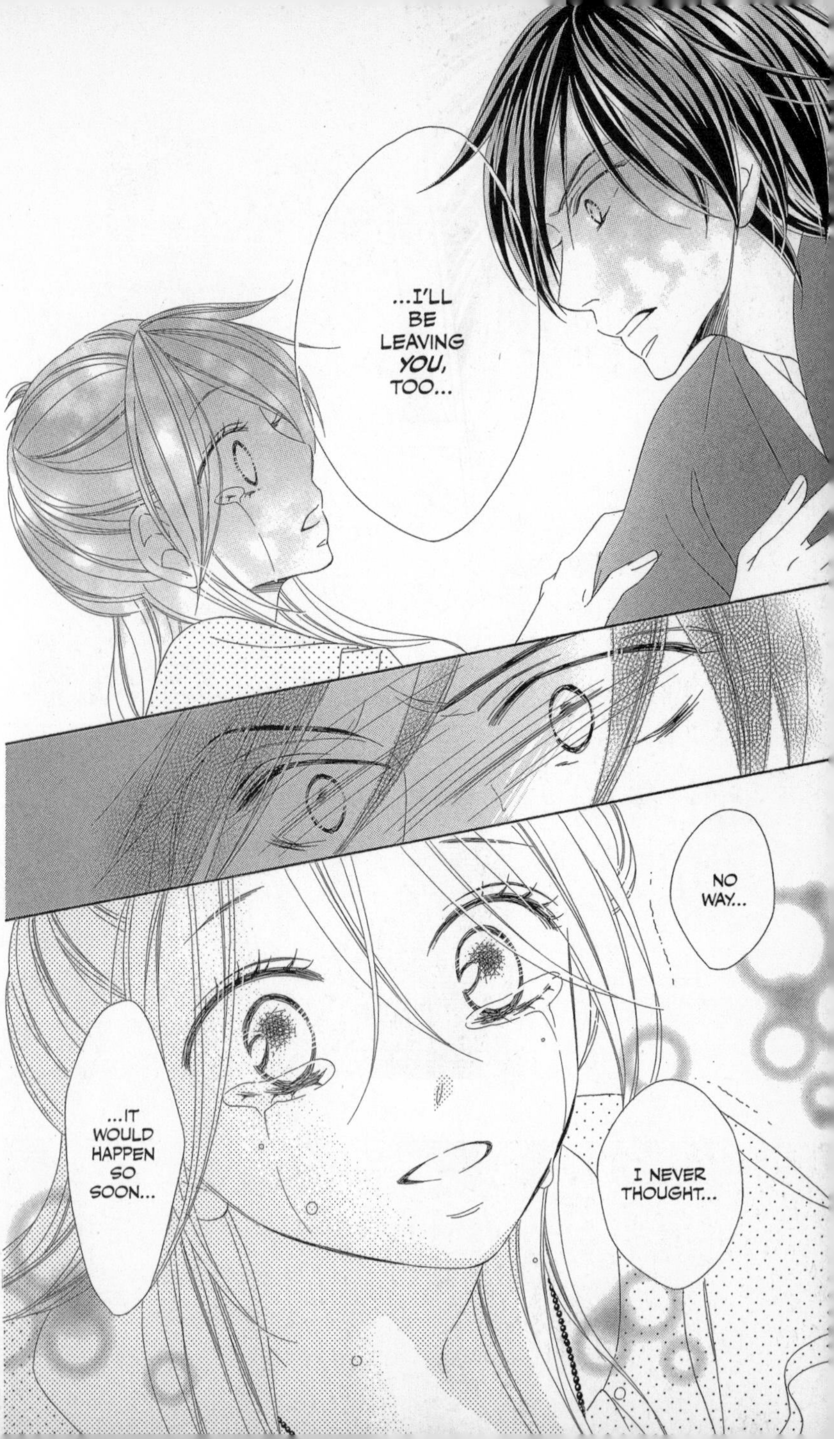
...I'LL BE LEAVING *YOU*, TOO...
NO WAY...
I NEVER THOUGHT...
...IT WOULD HAPPEN SO SOON...

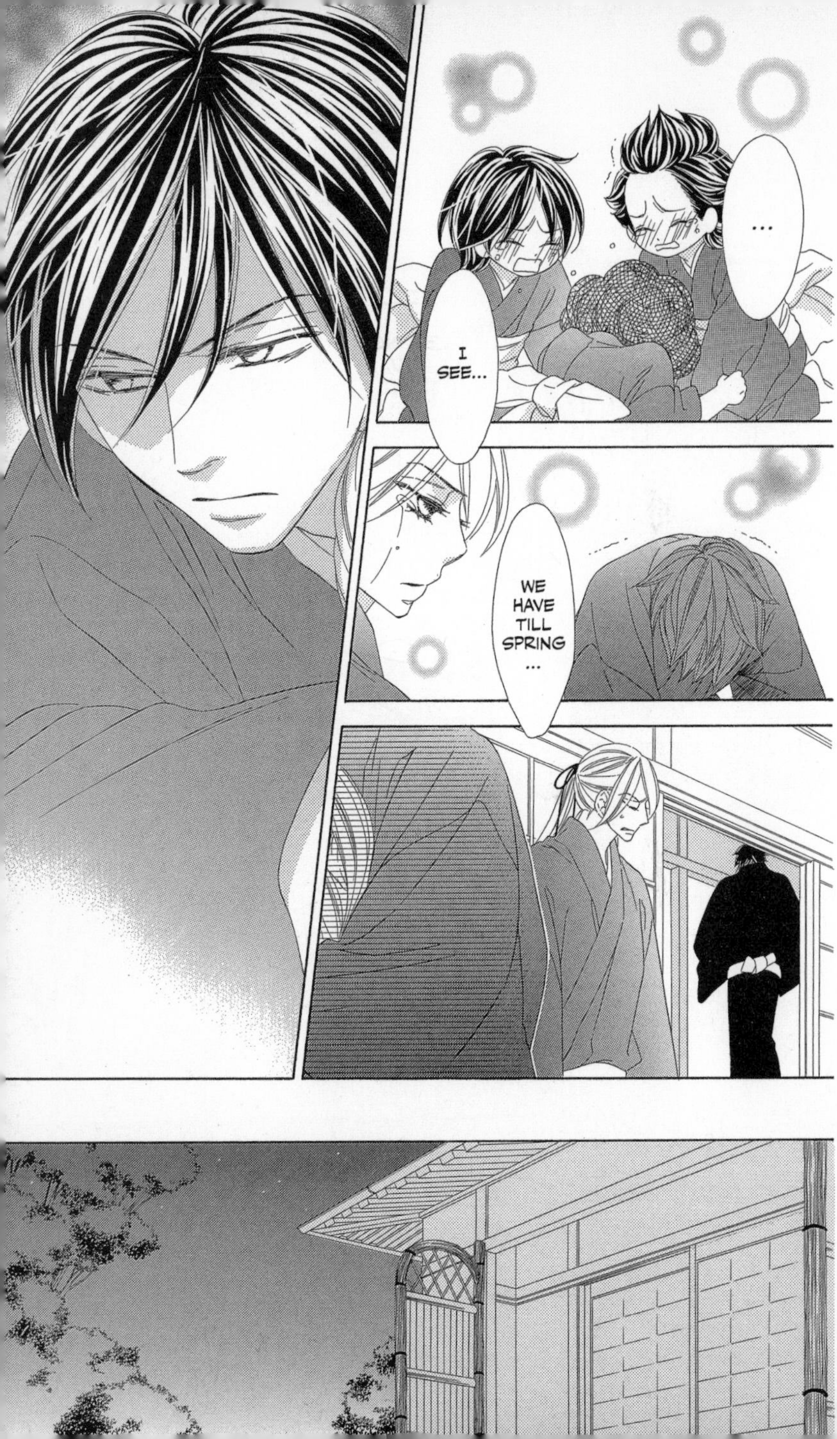
...
I SEE...
WE HAVE TILL SPRING ...

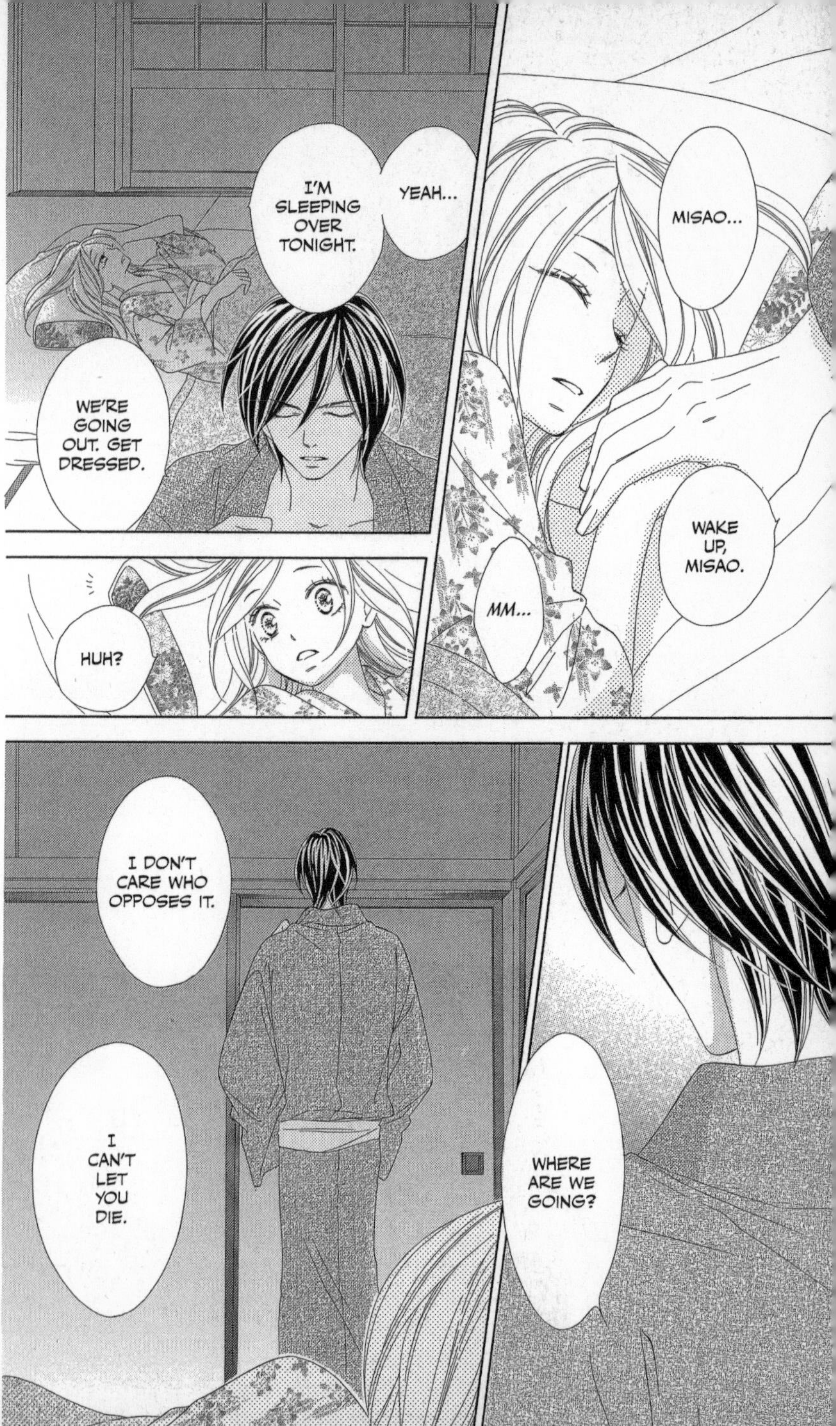
MISAO...
WAKE UP, MISAO.
MM...
YEAH...
I'M SLEEPING OVER TONIGHT.
WE'RE GOING OUT. GET DRESSED.
HUH?
WHERE ARE WE GOING?
I DON'T CARE WHO OPPOSES IT.
I CAN'T LET YOU DIE.

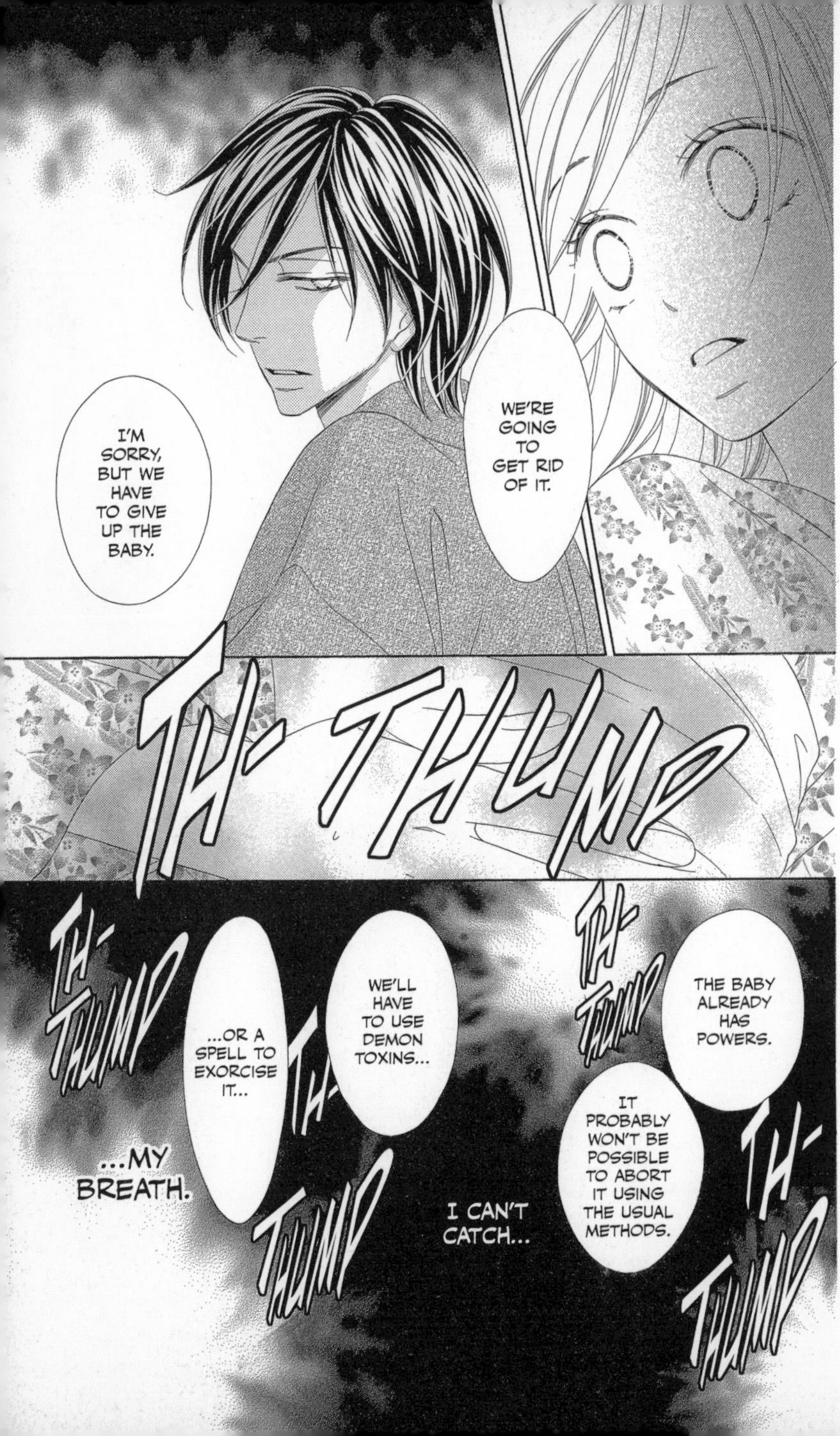
WE'RE GOING TO GET RID OF IT.
I'M SORRY, BUT WE HAVE TO GIVE UP THE BABY.
TH-THUMP
TH-THUMP
TH-THUMP
THE BABY ALREADY HAS POWERS.
IT PROBABLY WON'T BE POSSIBLE TO ABORT IT USING THE USUAL METHODS.
I CAN'T CATCH...
WE'LL HAVE TO USE DEMON TOXINS...
TH-THUMP
...OR A SPELL TO EXORCISE IT...
TH-THUMP
...MY BREATH.

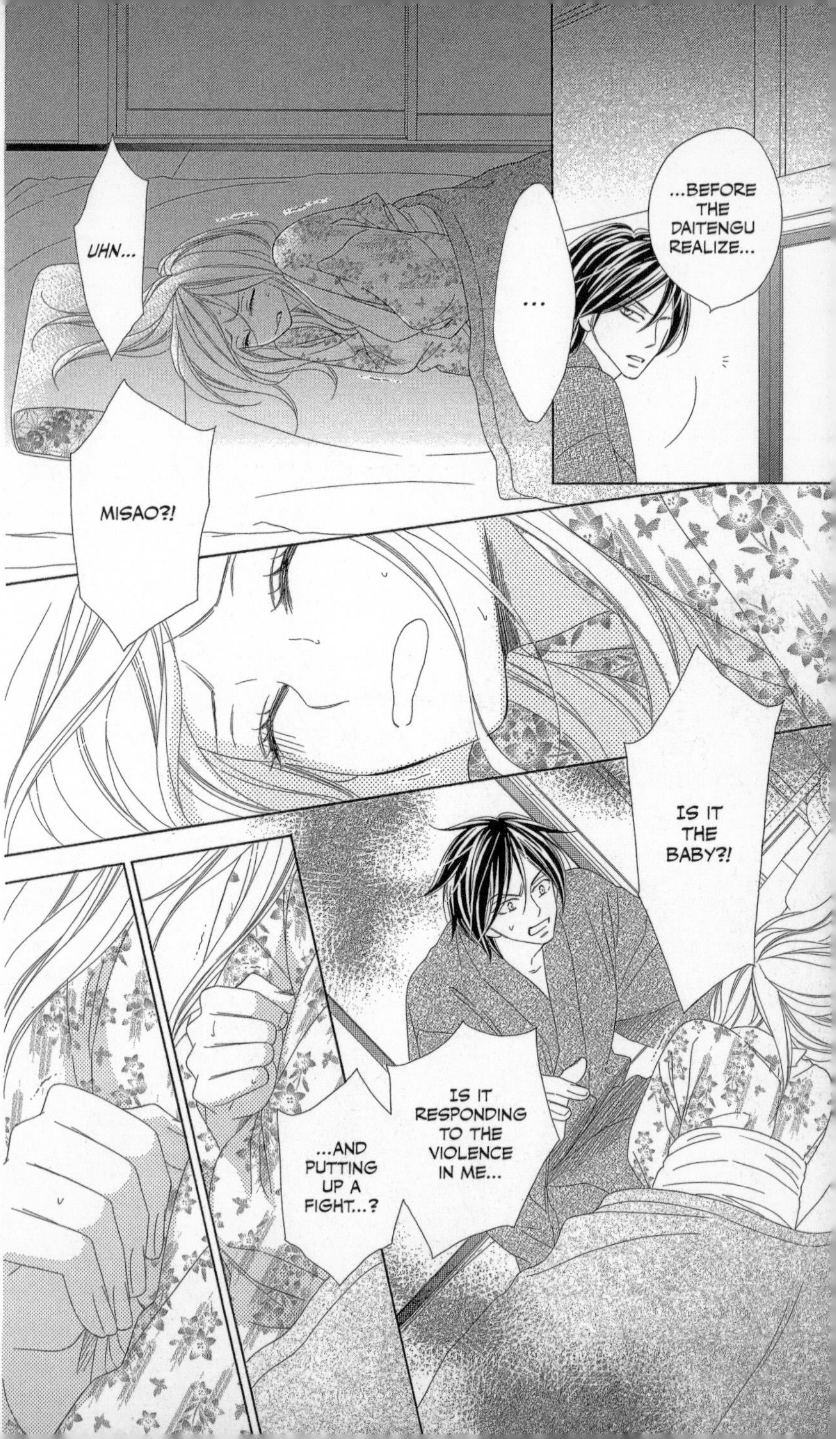
...BEFORE THE DAITENGU REALIZE...
...
UHN...
MISAO?!
IS IT THE BABY?!
IS IT RESPONDING TO THE VIOLENCE IN ME...
...AND PUTTING UP A FIGHT...?

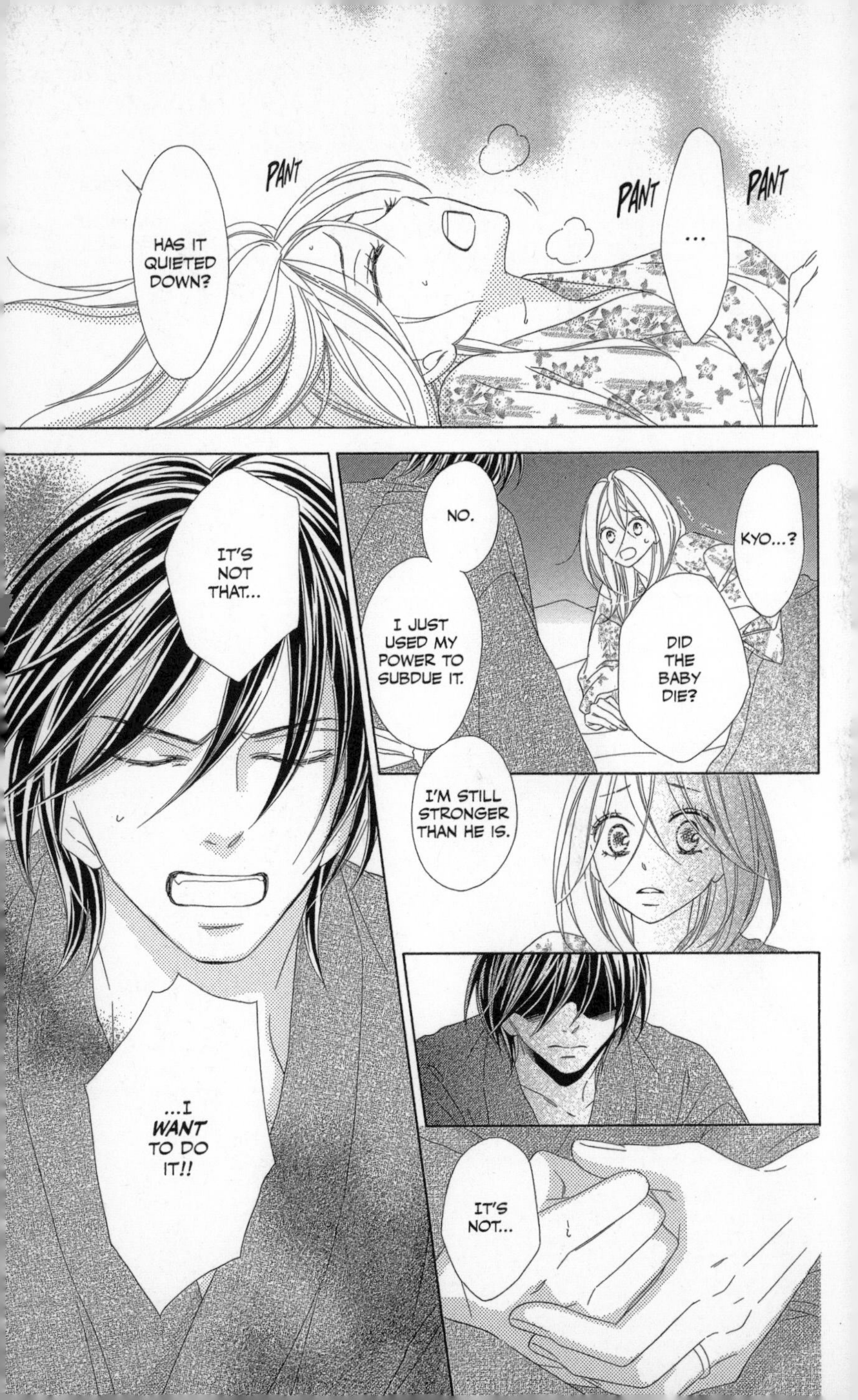
PANT
...
PANT
PANT
HAS IT QUIETED DOWN?
KYO...?
DID THE BABY DIE?
NO.
I JUST USED MY POWER TO SUBDUE IT.
I'M STILL STRONGER THAN HE IS.
IT'S NOT...
IT'S NOT THAT...
...I *WANT* TO DO IT!!

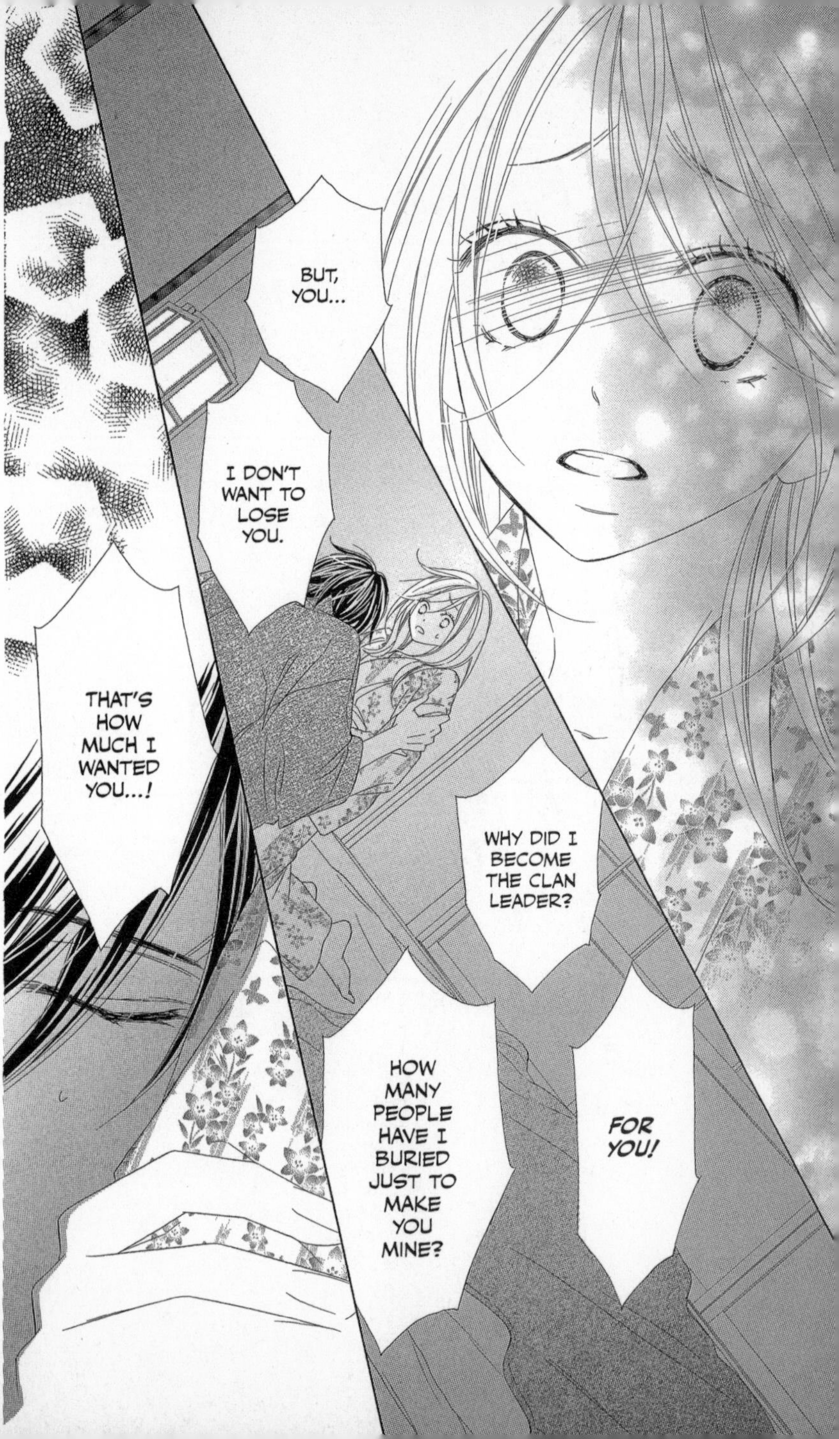
BUT, YOU...
I DON'T WANT TO LOSE YOU.
WHY DID I BECOME THE CLAN LEADER?
FOR YOU!
HOW MANY PEOPLE HAVE I BURIED JUST TO MAKE YOU MINE?
THAT'S HOW MUCH I WANTED YOU...!

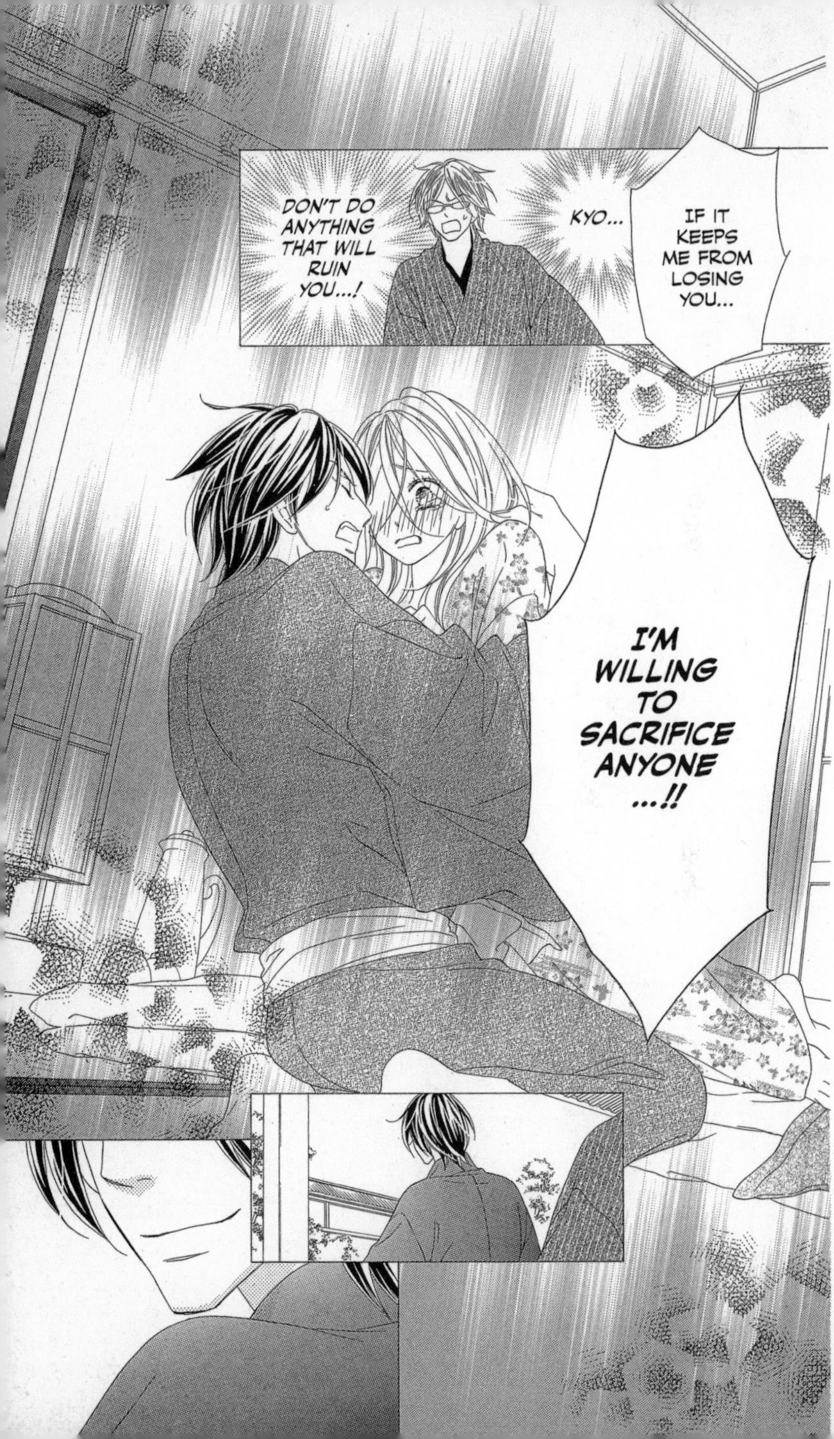
IF IT KEEPS ME FROM LOSING YOU...
KYO...
DON'T DO ANYTHING THAT WILL RUIN YOU...!
I'M WILLING TO SACRIFICE ANYONE ...!!

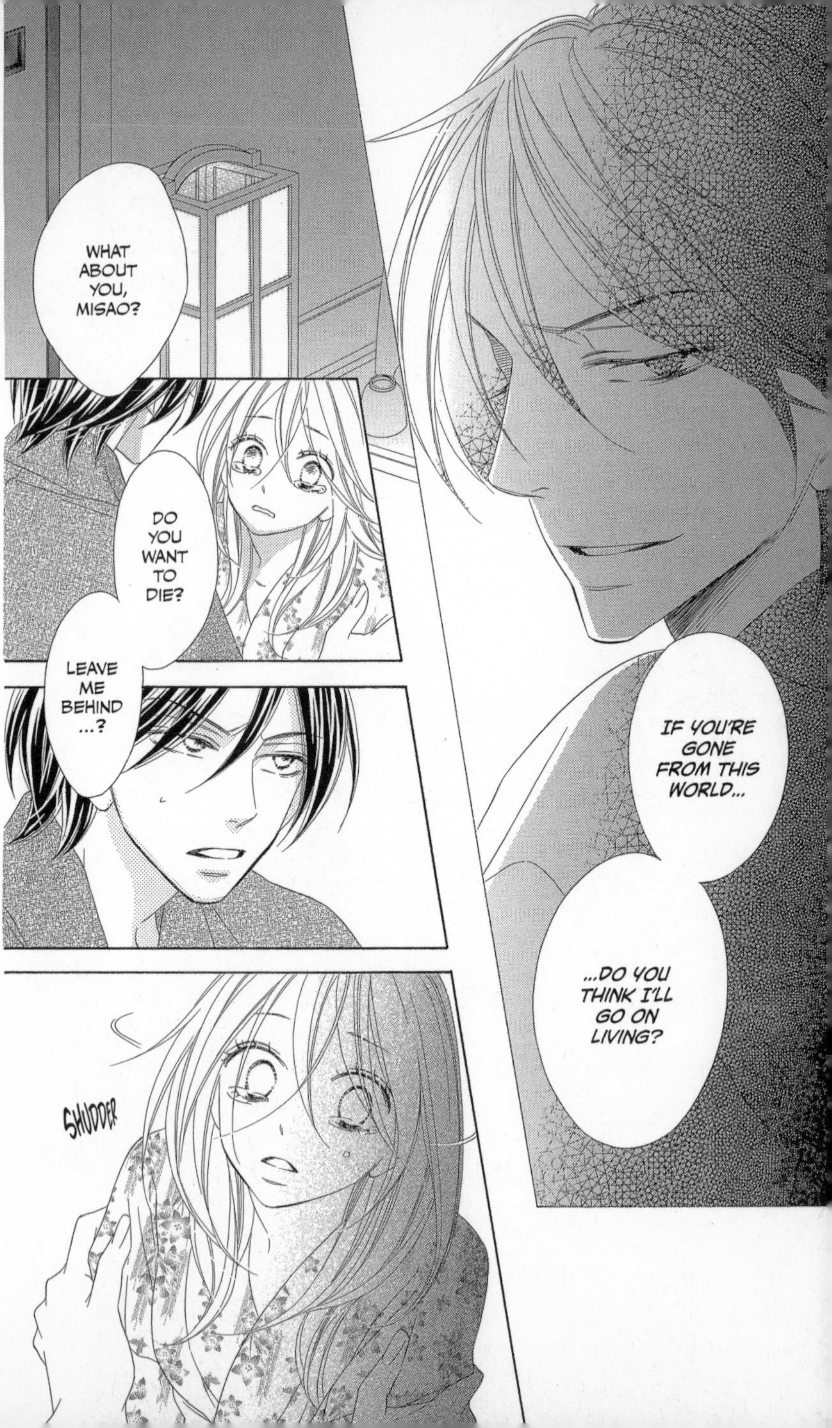
IF YOU'RE GONE FROM THIS WORLD...
...DO YOU THINK I'LL GO ON LIVING?
WHAT ABOUT YOU, MISAO?
DO YOU WANT TO DIE?
LEAVE ME BEHIND ...?
SHUDDER

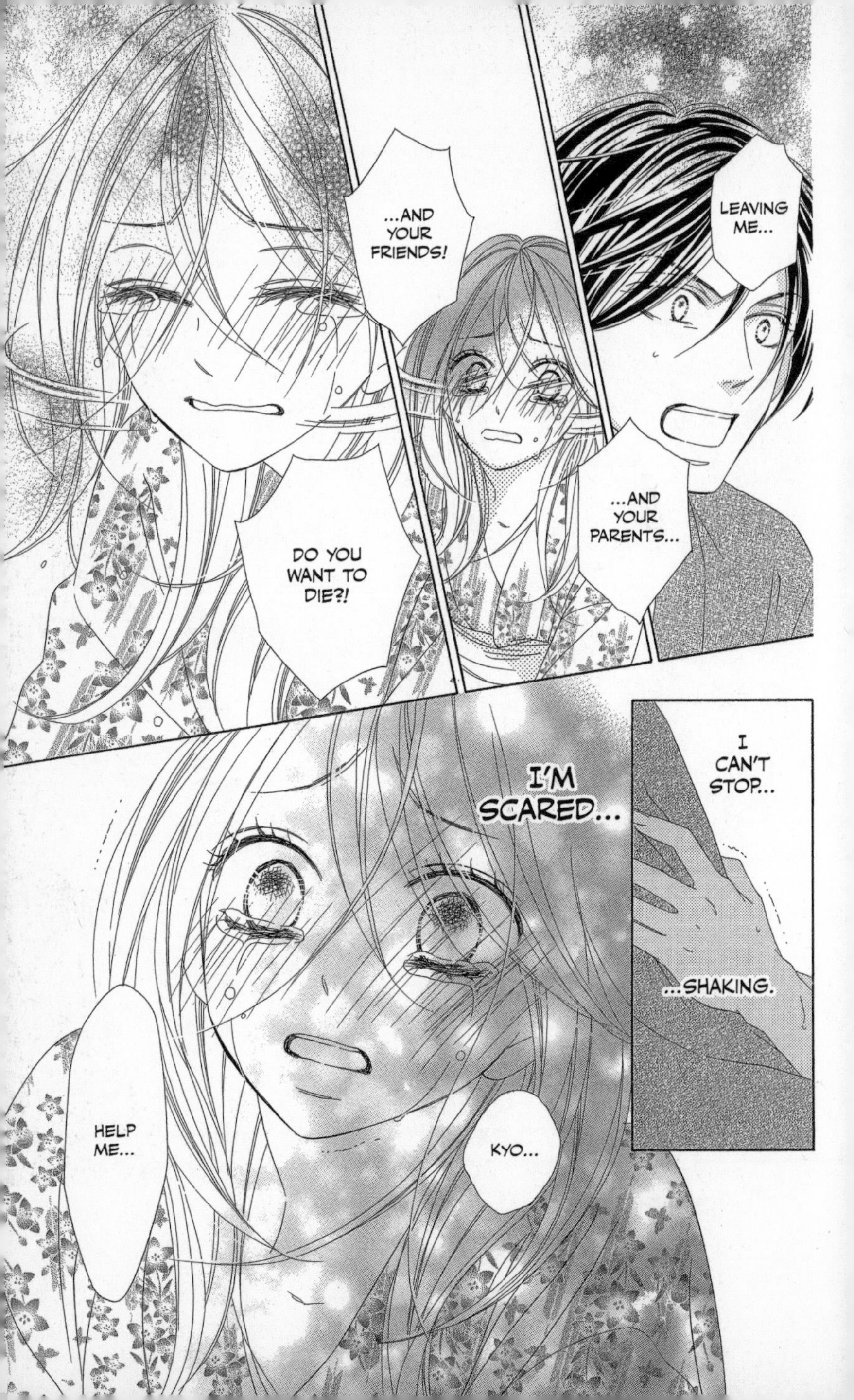
LEAVING ME...
...AND YOUR PARENTS...
...AND YOUR FRIENDS!
DO YOU WANT TO DIE?!
I CAN'T STOP...
...SHAKING.
I'M SCARED...
KYO...
HELP ME...

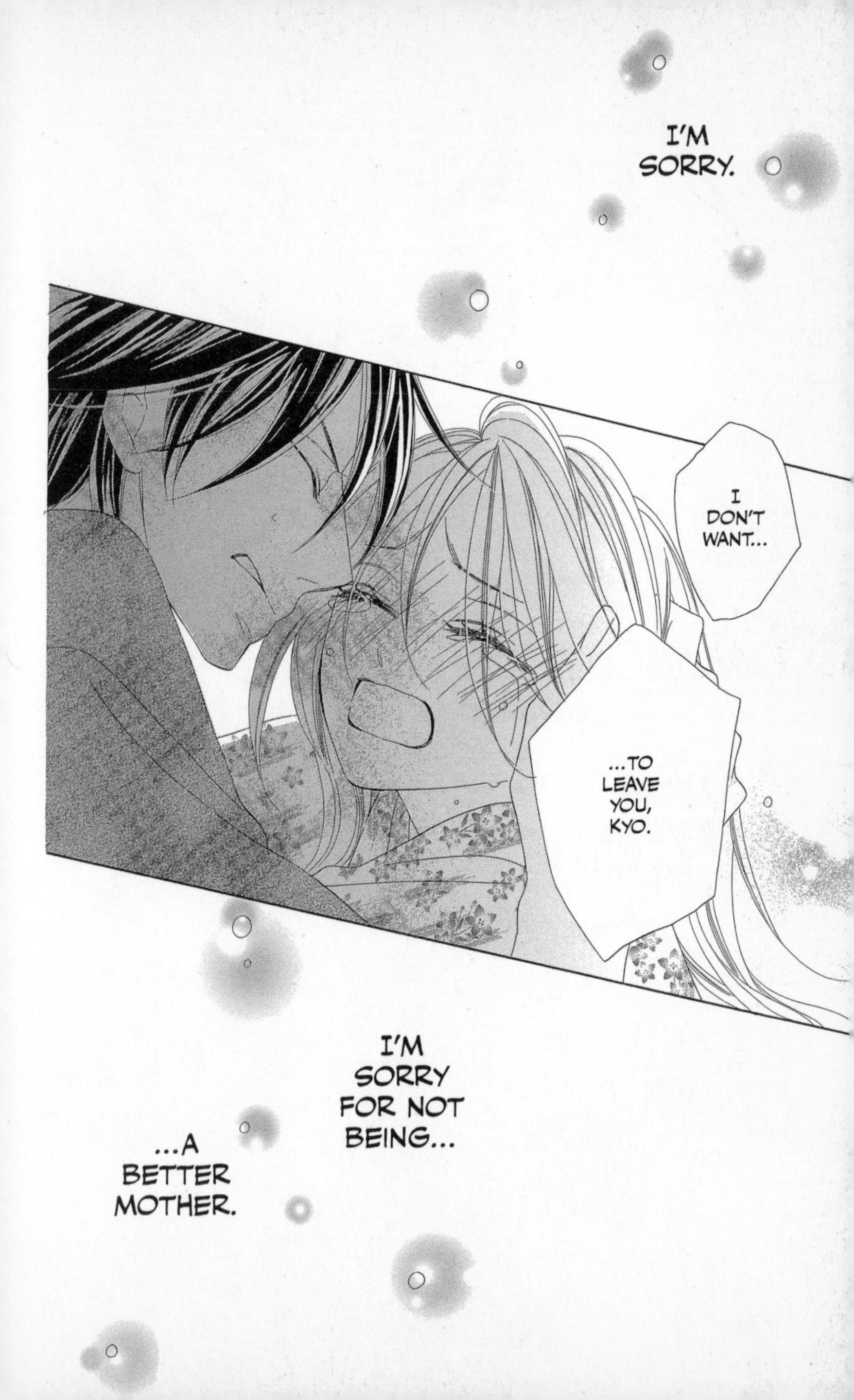
I'M SORRY.
I DON'T WANT...
...TO LEAVE YOU, KYO.
I'M SORRY FOR NOT BEING...
...A BETTER MOTHER.

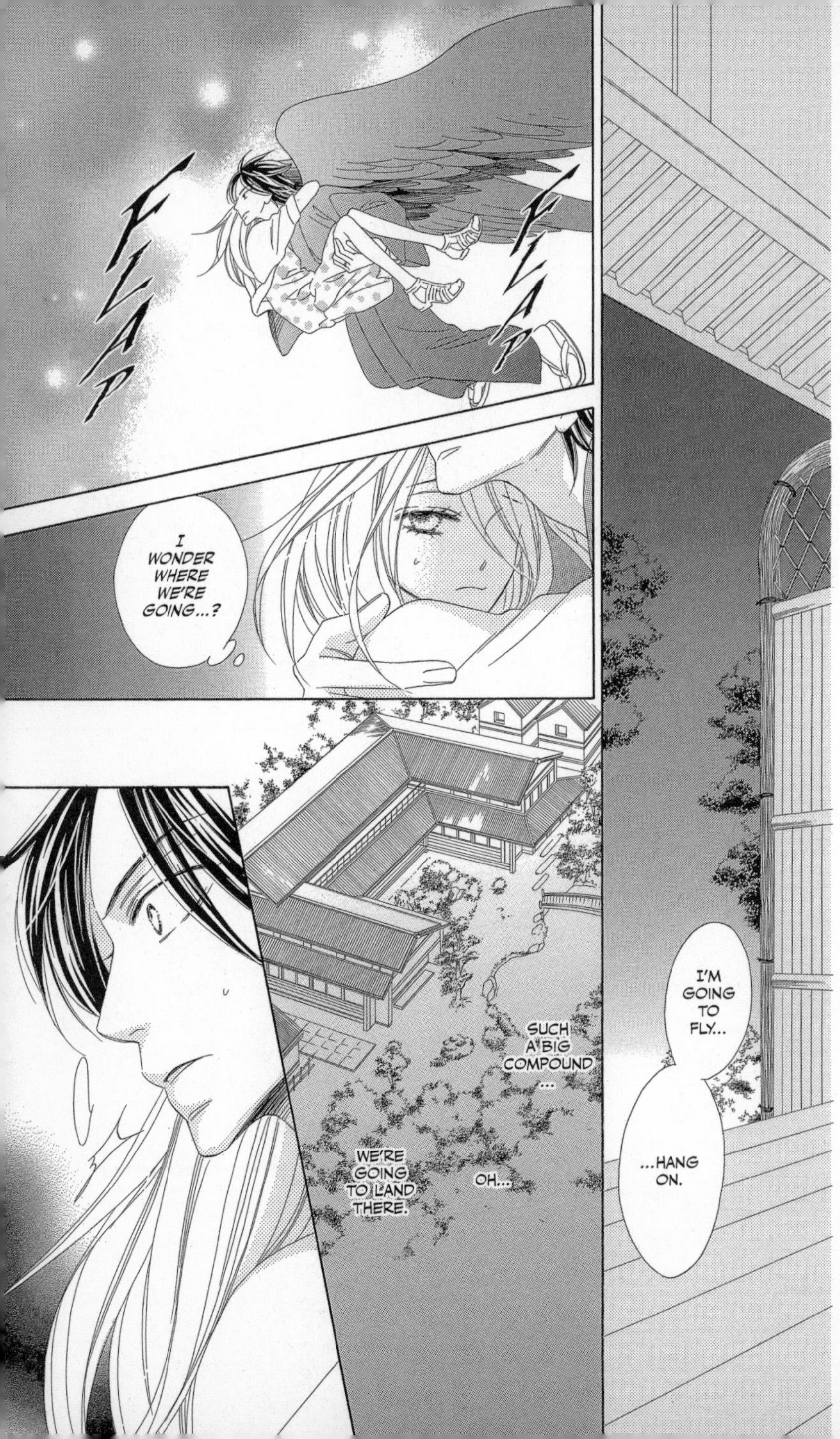
I'M GOING TO FLY...
...HANG ON.
FLAP
FLAP
I WONDER WHERE WE'RE GOING...?
SUCH A BIG COMPOUND...
OH...
WE'RE GOING TO LAND THERE.

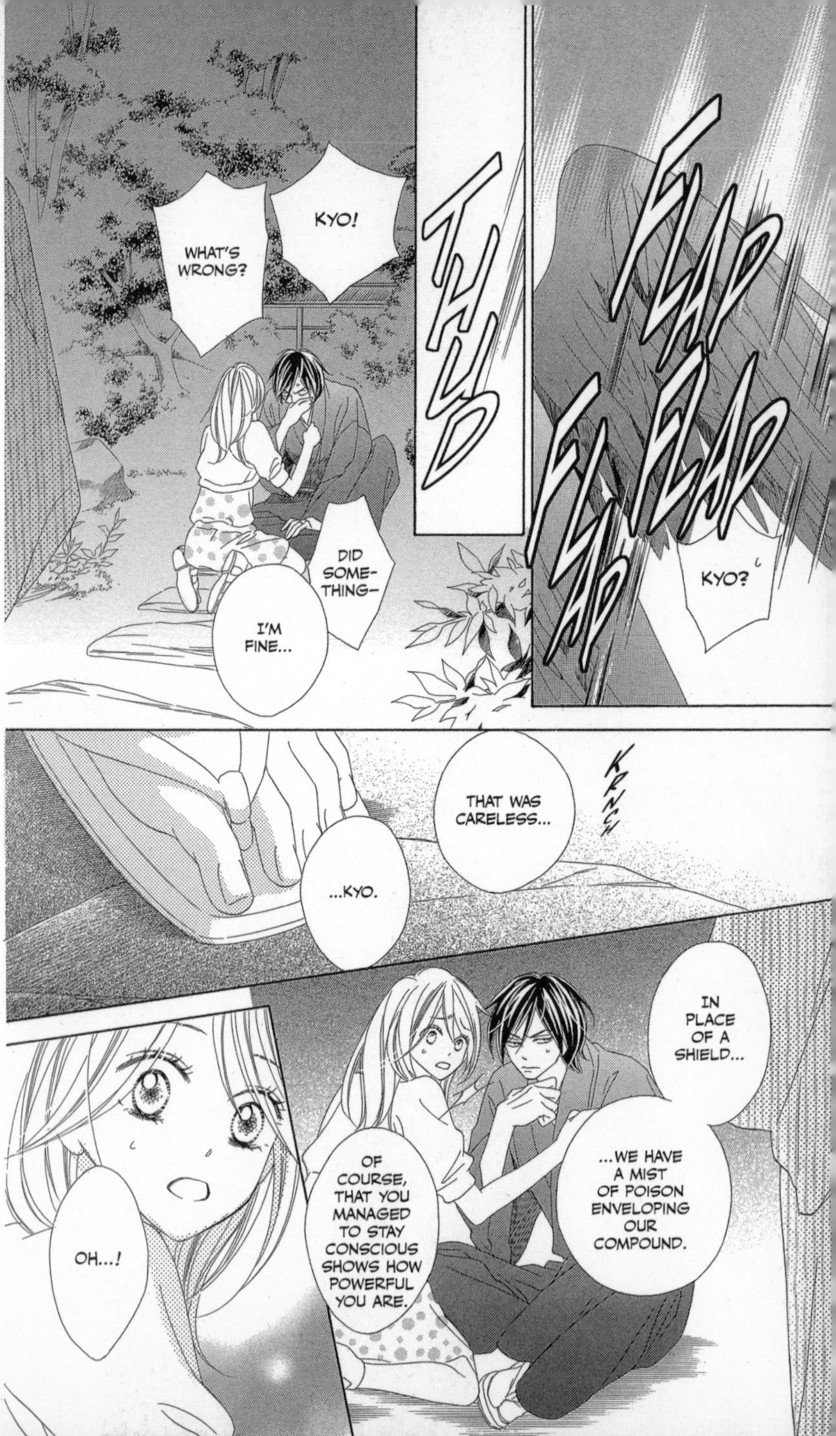
FLAP FLAP
FLAP
KYO?
THUD
KYO!
WHAT'S WRONG?
DID SOME-THING—
I'M FINE...
KRNCH
THAT WAS CARELESS...
...KYO.
IN PLACE OF A SHIELD...
...WE HAVE A MIST OF POISON ENVELOPING OUR COMPOUND.
OF COURSE, THAT YOU MANAGED TO STAY CONSCIOUS SHOWS HOW POWERFUL YOU ARE.
OH...!

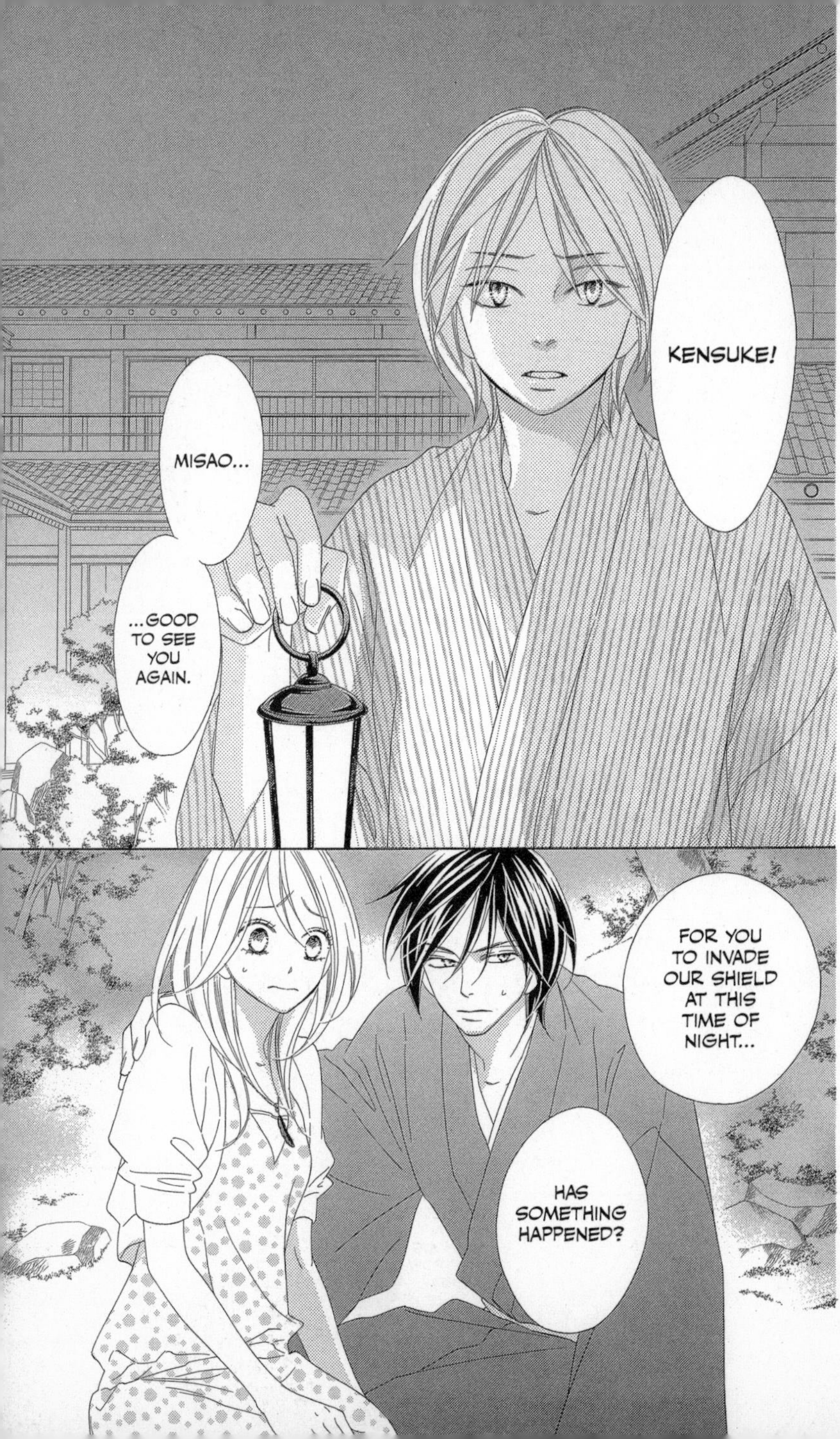
KENSUKE!
MISAO...
...GOOD TO SEE YOU AGAIN.
FOR YOU TO INVADE OUR SHIELD AT THIS TIME OF NIGHT...
HAS SOMETHING HAPPENED?

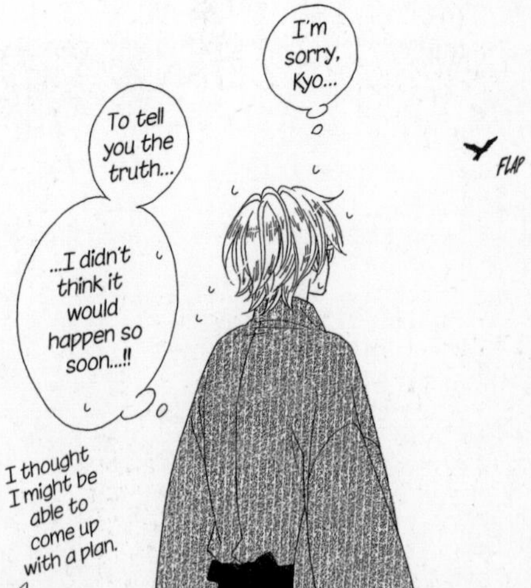
I'm sorry, Kyo...
FLAP
To tell you the truth...
...I didn't think it would happen so soon...!!
I thought I might be able to come up with a plan.

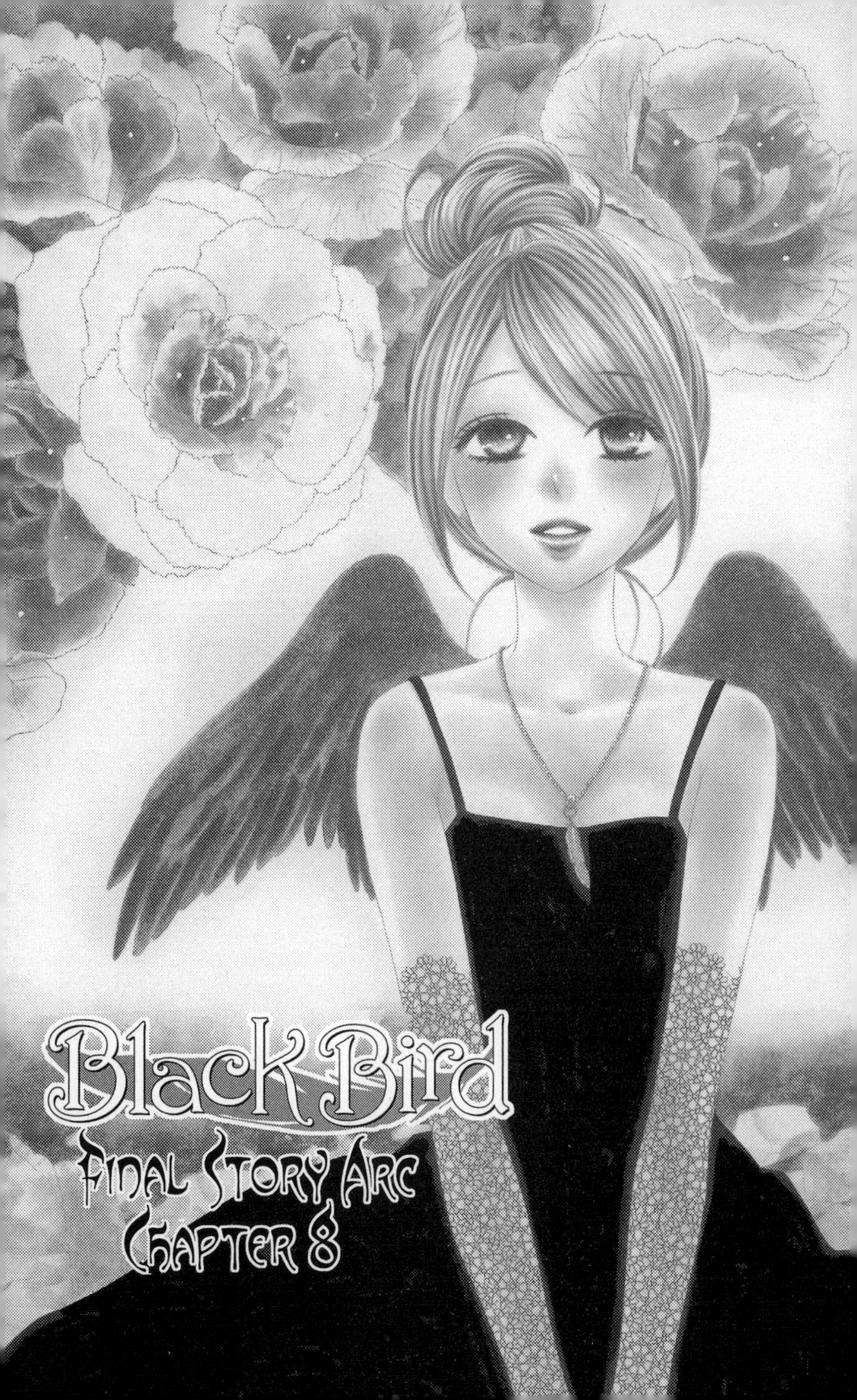
Black Bird
Final Story Arc
Chapter 8

MISAO
hand-riding
size

Black Bird

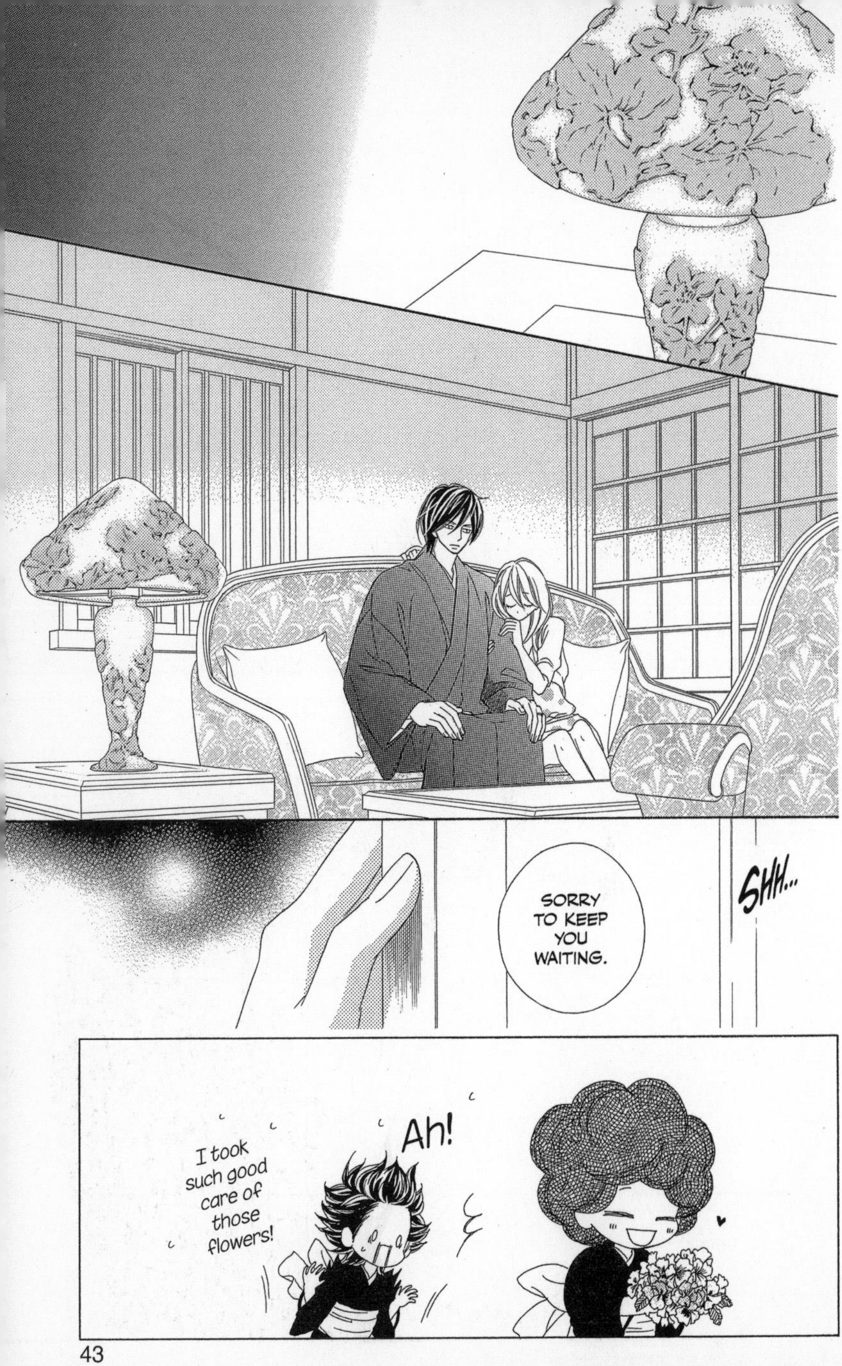
SHH...
SORRY TO KEEP YOU WAITING.
Ah!
I took such good care of those flowers!

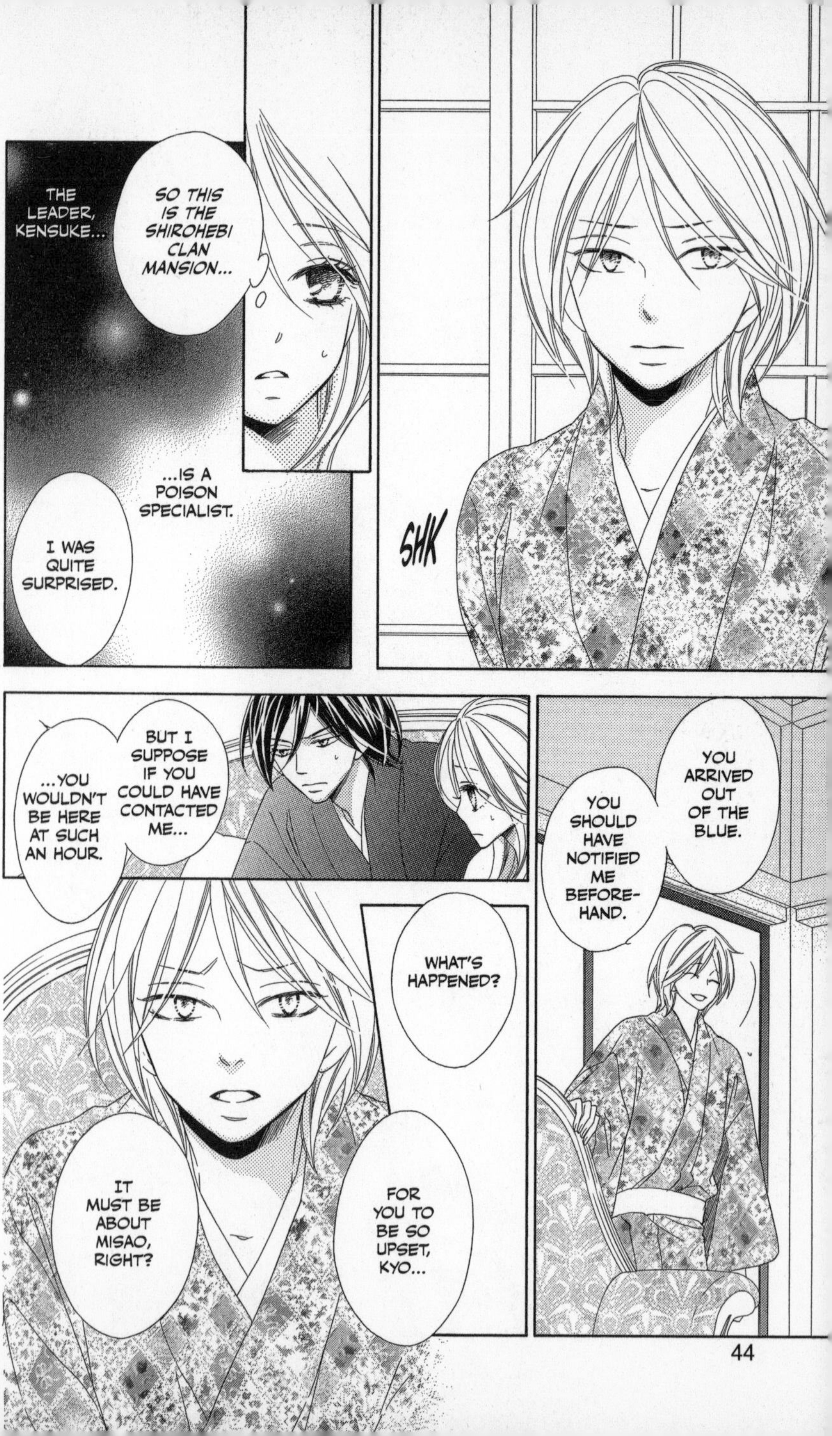
SHK
SO THIS IS THE SHIROHEBI CLAN MANSION...
THE LEADER, KENSUKE...
...IS A POISON SPECIALIST.
I WAS QUITE SURPRISED.
YOU ARRIVED OUT OF THE BLUE.
YOU SHOULD HAVE NOTIFIED ME BEFORE-HAND.
BUT I SUPPOSE IF YOU COULD HAVE CONTACTED ME...
...YOU WOULDN'T BE HERE AT SUCH AN HOUR.
WHAT'S HAPPENED?
FOR YOU TO BE SO UPSET, KYO...
IT MUST BE ABOUT MISAO, RIGHT?

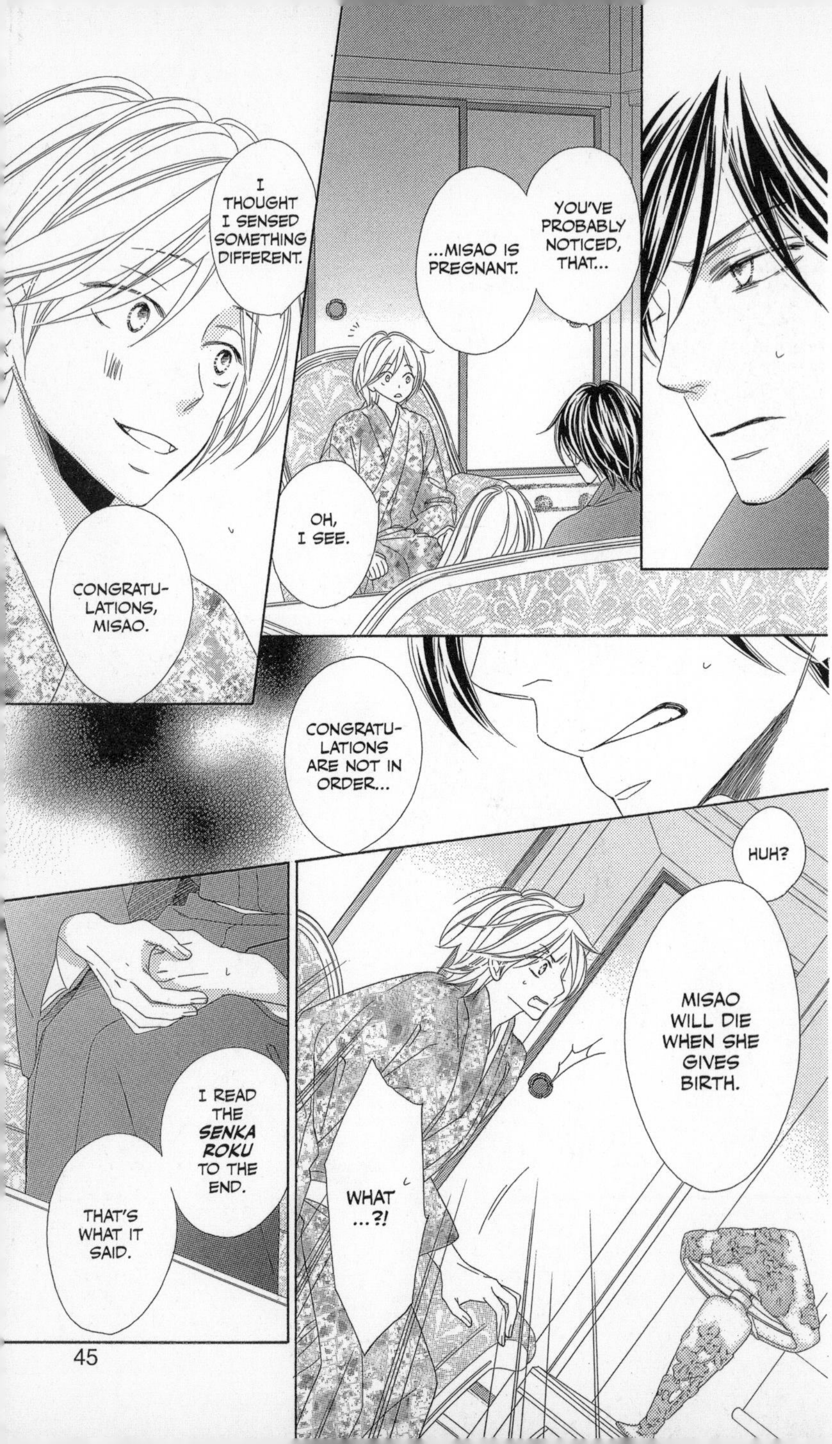
YOU'VE PROBABLY NOTICED, THAT...
...MISAO IS PREGNANT.
OH, I SEE.
I THOUGHT I SENSED SOMETHING DIFFERENT.
CONGRATULATIONS, MISAO.
CONGRATULATIONS ARE NOT IN ORDER...
HUH?
MISAO WILL DIE WHEN SHE GIVES BIRTH.
WHAT...?!
I READ THE *SENKA ROKU* TO THE END.
THAT'S WHAT IT SAID.

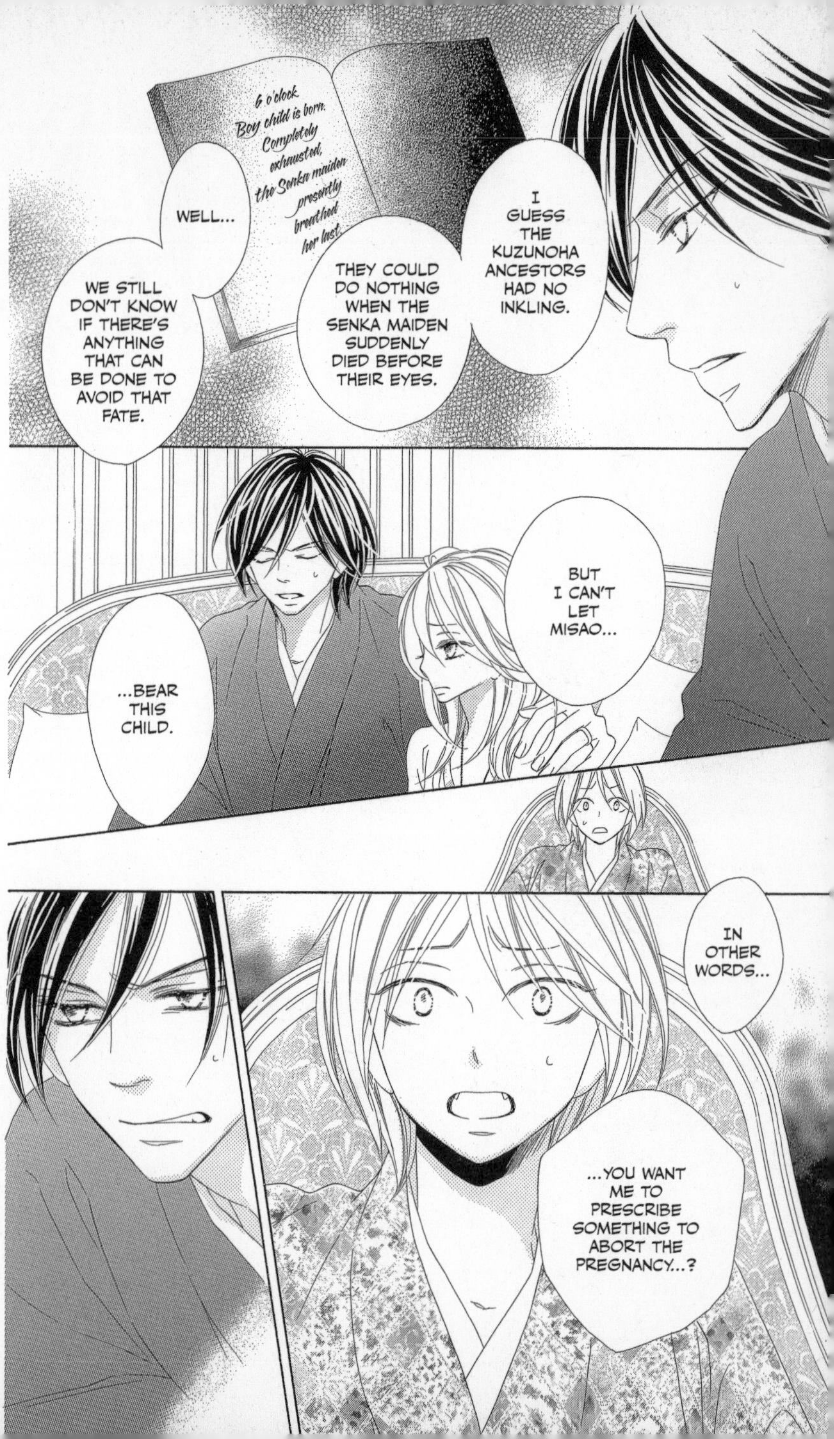
I GUESS THE KUZUNOHA ANCESTORS HAD NO INKLING.
THEY COULD DO NOTHING WHEN THE SENKA MAIDEN SUDDENLY DIED BEFORE THEIR EYES.
6 o'clock Boy child is born. Completely exhausted, the Senka maiden presently breathed her last.
WELL...
WE STILL DON'T KNOW IF THERE'S ANYTHING THAT CAN BE DONE TO AVOID THAT FATE.
BUT I CAN'T LET MISAO...
...BEAR THIS CHILD.
IN OTHER WORDS...
...YOU WANT ME TO PRESCRIBE SOMETHING TO ABORT THE PREGNANCY...?

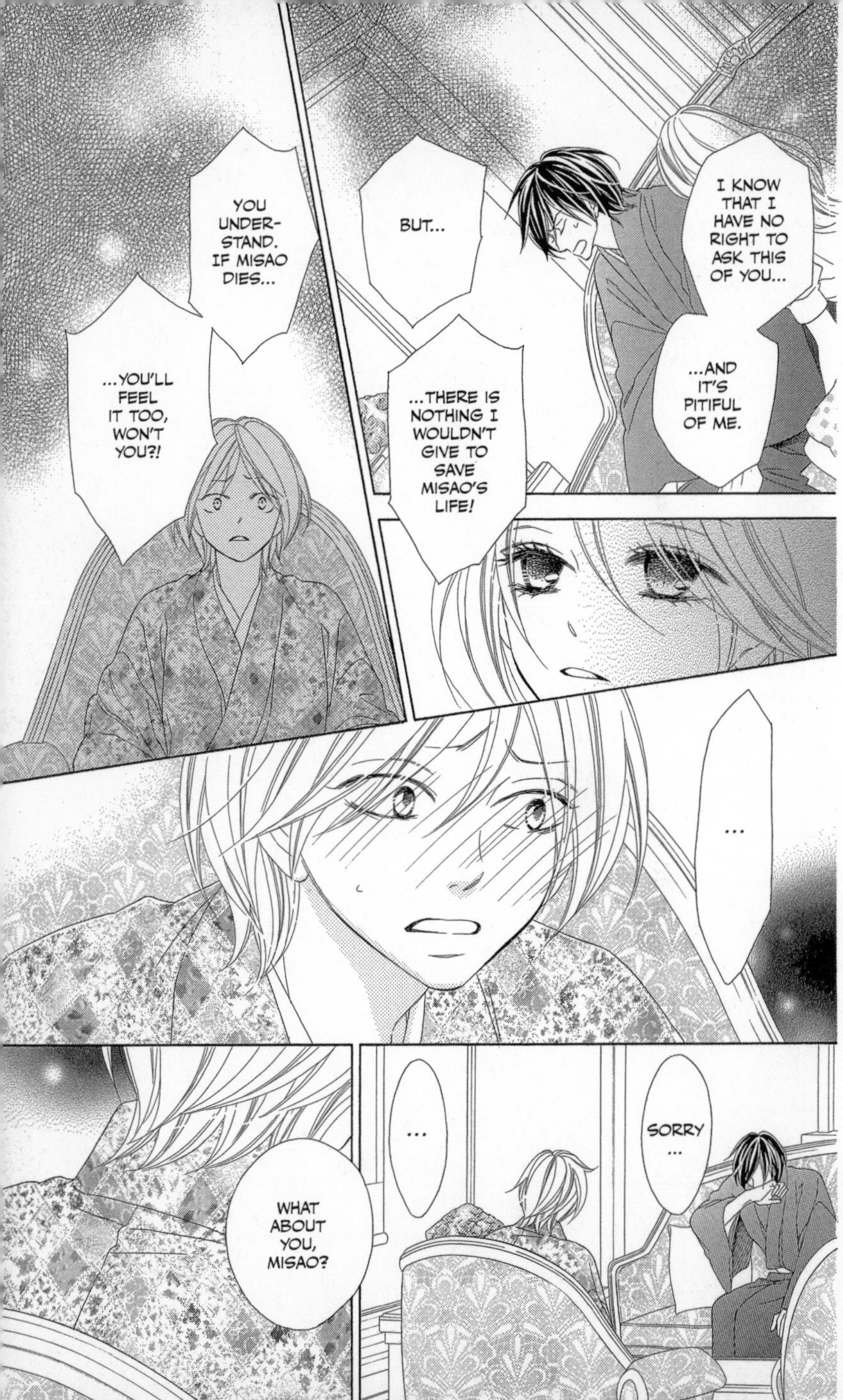
I KNOW THAT I HAVE NO RIGHT TO ASK THIS OF YOU...
...AND IT'S PITIFUL OF ME.
BUT...
...THERE IS NOTHING I WOULDN'T GIVE TO SAVE MISAO'S LIFE!
YOU UNDER-STAND. IF MISAO DIES...
...YOU'LL FEEL IT TOO, WON'T YOU?!
...
SORRY ...
...
WHAT ABOUT YOU, MISAO?

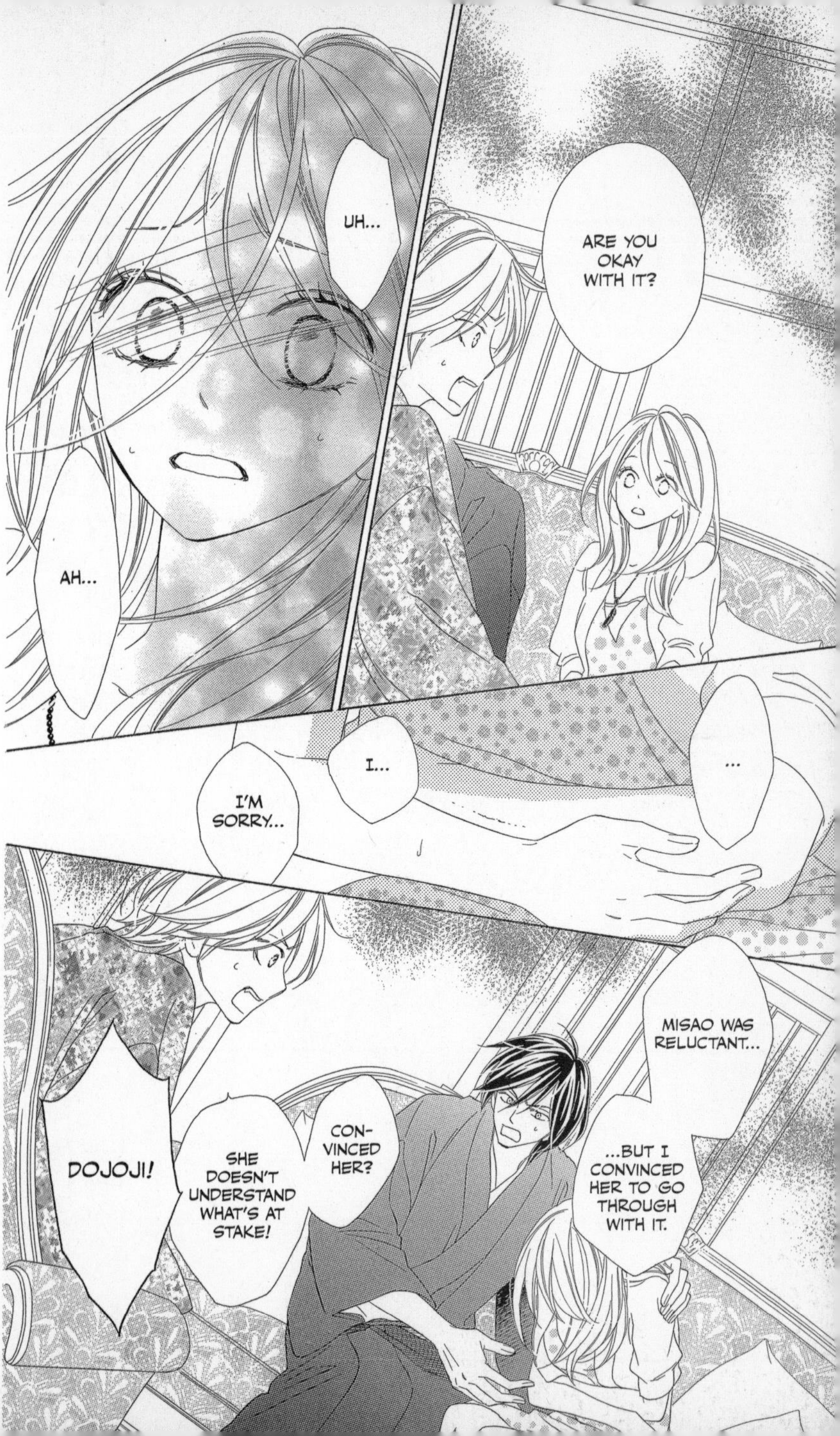
ARE YOU OKAY WITH IT?
UH...
AH...
...
I...
I'M SORRY...
MISAO WAS RELUCTANT...
...BUT I CONVINCED HER TO GO THROUGH WITH IT.
CON-VINCED HER?
SHE DOESN'T UNDERSTAND WHAT'S AT STAKE!
DOJOJI!

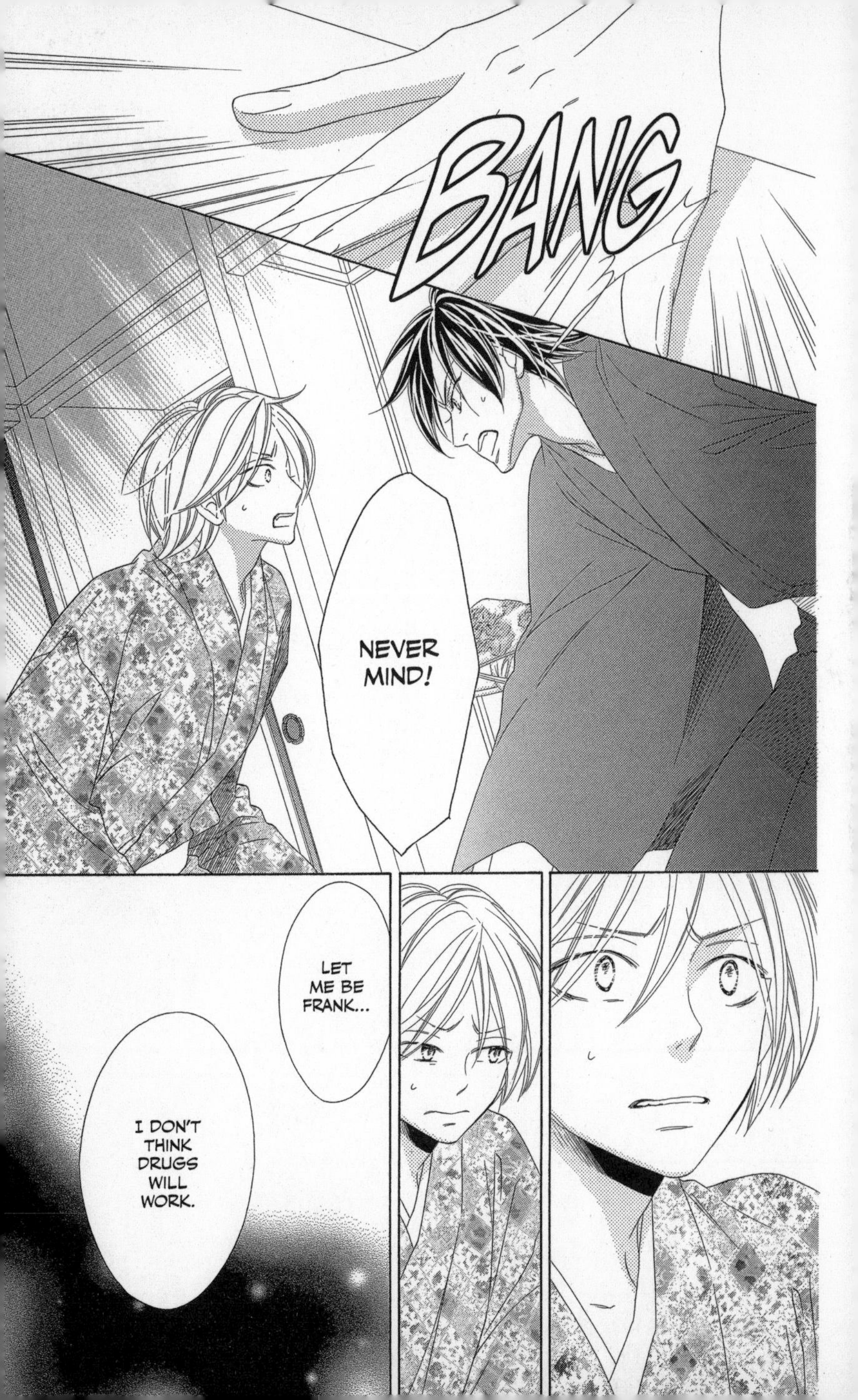
BANG
NEVER MIND!
LET ME BE FRANK...
I DON'T THINK DRUGS WILL WORK.

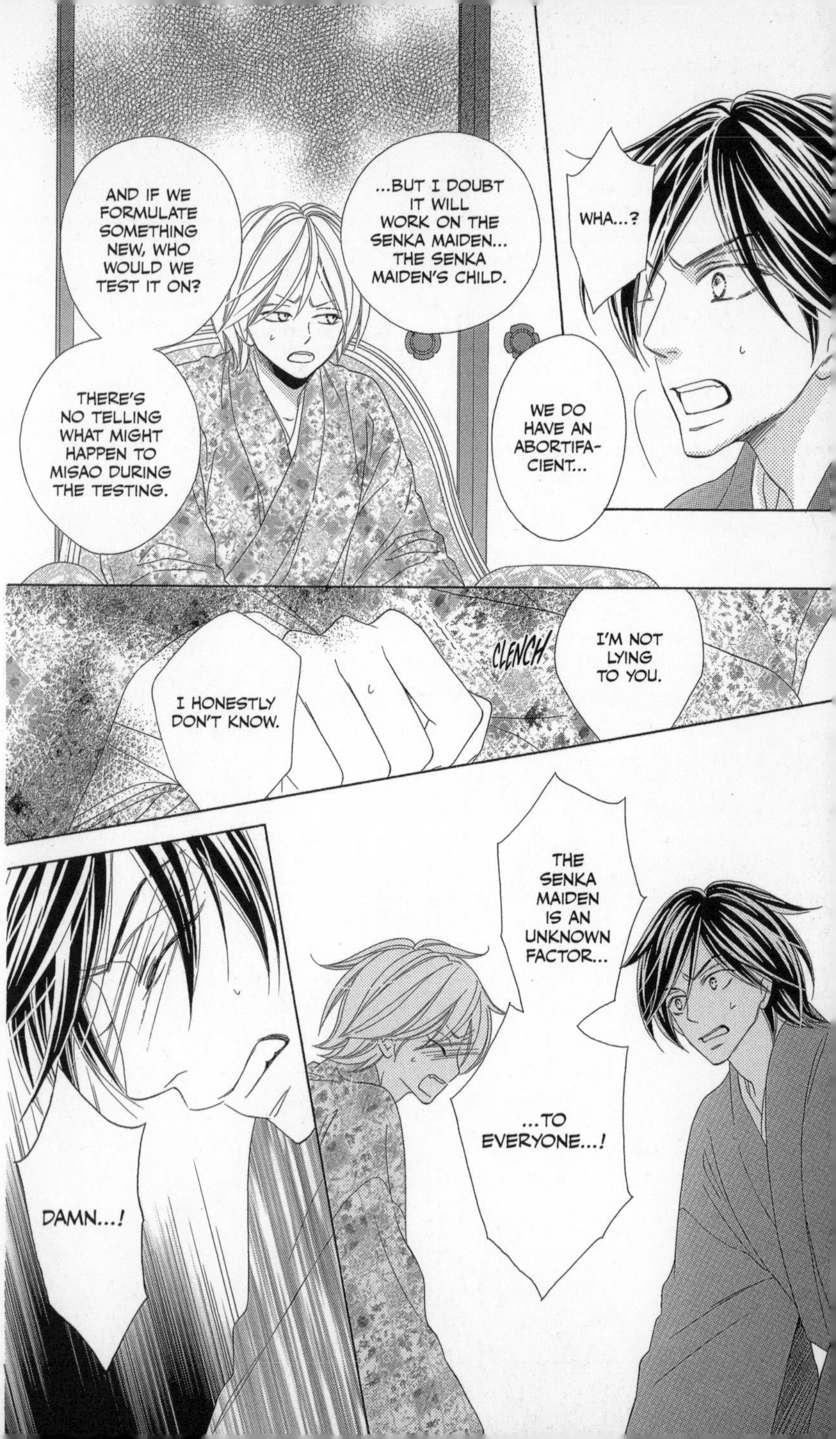
WHA...?
WE DO HAVE AN ABORTIFA-CIENT...
...BUT I DOUBT IT WILL WORK ON THE SENKA MAIDEN... THE SENKA MAIDEN'S CHILD.
AND IF WE FORMULATE SOMETHING NEW, WHO WOULD WE TEST IT ON?
THERE'S NO TELLING WHAT MIGHT HAPPEN TO MISAO DURING THE TESTING.
I'M NOT LYING TO YOU.
CLENCH
I HONESTLY DON'T KNOW.
THE SENKA MAIDEN IS AN UNKNOWN FACTOR...
...TO EVERYONE...!
DAMN...!

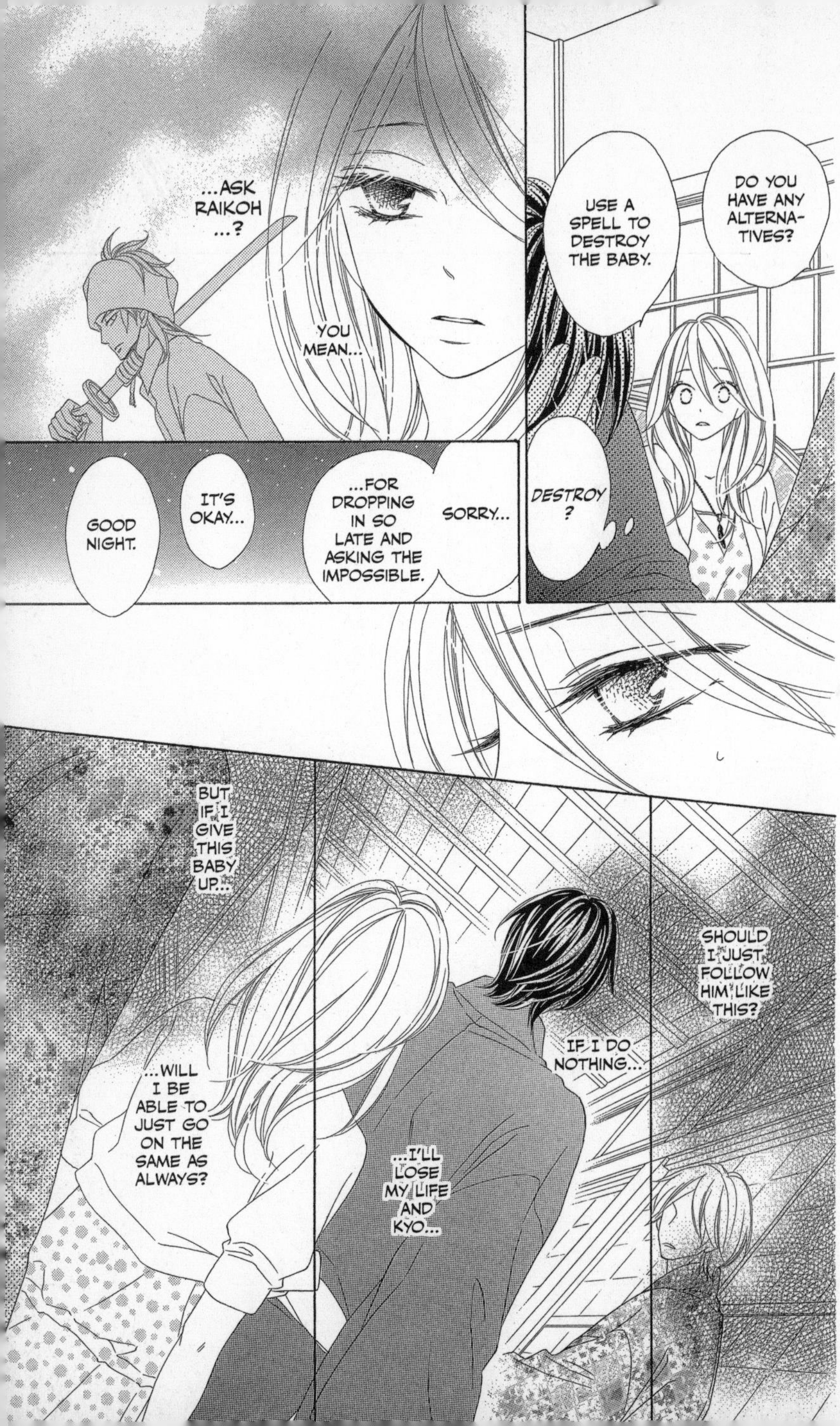
DO YOU HAVE ANY ALTERNA-TIVES?
USE A SPELL TO DESTROY THE BABY.
DESTROY?
YOU MEAN...
...ASK RAIKOH...?
SORRY...
...FOR DROPPING IN SO LATE AND ASKING THE IMPOSSIBLE.
IT'S OKAY...
GOOD NIGHT.
SHOULD I JUST FOLLOW HIM LIKE THIS?
IF I DO NOTHING...
...I'LL LOSE MY LIFE AND KYO...
BUT IF I GIVE THIS BABY UP...
...WILL I BE ABLE TO JUST GO ON THE SAME AS ALWAYS?

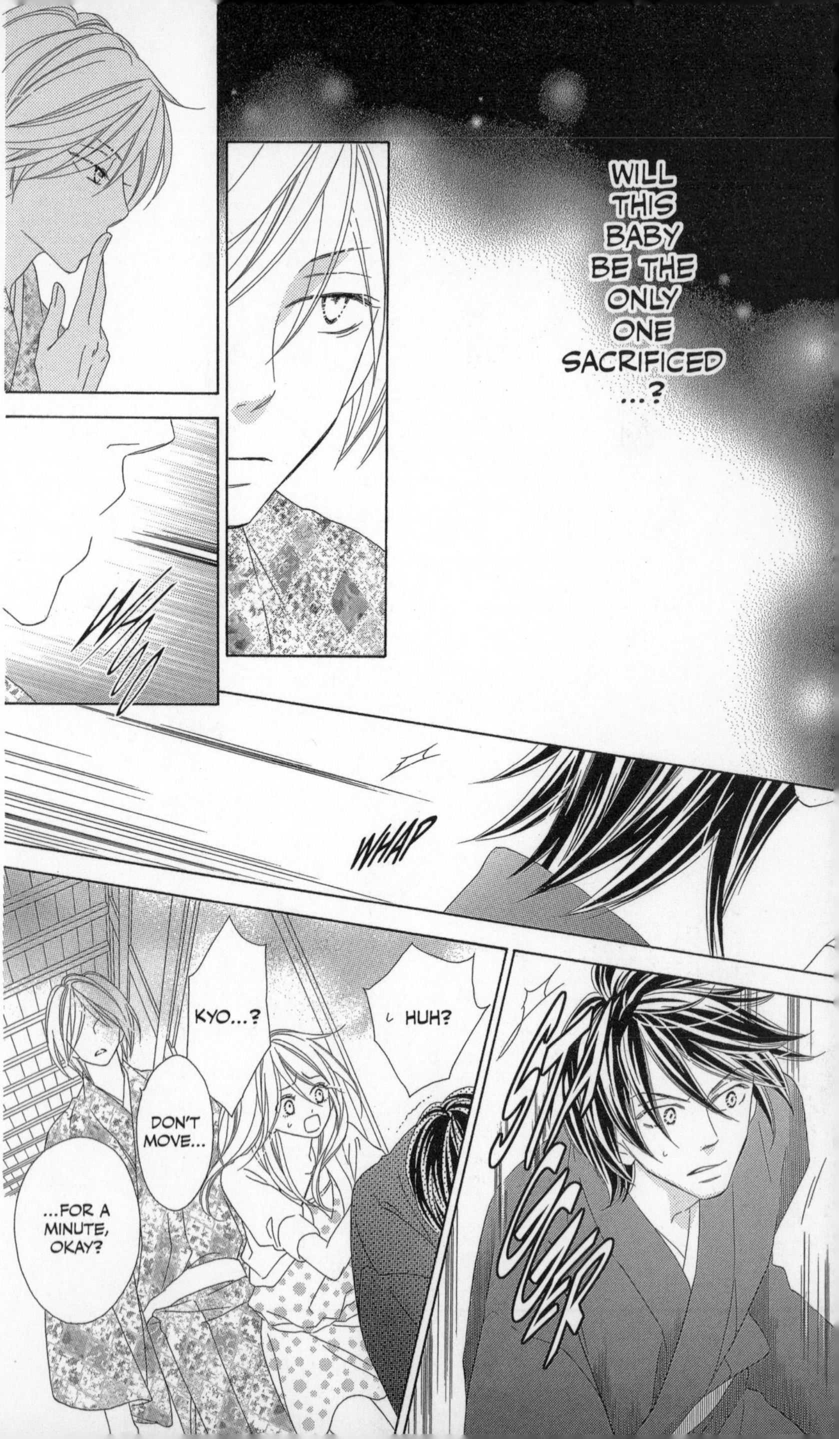
WILL THIS BABY BE THE ONLY ONE SACRIFICED ...?
WHAP
HUH?
KYO...?
DON'T MOVE...
...FOR A MINUTE, OKAY?

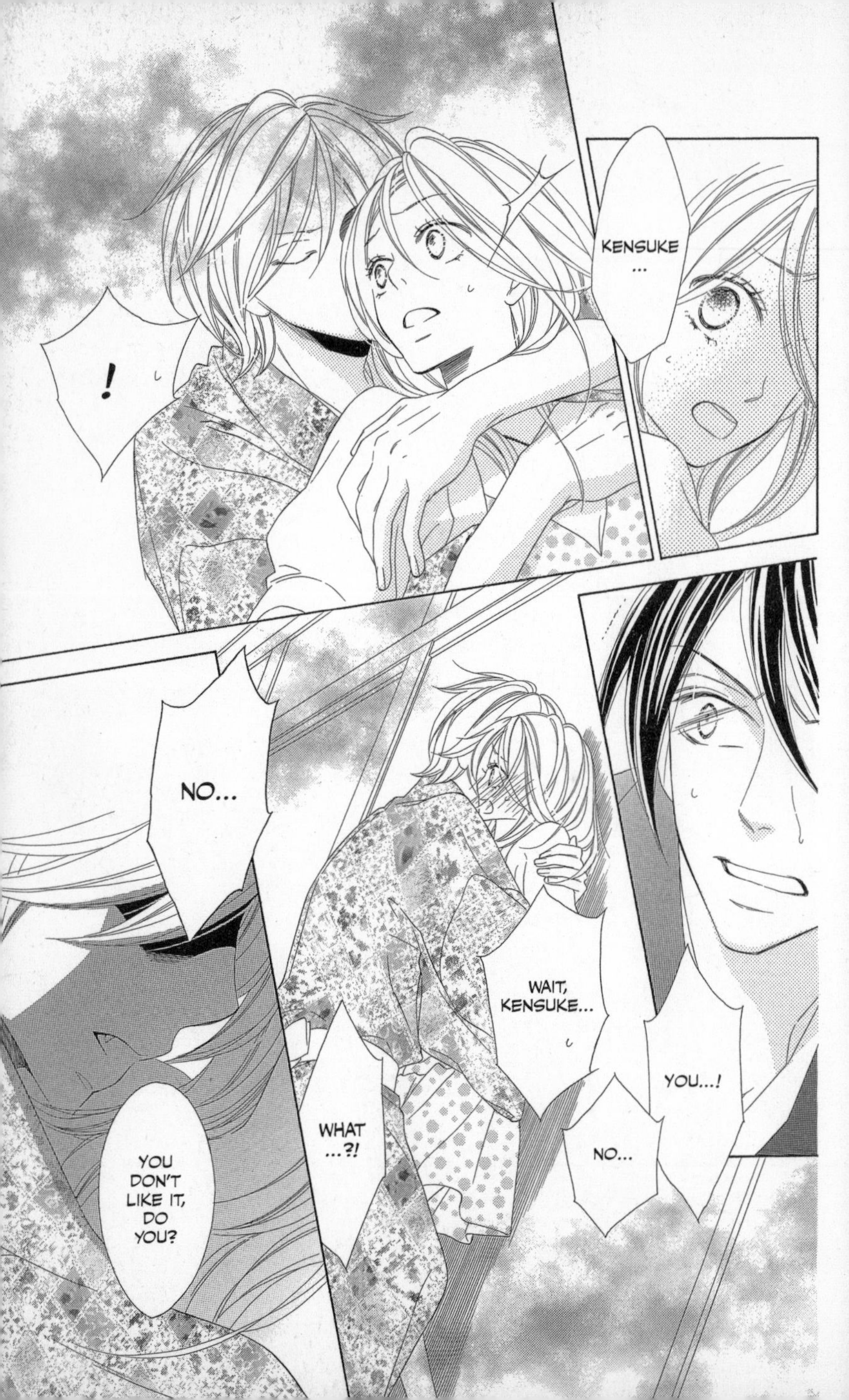
KENSUKE ...
!
YOU...!
WAIT, KENSUKE...
NO...
WHAT ...?!
NO...
YOU DON'T LIKE IT, DO YOU?

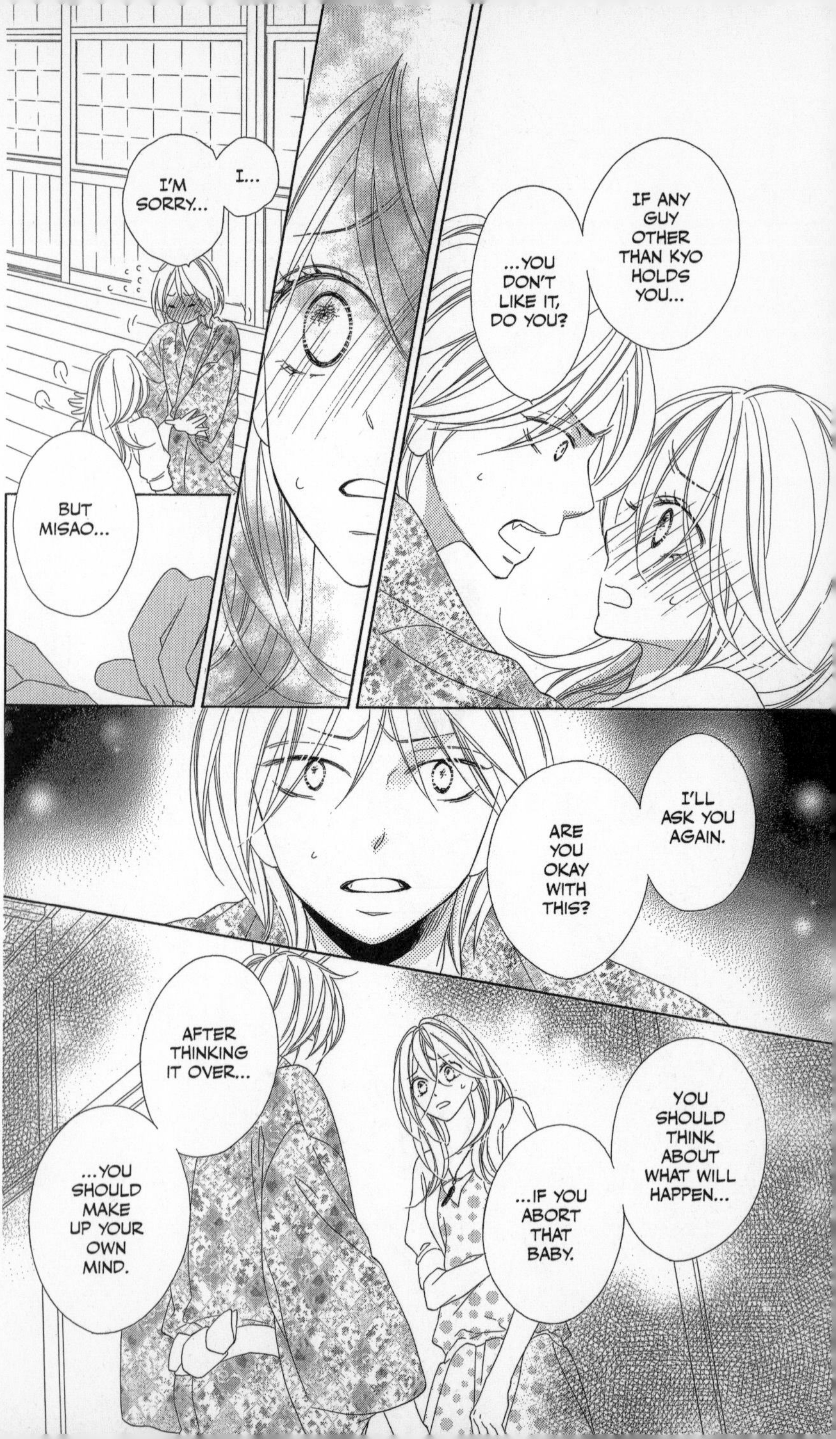
IF ANY GUY OTHER THAN KYO HOLDS YOU...
...YOU DON'T LIKE IT, DO YOU?
I...
I'M SORRY...
BUT MISAO...
I'LL ASK YOU AGAIN.
ARE YOU OKAY WITH THIS?
YOU SHOULD THINK ABOUT WHAT WILL HAPPEN...
...IF YOU ABORT THAT BABY.
AFTER THINKING IT OVER...
...YOU SHOULD MAKE UP YOUR OWN MIND.

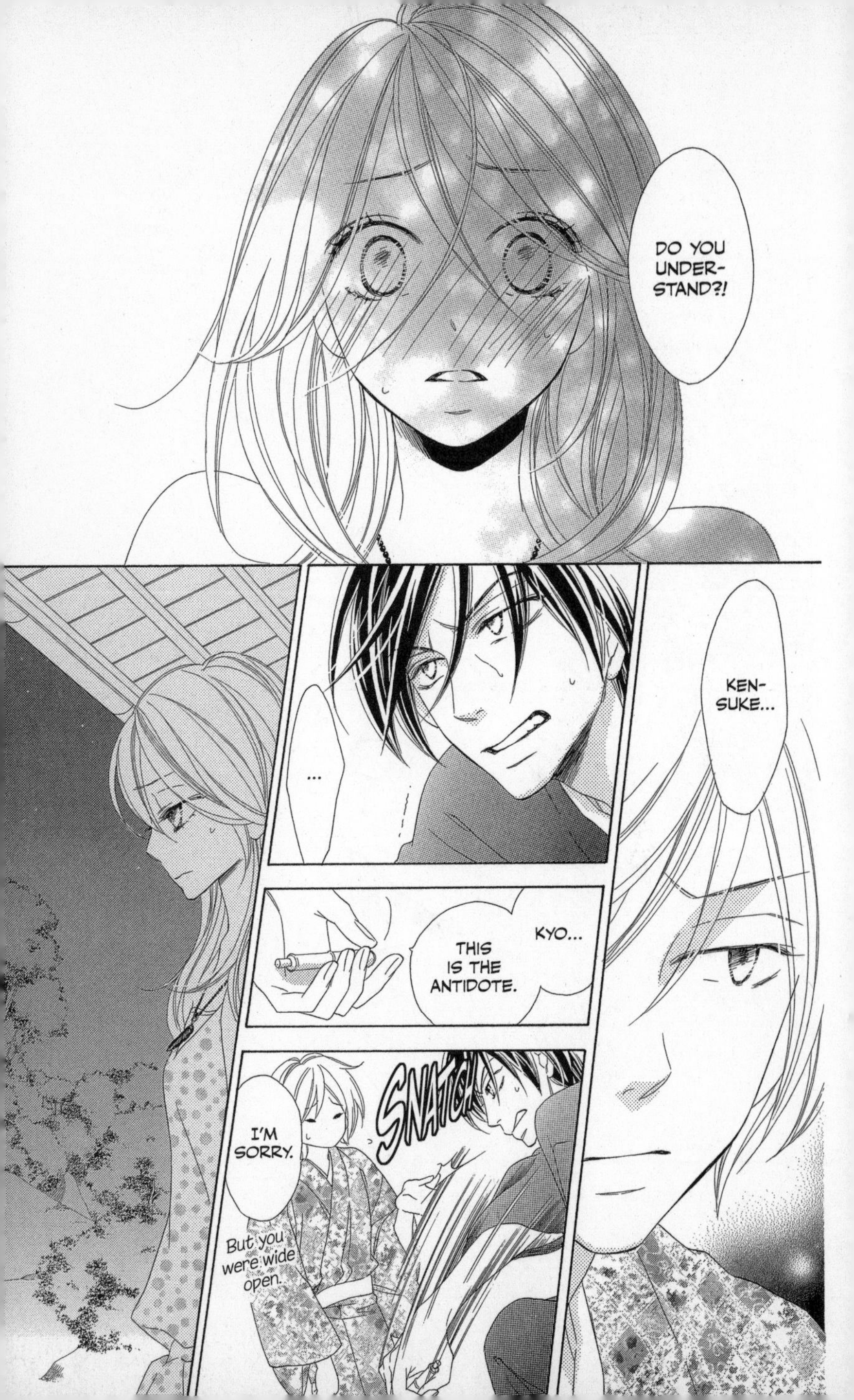
DO YOU UNDERSTAND?!
KEN-SUKE...
...
KYO...
THIS IS THE ANTIDOTE.
SNATCH
I'M SORRY.
But you were wide open.

WHAT WILL HAPPEN IF I...
...ABORT THIS BABY...?
FLAP
FLAP
I NEVER INTENDED ...
...TO SEE HER AGAIN.

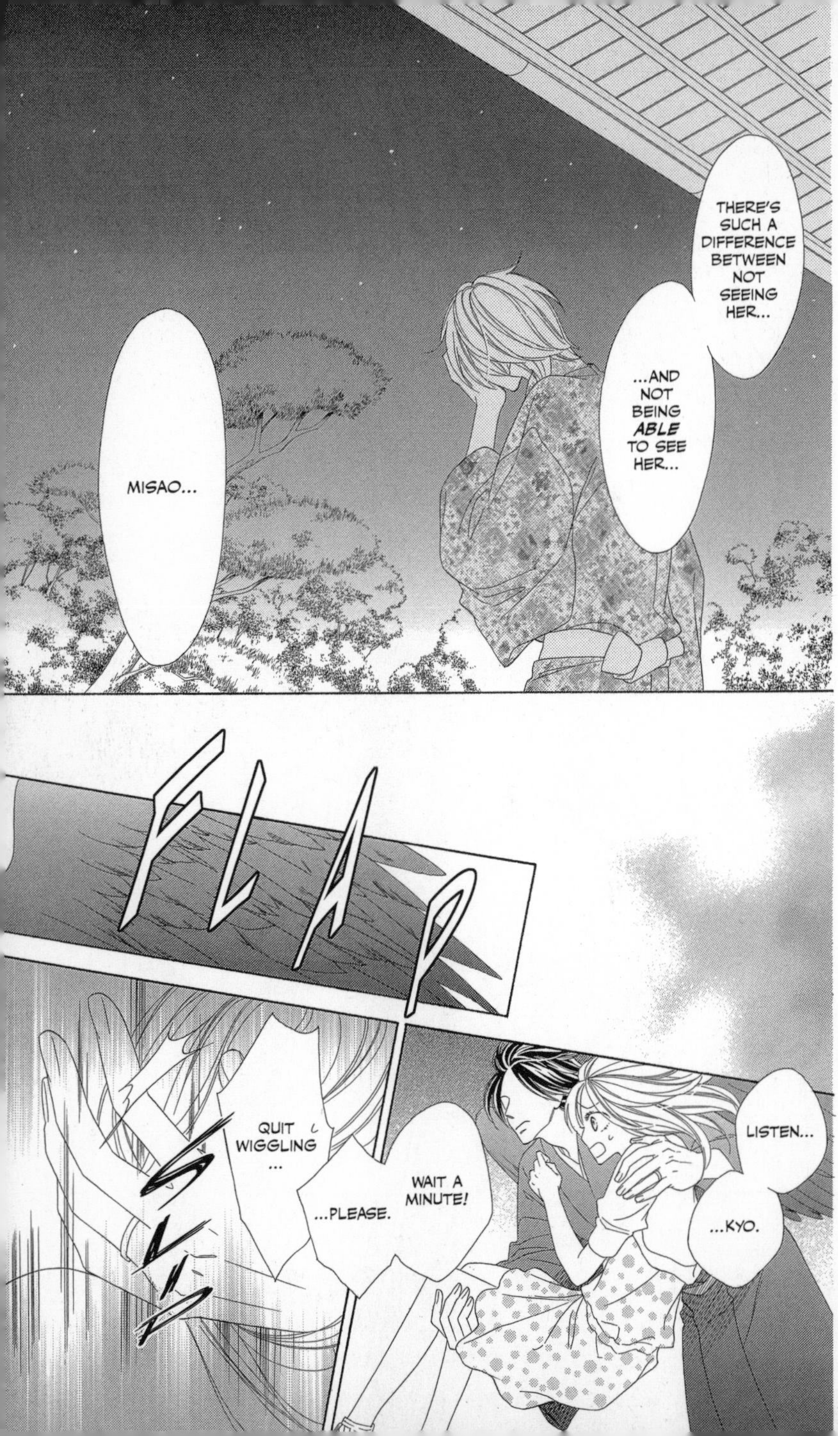
THERE'S SUCH A DIFFERENCE BETWEEN NOT SEEING HER...
...AND NOT BEING ***ABLE*** TO SEE HER...
MISAO...
FLAP
LISTEN...
...KYO.
WAIT A MINUTE!
...PLEASE.
QUIT WIGGLING ...

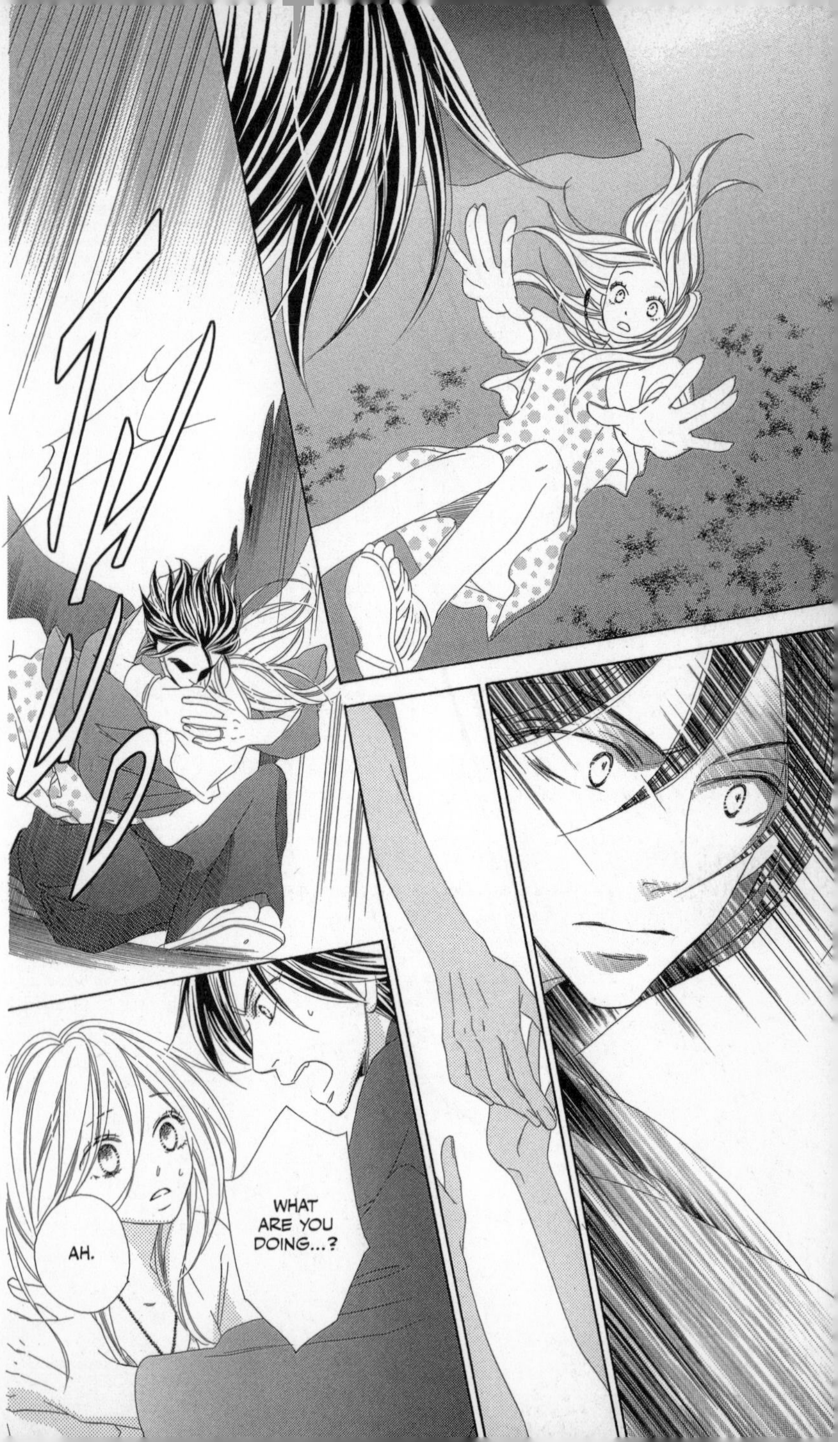
WHAT ARE YOU DOING...?
AH.

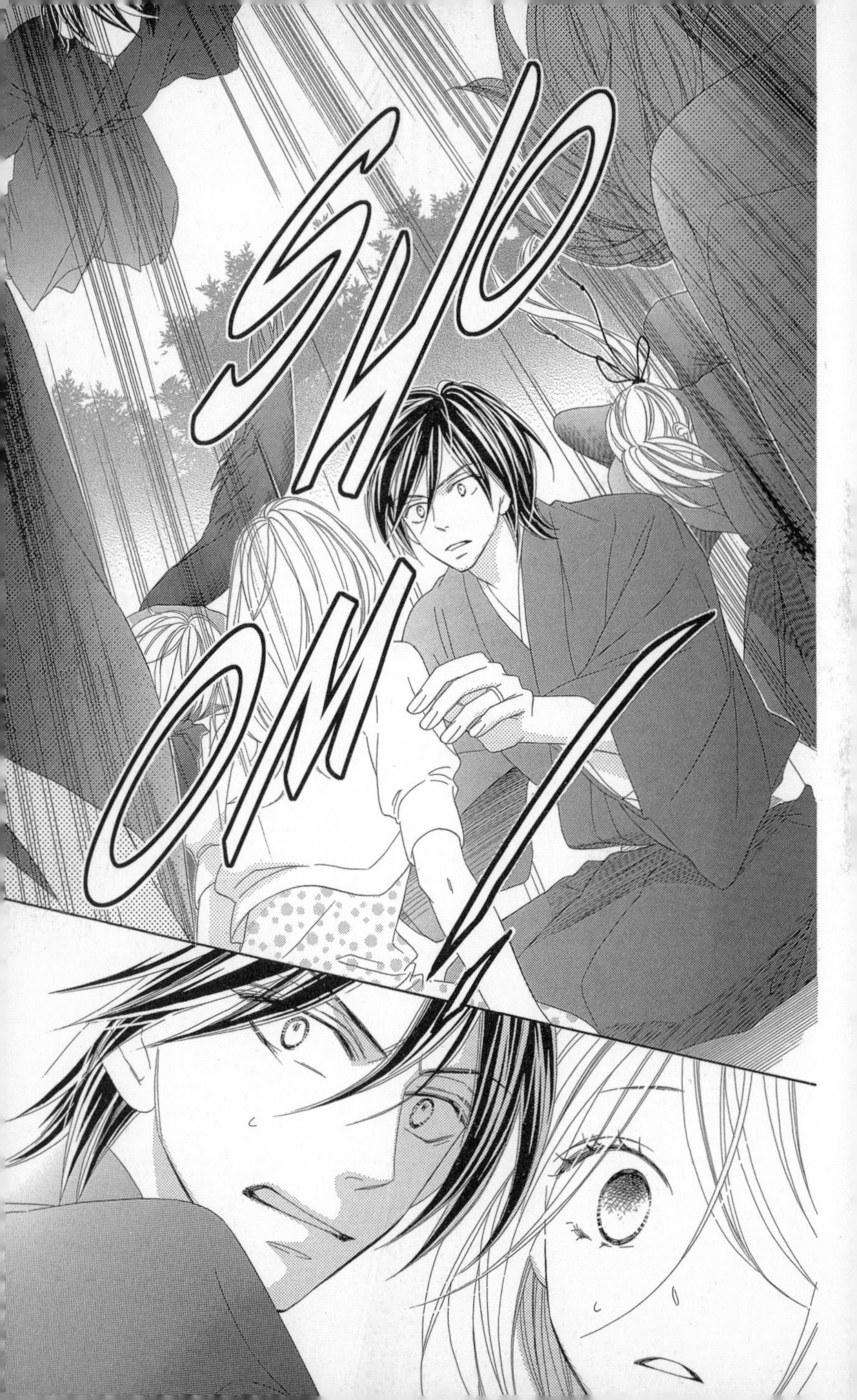

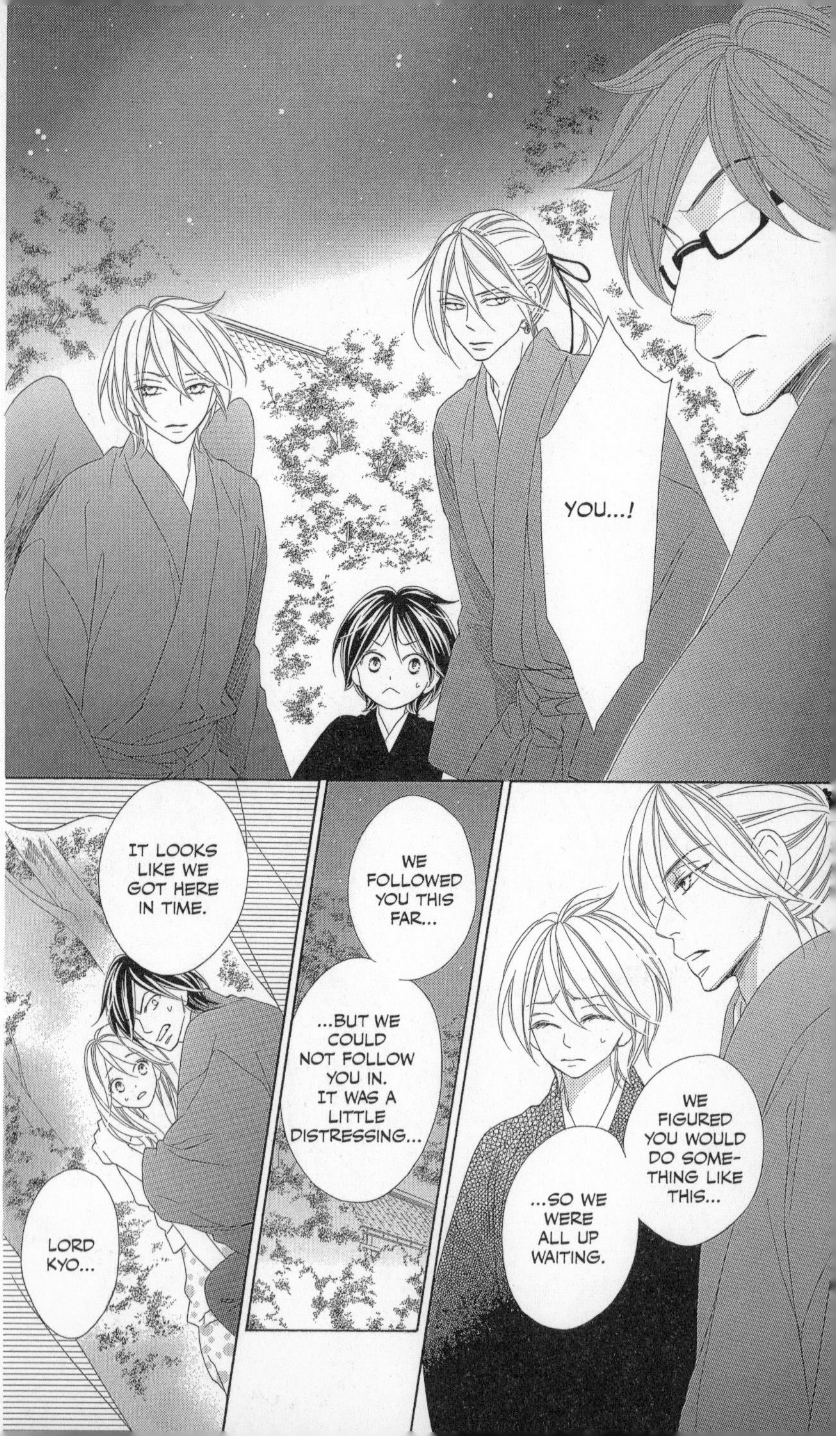
YOU...!
WE FIGURED YOU WOULD DO SOME-THING LIKE THIS...
...SO WE WERE ALL UP WAITING.
WE FOLLOWED YOU THIS FAR...
...BUT WE COULD NOT FOLLOW YOU IN. IT WAS A LITTLE DISTRESSING...
IT LOOKS LIKE WE GOT HERE IN TIME.
LORD KYO...

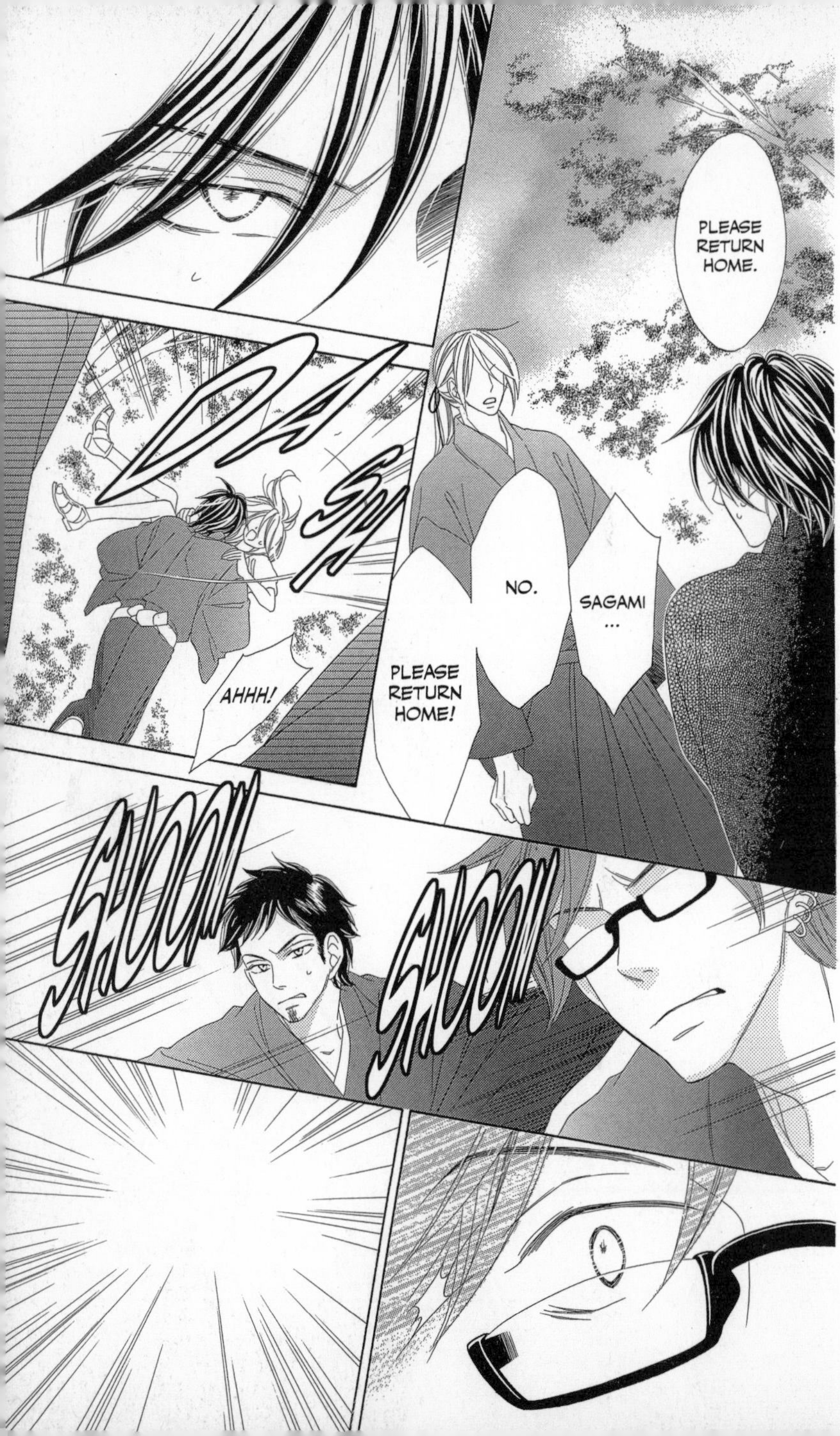
PLEASE RETURN HOME.
SAGAMI ...
NO.
PLEASE RETURN HOME!
DASH
AHHH!

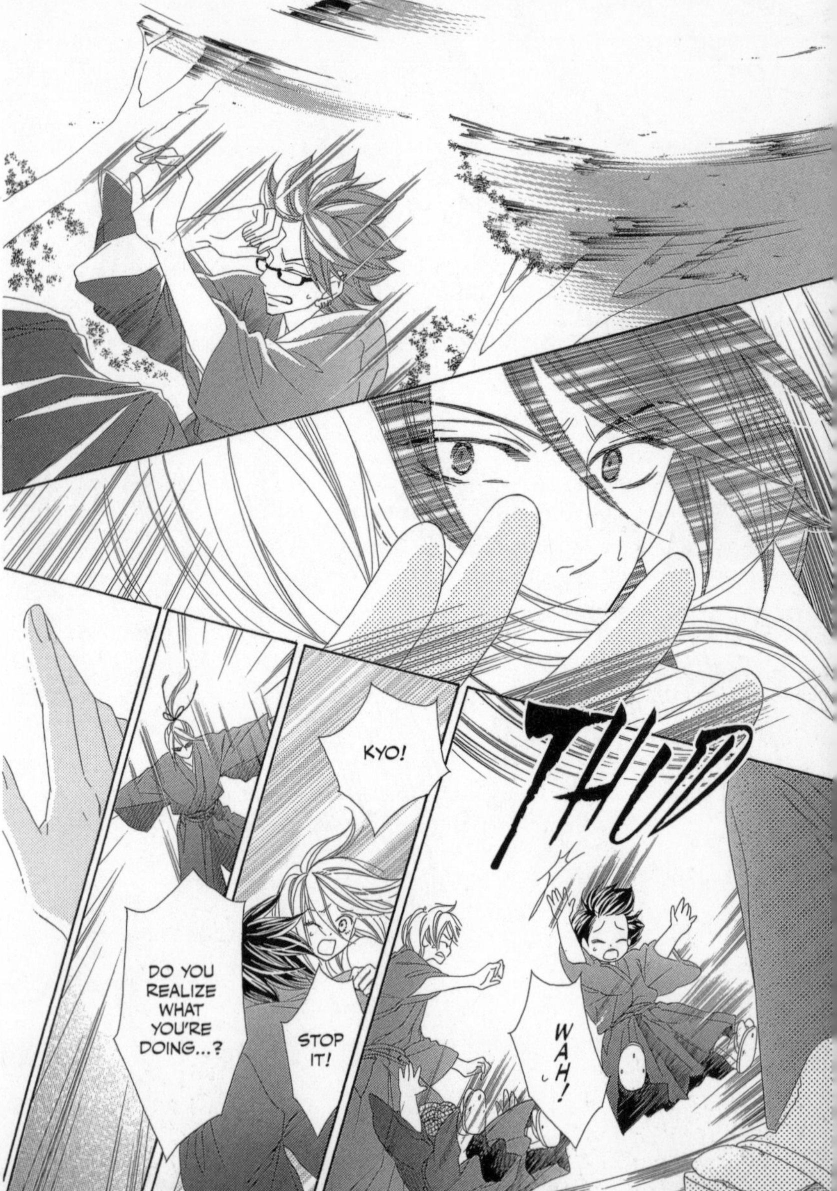
THUD
WAH!
KYO!
STOP IT!
DO YOU REALIZE WHAT YOU'RE DOING...?

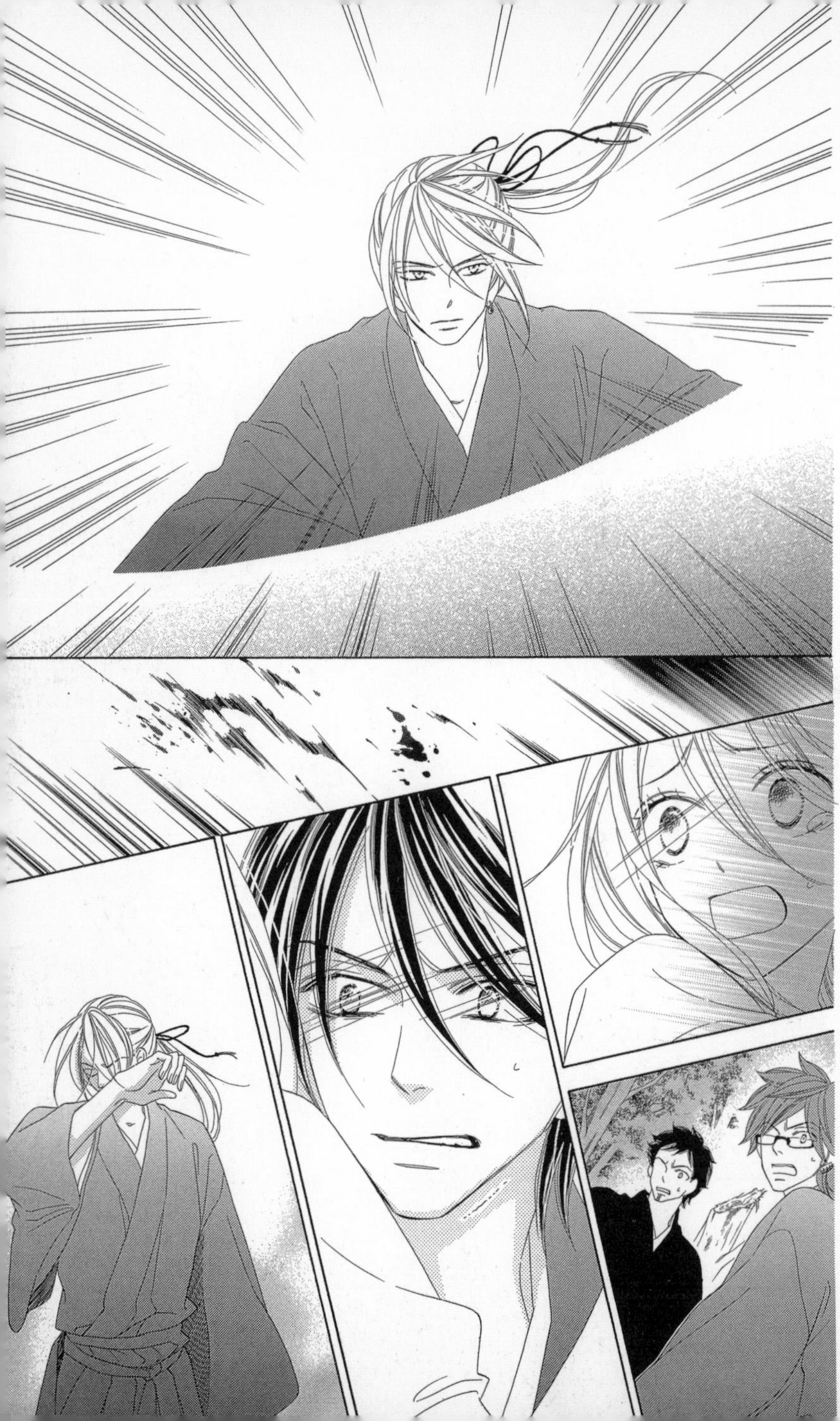

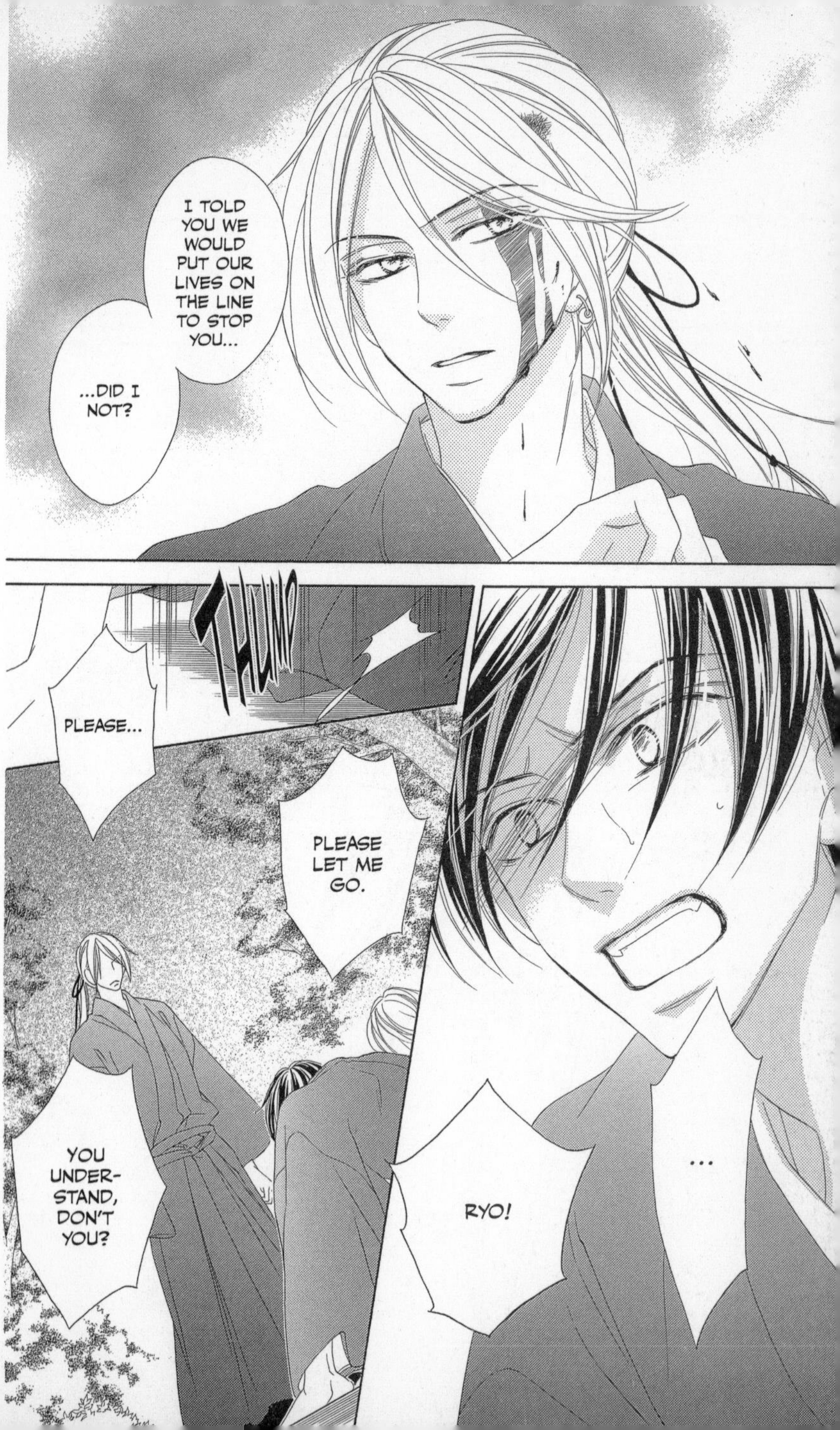
I TOLD YOU WE WOULD PUT OUR LIVES ON THE LINE TO STOP YOU...
...DID I NOT?
...
RYO!
THUMP
PLEASE...
PLEASE LET ME GO.
YOU UNDER-STAND, DON'T YOU?

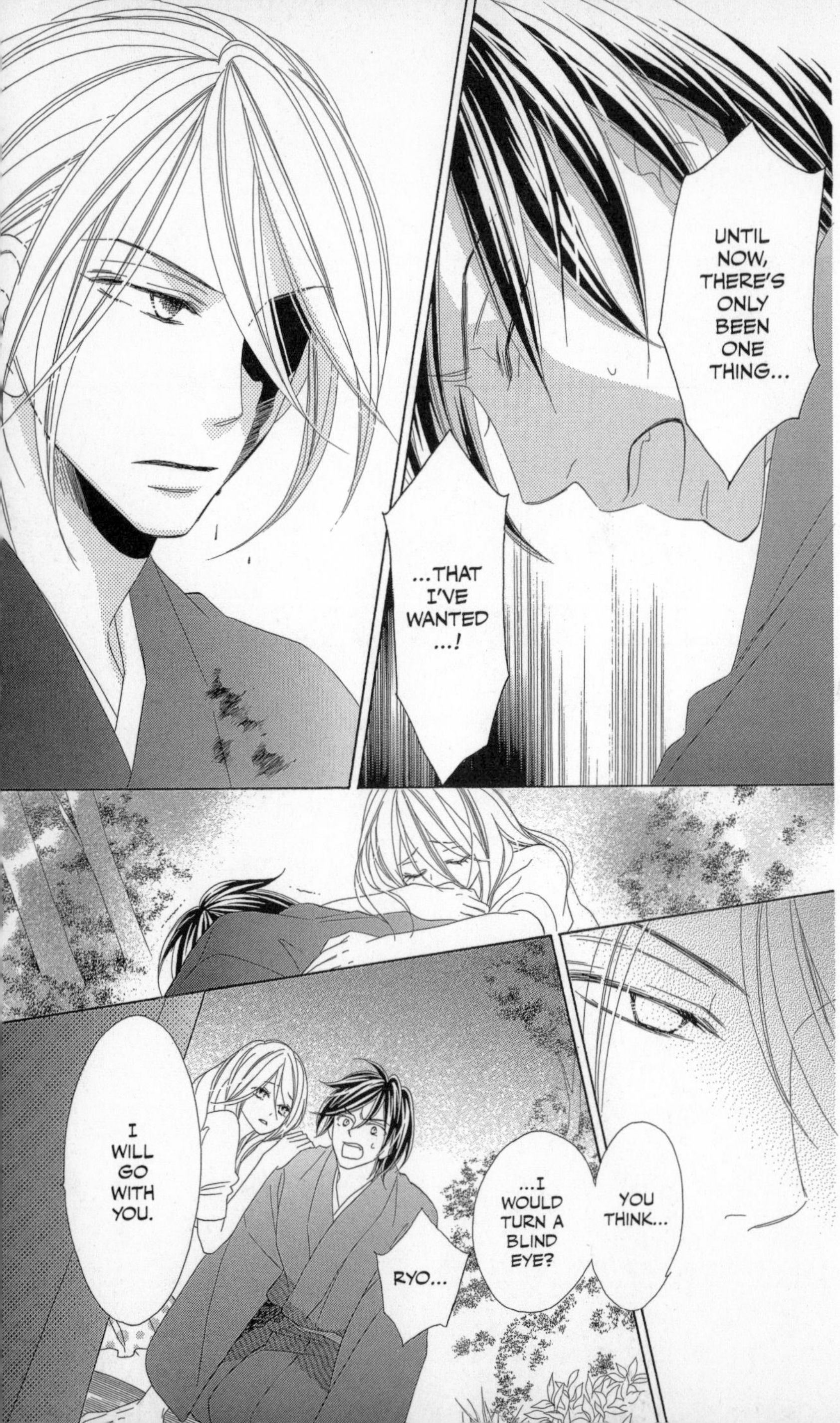
UNTIL NOW, THERE'S ONLY BEEN ONE THING...
...THAT I'VE WANTED ...!
YOU THINK...
...I WOULD TURN A BLIND EYE?
RYO...
I WILL GO WITH YOU.

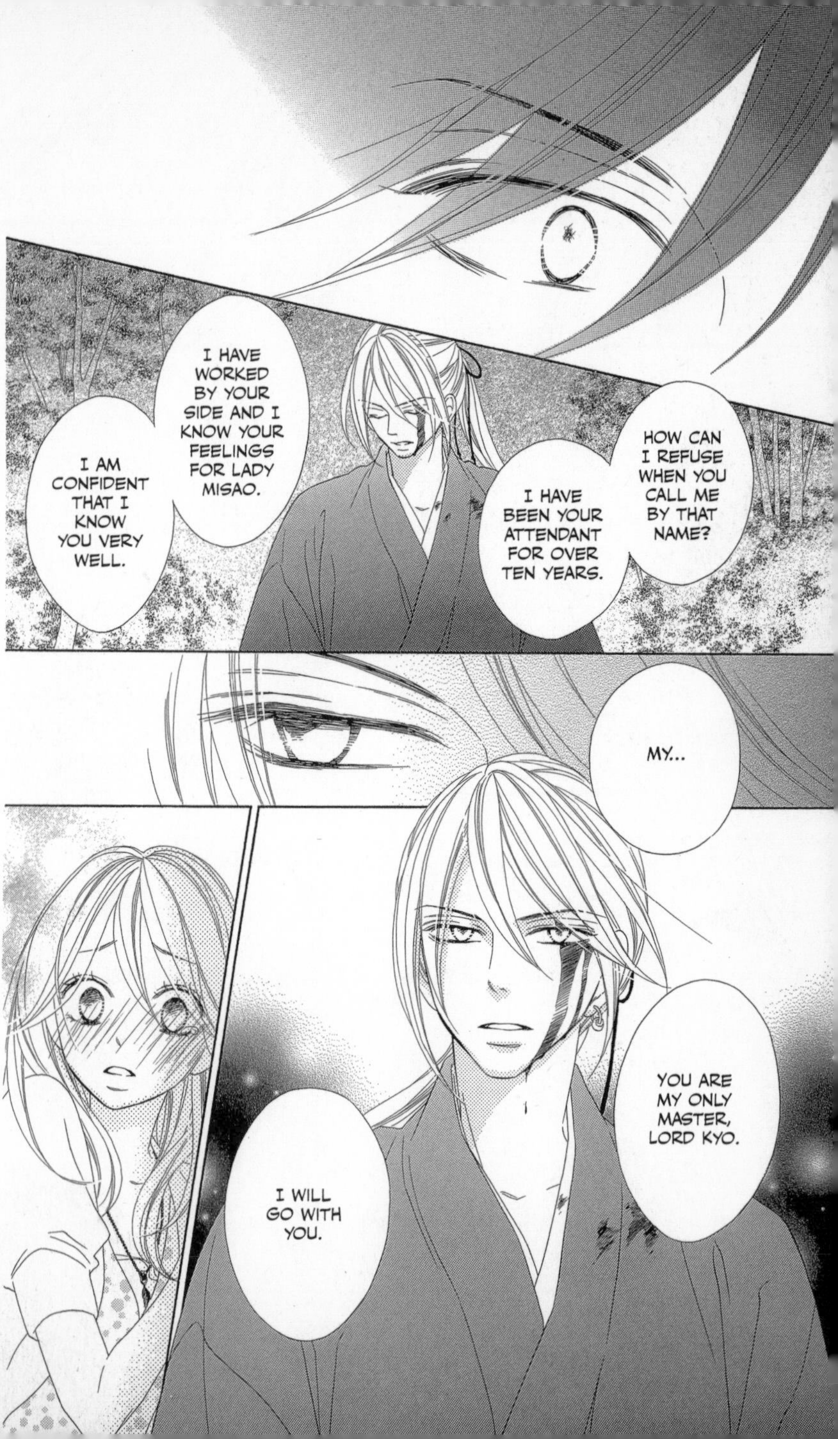
HOW CAN I REFUSE WHEN YOU CALL ME BY THAT NAME?
I HAVE BEEN YOUR ATTENDANT FOR OVER TEN YEARS.
I HAVE WORKED BY YOUR SIDE AND I KNOW YOUR FEELINGS FOR LADY MISAO.
I AM CONFIDENT THAT I KNOW YOU VERY WELL.
MY...
YOU ARE MY ONLY MASTER, LORD KYO.
I WILL GO WITH YOU.

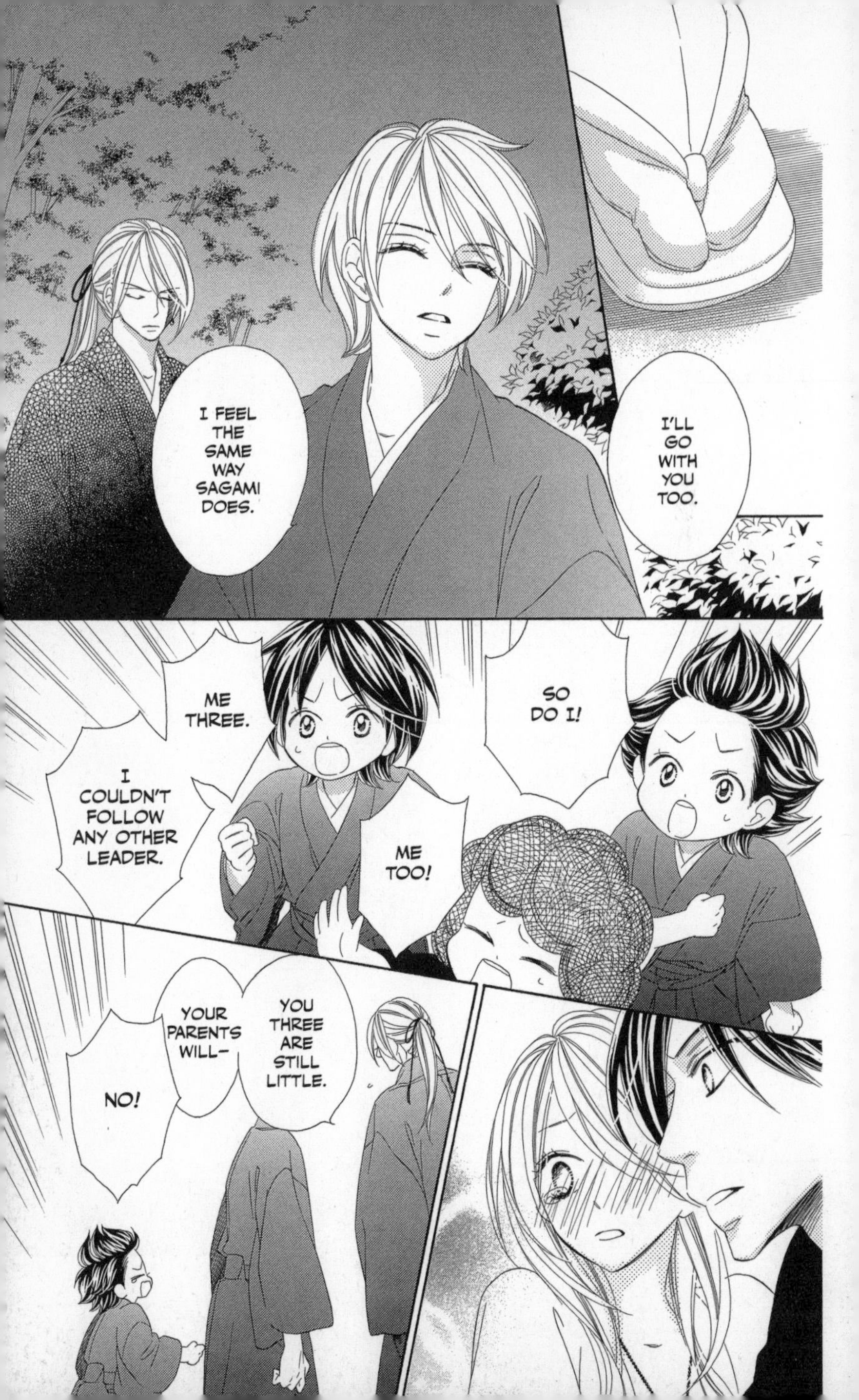
I'LL GO WITH YOU TOO.
I FEEL THE SAME WAY SAGAMI DOES.
SO DO I!
ME THREE.
ME TOO!
I COULDN'T FOLLOW ANY OTHER LEADER.
YOU THREE ARE STILL LITTLE.
YOUR PARENTS WILL—
NO!

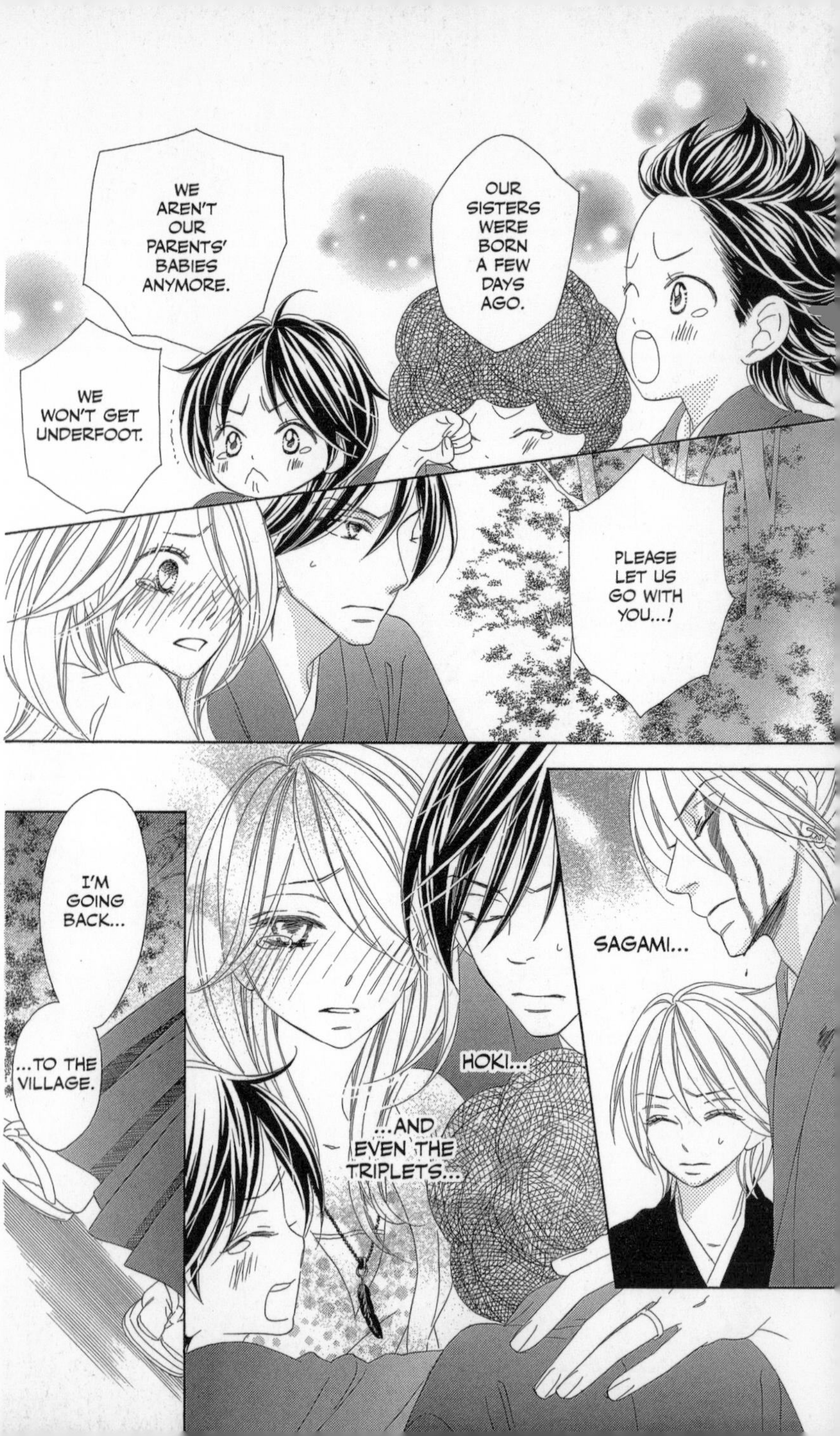
OUR SISTERS WERE BORN A FEW DAYS AGO.
WE AREN'T OUR PARENTS' BABIES ANYMORE.
WE WON'T GET UNDERFOOT.
PLEASE LET US GO WITH YOU...!
SAGAMI...
HOKI...
...AND EVEN THE TRIPLETS...
I'M GOING BACK...
...TO THE VILLAGE.

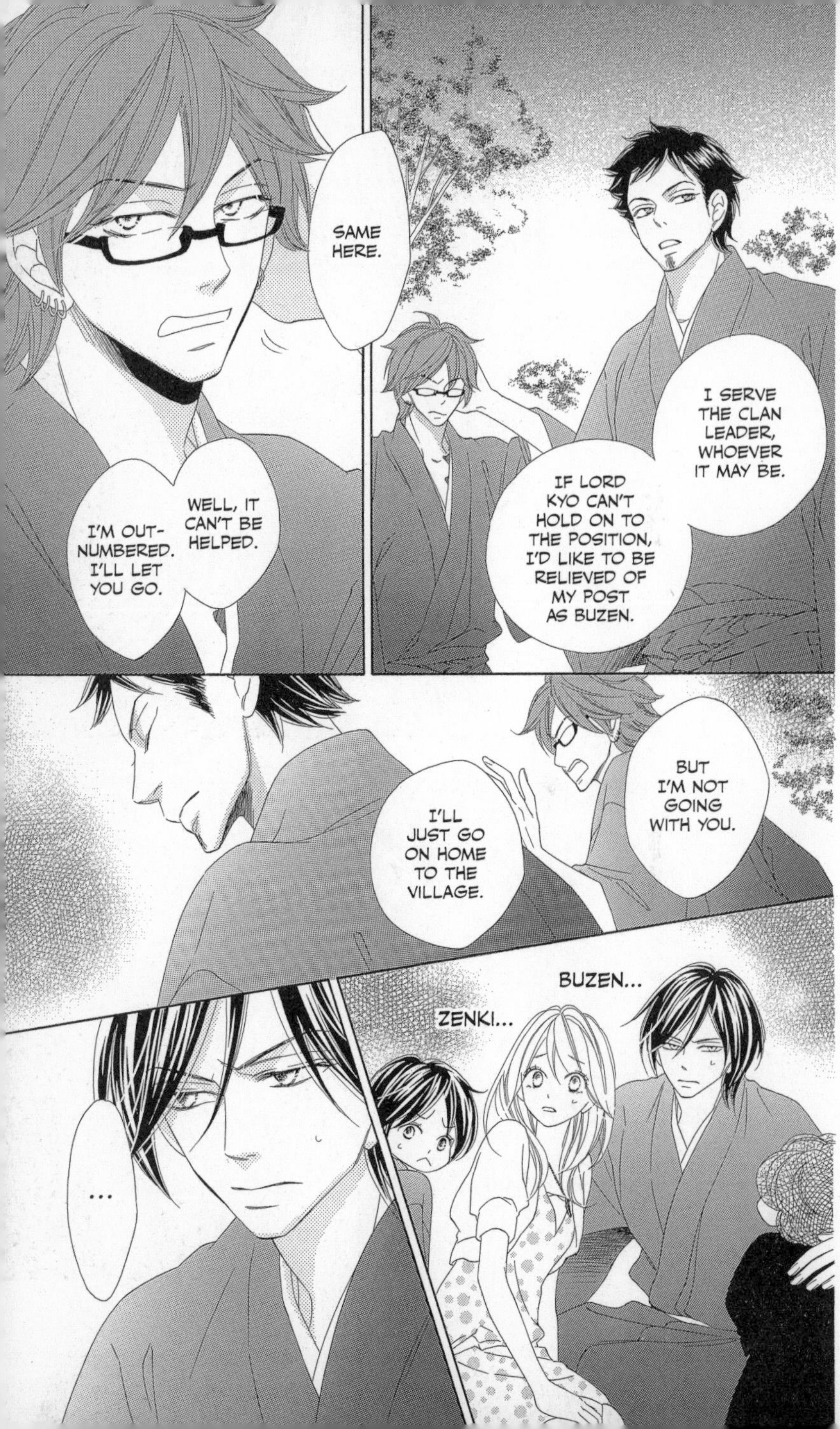
I SERVE THE CLAN LEADER, WHOEVER IT MAY BE.
IF LORD KYO CAN'T HOLD ON TO THE POSITION, I'D LIKE TO BE RELIEVED OF MY POST AS BUZEN.
SAME HERE.
WELL, IT CAN'T BE HELPED.
I'M OUT-NUMBERED. I'LL LET YOU GO.
BUT I'M NOT GOING WITH YOU.
I'LL JUST GO ON HOME TO THE VILLAGE.
BUZEN...
ZENKI...
...

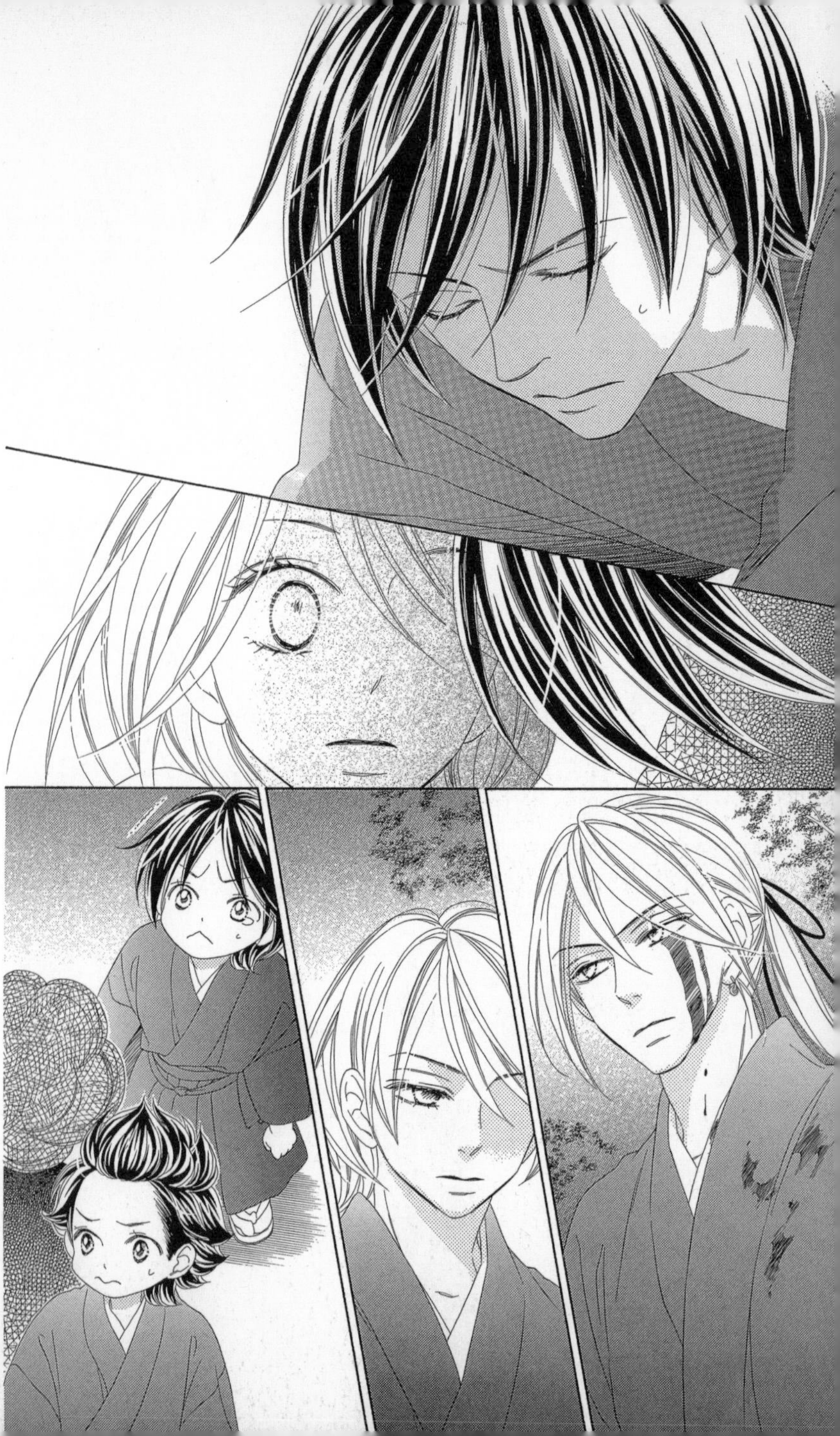

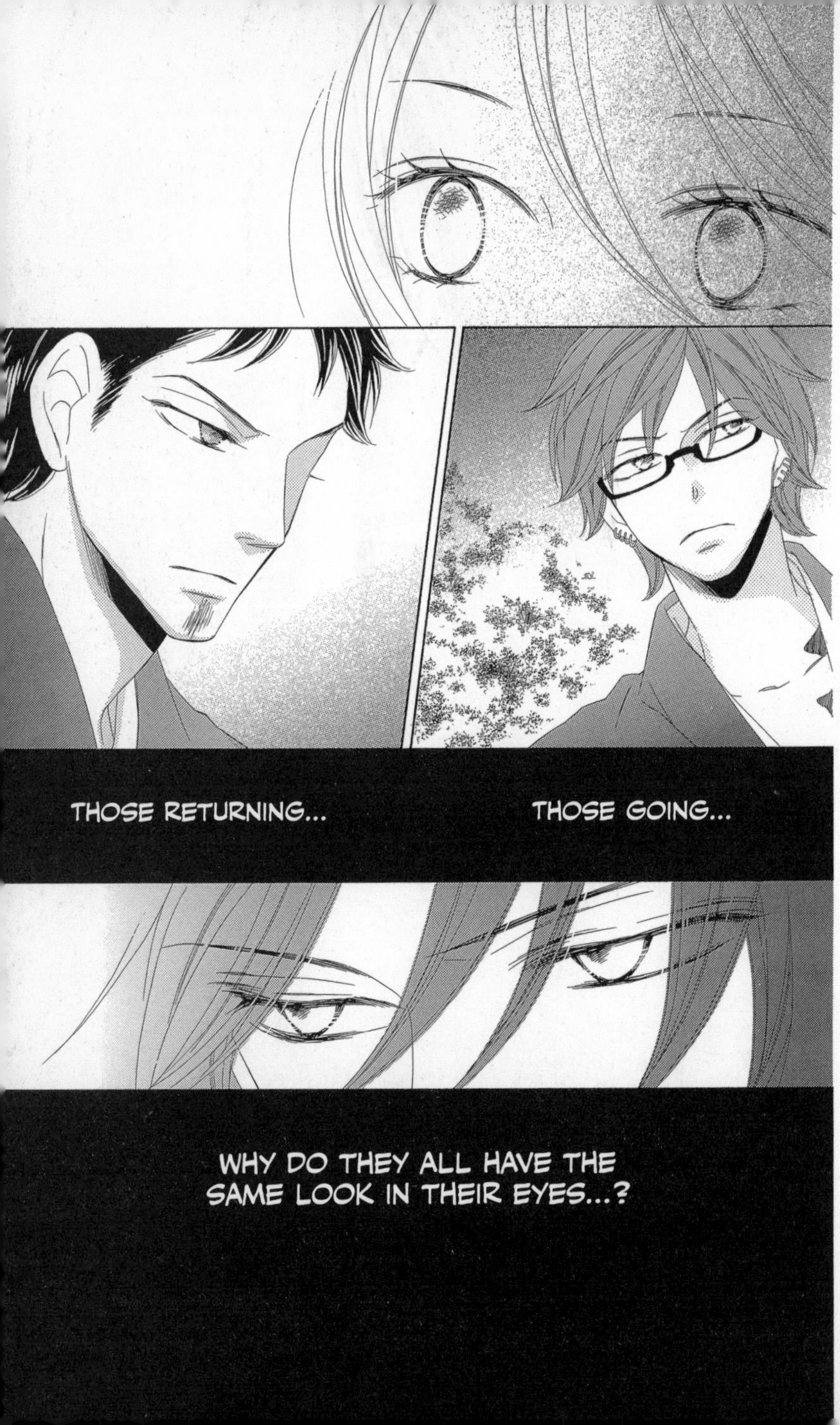

THOSE GOING...
THOSE RETURNING...
WHY DO THEY ALL HAVE THE SAME LOOK IN THEIR EYES...?

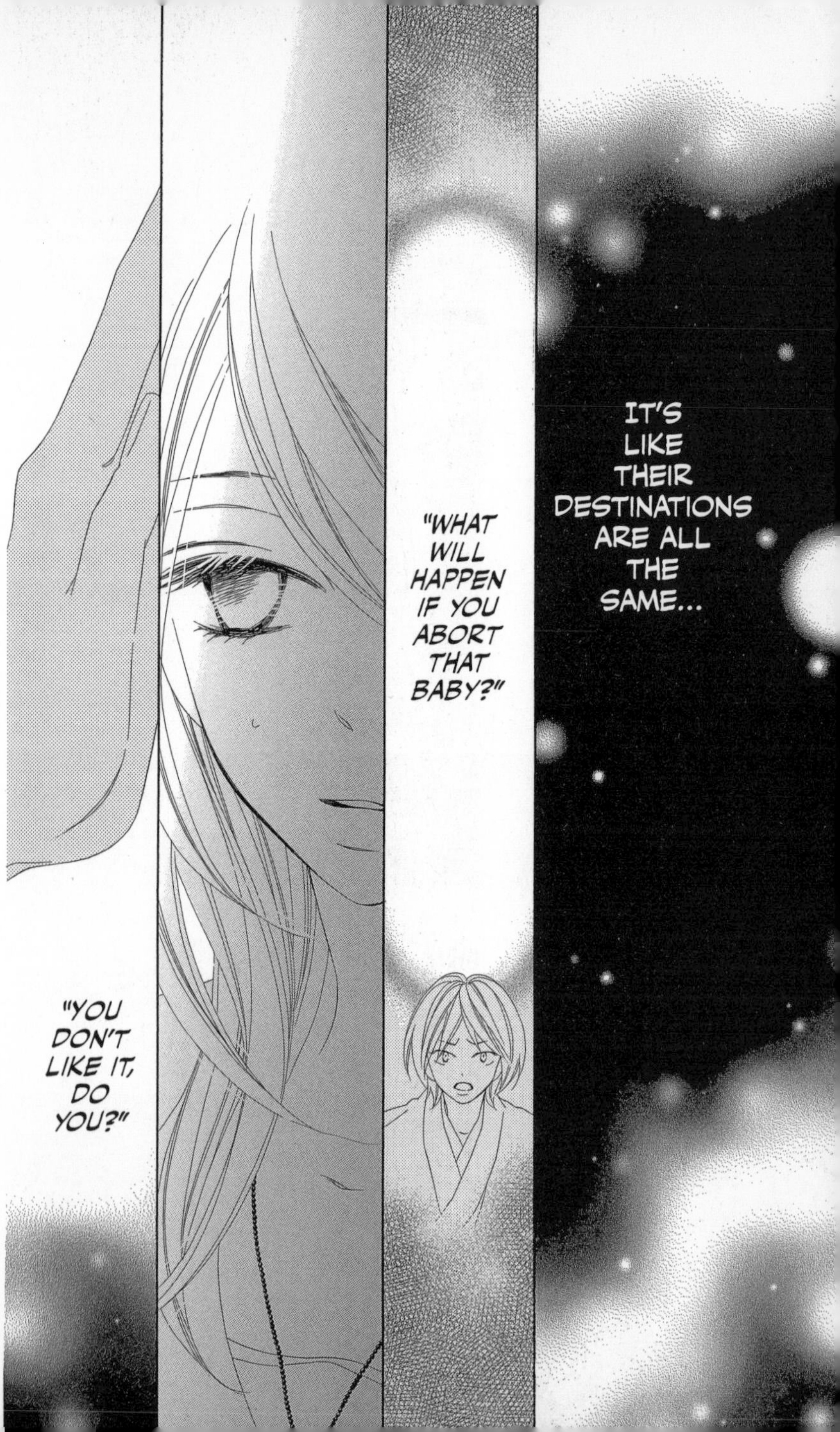
IT'S LIKE THEIR DESTINATIONS ARE ALL THE SAME...
"WHAT WILL HAPPEN IF YOU ABORT THAT BABY?"
"YOU DON'T LIKE IT, DO YOU?"

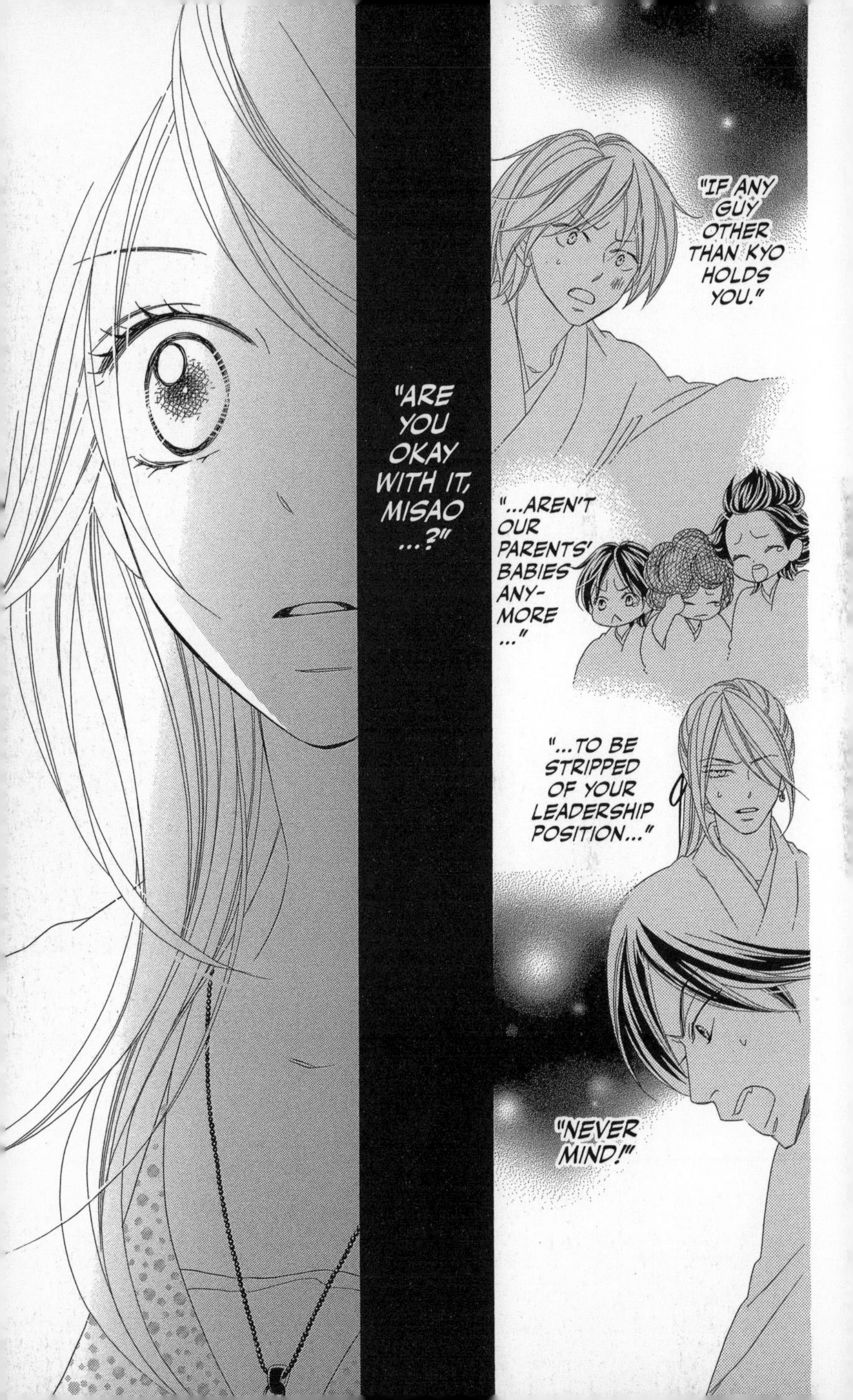
"IF ANY GUY OTHER THAN KYO HOLDS YOU."
"...AREN'T OUR PARENTS' BABIES ANY-MORE ..."
"...TO BE STRIPPED OF YOUR LEADERSHIP POSITION..."
"NEVER MIND!"
"ARE YOU OKAY WITH IT, MISAO ...?"

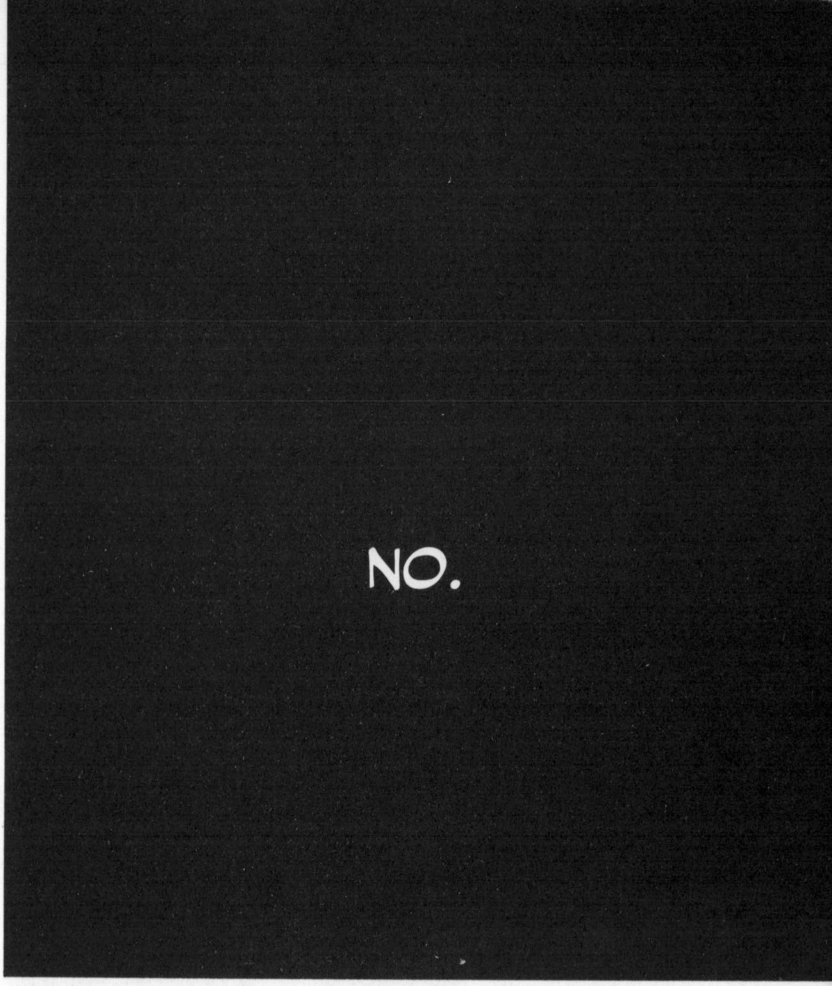
NO.

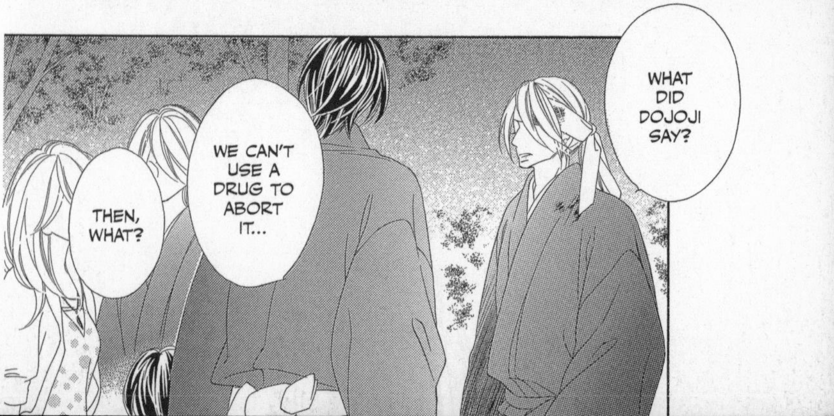
WHAT DID DOJOJI SAY?
WE CAN'T USE A DRUG TO ABORT IT...
THEN, WHAT?

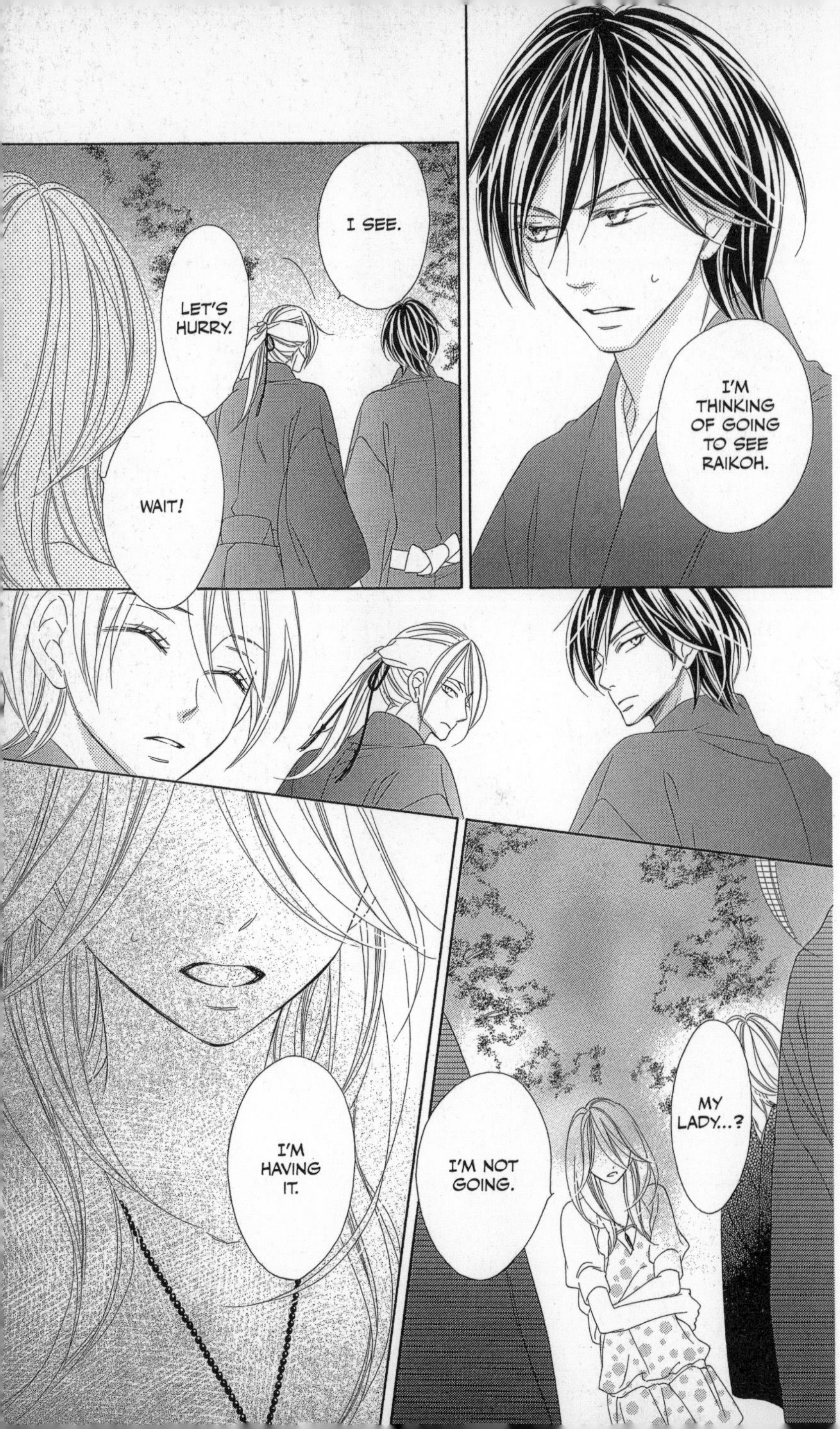
I'M THINKING OF GOING TO SEE RAIKOH.
I SEE.
LET'S HURRY.
WAIT!
MY LADY...?
I'M NOT GOING.
I'M HAVING IT.

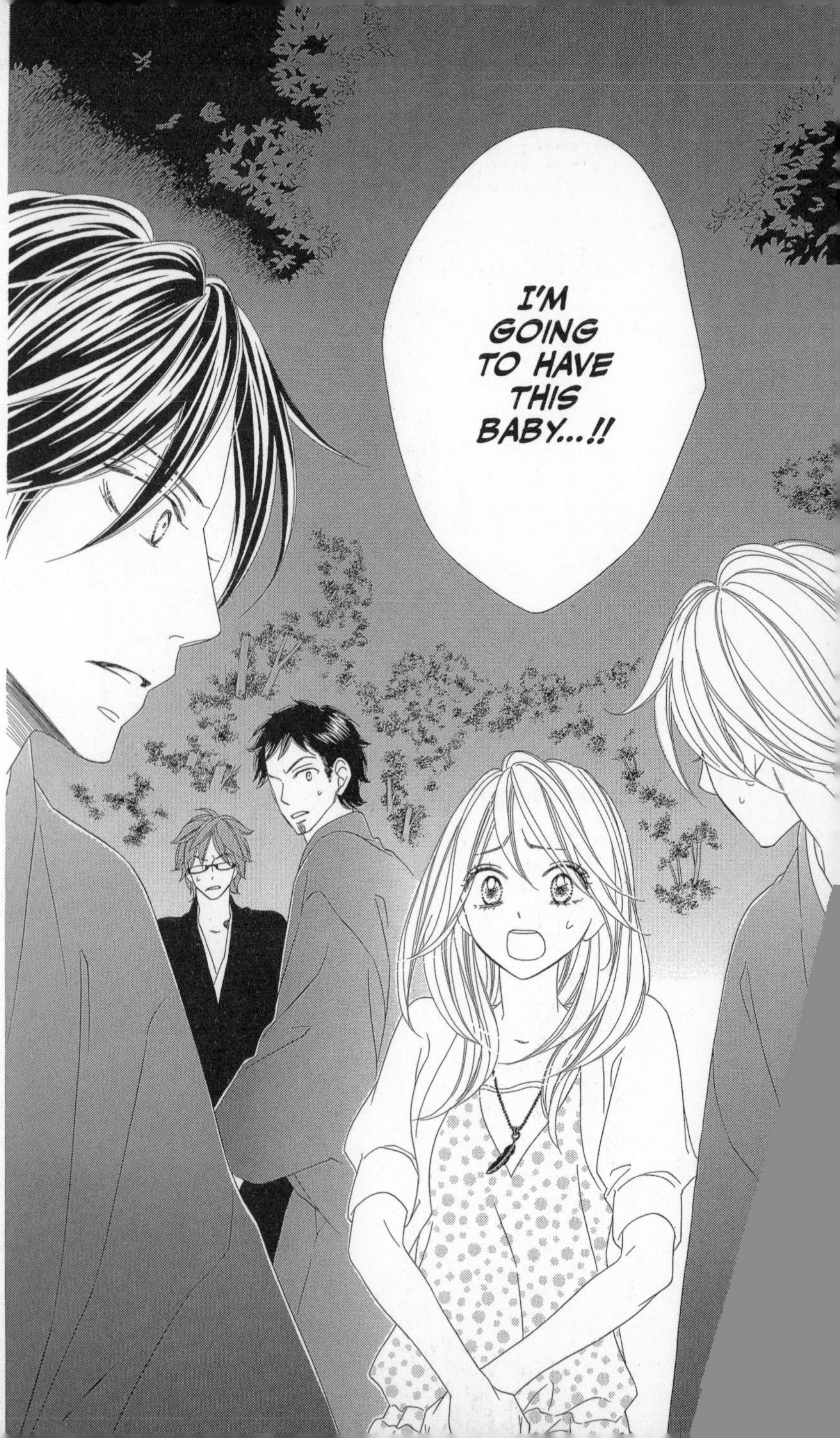
I'M GOING TO HAVE THIS BABY...!!

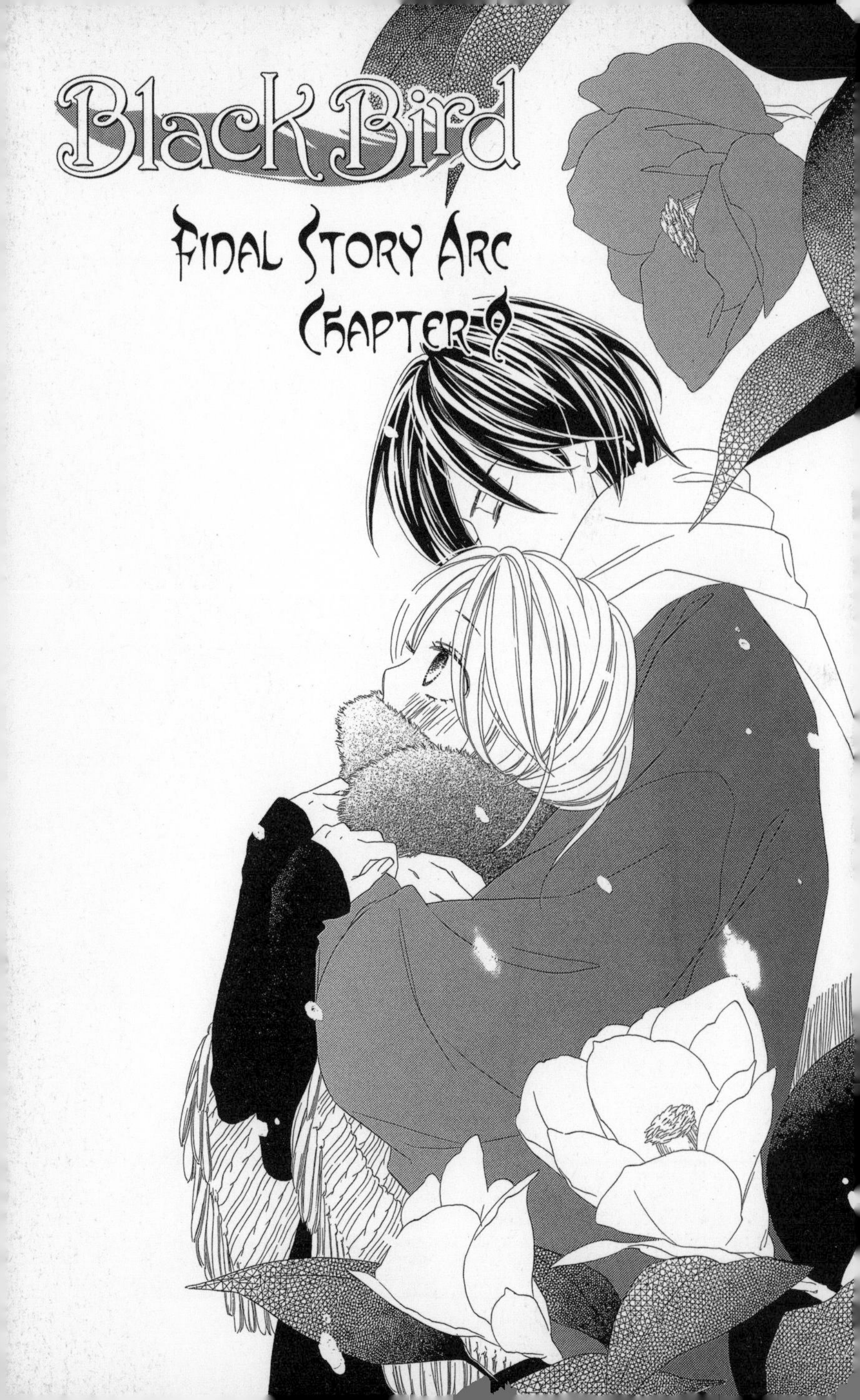
Black Bird
Final Story Arc
Chapter 9

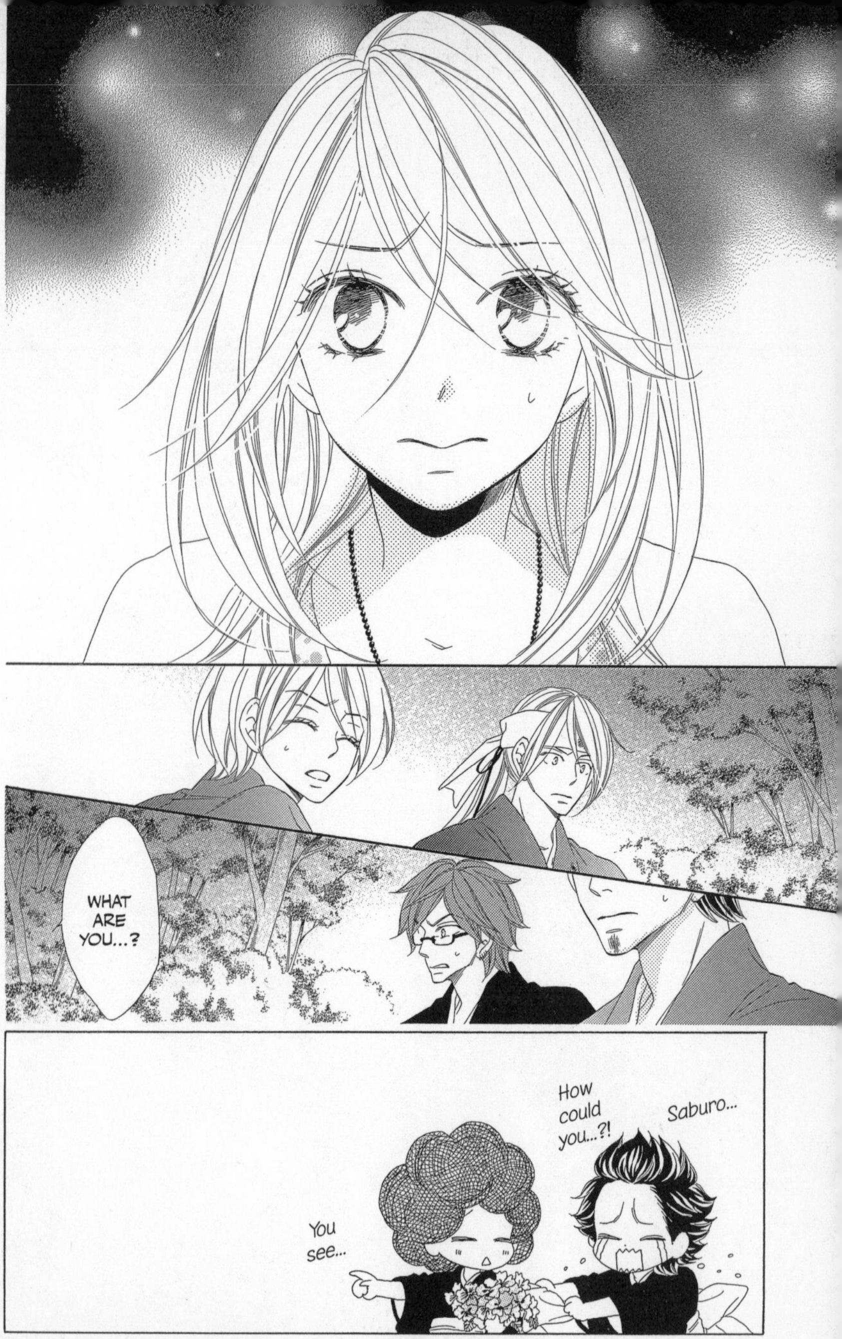
WHAT ARE YOU...?
Saburo...
How could you...?!
You see...

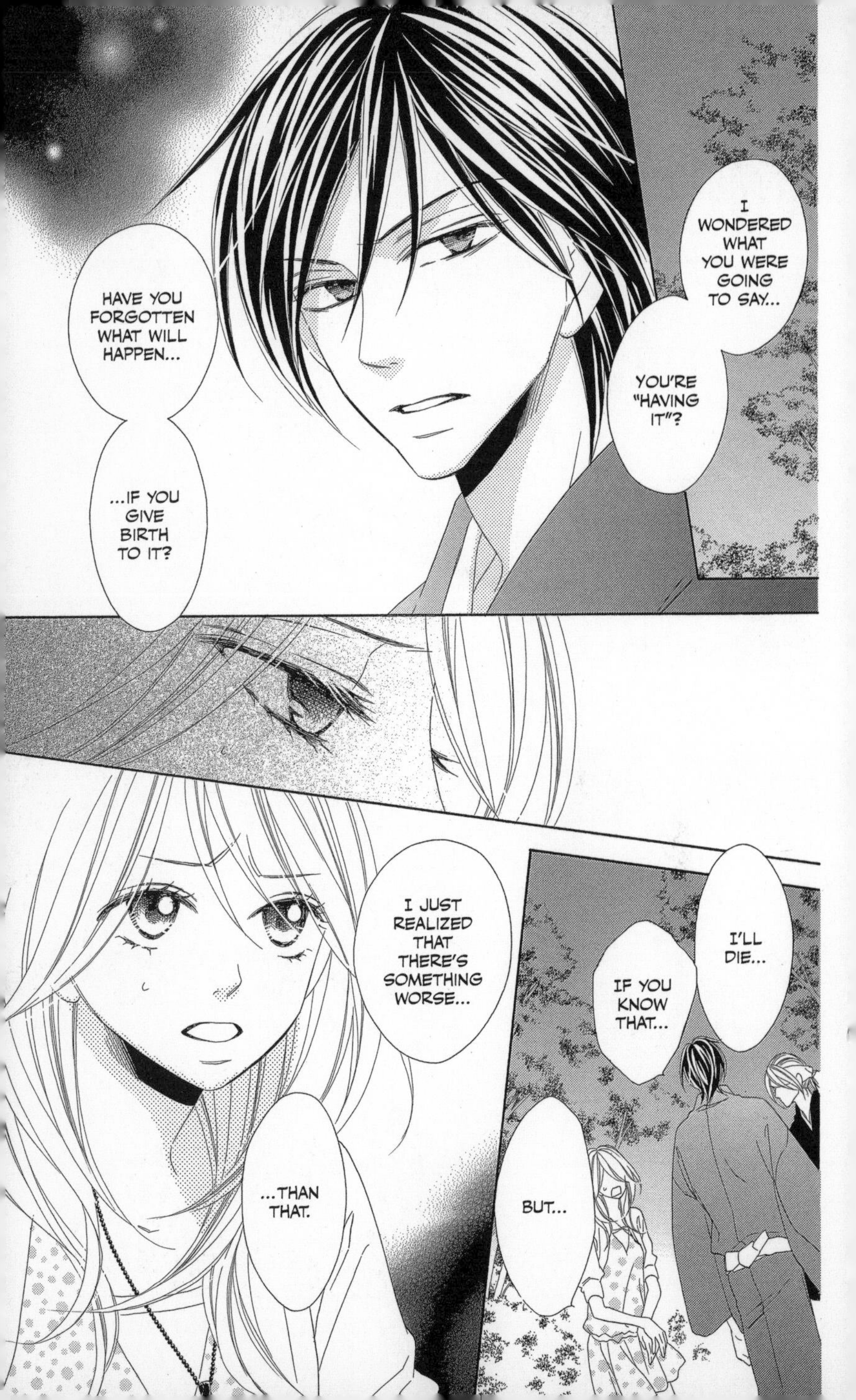
I WONDERED WHAT YOU WERE GOING TO SAY...
YOU'RE "HAVING IT"?
HAVE YOU FORGOTTEN WHAT WILL HAPPEN...
...IF YOU GIVE BIRTH TO IT?
I'LL DIE...
IF YOU KNOW THAT...
BUT...
I JUST REALIZED THAT THERE'S SOMETHING WORSE...
...THAN THAT.

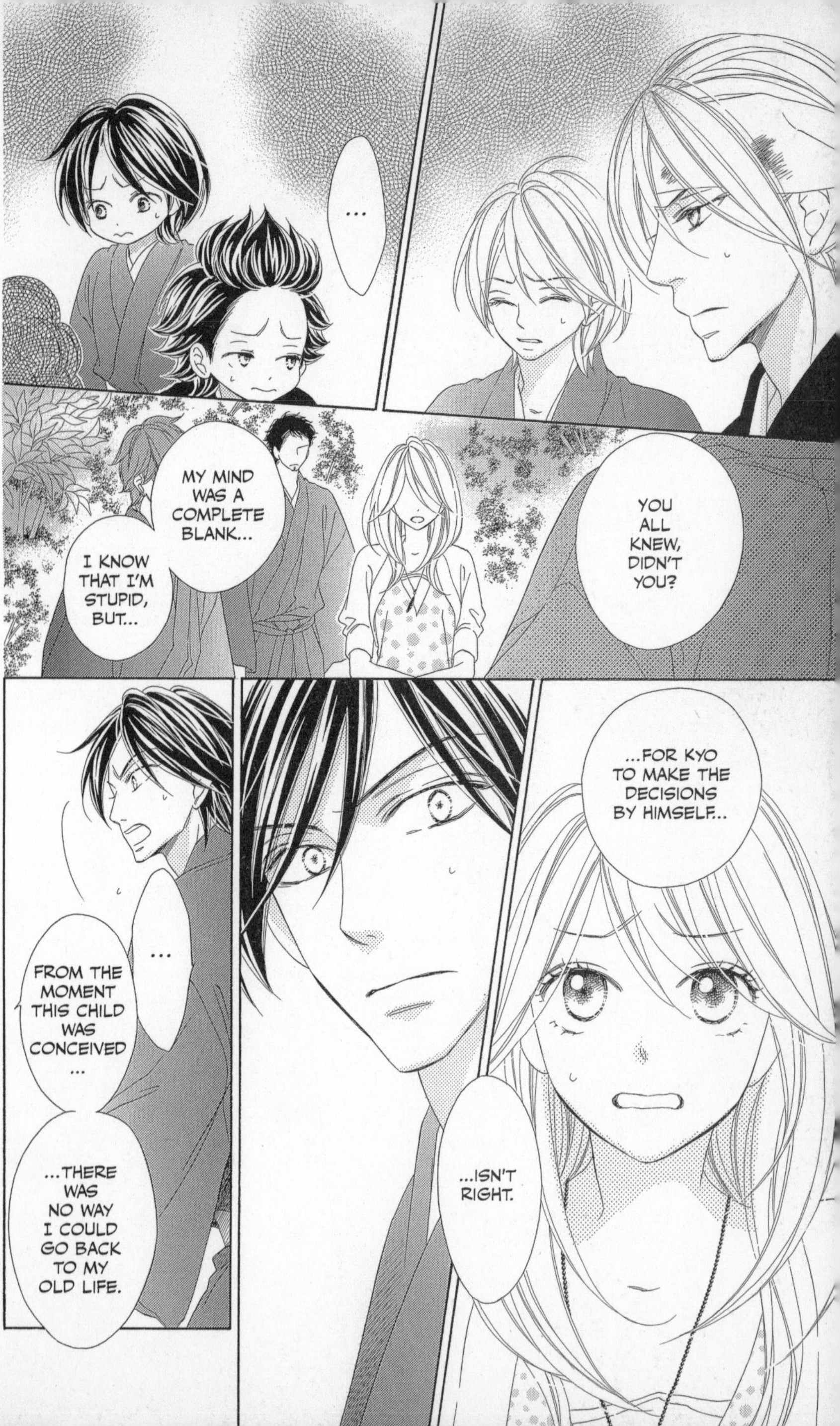
...
YOU ALL KNEW, DIDN'T YOU?
MY MIND WAS A COMPLETE BLANK...
I KNOW THAT I'M STUPID, BUT...
...FOR KYO TO MAKE THE DECISIONS BY HIMSELF...
...ISN'T RIGHT.
...
FROM THE MOMENT THIS CHILD WAS CONCEIVED ...
...THERE WAS NO WAY I COULD GO BACK TO MY OLD LIFE.

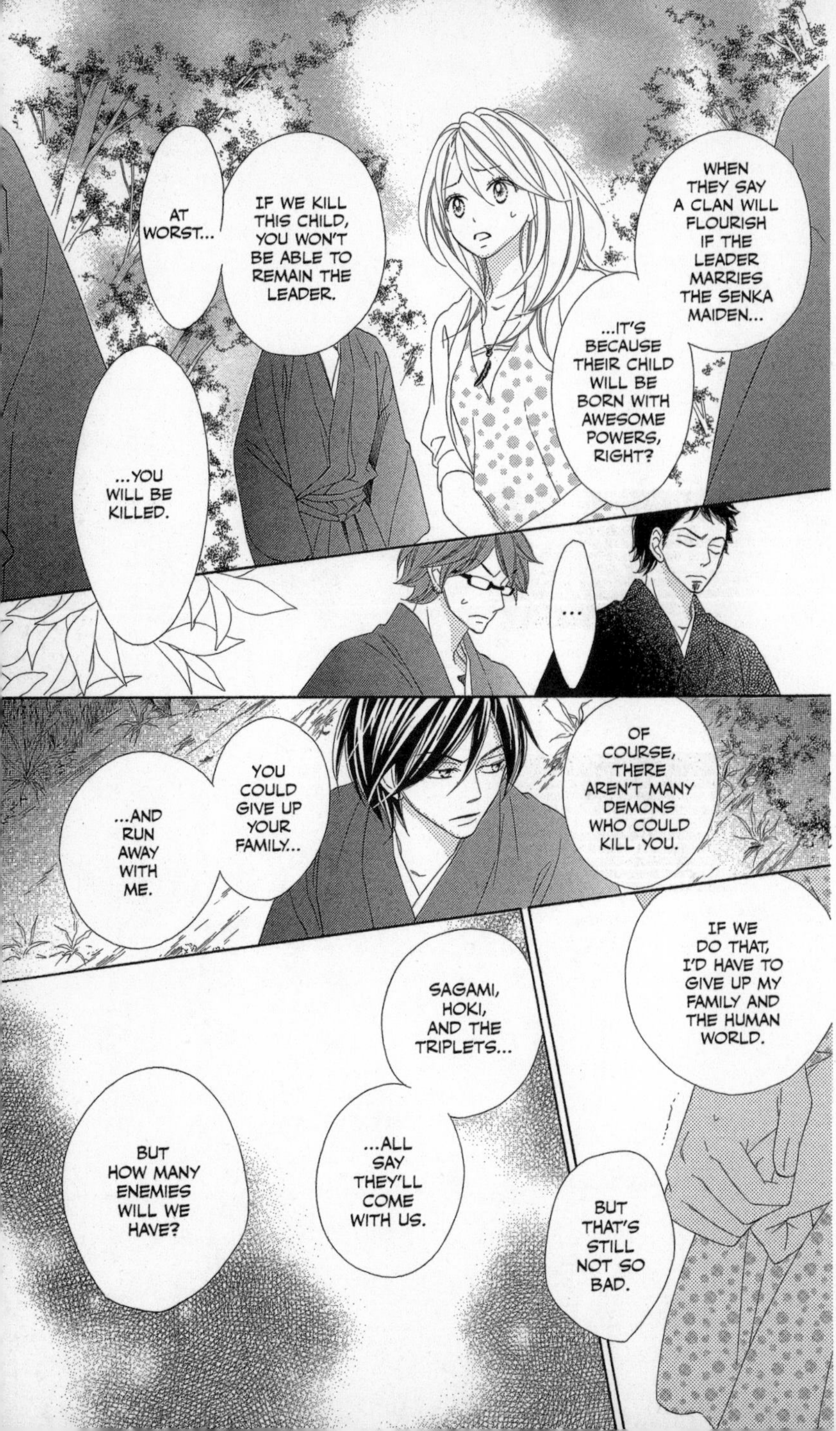
WHEN THEY SAY A CLAN WILL FLOURISH IF THE LEADER MARRIES THE SENKA MAIDEN...
...IT'S BECAUSE THEIR CHILD WILL BE BORN WITH AWESOME POWERS, RIGHT?
IF WE KILL THIS CHILD, YOU WON'T BE ABLE TO REMAIN THE LEADER.
AT WORST...
...YOU WILL BE KILLED.
...
OF COURSE, THERE AREN'T MANY DEMONS WHO COULD KILL YOU.
YOU COULD GIVE UP YOUR FAMILY...
...AND RUN AWAY WITH ME.
IF WE DO THAT, I'D HAVE TO GIVE UP MY FAMILY AND THE HUMAN WORLD.
BUT THAT'S STILL NOT SO BAD.
SAGAMI, HOKI, AND THE TRIPLETS...
...ALL SAY THEY'LL COME WITH US.
BUT HOW MANY ENEMIES WILL WE HAVE?

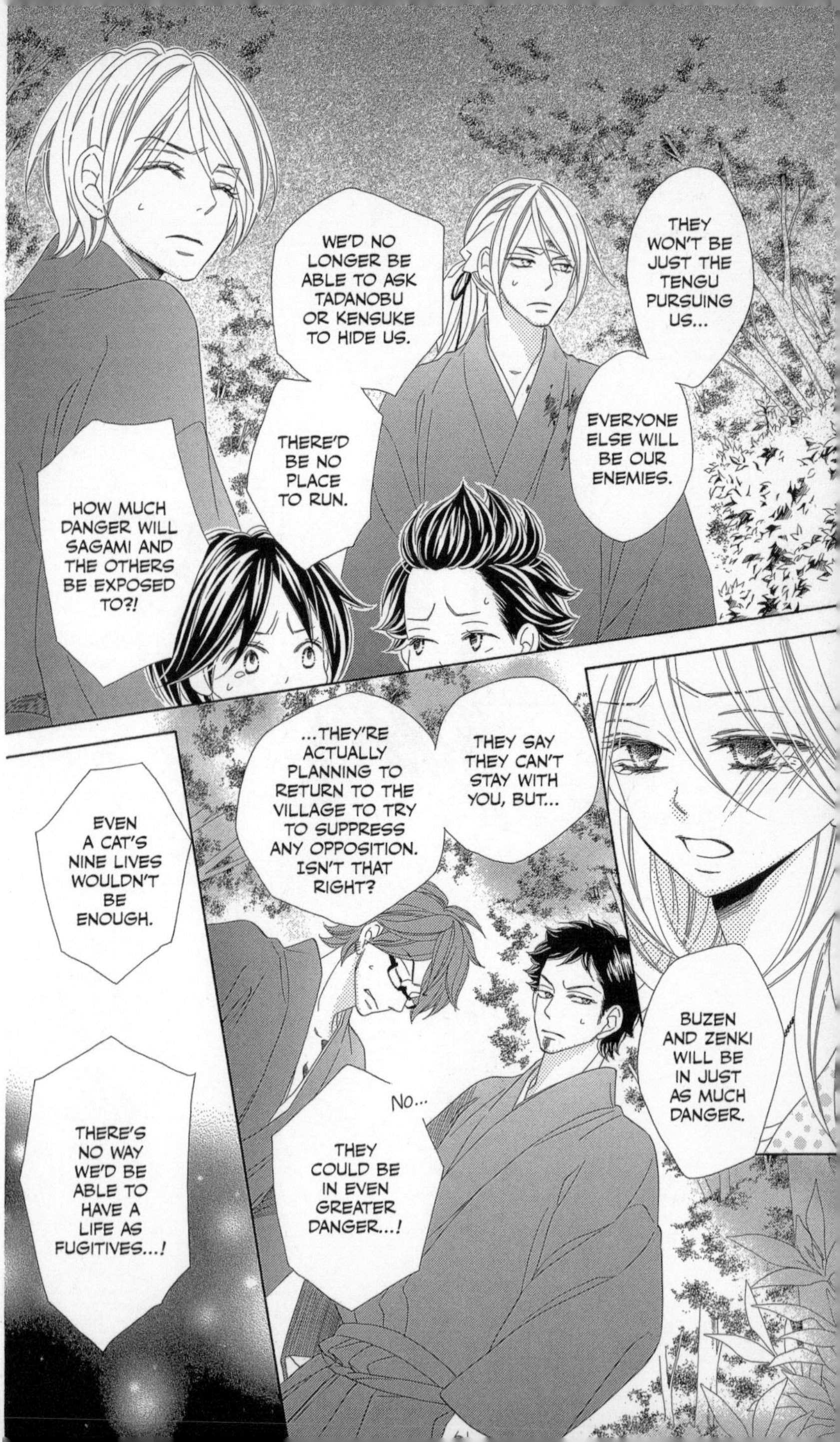
THEY WON'T BE JUST THE TENGU PURSUING US...
EVERYONE ELSE WILL BE OUR ENEMIES.
WE'D NO LONGER BE ABLE TO ASK TADANOBU OR KENSUKE TO HIDE US.
THERE'D BE NO PLACE TO RUN.
HOW MUCH DANGER WILL SAGAMI AND THE OTHERS BE EXPOSED TO?!
BUZEN AND ZENKI WILL BE IN JUST AS MUCH DANGER.
THEY SAY THEY CAN'T STAY WITH YOU, BUT...
...THEY'RE ACTUALLY PLANNING TO RETURN TO THE VILLAGE TO TRY TO SUPPRESS ANY OPPOSITION. ISN'T THAT RIGHT?
No...
THEY COULD BE IN EVEN GREATER DANGER...!
EVEN A CAT'S NINE LIVES WOULDN'T BE ENOUGH.
THERE'S NO WAY WE'D BE ABLE TO HAVE A LIFE AS FUGITIVES...!

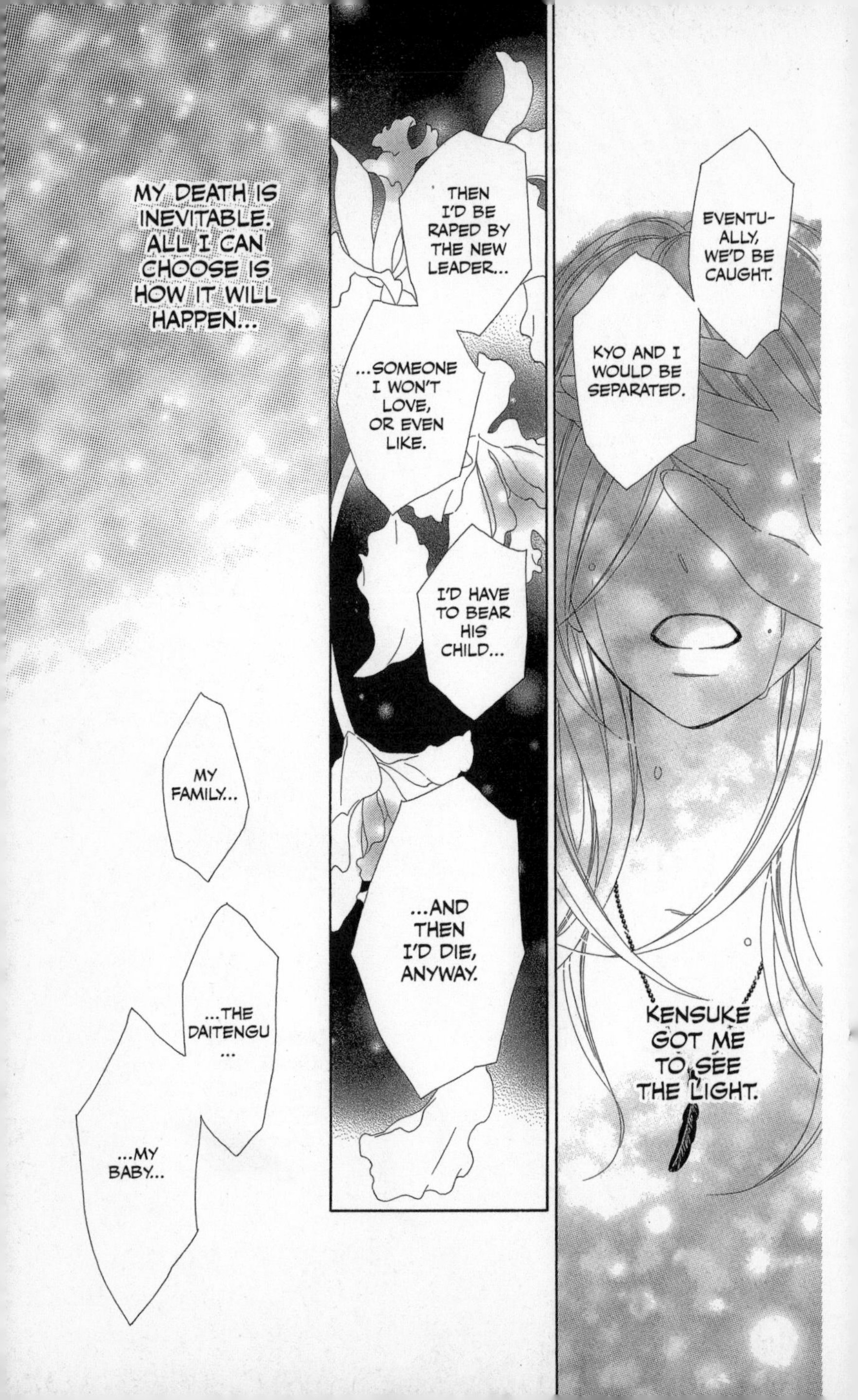
EVENTU-ALLY, WE'D BE CAUGHT.
KYO AND I WOULD BE SEPARATED.
KENSUKE GOT ME TO SEE THE LIGHT.
THEN I'D BE RAPED BY THE NEW LEADER...
...SOMEONE I WON'T LOVE, OR EVEN LIKE.
I'D HAVE TO BEAR HIS CHILD...
...AND THEN I'D DIE, ANYWAY.
MY DEATH IS INEVITABLE. ALL I CAN CHOOSE IS HOW IT WILL HAPPEN...
MY FAMILY...
...THE DAITENGU...
...MY BABY...

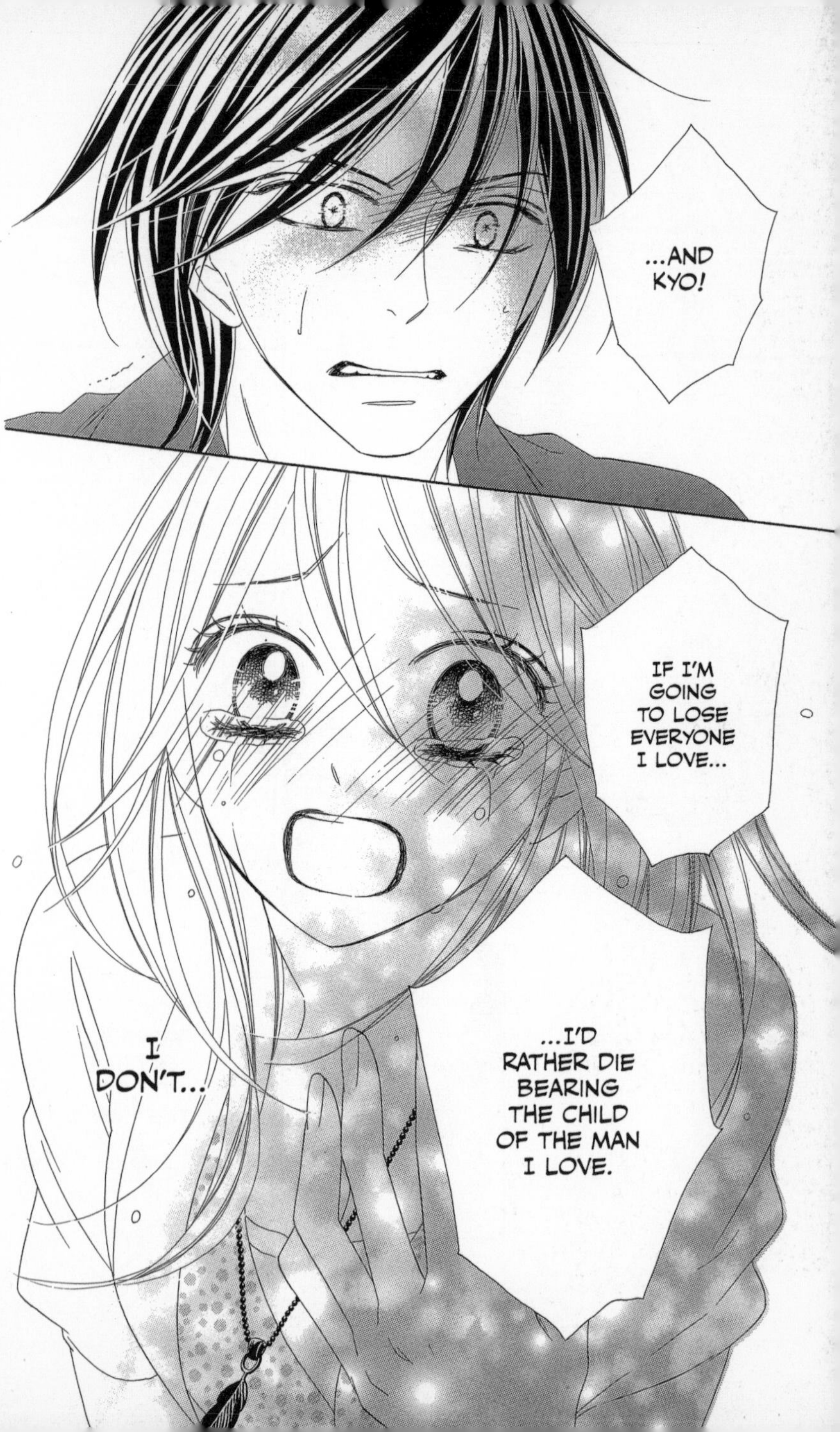
...AND KYO!
IF I'M GOING TO LOSE EVERYONE I LOVE...
...I'D RATHER DIE BEARING THE CHILD OF THE MAN I LOVE.
I DON'T...

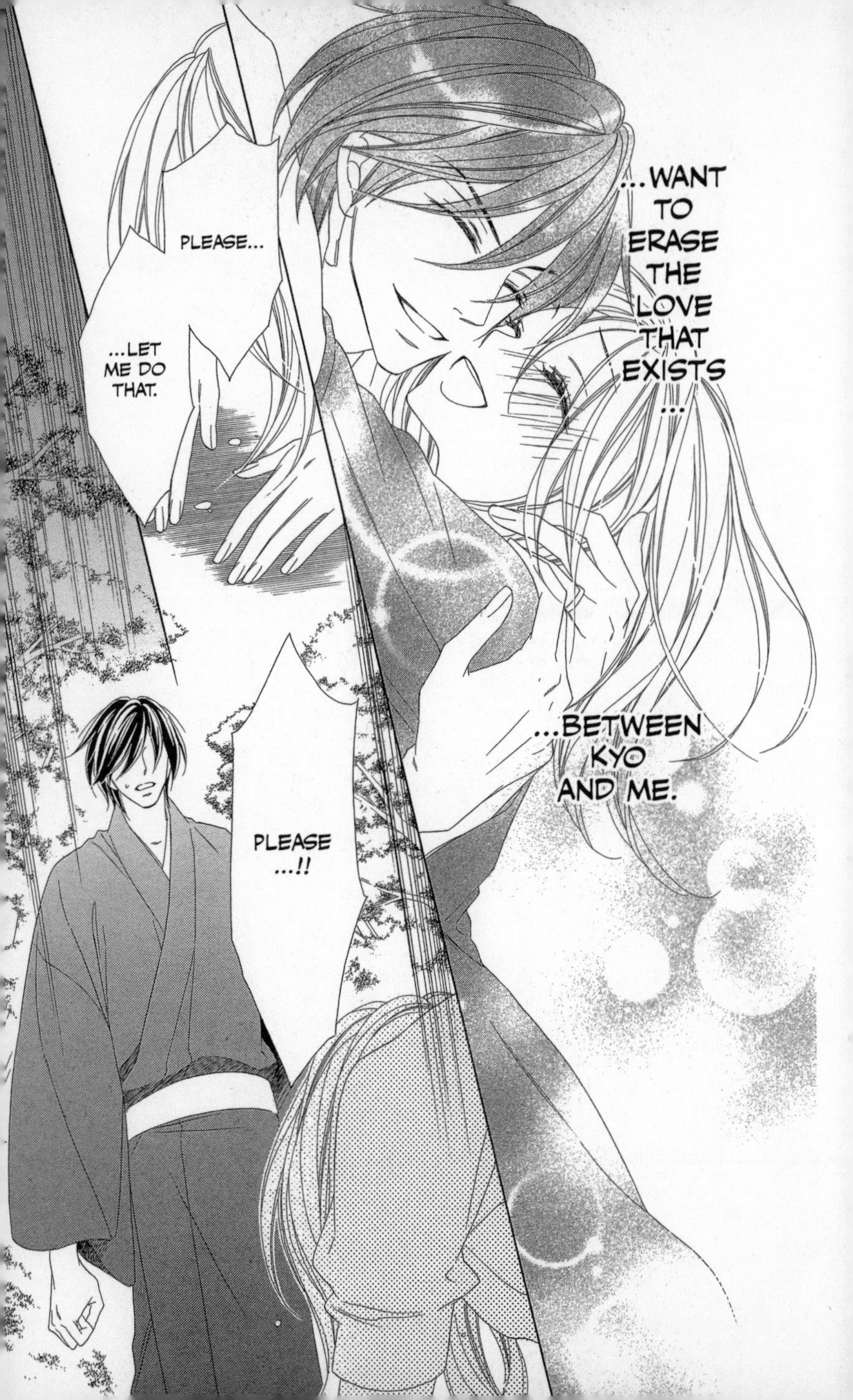
...WANT TO ERASE THE LOVE THAT EXISTS...
...BETWEEN KYO AND ME.
PLEASE...
...LET ME DO THAT.
PLEASE ...!!

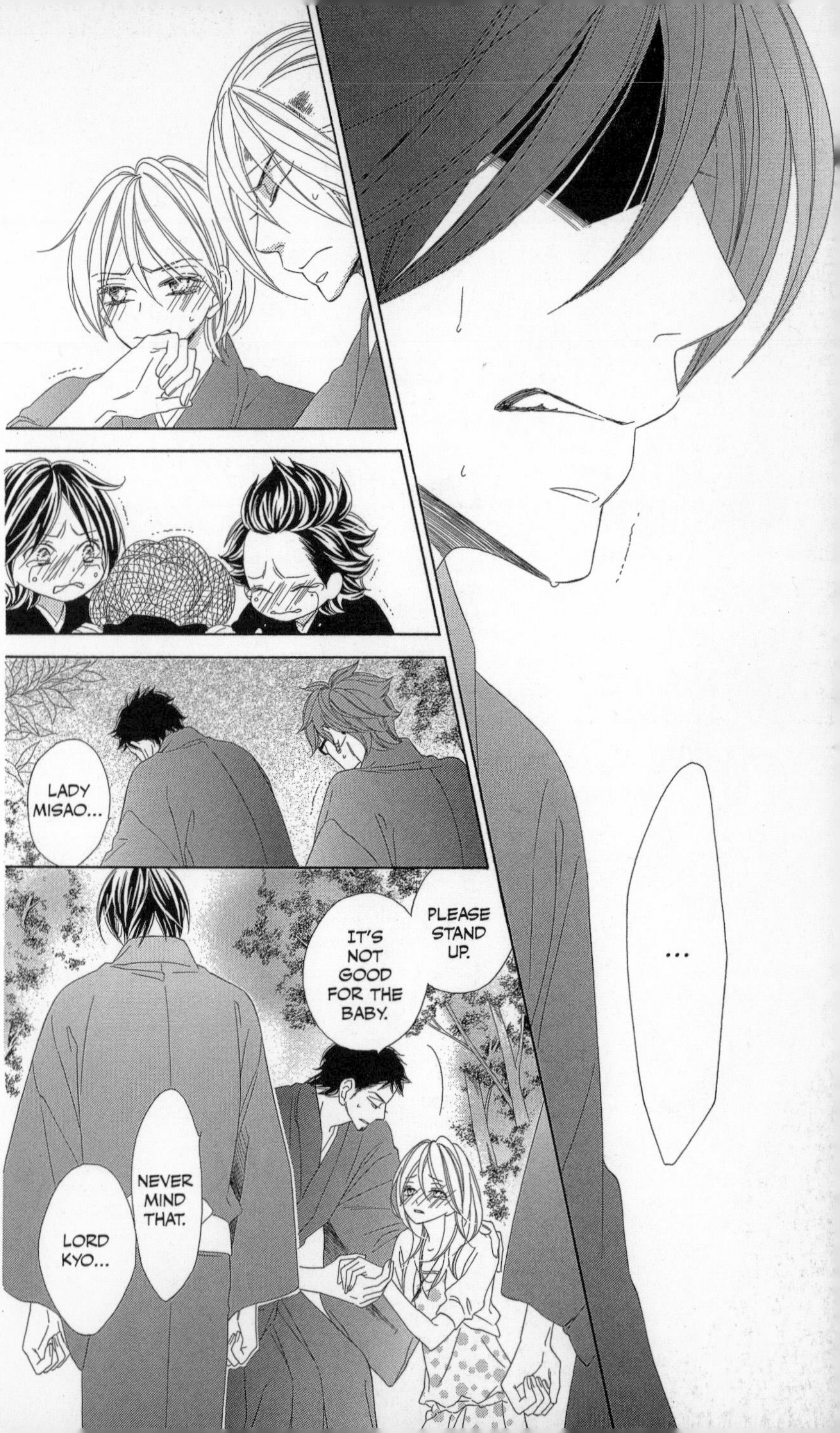
...
LADY MISAO...
PLEASE STAND UP.
IT'S NOT GOOD FOR THE BABY.
NEVER MIND THAT.
LORD KYO...

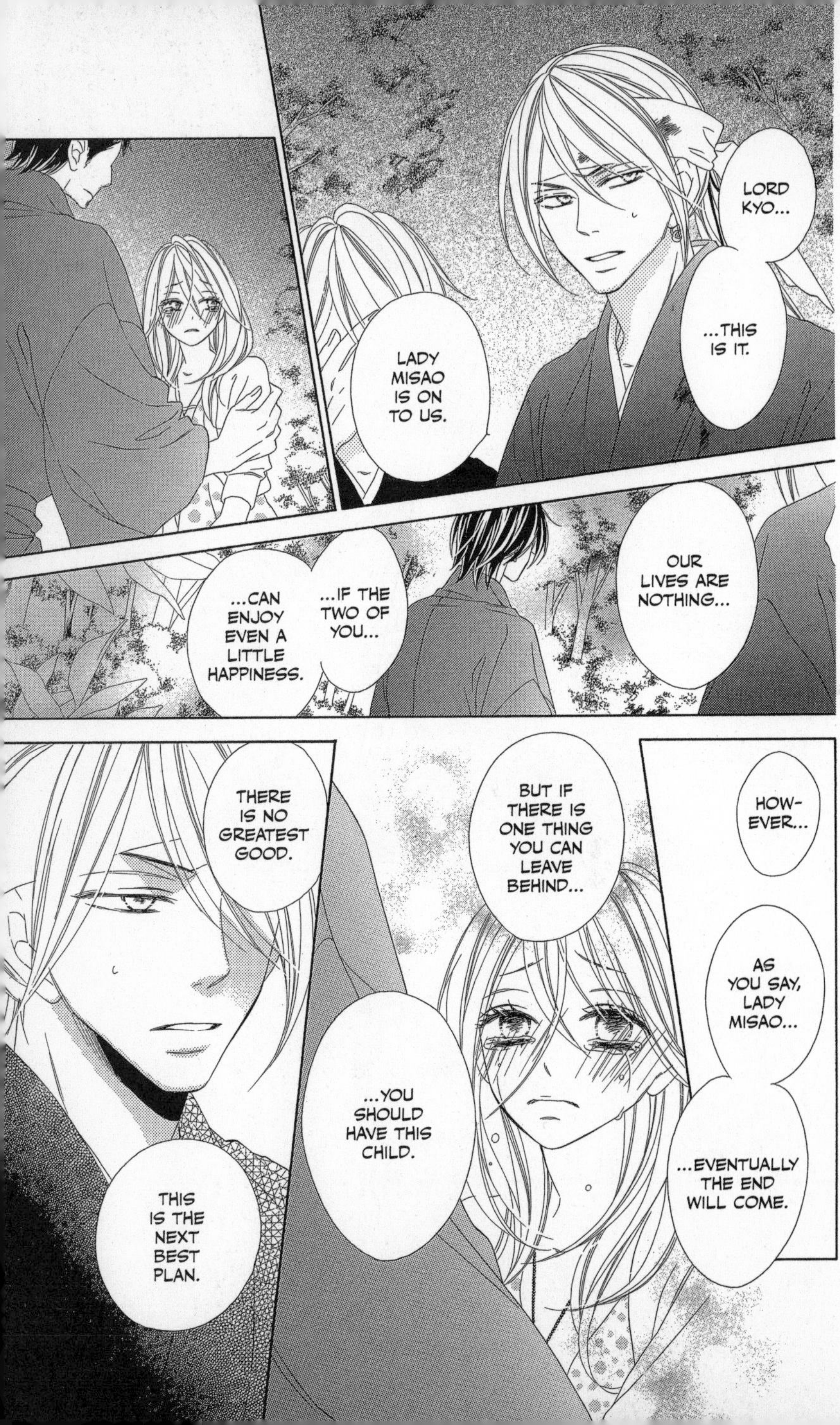
LORD KYO...
...THIS IS IT.
LADY MISAO IS ON TO US.
OUR LIVES ARE NOTHING...
...IF THE TWO OF YOU...
...CAN ENJOY EVEN A LITTLE HAPPINESS.
HOW-EVER...
AS YOU SAY, LADY MISAO...
...EVENTUALLY THE END WILL COME.
BUT IF THERE IS ONE THING YOU CAN LEAVE BEHIND...
...YOU SHOULD HAVE THIS CHILD.
THERE IS NO GREATEST GOOD.
THIS IS THE NEXT BEST PLAN.

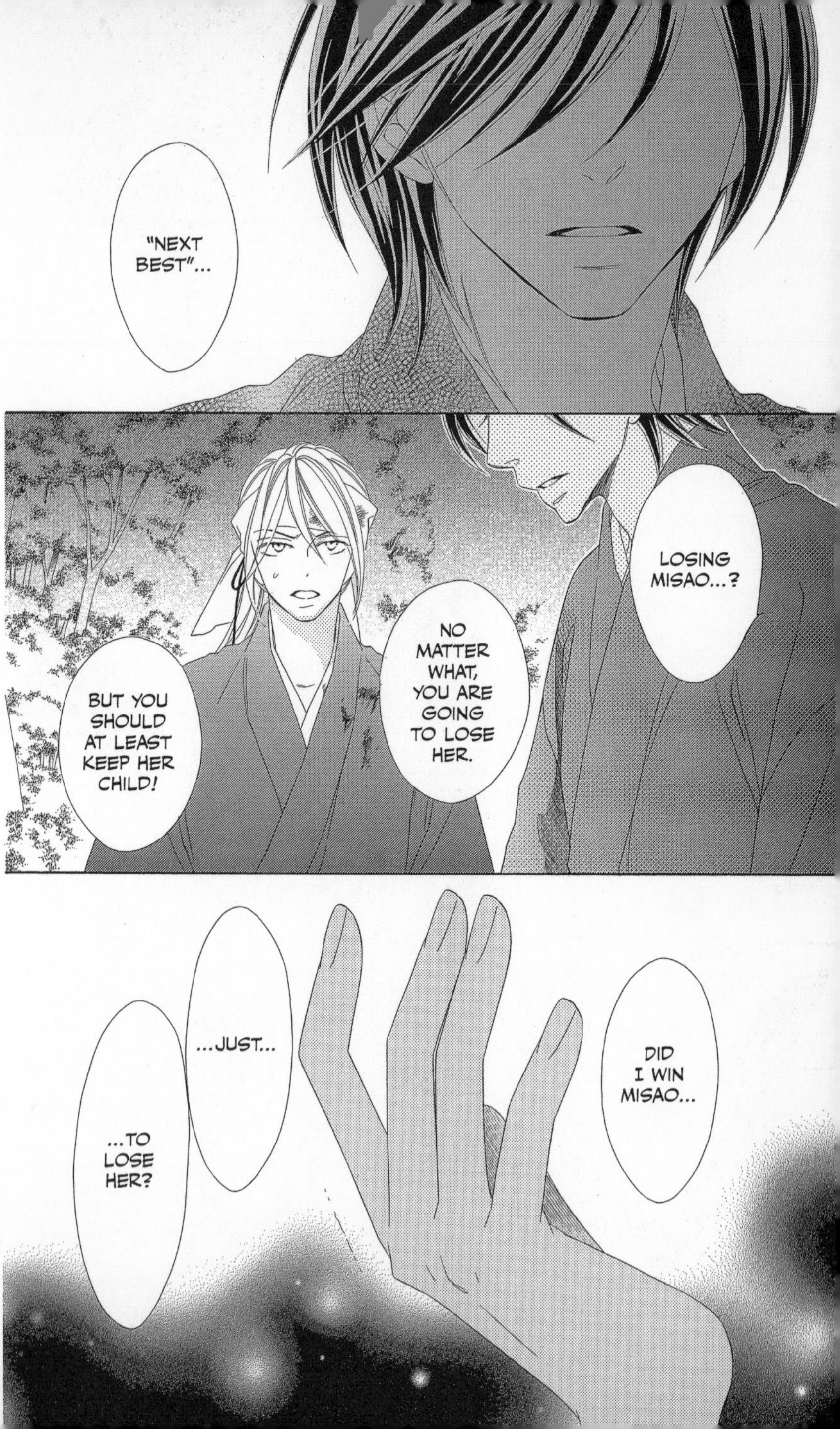
"NEXT BEST"...
LOSING MISAO...?
NO MATTER WHAT, YOU ARE GOING TO LOSE HER.
BUT YOU SHOULD AT LEAST KEEP HER CHILD!
DID I WIN MISAO...
...JUST...
...TO LOSE HER?

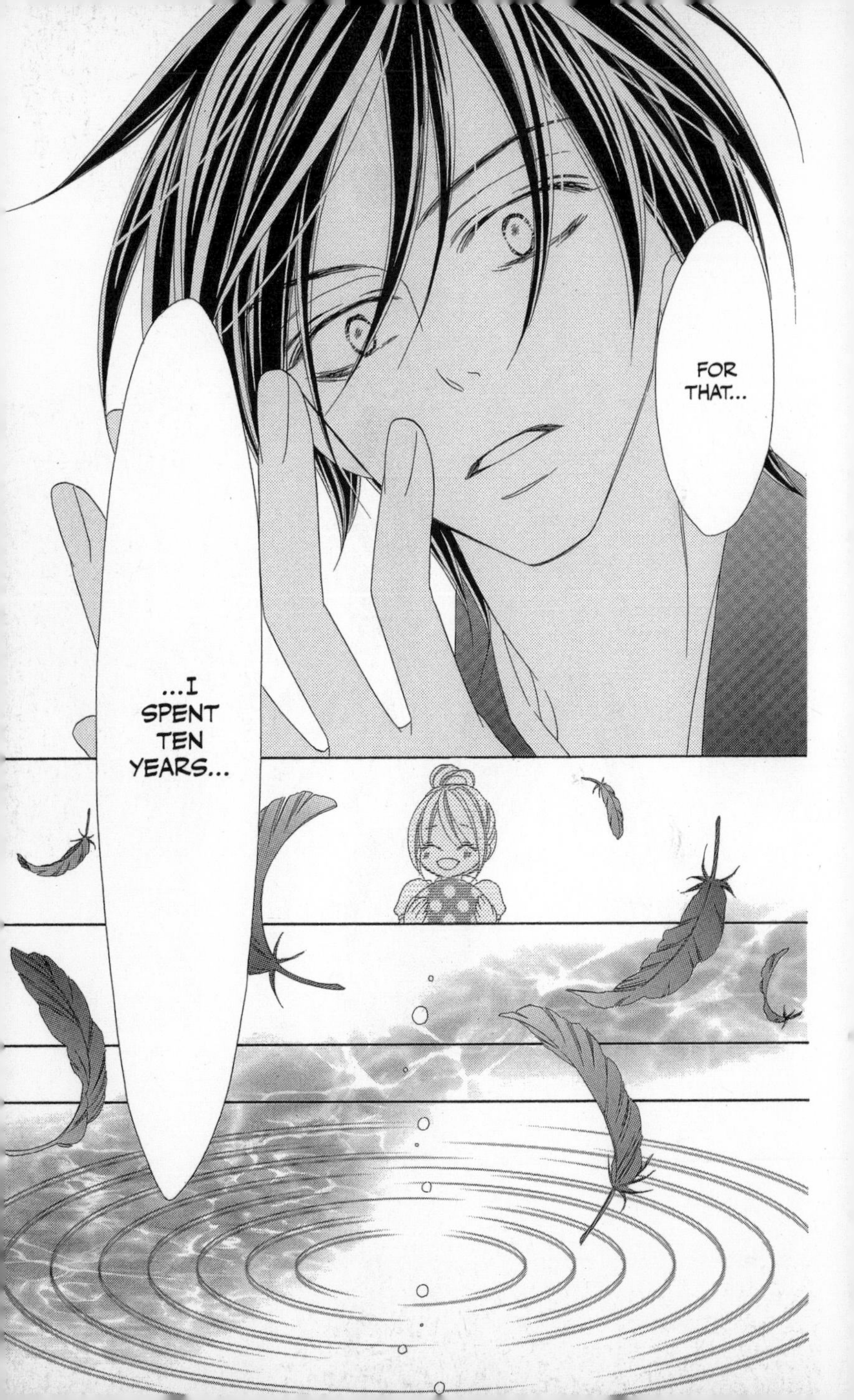
FOR THAT...
...I SPENT TEN YEARS...

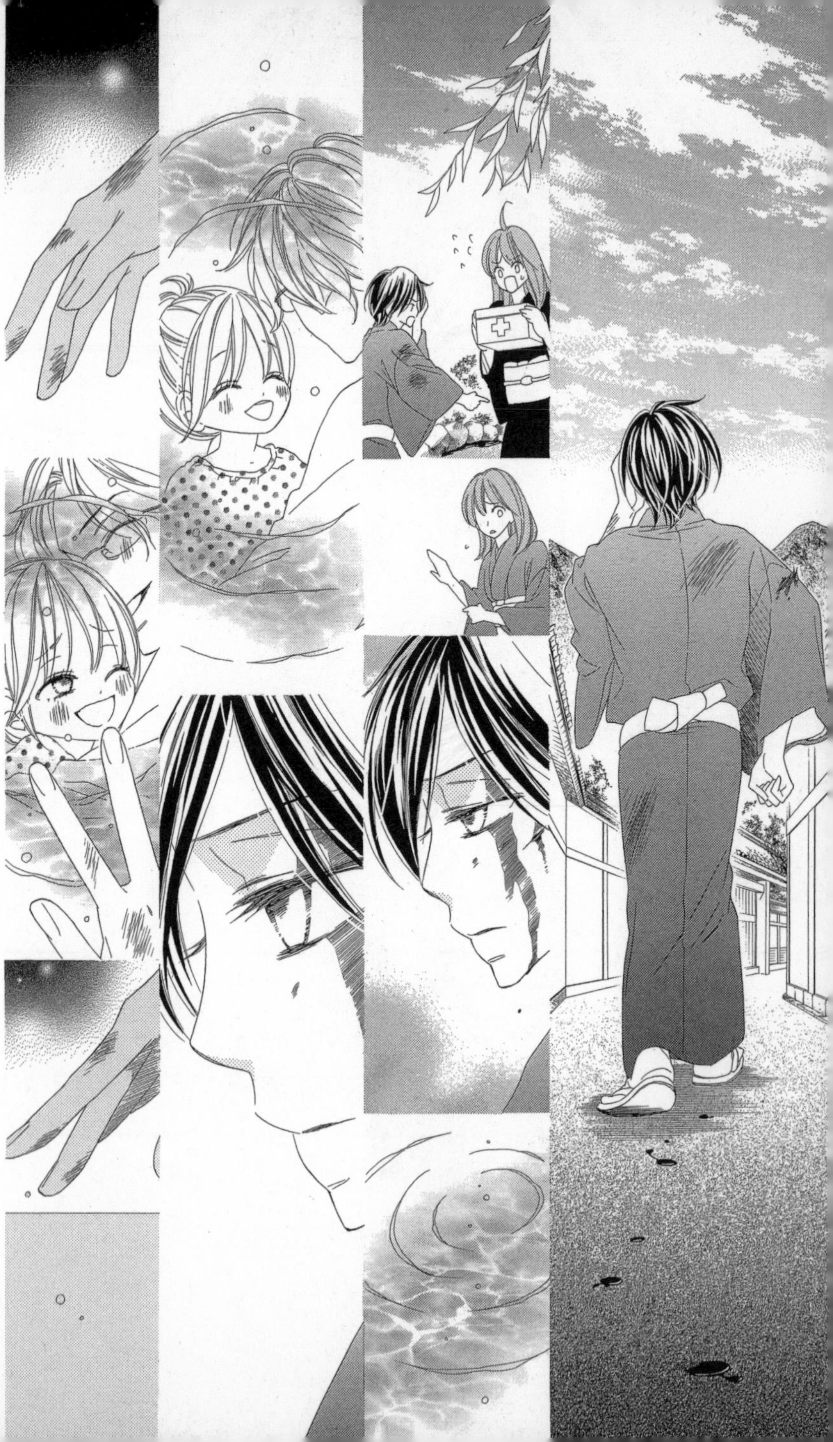

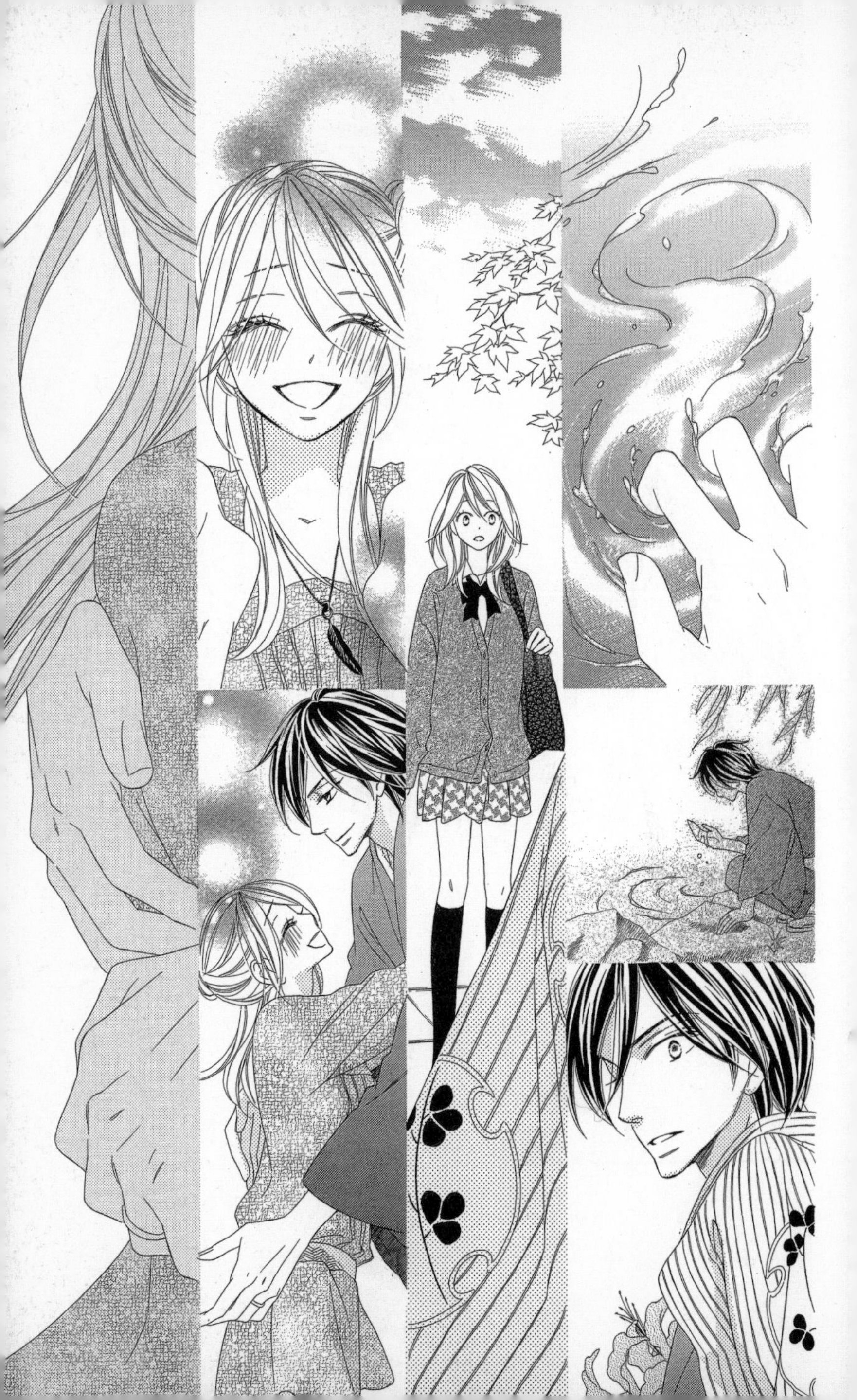

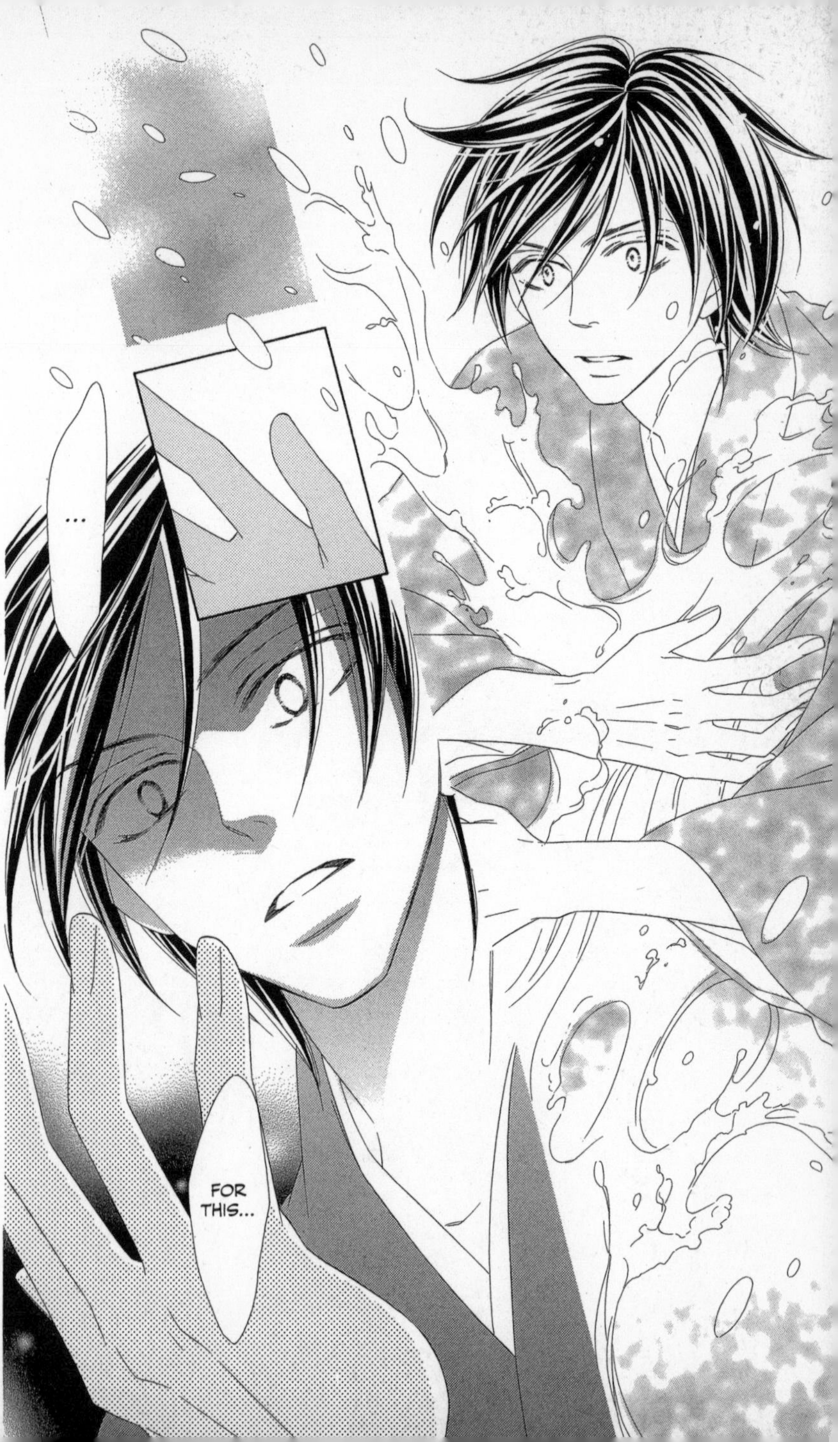
...
FOR THIS...

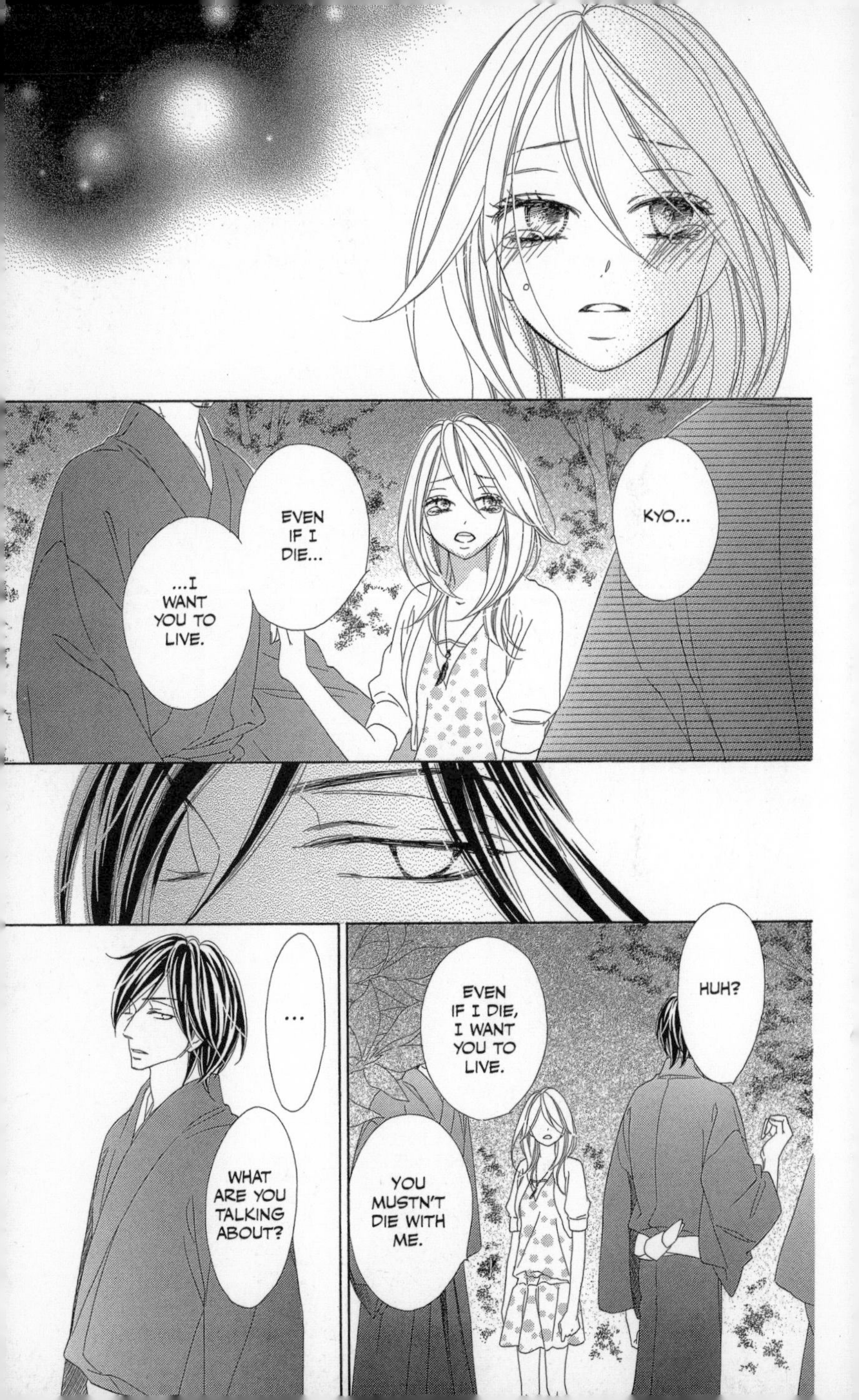
KYO...
EVEN IF I DIE...
...I WANT YOU TO LIVE.
HUH?
EVEN IF I DIE, I WANT YOU TO LIVE.
YOU MUSTN'T DIE WITH ME.
...
WHAT ARE YOU TALKING ABOUT?

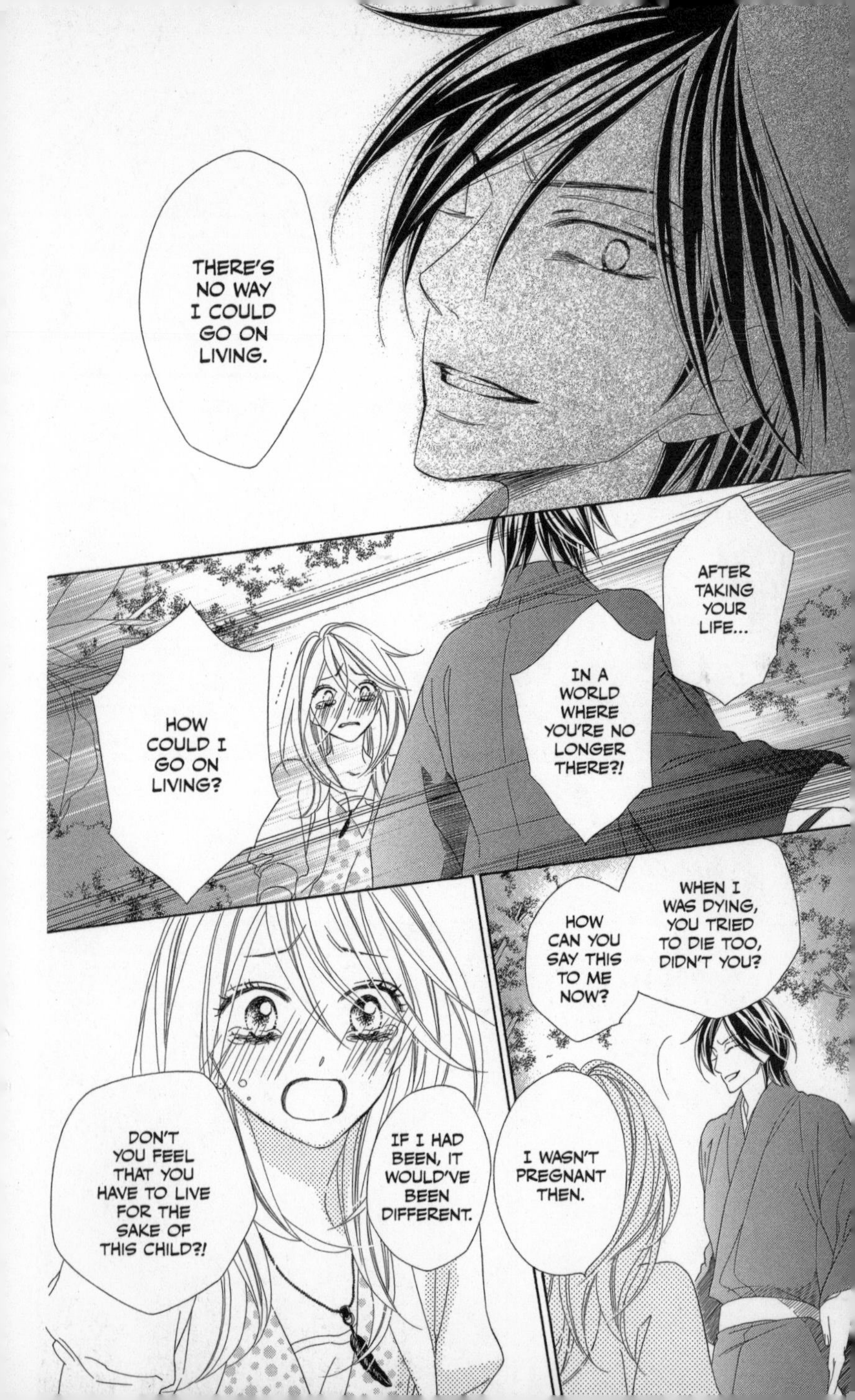
THERE'S NO WAY I COULD GO ON LIVING.
AFTER TAKING YOUR LIFE...
IN A WORLD WHERE YOU'RE NO LONGER THERE?!
HOW COULD I GO ON LIVING?
WHEN I WAS DYING, YOU TRIED TO DIE TOO, DIDN'T YOU?
HOW CAN YOU SAY THIS TO ME NOW?
I WASN'T PREGNANT THEN.
IF I HAD BEEN, IT WOULD'VE BEEN DIFFERENT.
DON'T YOU FEEL THAT YOU HAVE TO LIVE FOR THE SAKE OF THIS CHILD?!

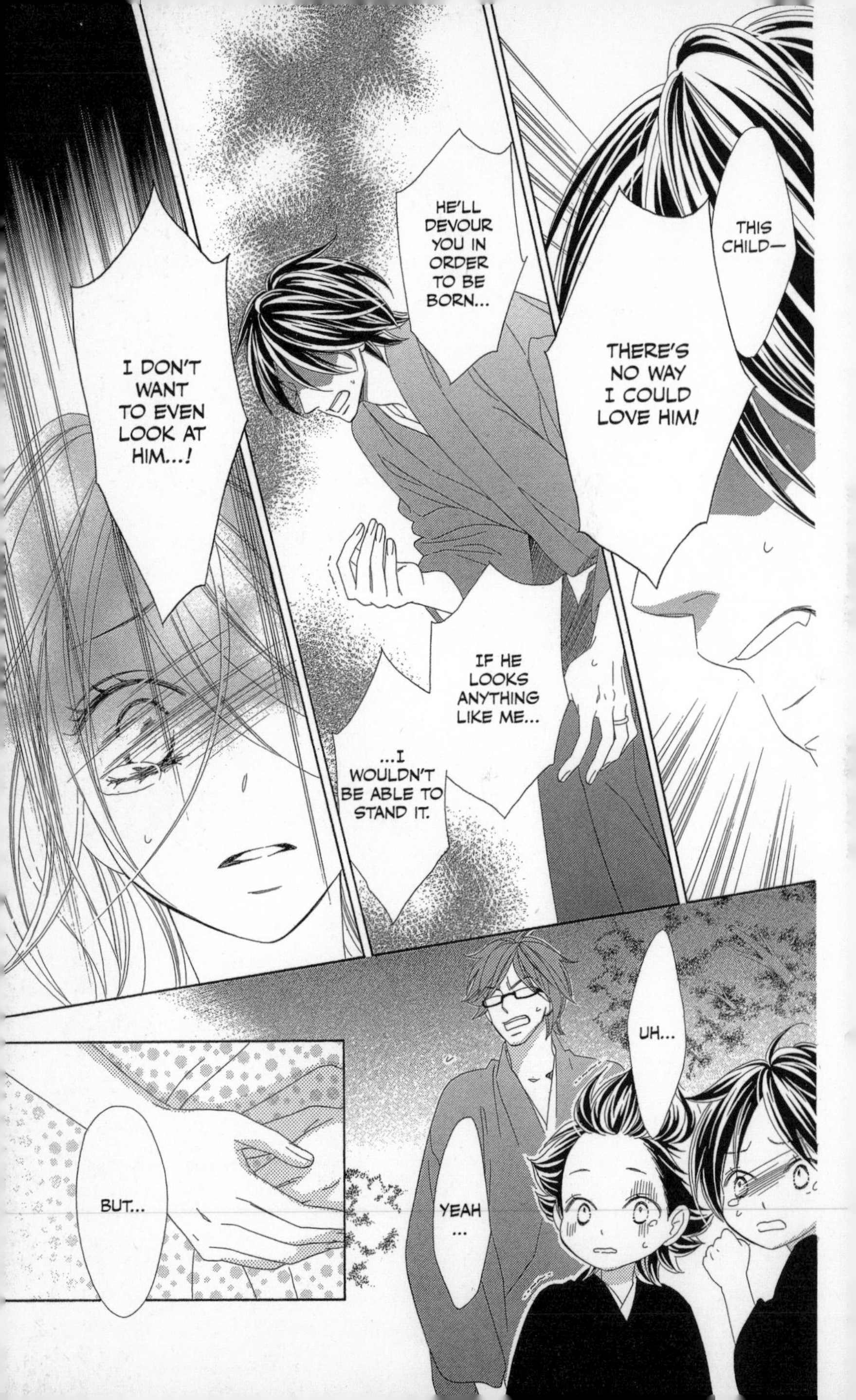
THIS CHILD—
THERE'S NO WAY I COULD LOVE HIM!
HE'LL DEVOUR YOU IN ORDER TO BE BORN...
IF HE LOOKS ANYTHING LIKE ME...
...I WOULDN'T BE ABLE TO STAND IT.
I DON'T WANT TO EVEN LOOK AT HIM...!
UH...
YEAH ...
BUT...

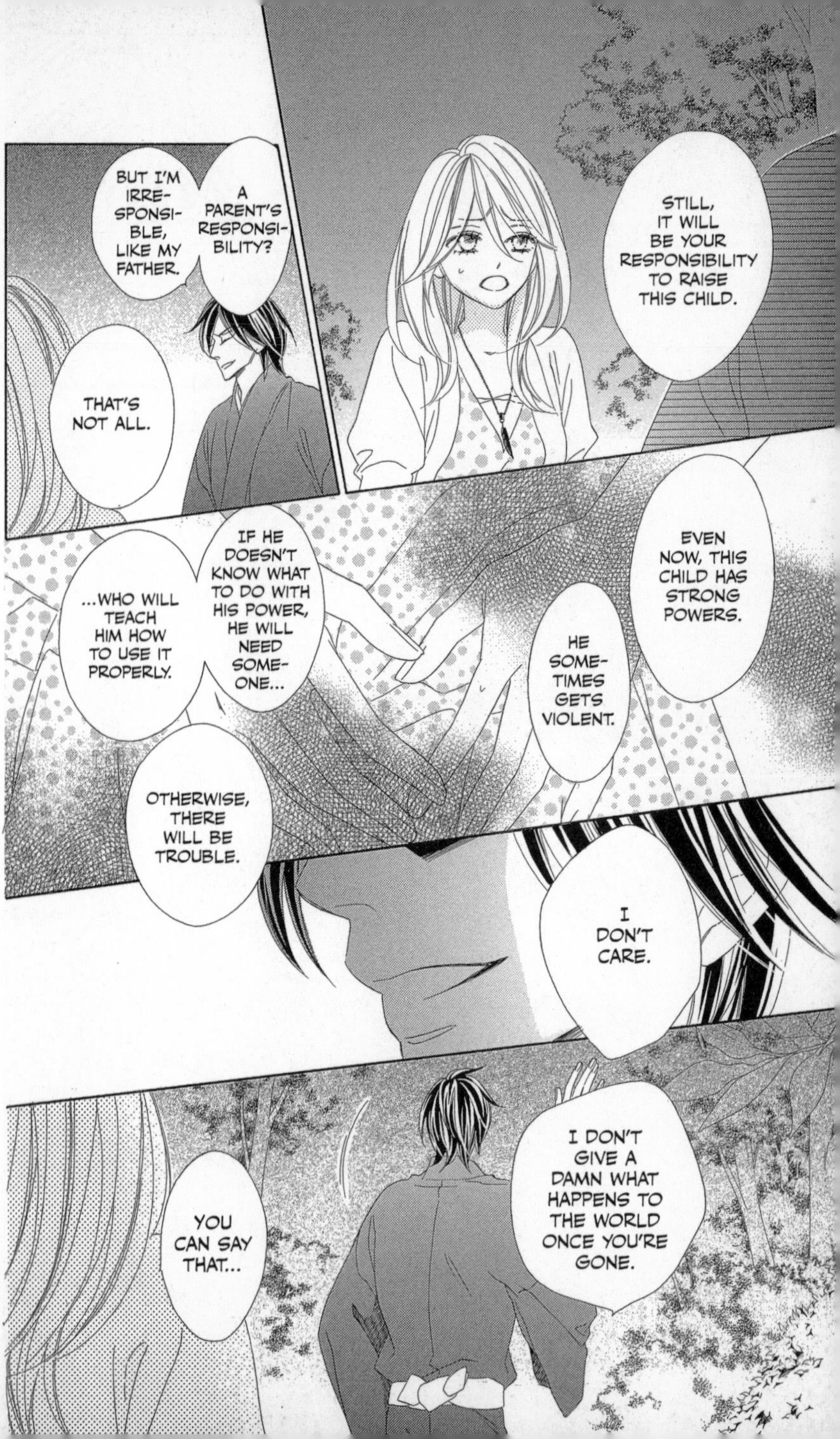
STILL, IT WILL BE YOUR RESPONSIBILITY TO RAISE THIS CHILD.
A PARENT'S RESPONSIBILITY?
BUT I'M IRRESPONSIBLE, LIKE MY FATHER.
THAT'S NOT ALL.
EVEN NOW, THIS CHILD HAS STRONG POWERS.
HE SOMETIMES GETS VIOLENT.
IF HE DOESN'T KNOW WHAT TO DO WITH HIS POWER, HE WILL NEED SOMEONE...
...WHO WILL TEACH HIM HOW TO USE IT PROPERLY.
OTHERWISE, THERE WILL BE TROUBLE.
I DON'T CARE.
I DON'T GIVE A DAMN WHAT HAPPENS TO THE WORLD ONCE YOU'RE GONE.
YOU CAN SAY THAT...

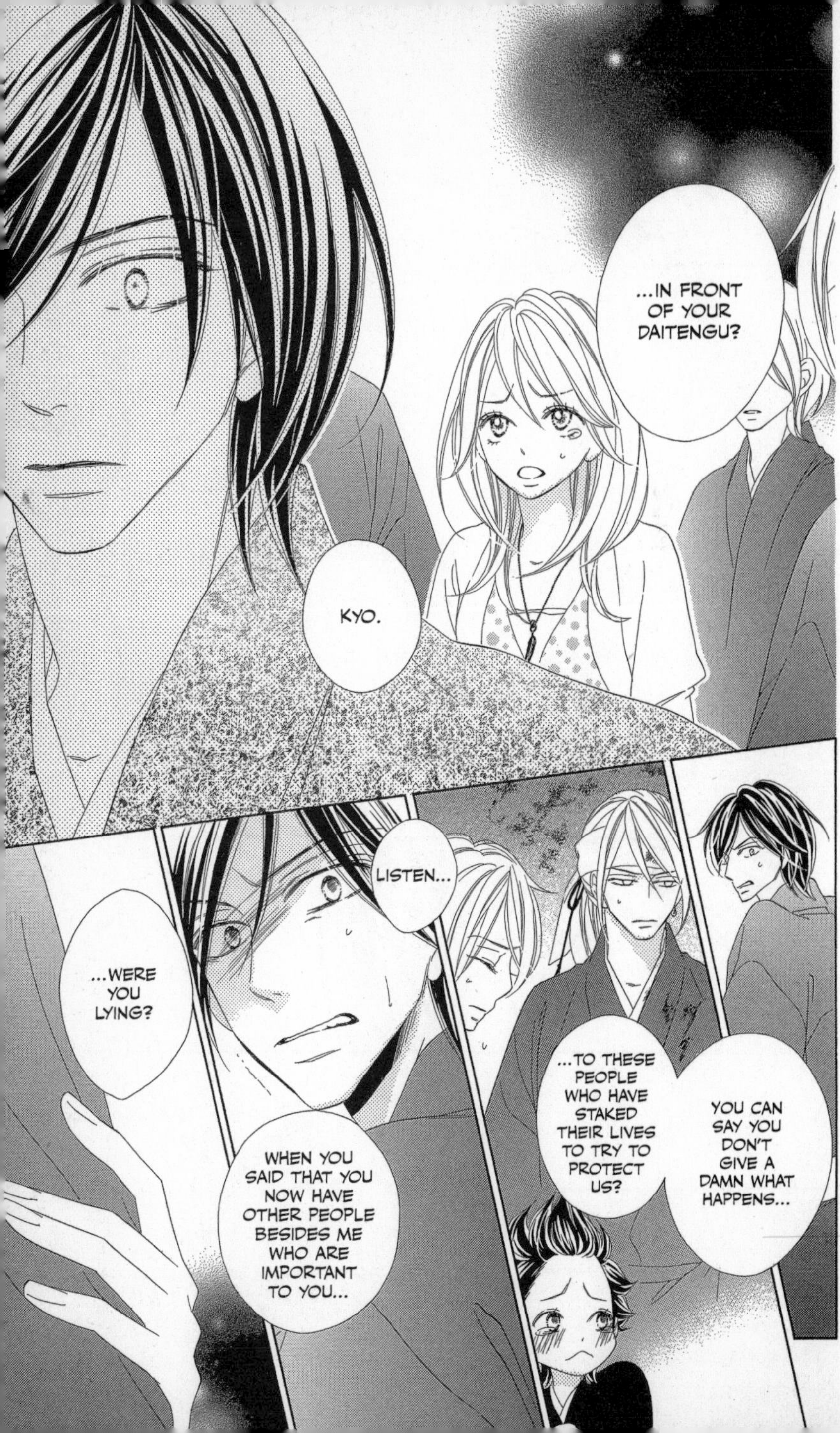
...IN FRONT OF YOUR DAITENGU?
KYO.
YOU CAN SAY YOU DON'T GIVE A DAMN WHAT HAPPENS...
...TO THESE PEOPLE WHO HAVE STAKED THEIR LIVES TO TRY TO PROTECT US?
LISTEN...
WHEN YOU SAID THAT YOU NOW HAVE OTHER PEOPLE BESIDES ME WHO ARE IMPORTANT TO YOU...
...WERE YOU LYING?

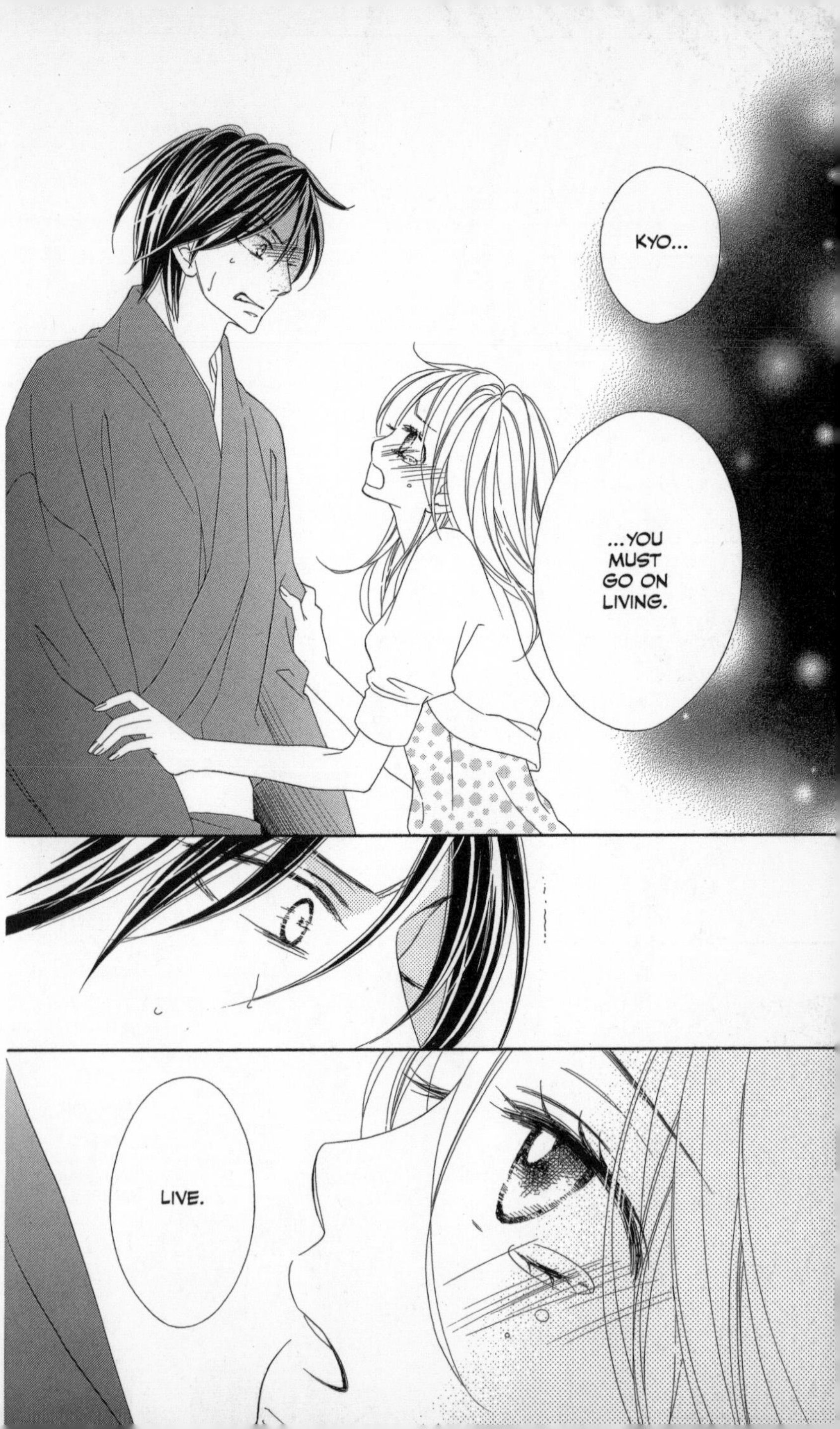
KYO...
...YOU MUST GO ON LIVING.
LIVE.

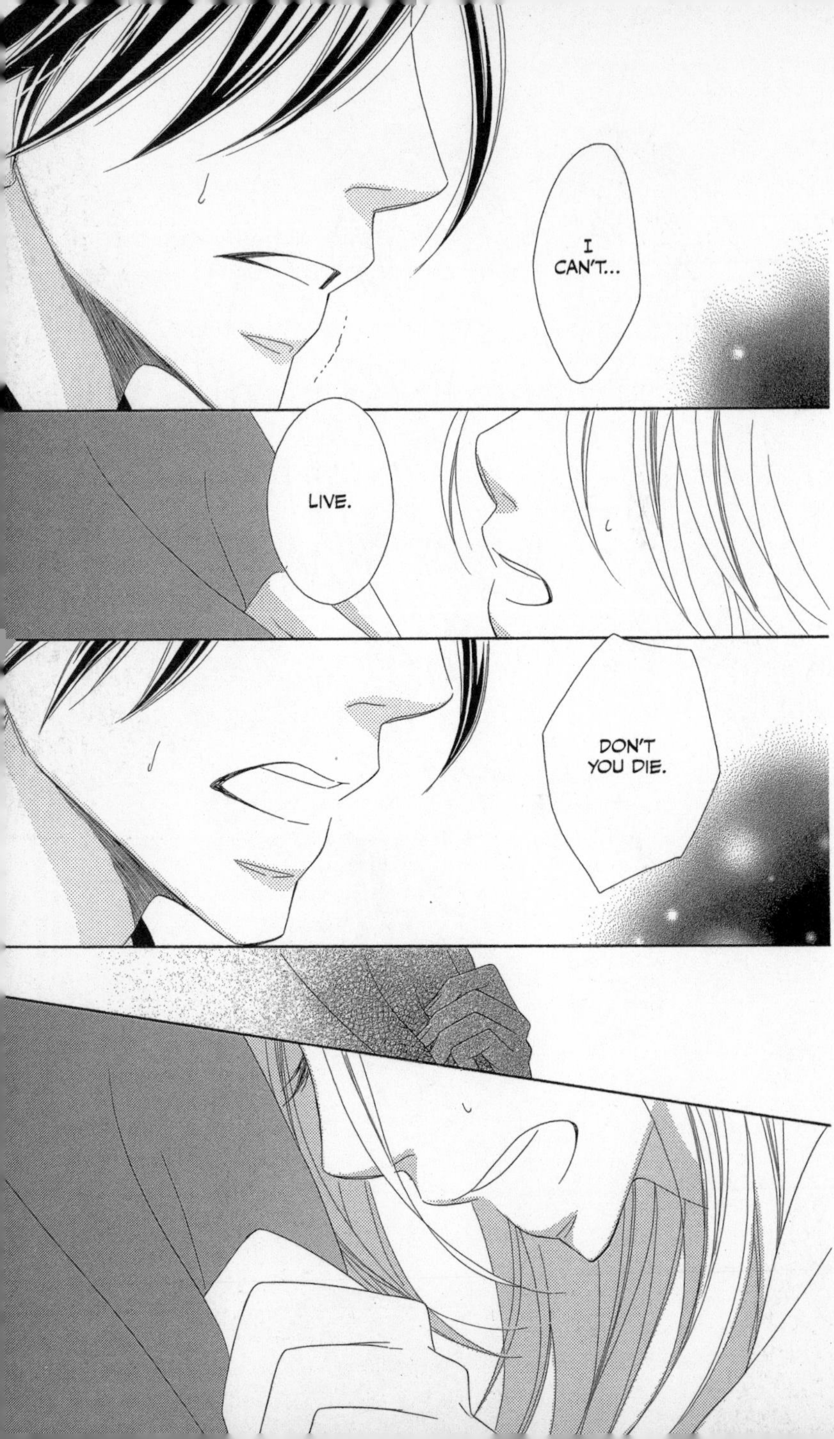
I CAN'T...
LIVE.
DON'T YOU DIE.

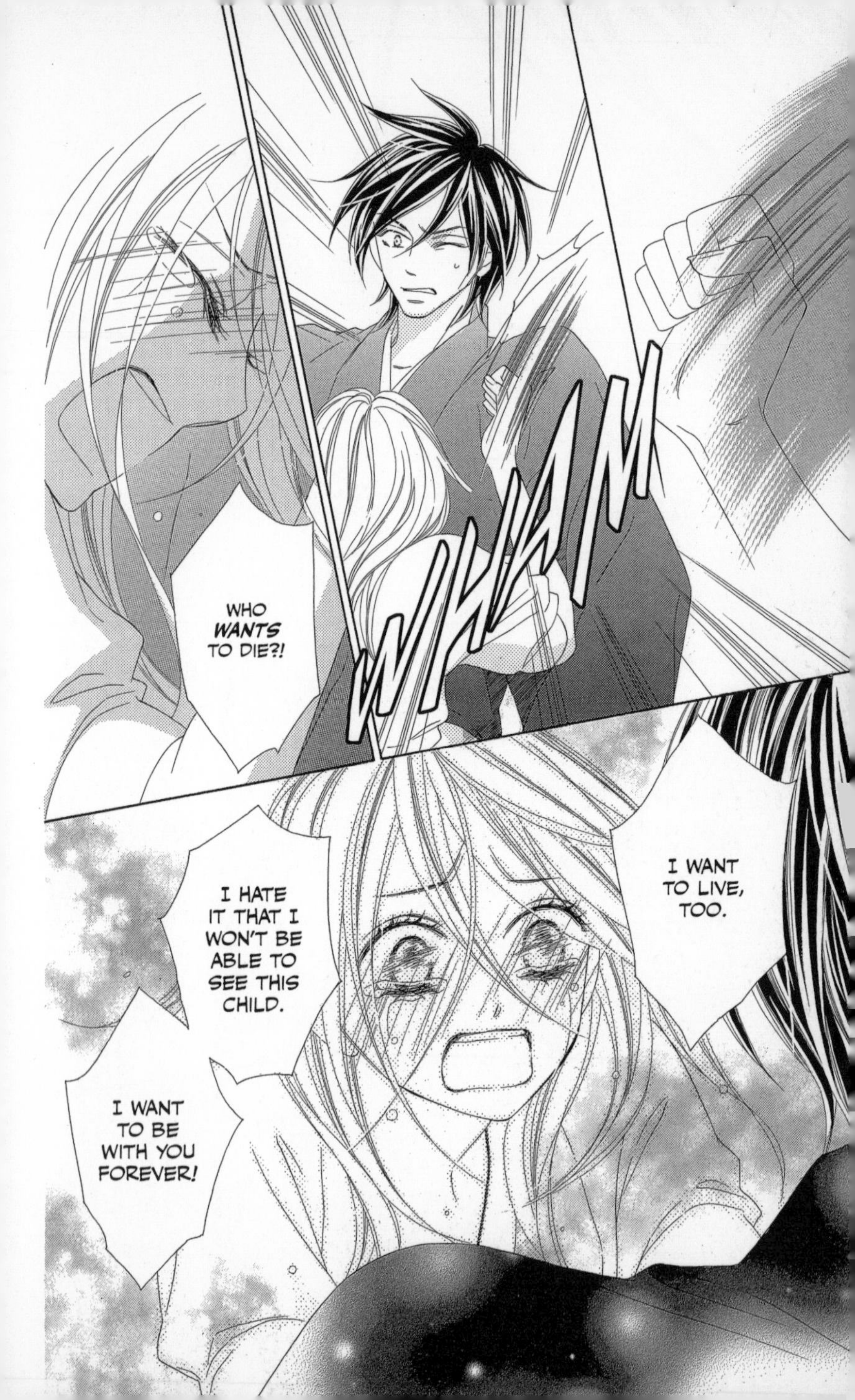
WHAM
WHO *WANTS* TO DIE?!
I WANT TO LIVE, TOO.
I HATE IT THAT I WON'T BE ABLE TO SEE THIS CHILD.
I WANT TO BE WITH YOU FOREVER!

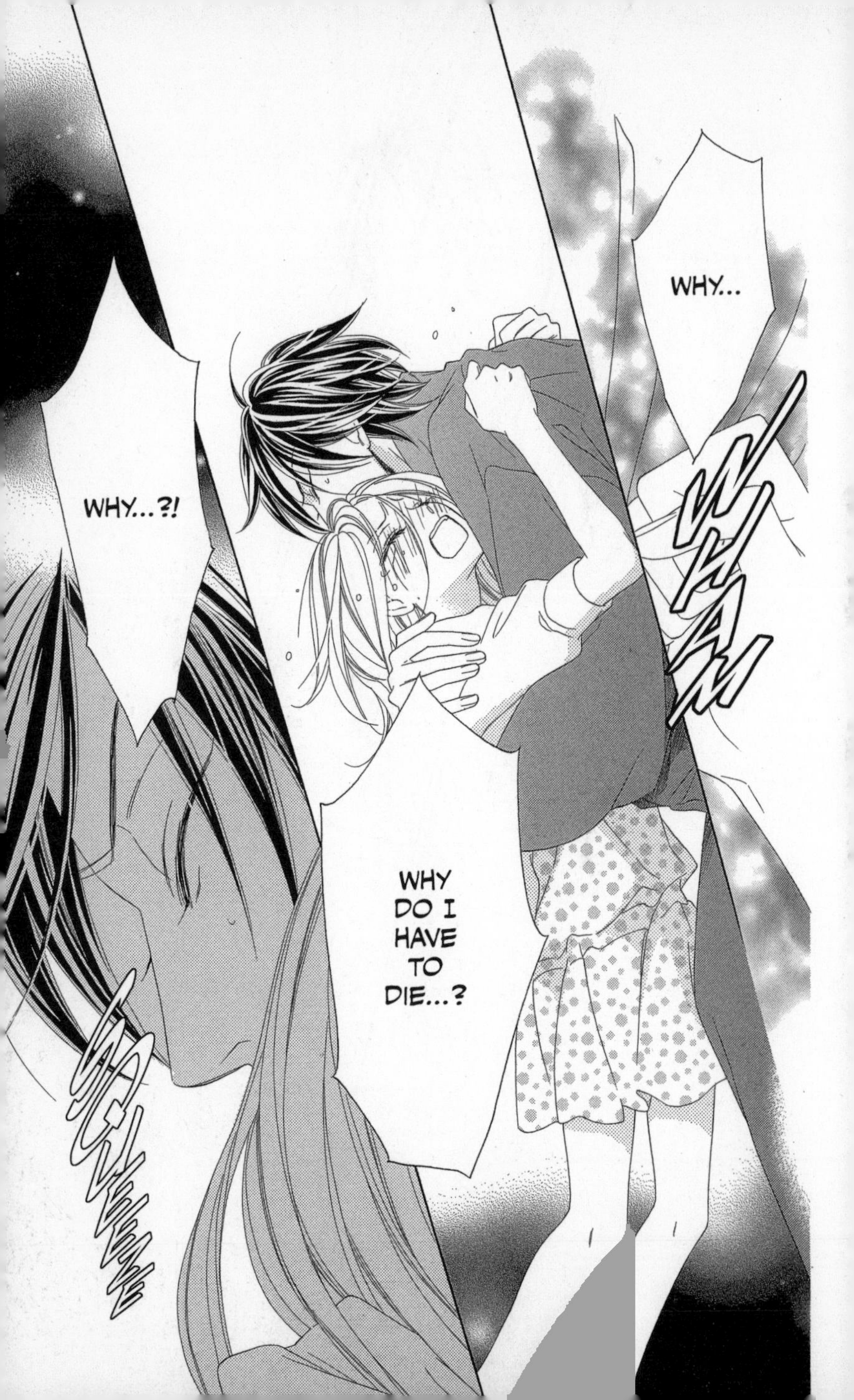
WHY...
WHY DO I HAVE TO DIE...?
WHY...?!

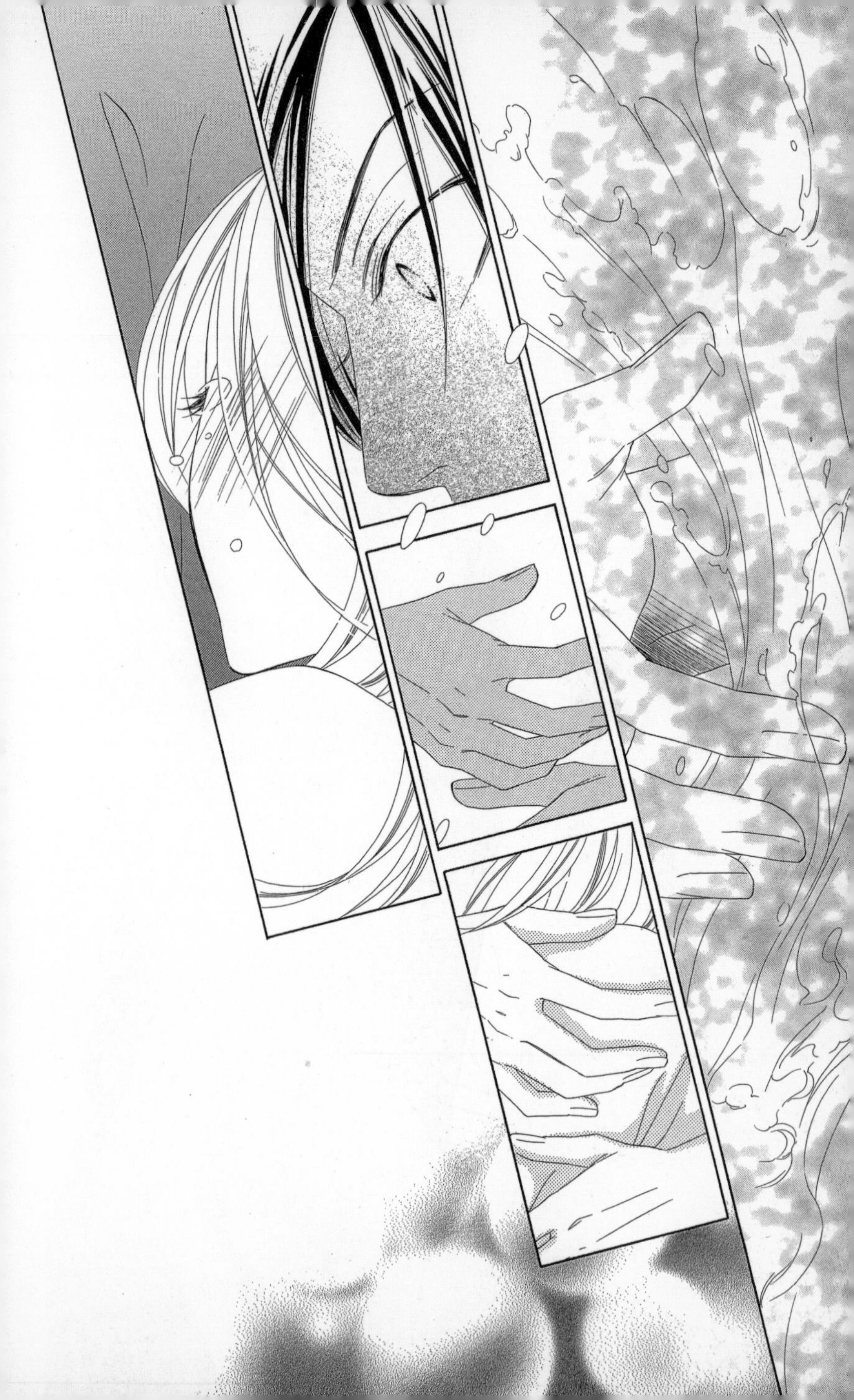

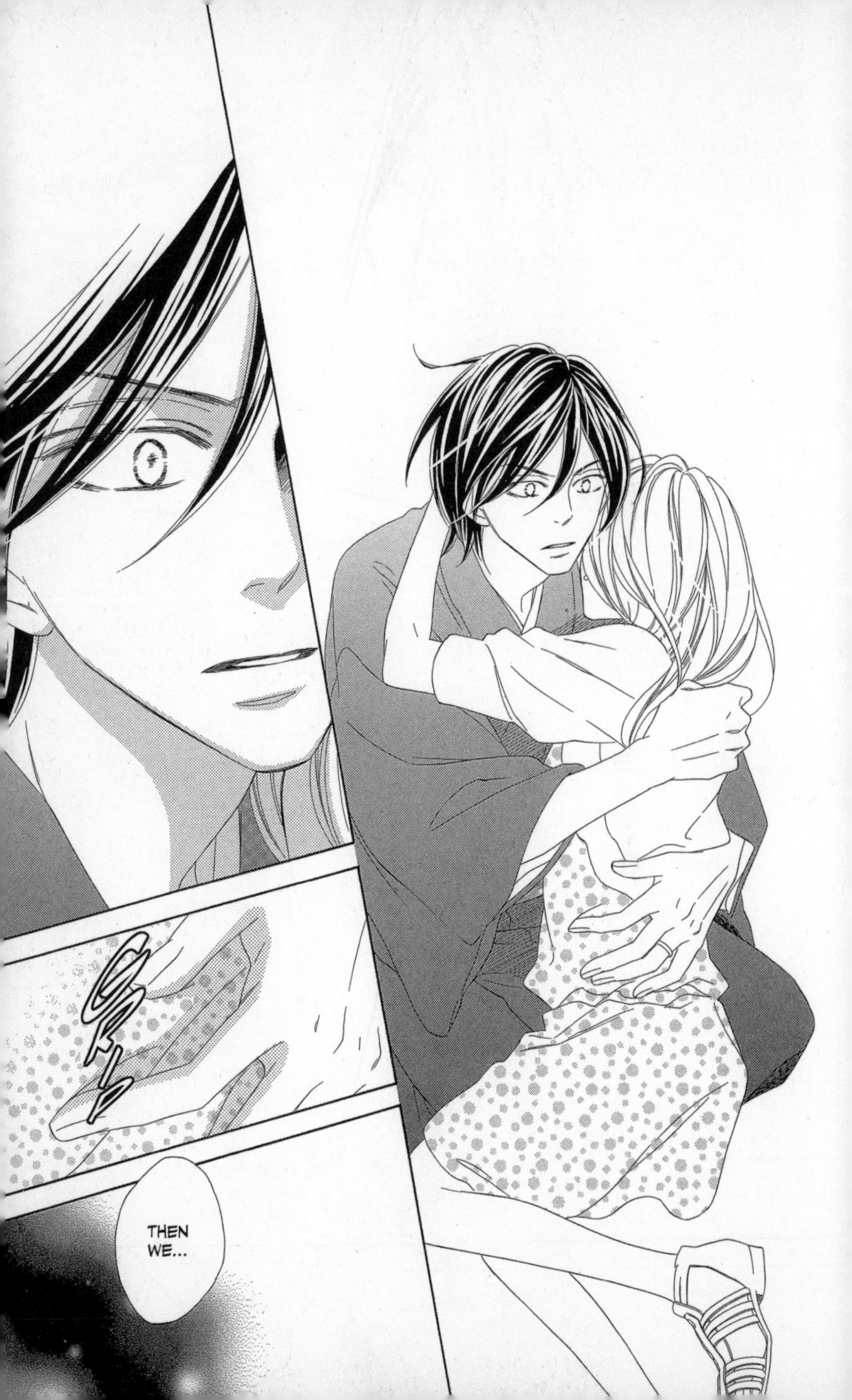
GRIP
THEN WE...

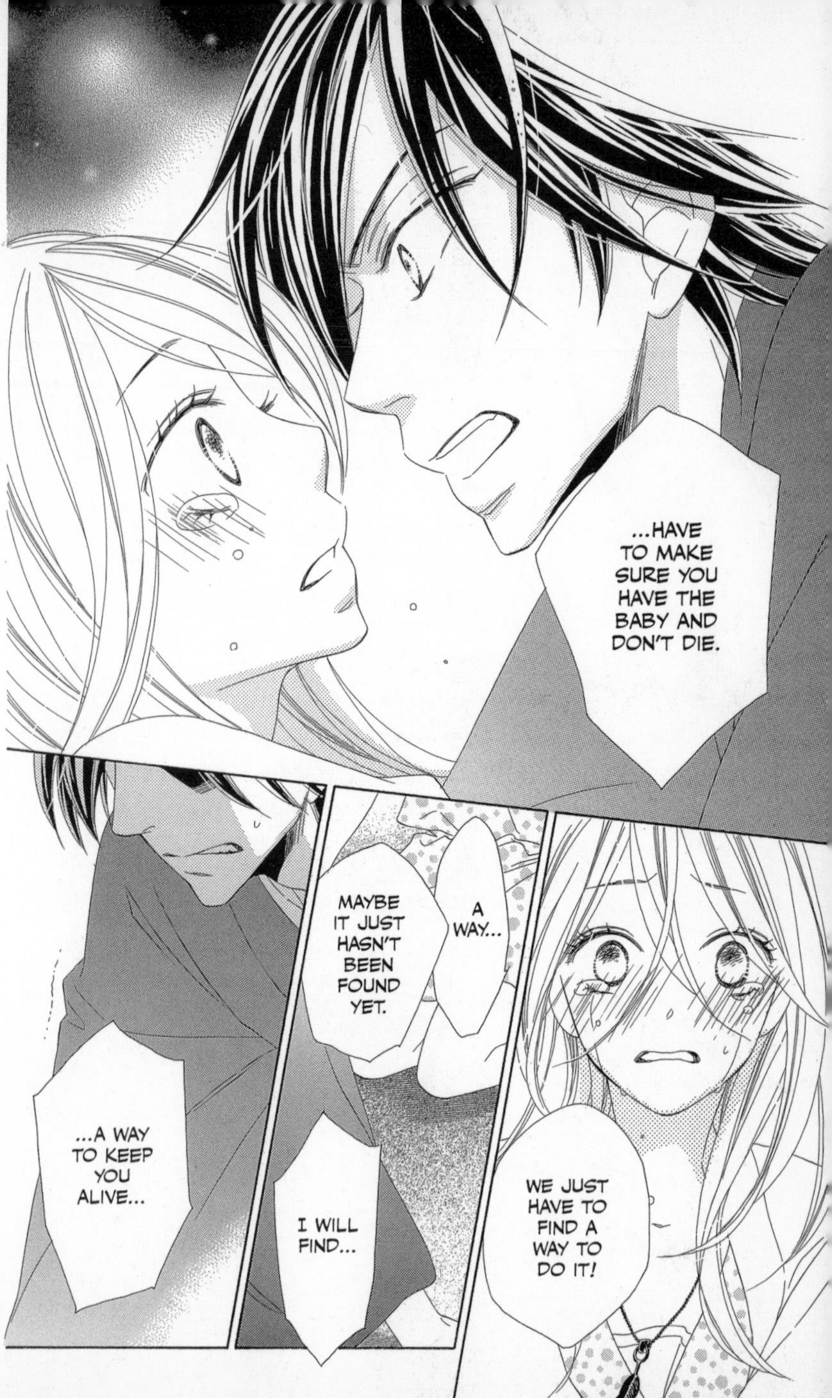
...HAVE TO MAKE SURE YOU HAVE THE BABY AND DON'T DIE.
WE JUST HAVE TO FIND A WAY TO DO IT!
A WAY...
MAYBE IT JUST HASN'T BEEN FOUND YET.
I WILL FIND...
...A WAY TO KEEP YOU ALIVE...

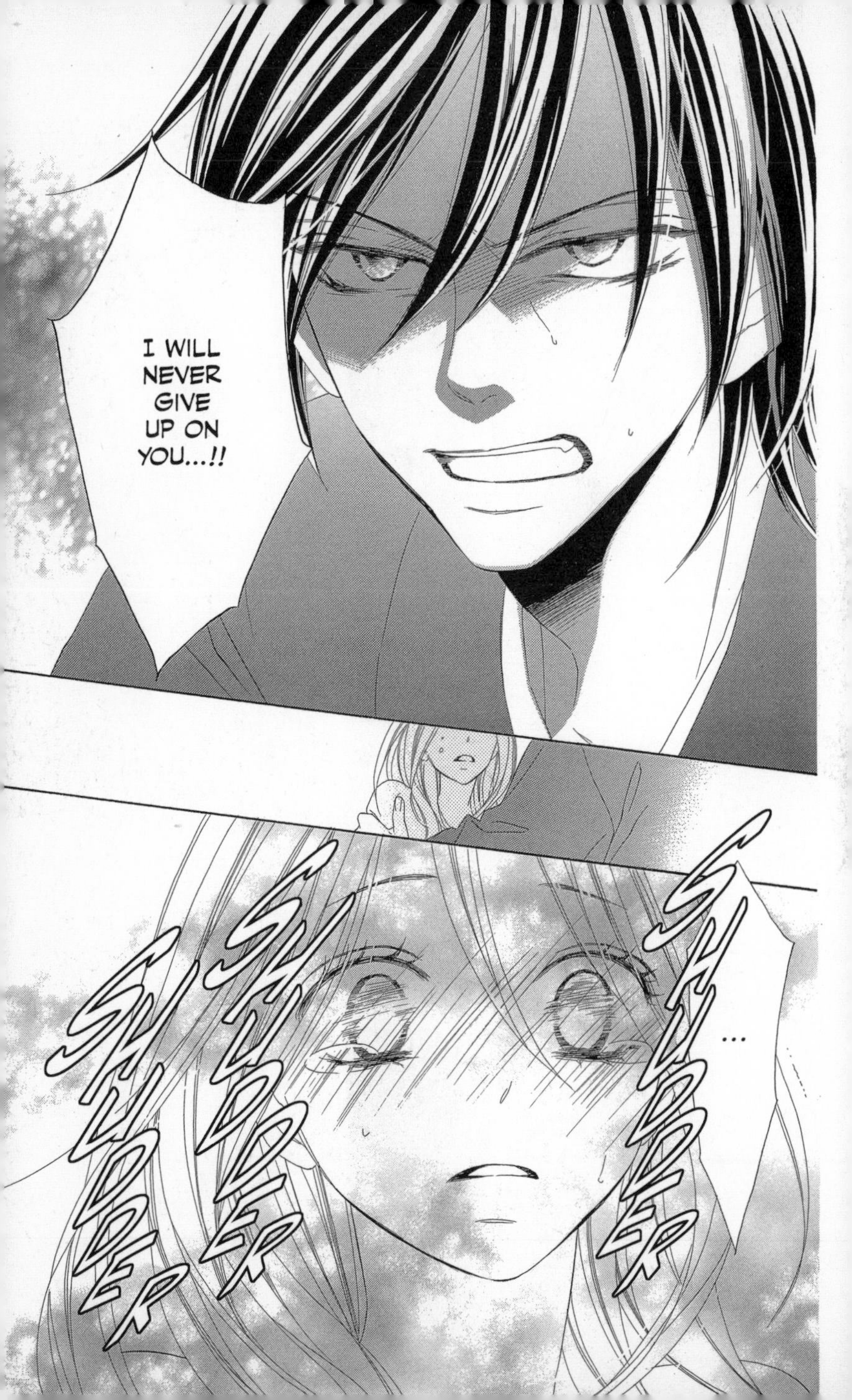
I WILL NEVER GIVE UP ON YOU...!!
SHUDDER
...
SHUDDER
SHUDDER

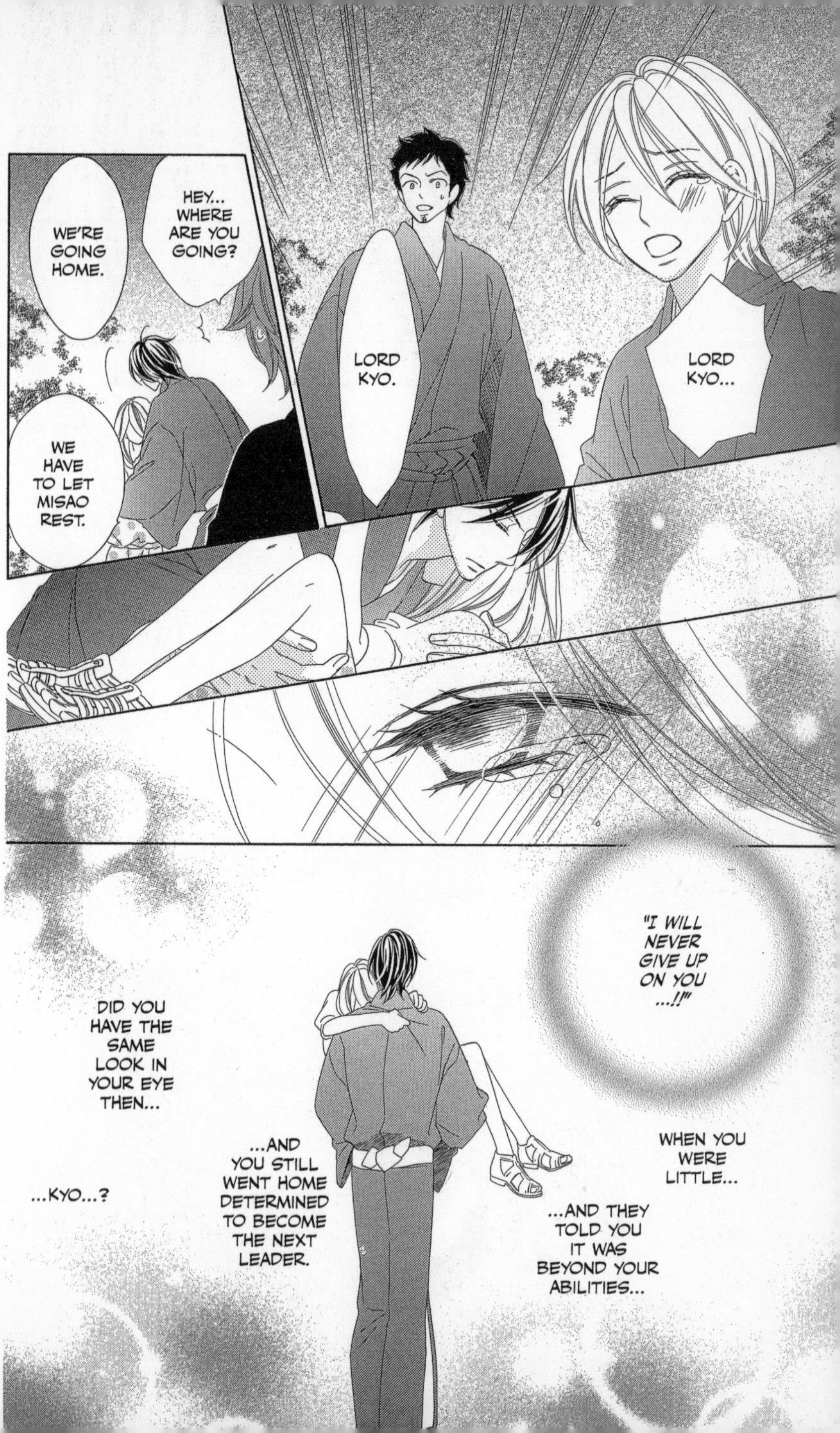
LORD KYO...
LORD KYO.
HEY... WHERE ARE YOU GOING?
WE'RE GOING HOME.
WE HAVE TO LET MISAO REST.
"I WILL NEVER GIVE UP ON YOU ...!!"
WHEN YOU WERE LITTLE...
...AND THEY TOLD YOU IT WAS BEYOND YOUR ABILITIES...
DID YOU HAVE THE SAME LOOK IN YOUR EYE THEN...
...AND YOU STILL WENT HOME DETERMINED TO BECOME THE NEXT LEADER.
...KYO...?

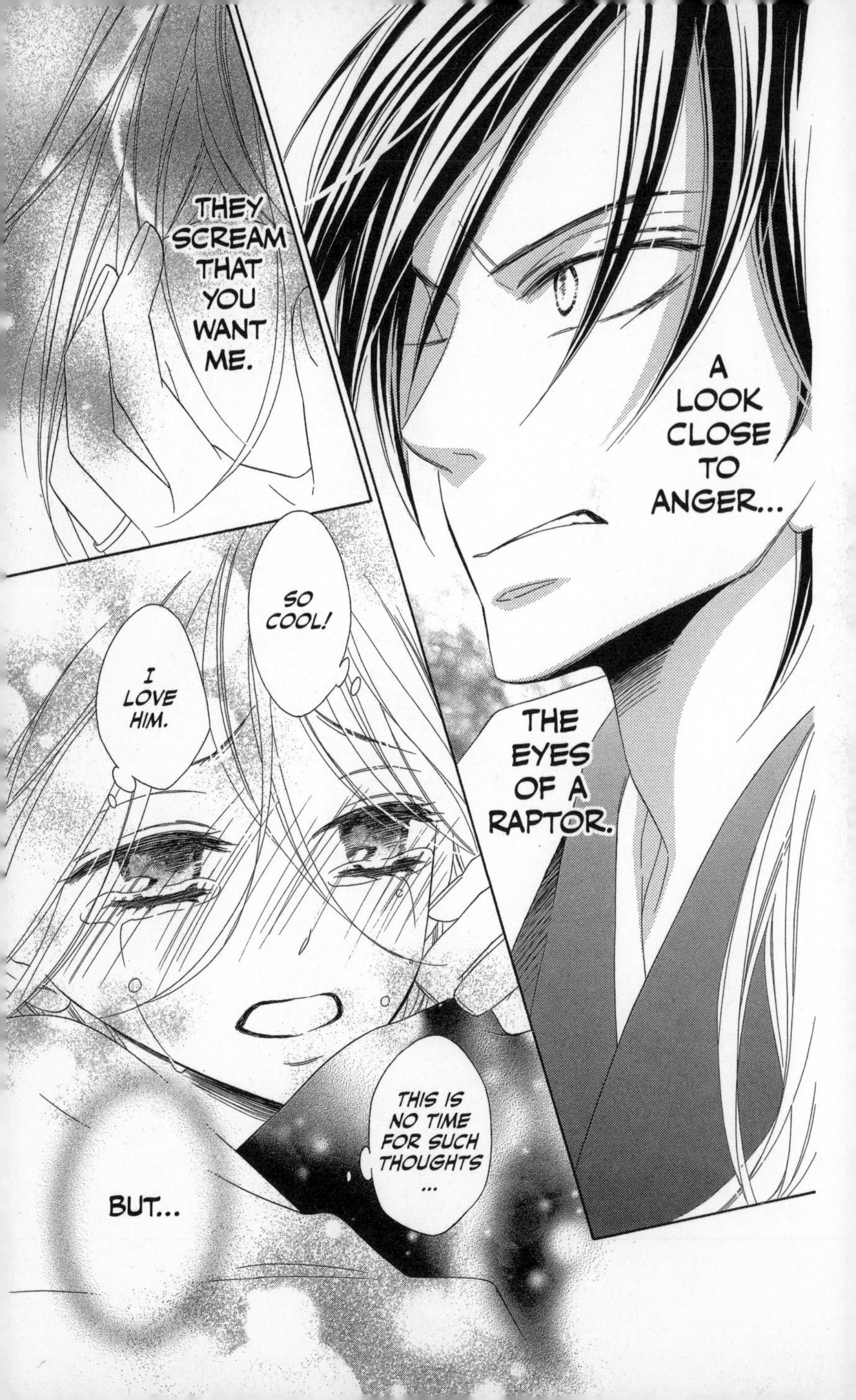
A LOOK CLOSE TO ANGER...
THE EYES OF A RAPTOR.
THEY SCREAM THAT YOU WANT ME.
SO COOL!
I LOVE HIM.
THIS IS NO TIME FOR SUCH THOUGHTS...
BUT...

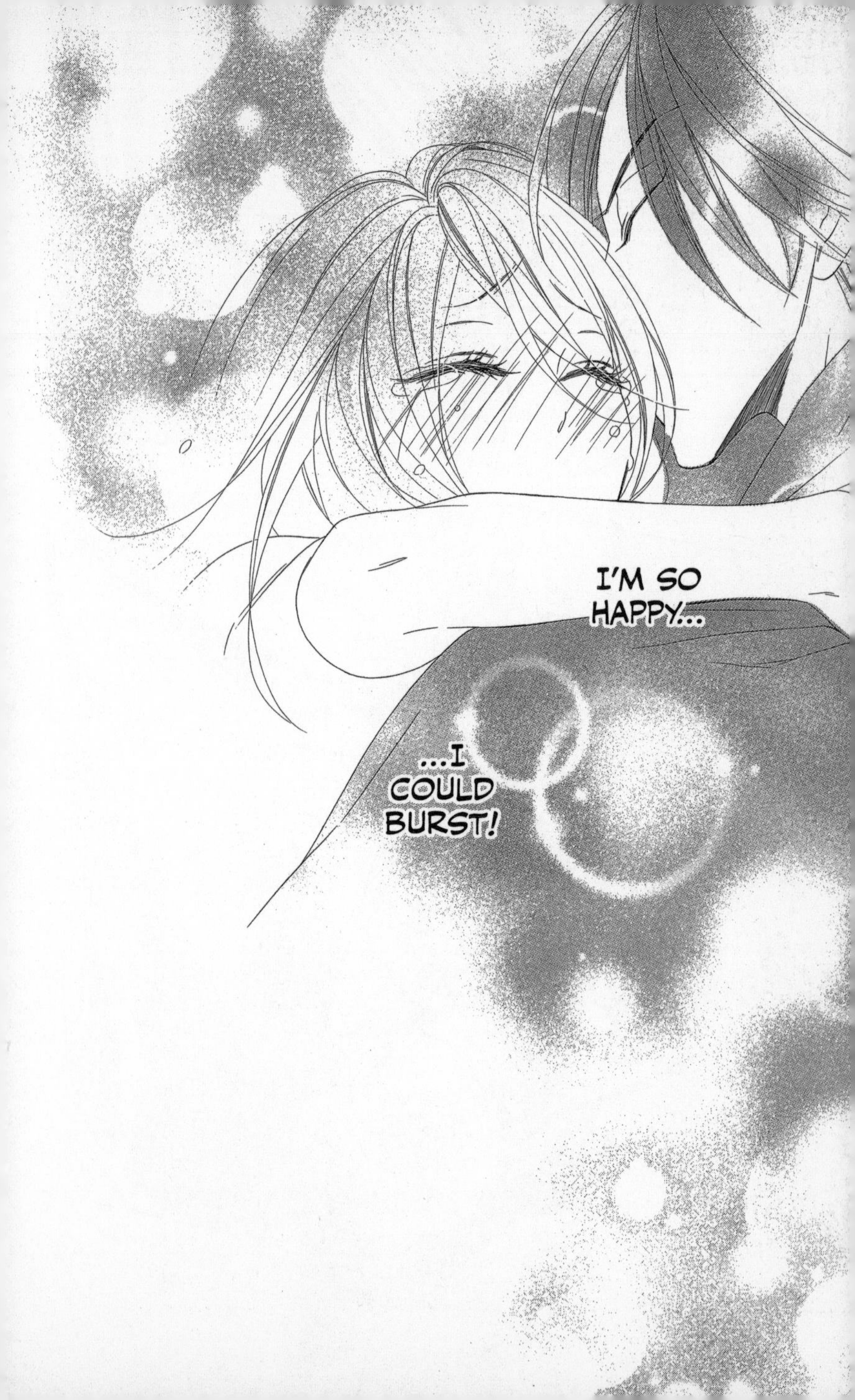
I'M SO HAPPY...
...I COULD BURST!

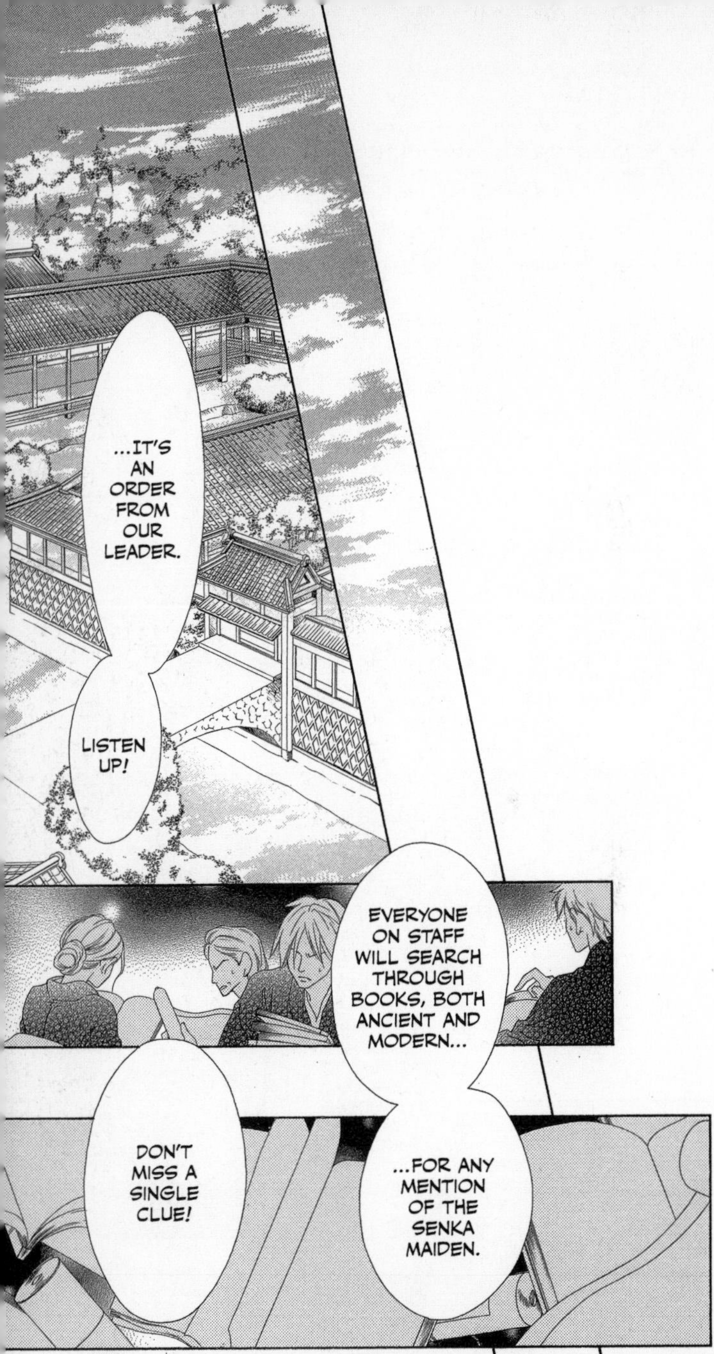
...IT'S AN ORDER FROM OUR LEADER.
LISTEN UP!
EVERYONE ON STAFF WILL SEARCH THROUGH BOOKS, BOTH ANCIENT AND MODERN...
...FOR ANY MENTION OF THE SENKA MAIDEN.
DON'T MISS A SINGLE CLUE!

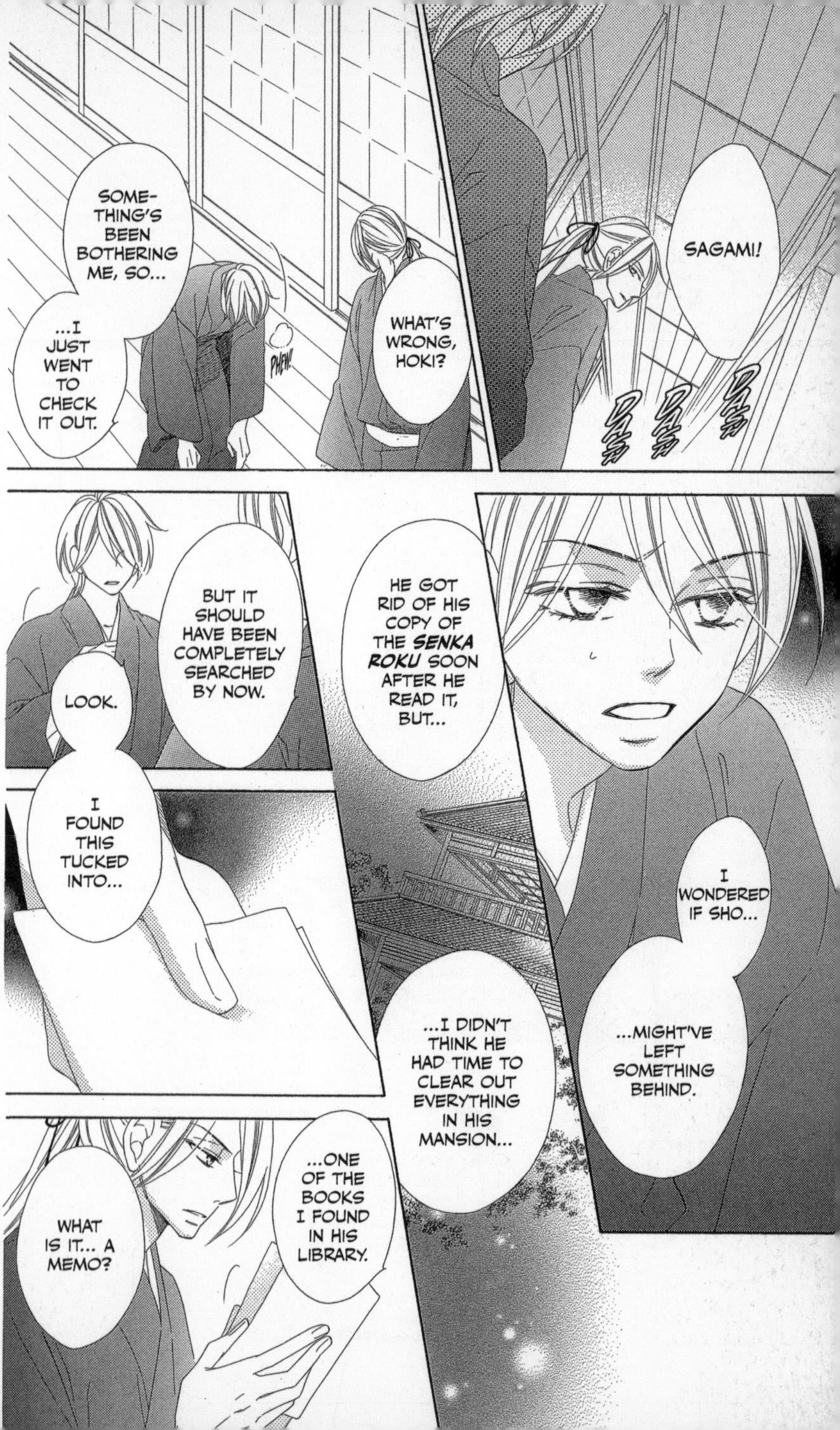
SAGAMI!
WHAT'S WRONG, HOKI?
PHEW!
SOMETHING'S BEEN BOTHERING ME, SO...
...I JUST WENT TO CHECK IT OUT.
HE GOT RID OF HIS COPY OF THE SENKA ROKU SOON AFTER HE READ IT, BUT...
I WONDERED IF SHO...
...MIGHT'VE LEFT SOMETHING BEHIND.
...I DIDN'T THINK HE HAD TIME TO CLEAR OUT EVERYTHING IN HIS MANSION...
BUT IT SHOULD HAVE BEEN COMPLETELY SEARCHED BY NOW.
LOOK.
I FOUND THIS TUCKED INTO...
...ONE OF THE BOOKS I FOUND IN HIS LIBRARY.
WHAT IS IT... A MEMO?

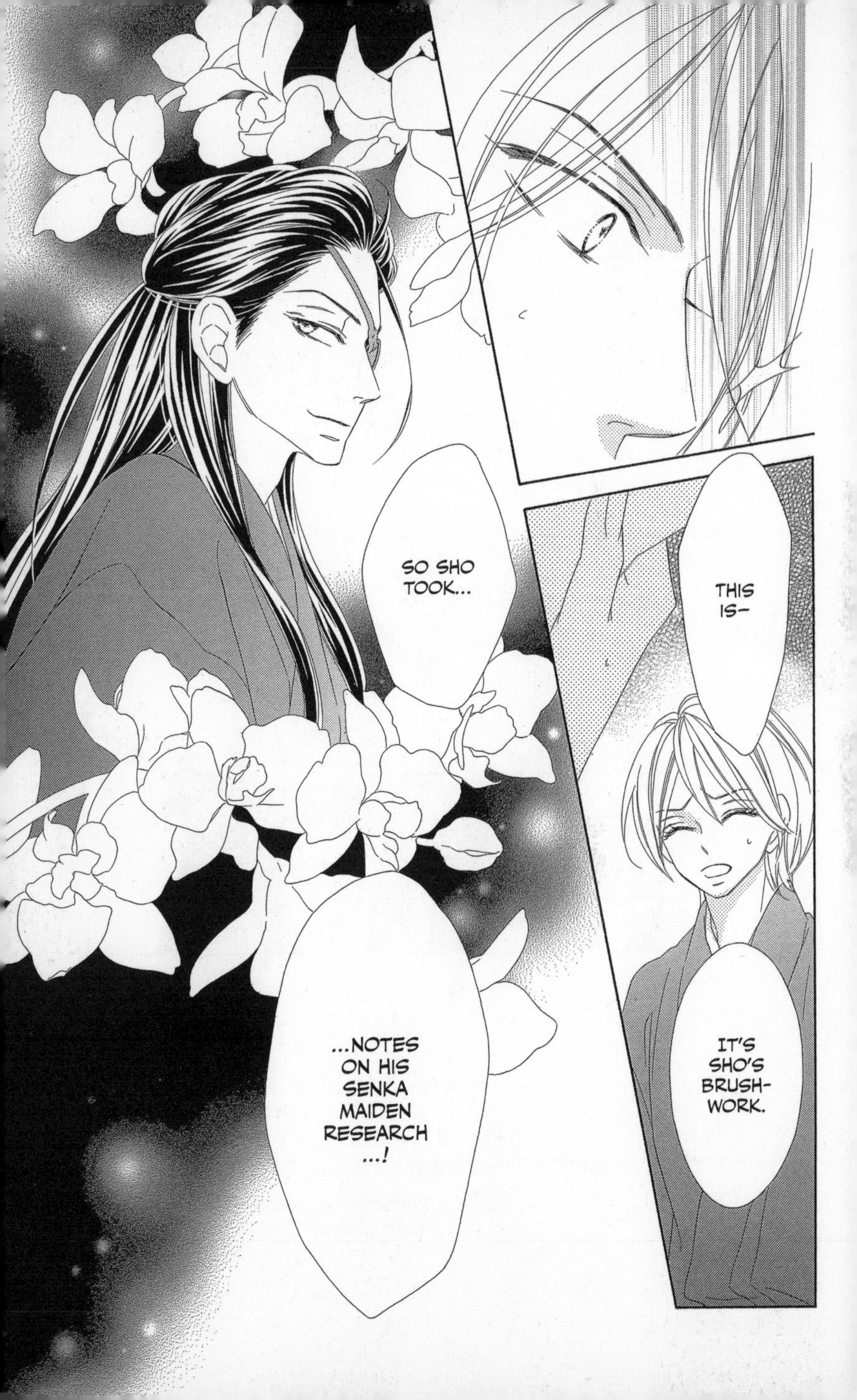
THIS IS—
IT'S SHO'S BRUSHWORK.
SO SHO TOOK...
...NOTES ON HIS SENKA MAIDEN RESEARCH ...!

Back after a hiatus!

Illustration Request Number 13

"Rock Band"

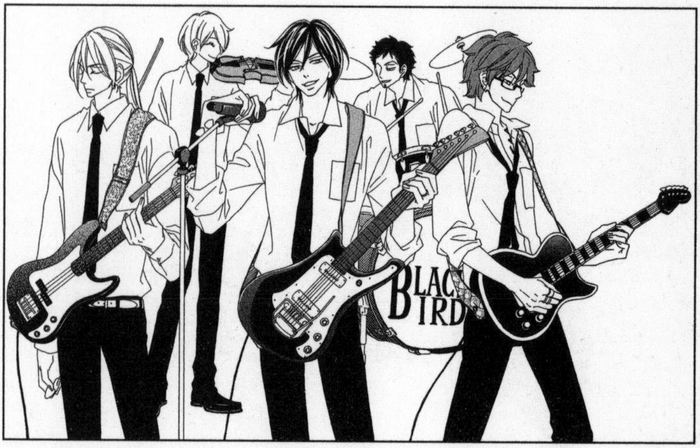
BLAC
IRD

It was easy assigning instruments to everyone, except for Hoki. I could've given him a keyboard, but I gave him a violin because I thought it would work better as a picture.

It's far from the music I imagine, but...
Drawing a 5-piece band is difficult!

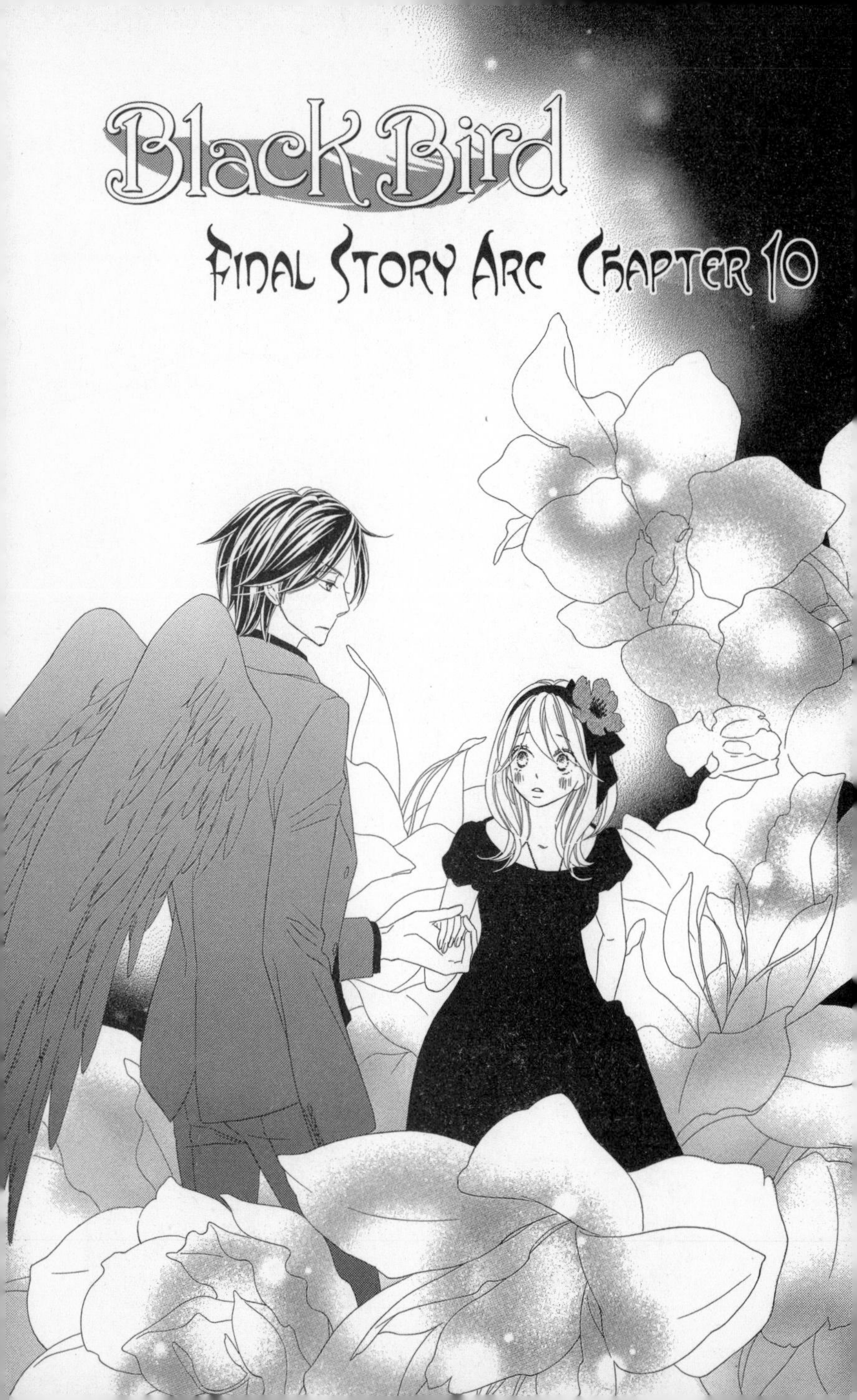
Black Bird
Final Story Arc Chapter 10

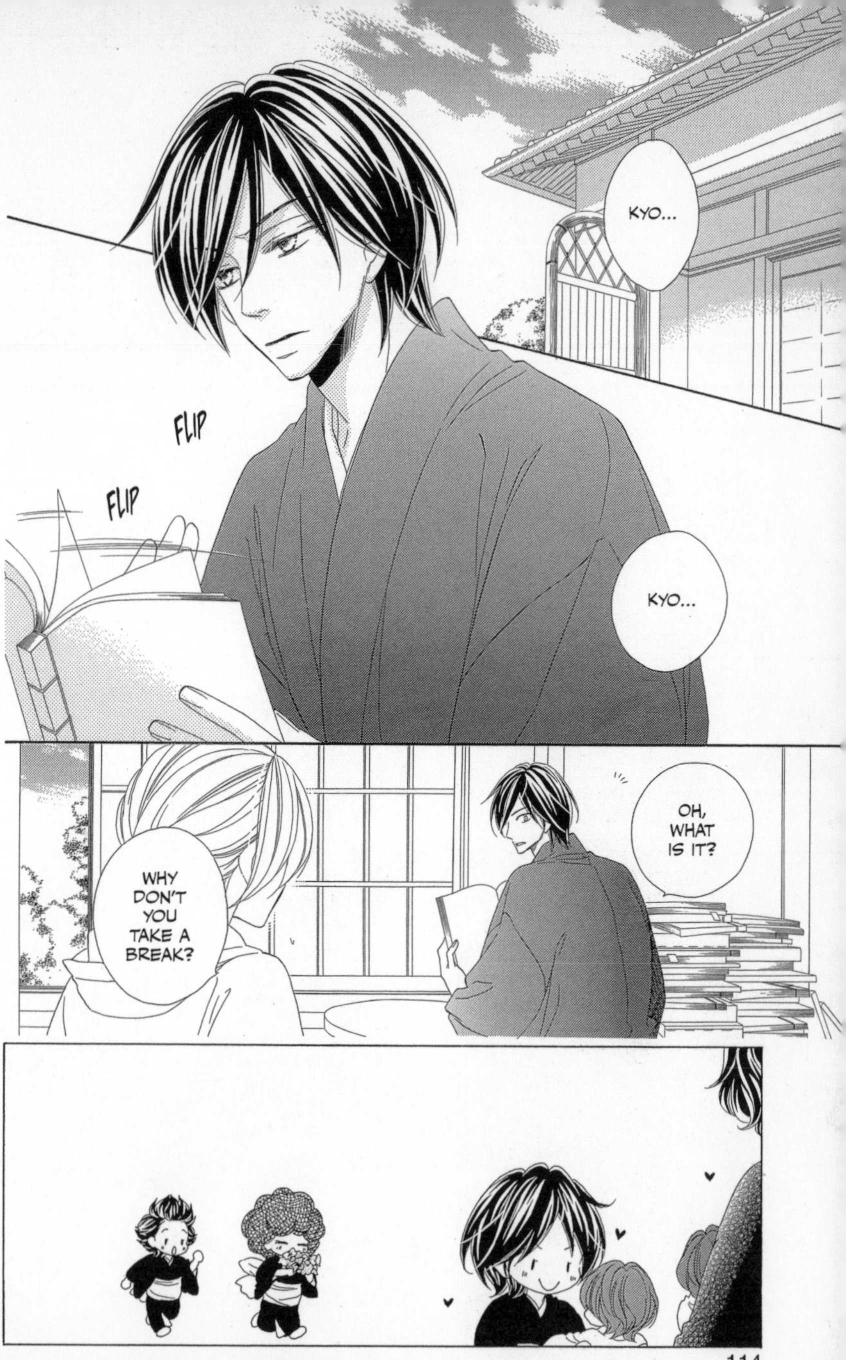
KYO...
KYO...
FLIP
FLIP
OH, WHAT IS IT?
WHY DON'T YOU TAKE A BREAK?

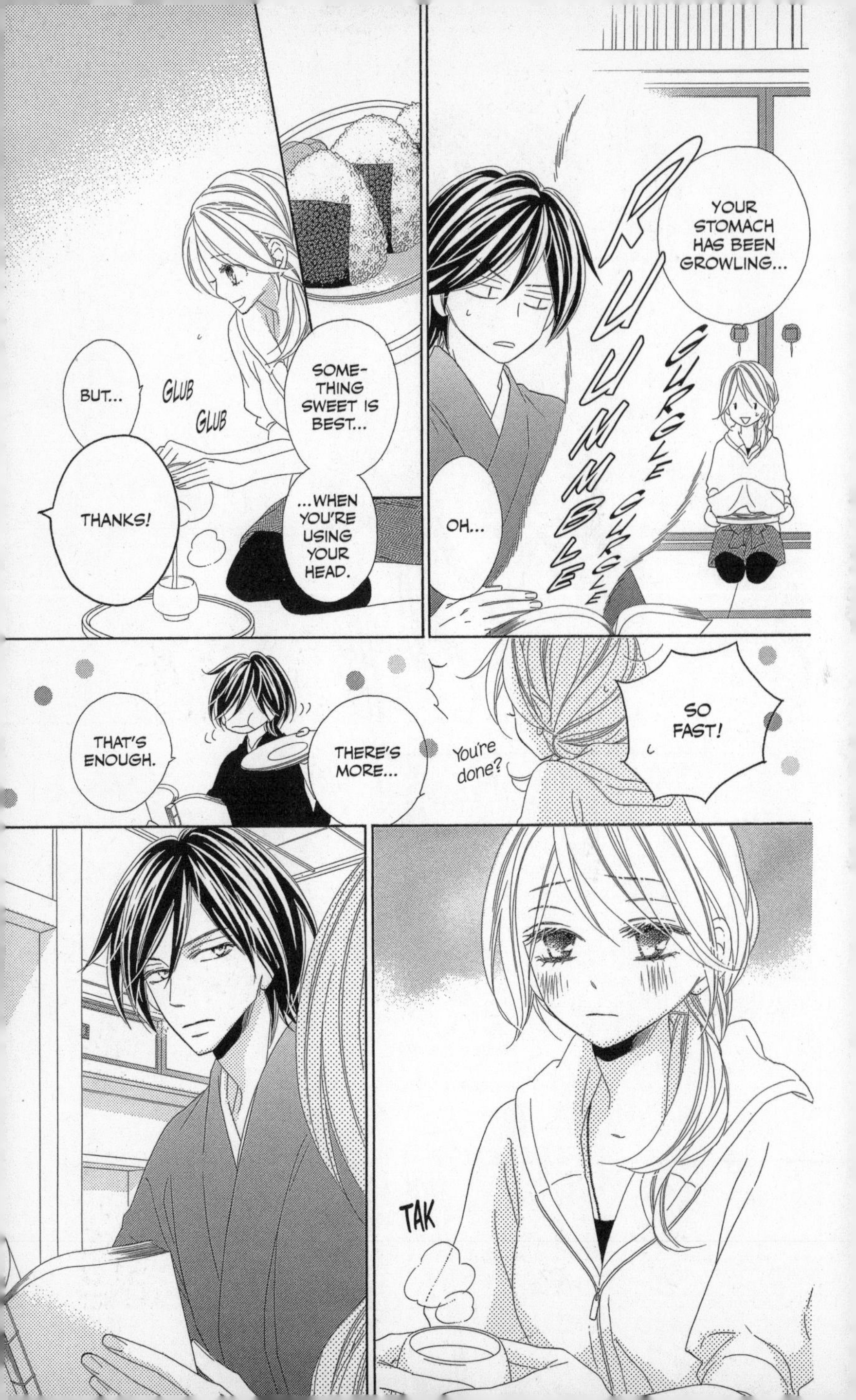
YOUR STOMACH HAS BEEN GROWLING...
RUUMMBLE
GURGLE GURGLE
OH...
SOME-THING SWEET IS BEST...
...WHEN YOU'RE USING YOUR HEAD.
BUT...
GLUB GLUB
THANKS!
SO FAST!
You're done?
THERE'S MORE...
THAT'S ENOUGH.
TAK

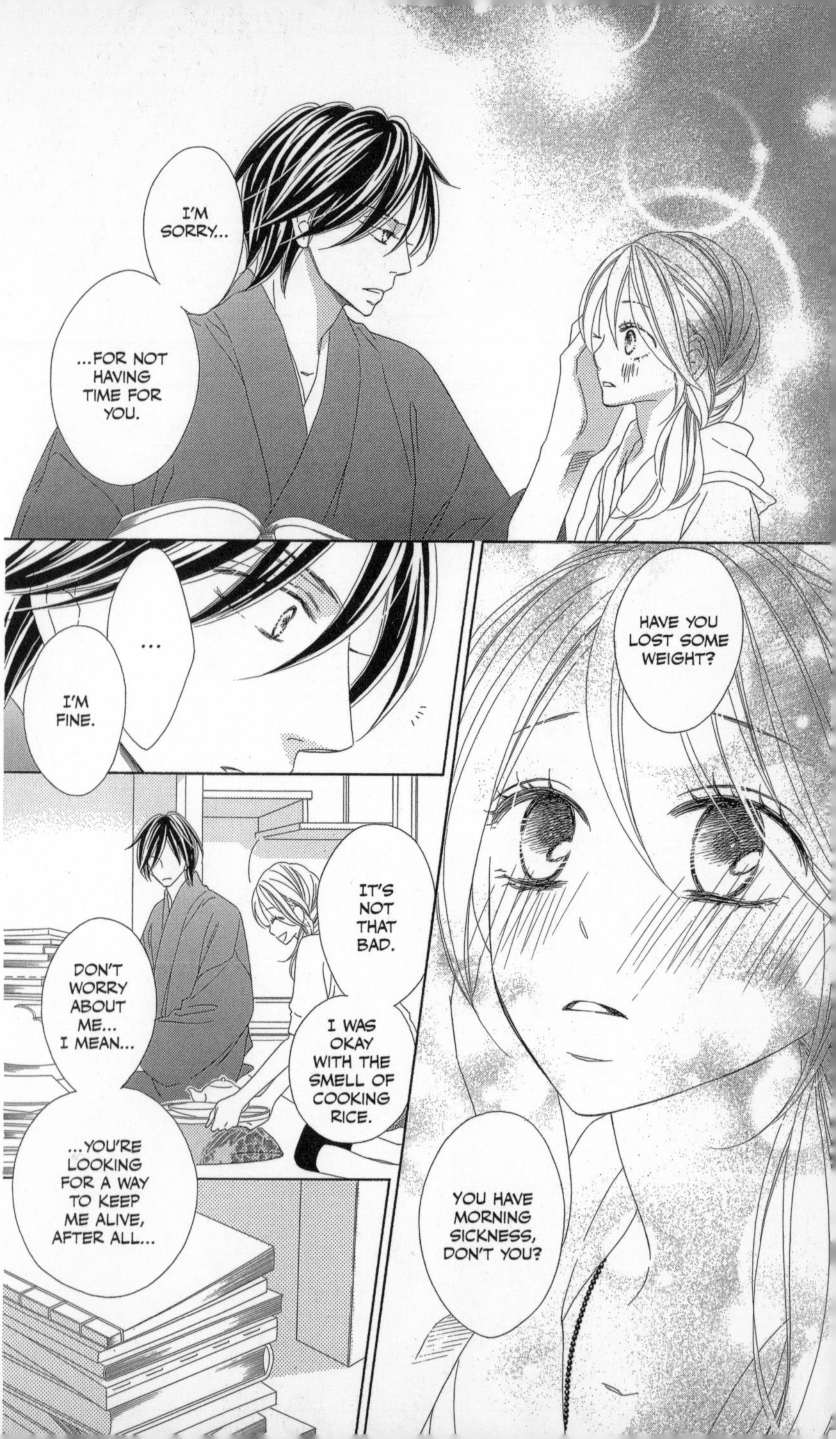
I'M SORRY...
...FOR NOT HAVING TIME FOR YOU.
HAVE YOU LOST SOME WEIGHT?
YOU HAVE MORNING SICKNESS, DON'T YOU?
...
I'M FINE.
IT'S NOT THAT BAD.
I WAS OKAY WITH THE SMELL OF COOKING RICE.
DON'T WORRY ABOUT ME... I MEAN...
...YOU'RE LOOKING FOR A WAY TO KEEP ME ALIVE, AFTER ALL...

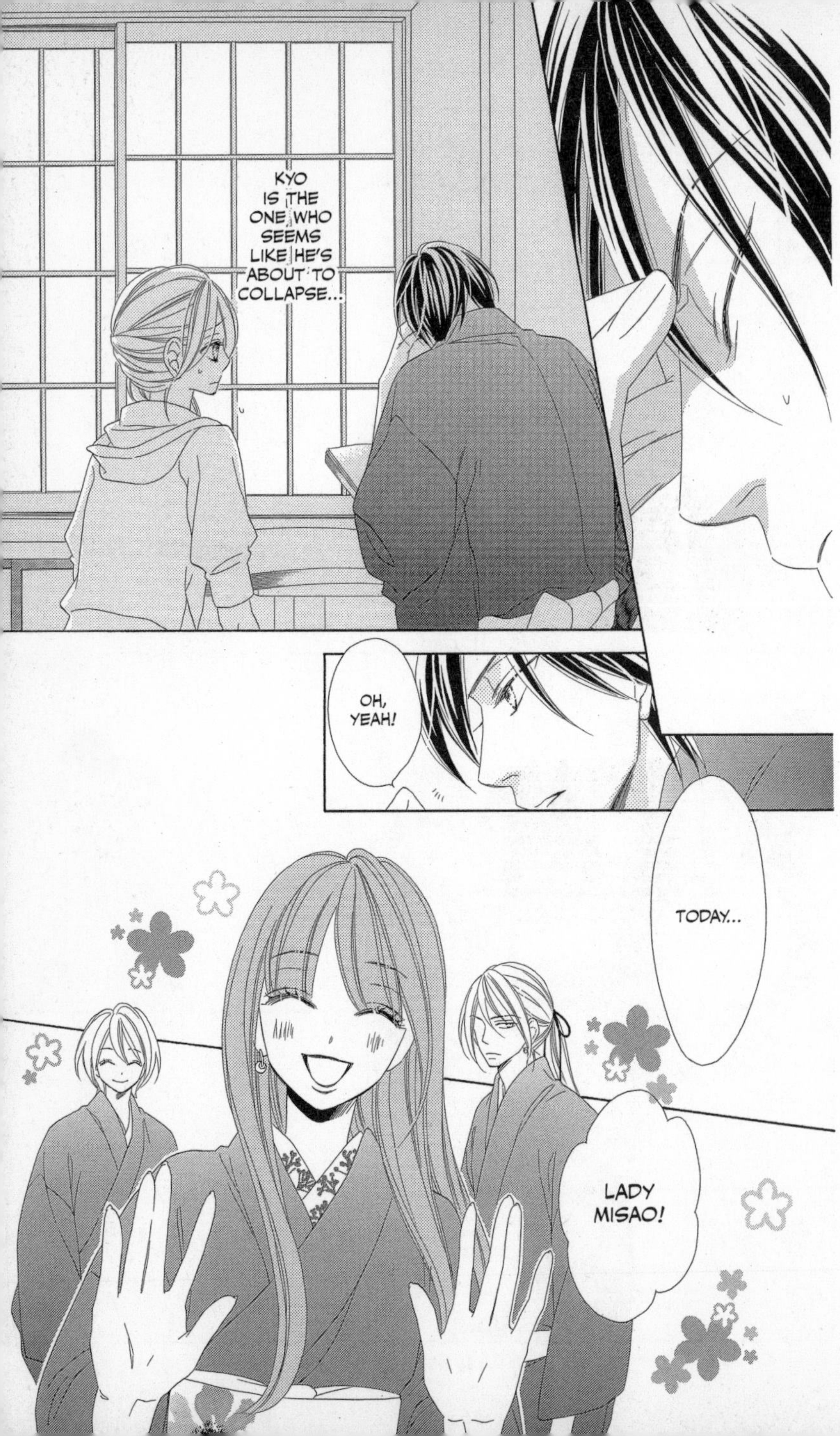
KYO IS THE ONE WHO SEEMS LIKE HE'S ABOUT TO COLLAPSE...
OH, YEAH!
TODAY...
LADY MISAO!

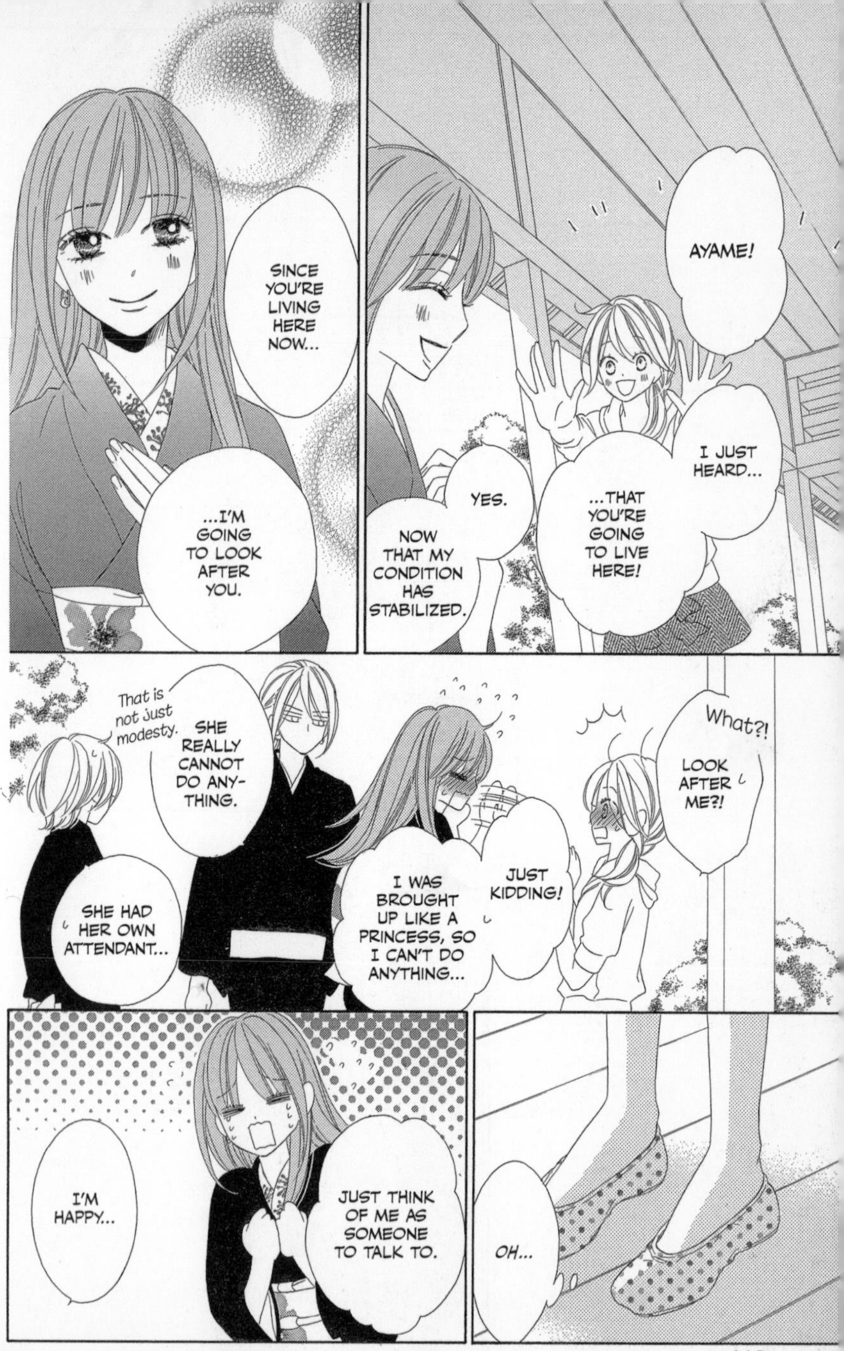
AYAME!
I JUST HEARD...
...THAT YOU'RE GOING TO LIVE HERE!
YES.
NOW THAT MY CONDITION HAS STABILIZED.
SINCE YOU'RE LIVING HERE NOW...
...I'M GOING TO LOOK AFTER YOU.
What?!
LOOK AFTER ME?!
JUST KIDDING!
I WAS BROUGHT UP LIKE A PRINCESS, SO I CAN'T DO ANYTHING...
SHE REALLY CANNOT DO ANYTHING.
That is not just modesty.
SHE HAD HER OWN ATTENDANT...
OH...
JUST THINK OF ME AS SOMEONE TO TALK TO.
I'M HAPPY...

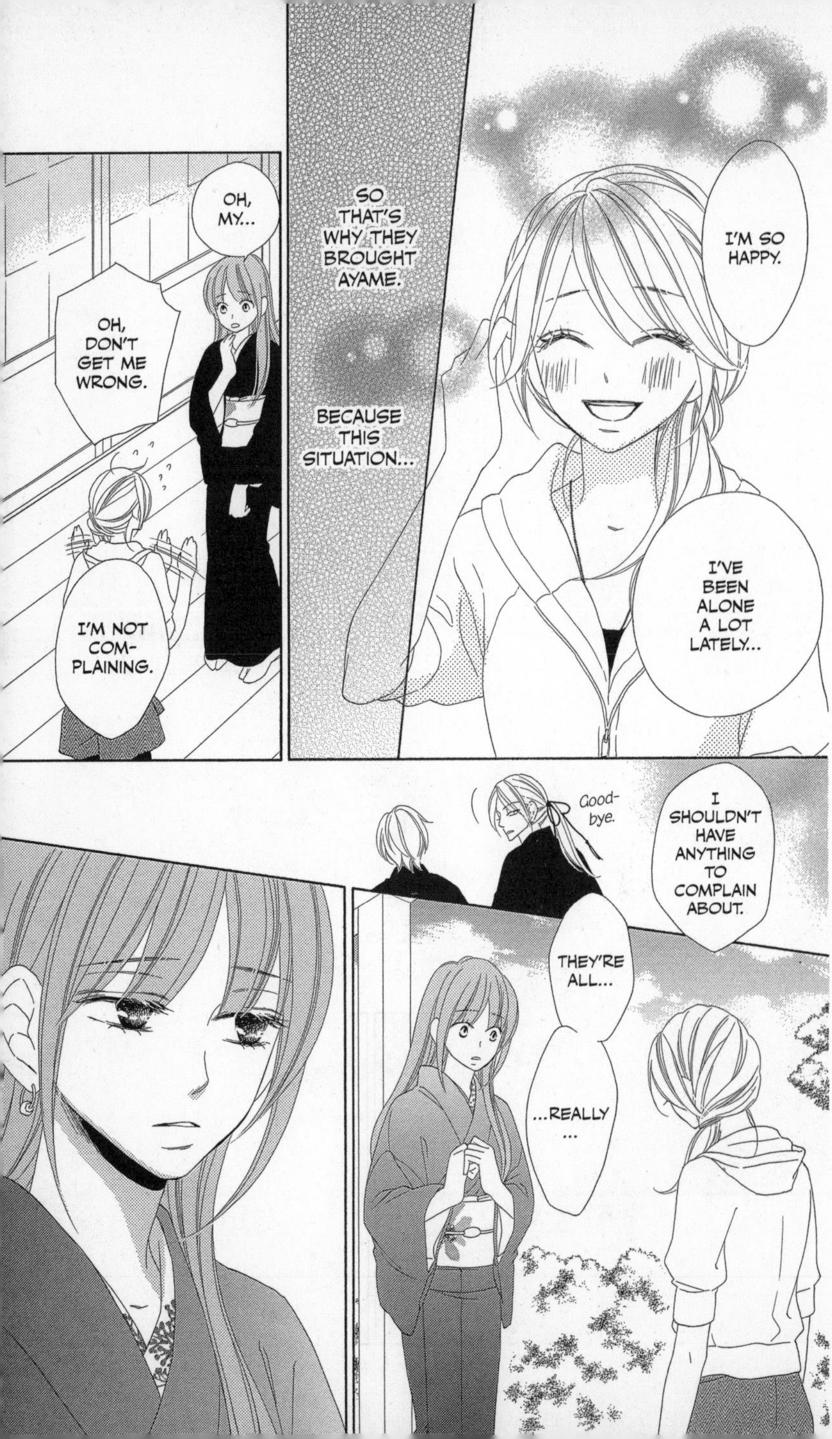
I'M SO HAPPY.
I'VE BEEN ALONE A LOT LATELY...
SO THAT'S WHY THEY BROUGHT AYAME.
BECAUSE THIS SITUATION...
OH, MY...
OH, DON'T GET ME WRONG.
I'M NOT COMPLAINING.
I SHOULDN'T HAVE ANYTHING TO COMPLAIN ABOUT.
Good-bye.
THEY'RE ALL...
...REALLY...

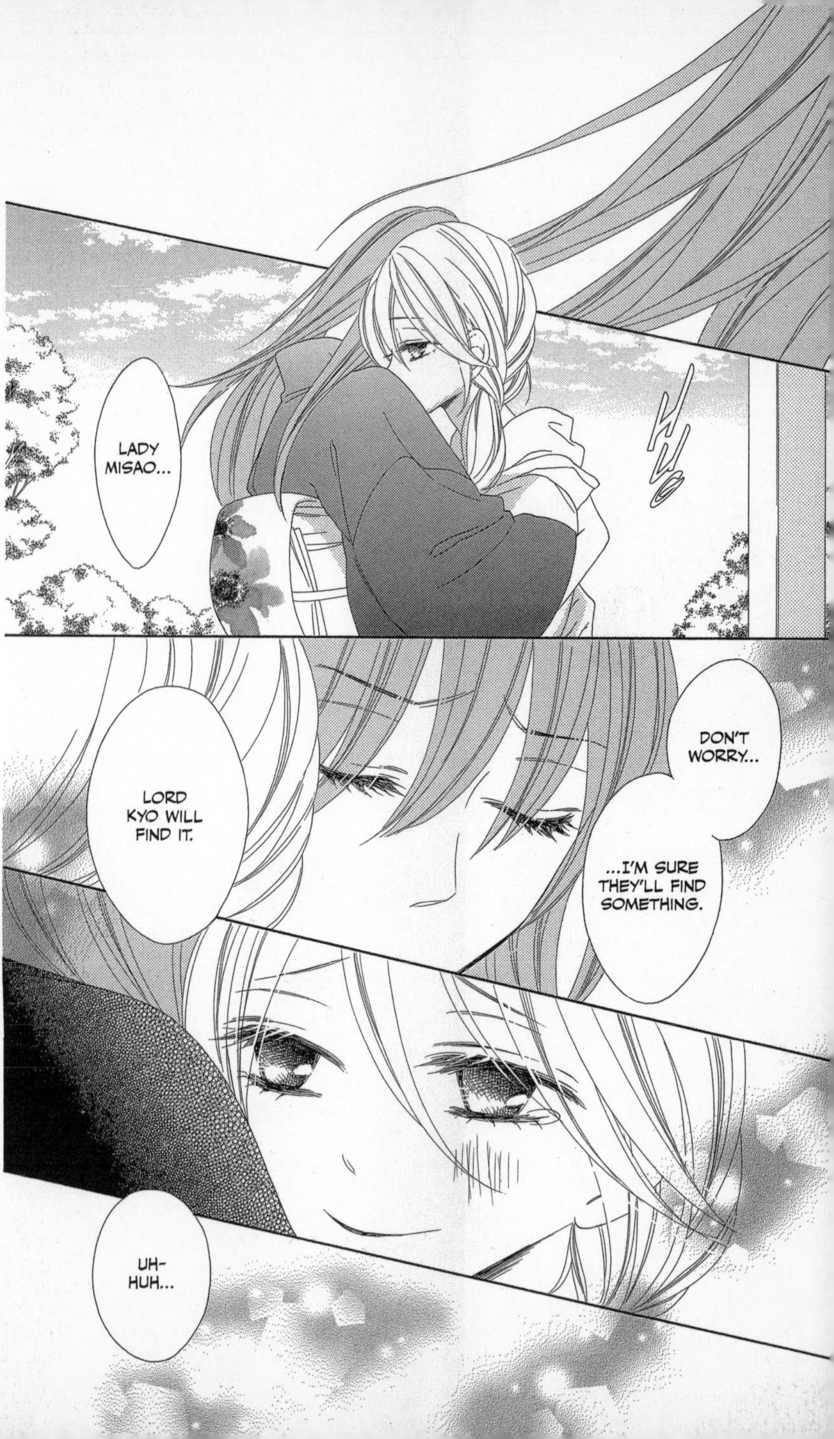
HUG
LADY MISAO...
DON'T WORRY...
...I'M SURE THEY'LL FIND SOMETHING.
LORD KYO WILL FIND IT.
UH-HUH...

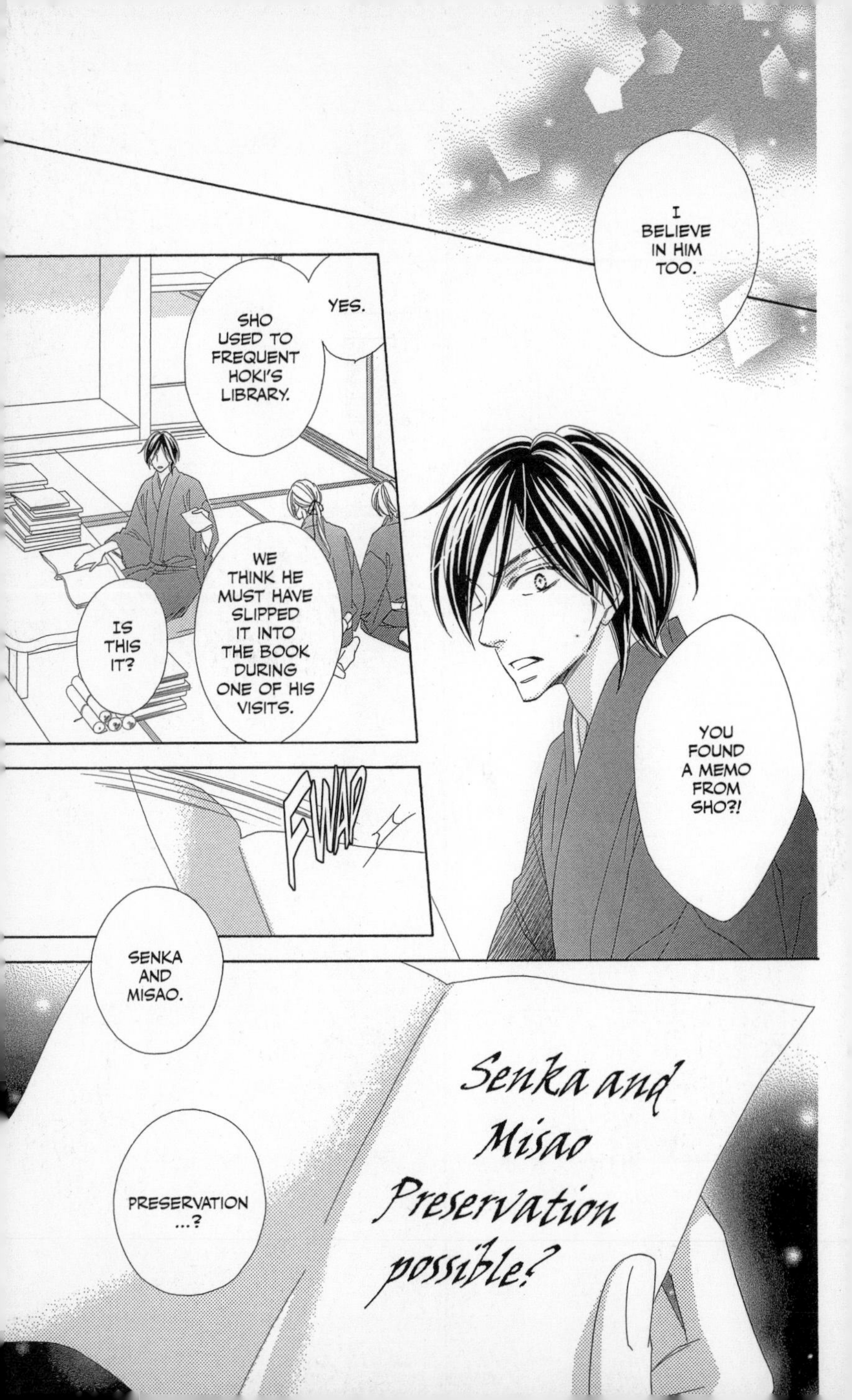
I BELIEVE IN HIM TOO.
YOU FOUND A MEMO FROM SHO?!
YES.
SHO USED TO FREQUENT HOKI'S LIBRARY.
WE THINK HE MUST HAVE SLIPPED IT INTO THE BOOK DURING ONE OF HIS VISITS.
IS THIS IT?
SWAP
Senka and Misao Preservation possible?
SENKA AND MISAO.
PRESERVATION ...?

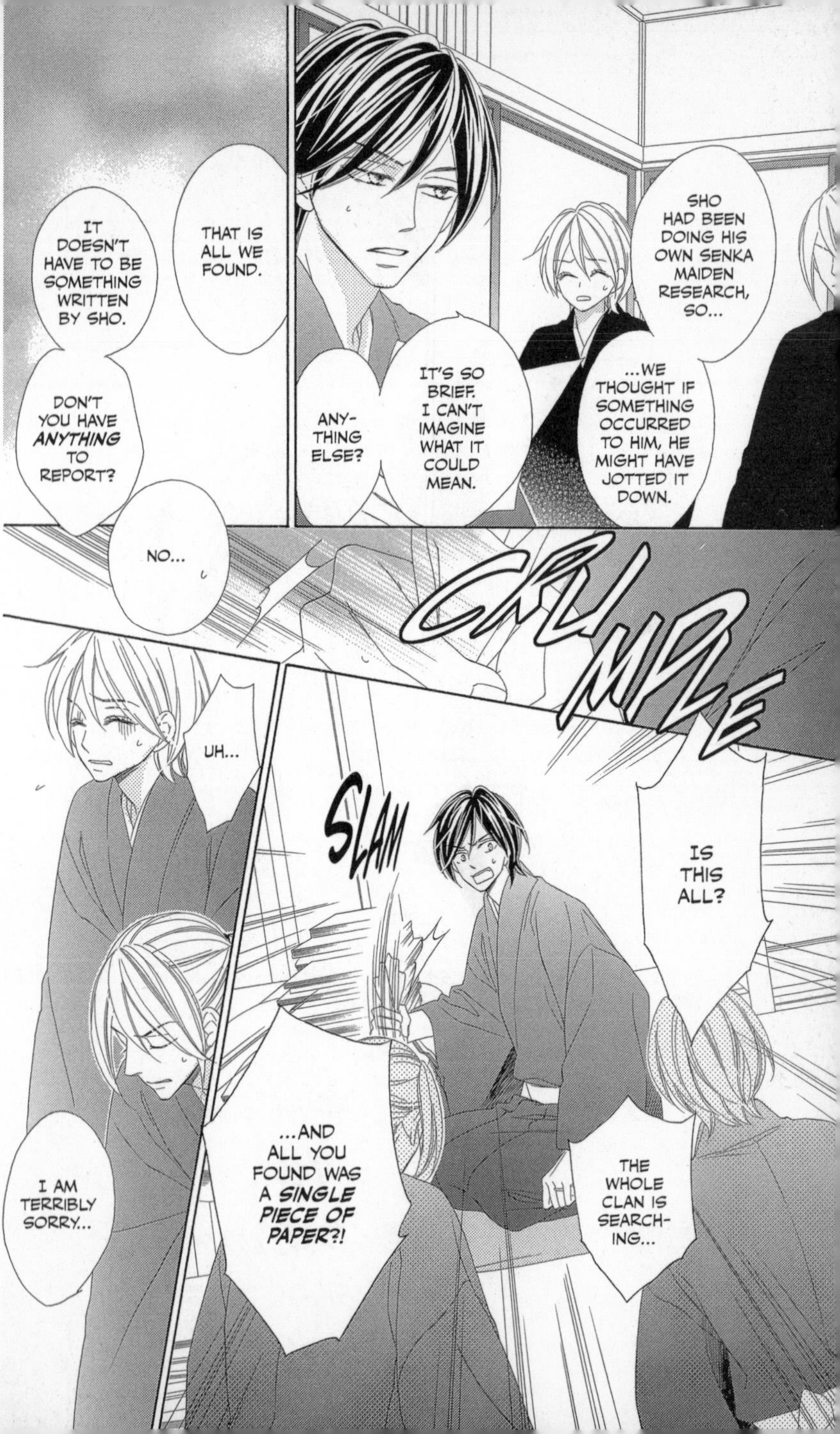
SHO HAD BEEN DOING HIS OWN SENKA MAIDEN RESEARCH, SO...
...WE THOUGHT IF SOMETHING OCCURRED TO HIM, HE MIGHT HAVE JOTTED IT DOWN.
IT'S SO BRIEF. I CAN'T IMAGINE WHAT IT COULD MEAN.
ANY-THING ELSE?
THAT IS ALL WE FOUND.
IT DOESN'T HAVE TO BE SOMETHING WRITTEN BY SHO.
DON'T YOU HAVE *ANYTHING* TO REPORT?
NO...
CRUMPLE
IS THIS ALL?
SLAM
THE WHOLE CLAN IS SEARCH-ING...
...AND ALL YOU FOUND WAS A *SINGLE PIECE OF PAPER?!*
UH...
I AM TERRIBLY SORRY...

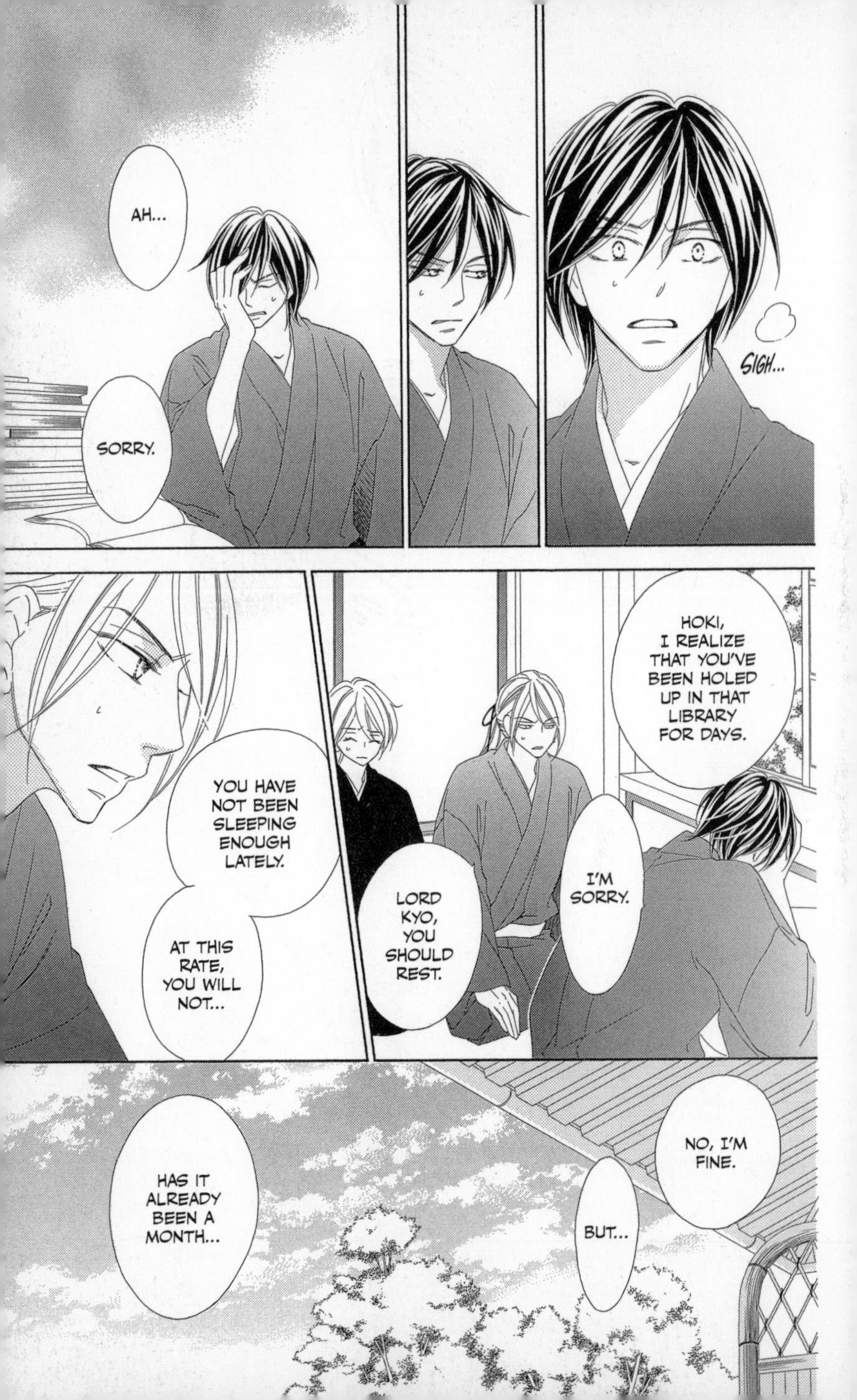
SIGH...
AH...
SORRY.
HOKI, I REALIZE THAT YOU'VE BEEN HOLED UP IN THAT LIBRARY FOR DAYS.
I'M SORRY.
LORD KYO, YOU SHOULD REST.
YOU HAVE NOT BEEN SLEEPING ENOUGH LATELY.
AT THIS RATE, YOU WILL NOT...
NO, I'M FINE.
BUT...
HAS IT ALREADY BEEN A MONTH...

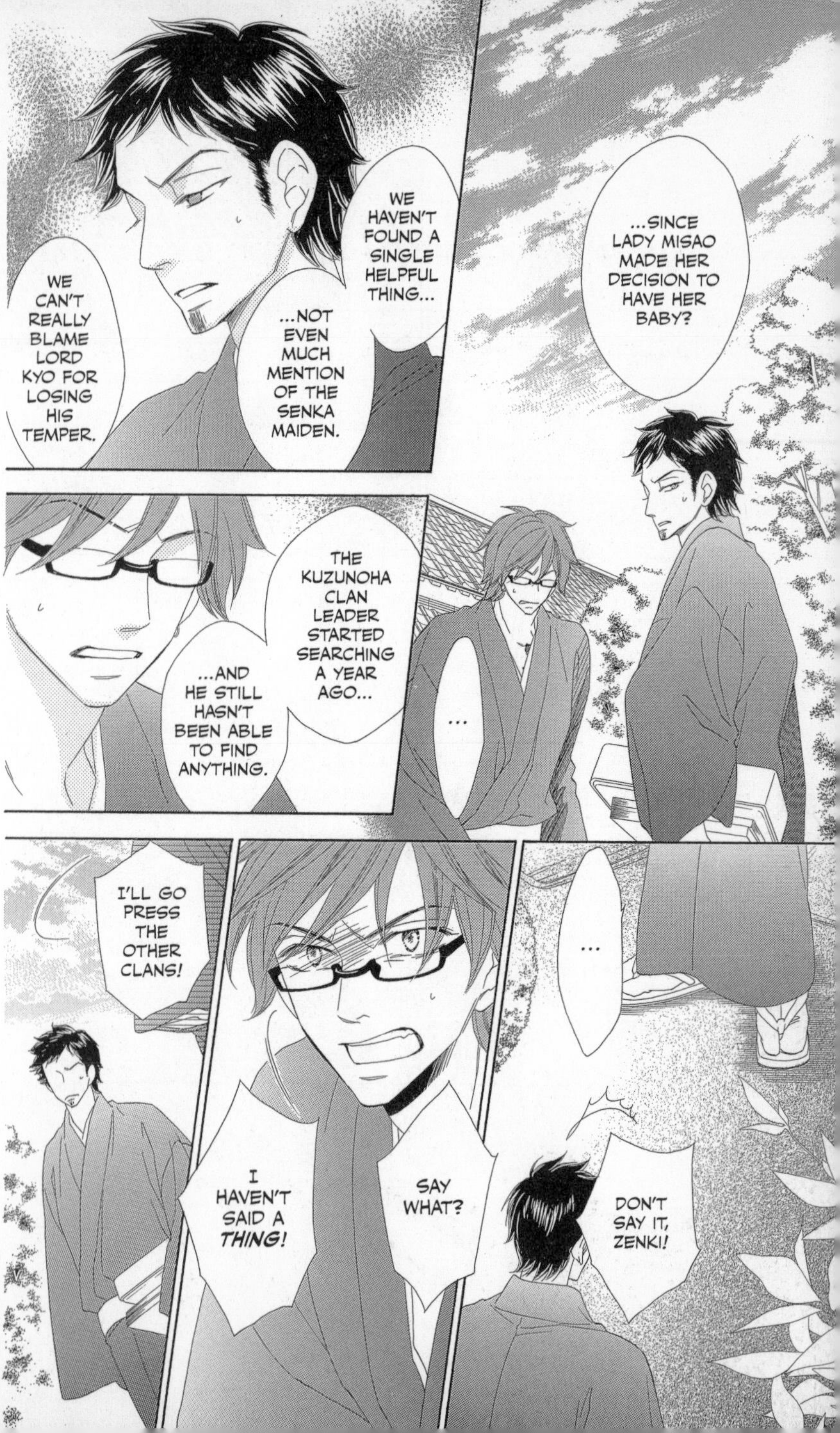
...SINCE LADY MISAO MADE HER DECISION TO HAVE HER BABY?
...
WE HAVEN'T FOUND A SINGLE HELPFUL THING...
...NOT EVEN MUCH MENTION OF THE SENKA MAIDEN.
WE CAN'T REALLY BLAME LORD KYO FOR LOSING HIS TEMPER.
THE KUZUNOHA CLAN LEADER STARTED SEARCHING A YEAR AGO...
...AND HE STILL HASN'T BEEN ABLE TO FIND ANYTHING.
...
DON'T SAY IT, ZENKI!
SAY WHAT?
I HAVEN'T SAID A *THING*!
I'LL GO PRESS THE OTHER CLANS!

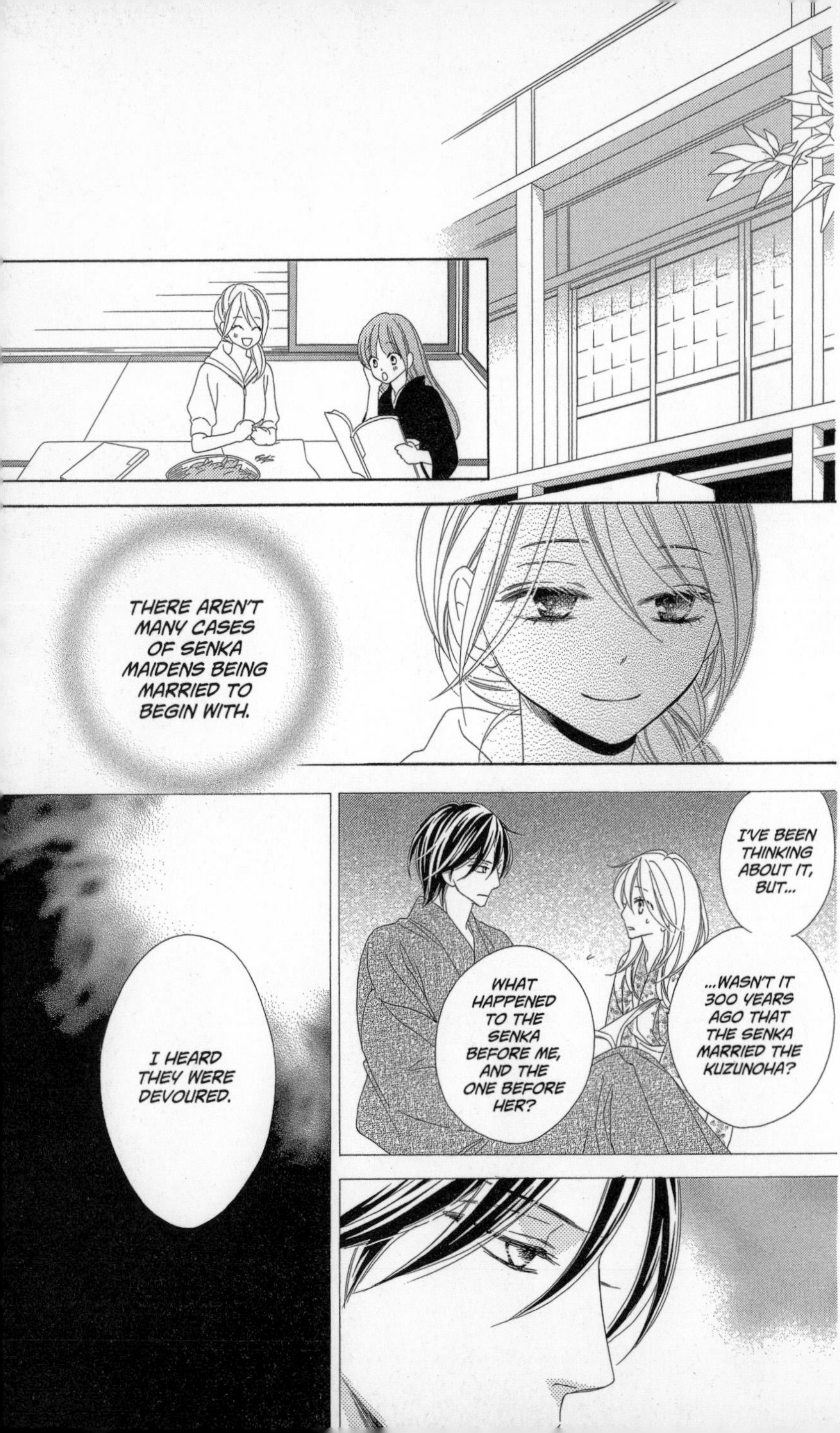
THERE AREN'T MANY CASES OF SENKA MAIDENS BEING MARRIED TO BEGIN WITH.
I'VE BEEN THINKING ABOUT IT, BUT...
...WASN'T IT 300 YEARS AGO THAT THE SENKA MARRIED THE KUZUNOHA?
WHAT HAPPENED TO THE SENKA BEFORE ME, AND THE ONE BEFORE HER?
I HEARD THEY WERE DEVOURED.

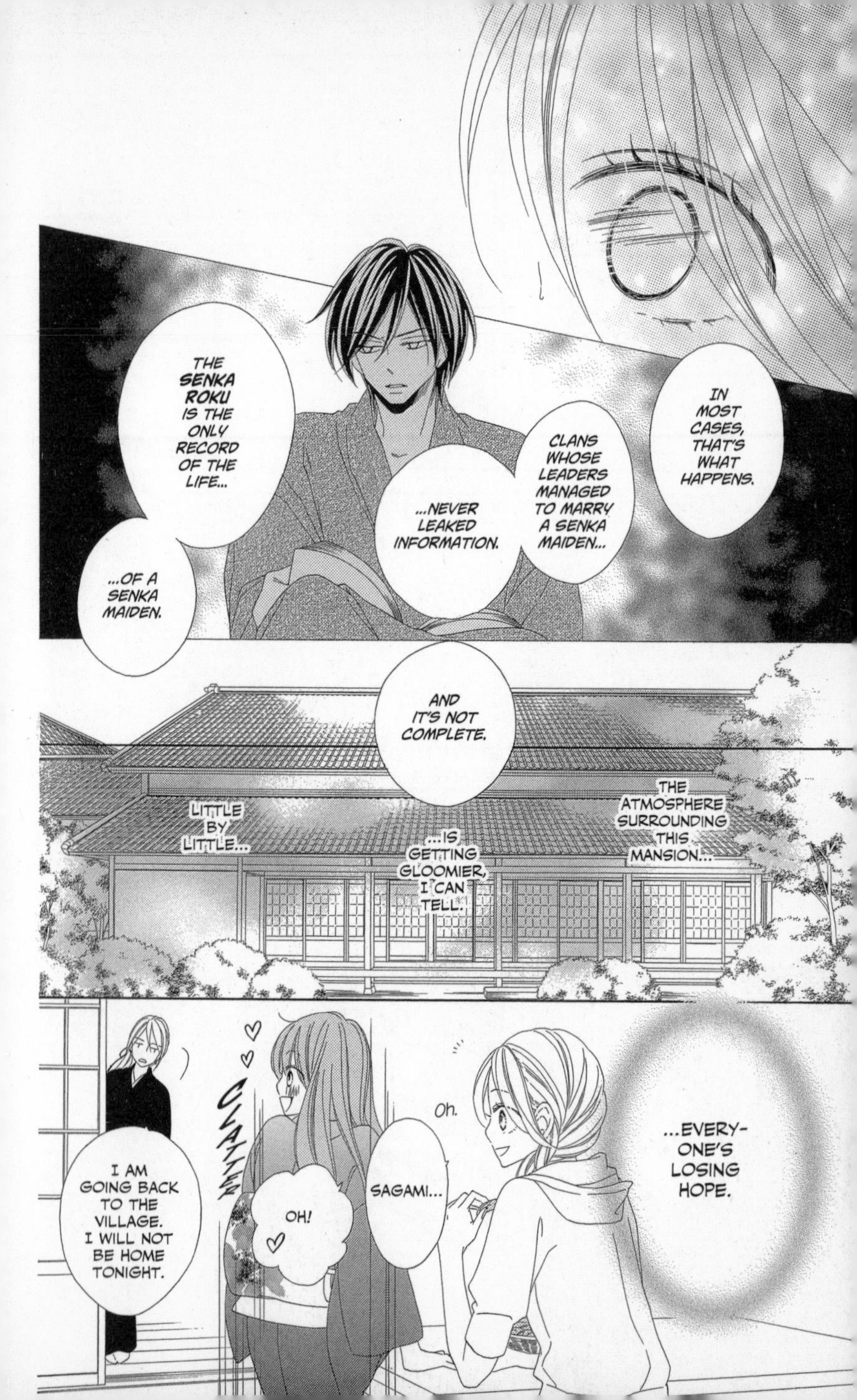
IN MOST CASES, THAT'S WHAT HAPPENS.
CLANS WHOSE LEADERS MANAGED TO MARRY A SENKA MAIDEN...
...NEVER LEAKED INFORMATION.
THE SENKA ROKU IS THE ONLY RECORD OF THE LIFE...
...OF A SENKA MAIDEN.
AND IT'S NOT COMPLETE.
THE ATMOSPHERE SURROUNDING THIS MANSION...
...IS GETTING GLOOMIER, I CAN TELL.
LITTLE BY LITTLE...
...EVERY-ONE'S LOSING HOPE.
Oh.
SAGAMI...
OH!
CLATTER
I AM GOING BACK TO THE VILLAGE. I WILL NOT BE HOME TONIGHT.

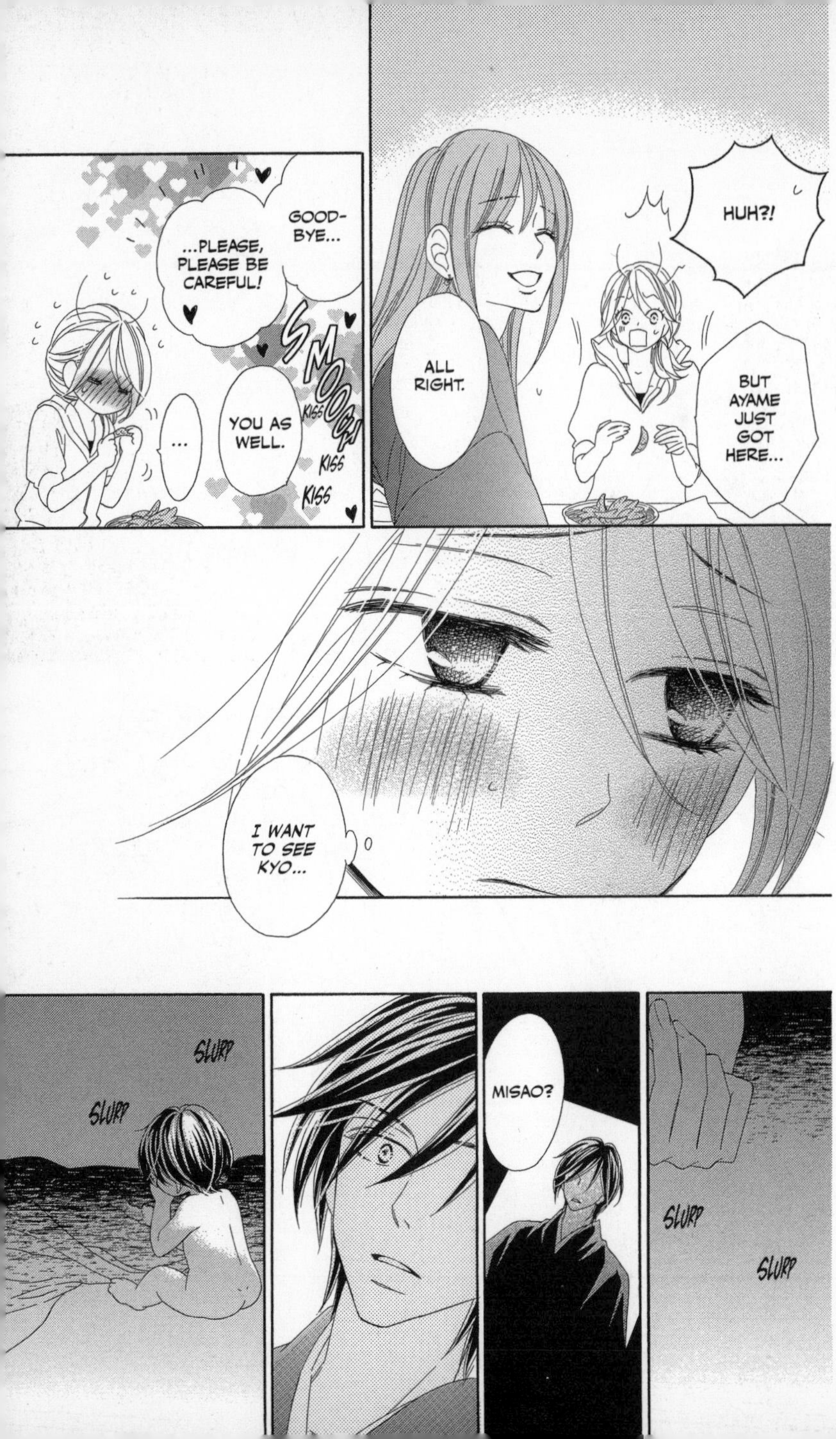
HUH?!
BUT AYAME JUST GOT HERE...
ALL RIGHT.
GOOD-BYE...
...PLEASE, PLEASE BE CAREFUL!
SMOOCH
KISS KISS KISS
YOU AS WELL.
...
I WANT TO SEE KYO...
SLURP
SLURP
MISAO?
SLURP
SLURP

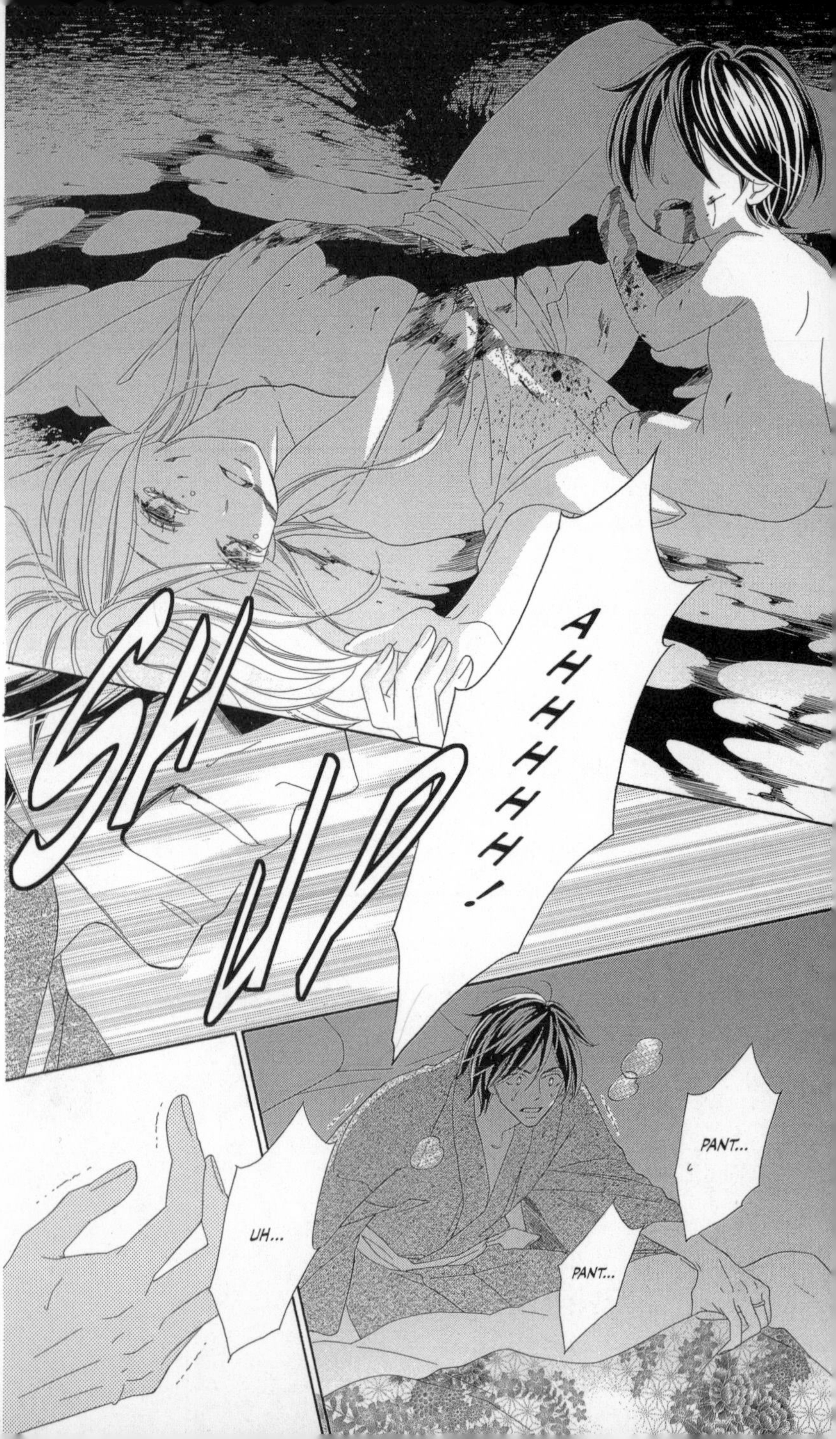
SHUP
AHHHHHH!
PANT...
PANT...
UH...

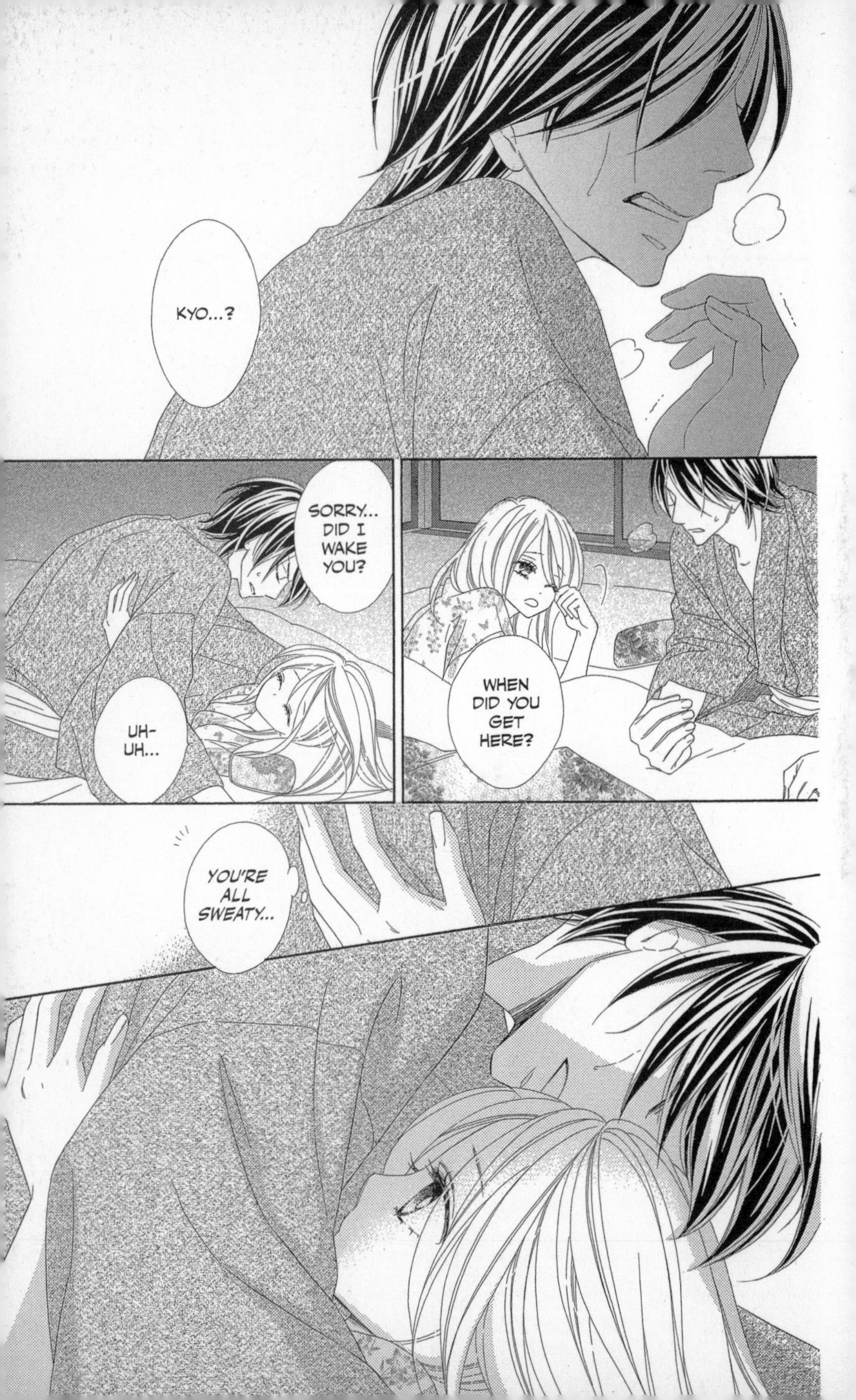
KYO...?
WHEN DID YOU GET HERE?
SORRY... DID I WAKE YOU?
UH-UH...
YOU'RE ALL SWEATY...

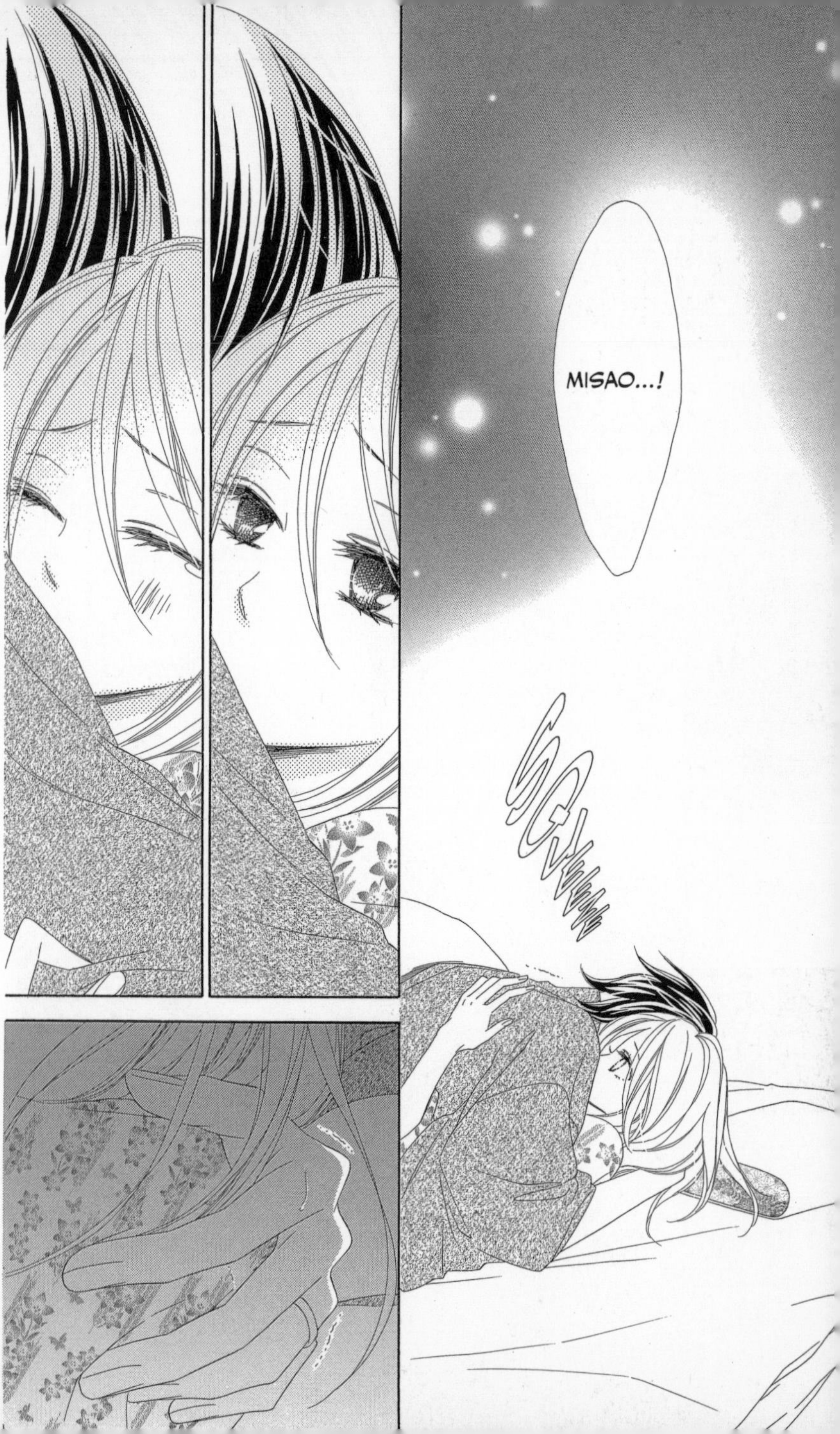
MISAO...!
SQUEEZE

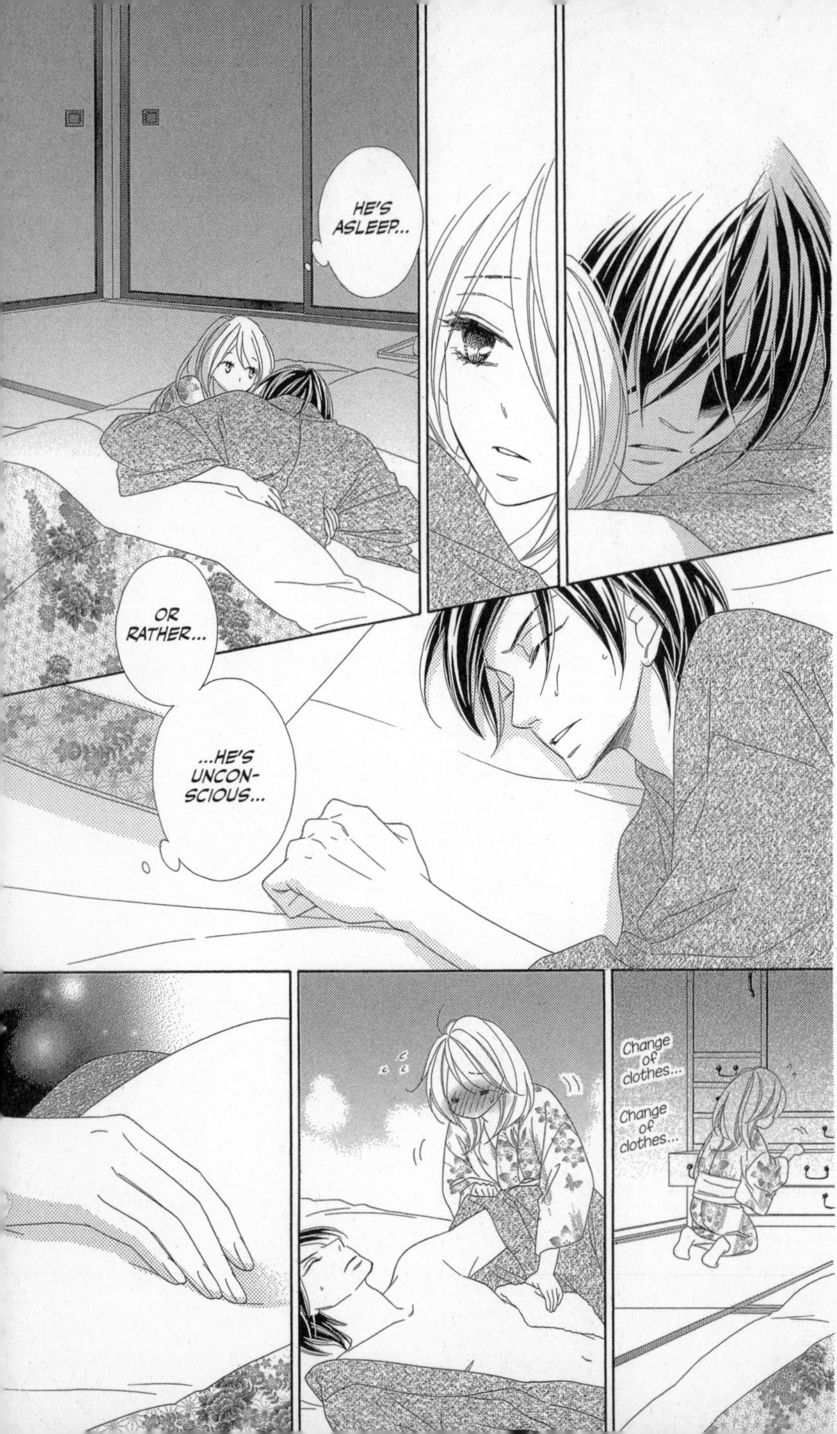
HE'S ASLEEP...
OR RATHER...
...HE'S UNCON-SCIOUS...
Change of clothes...
Change of clothes...

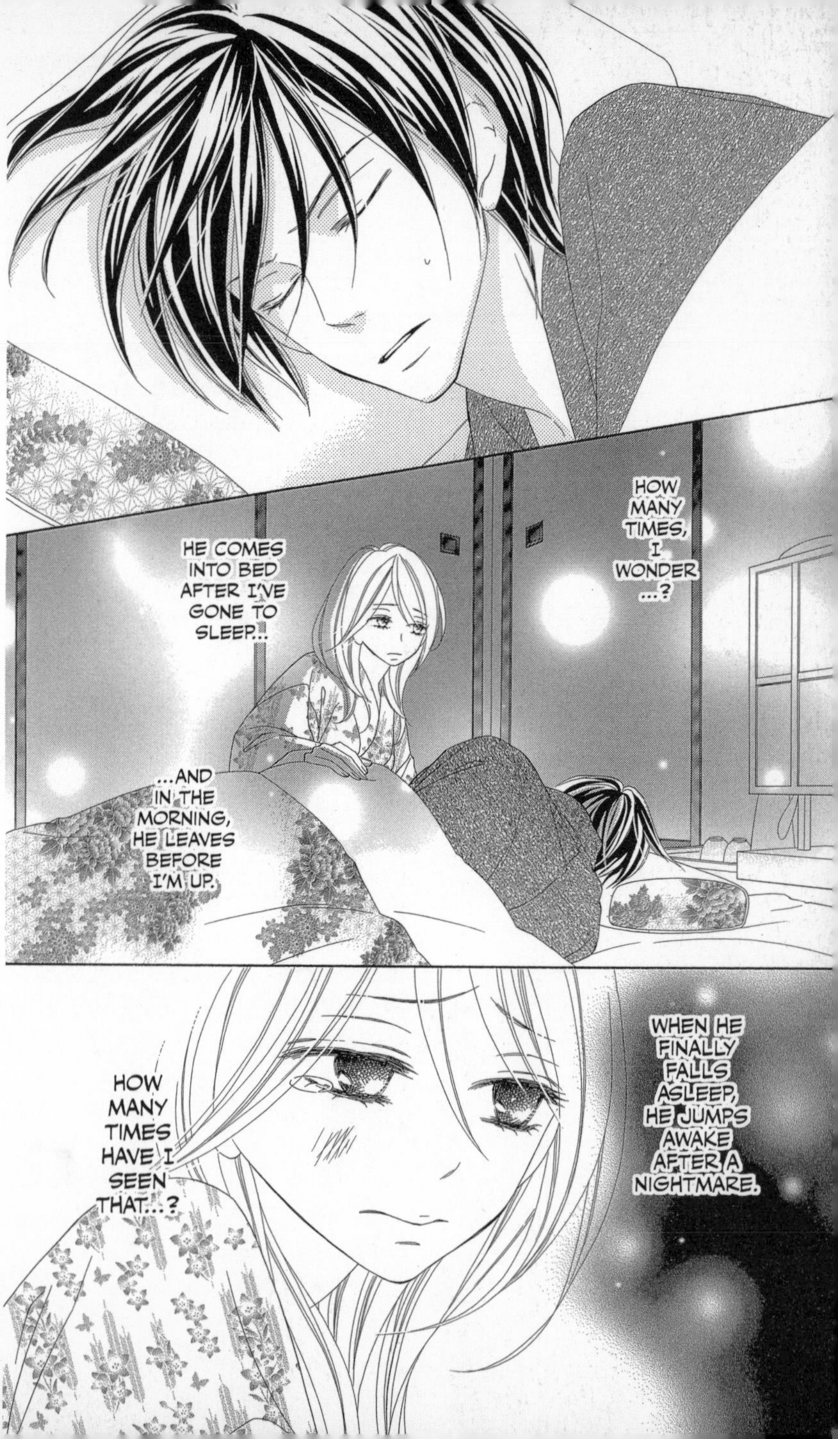
HOW MANY TIMES, I WONDER ...?
HE COMES INTO BED AFTER I'VE GONE TO SLEEP...
...AND IN THE MORNING, HE LEAVES BEFORE I'M UP.
WHEN HE FINALLY FALLS ASLEEP, HE JUMPS AWAKE AFTER A NIGHTMARE.
HOW MANY TIMES HAVE I SEEN THAT...?

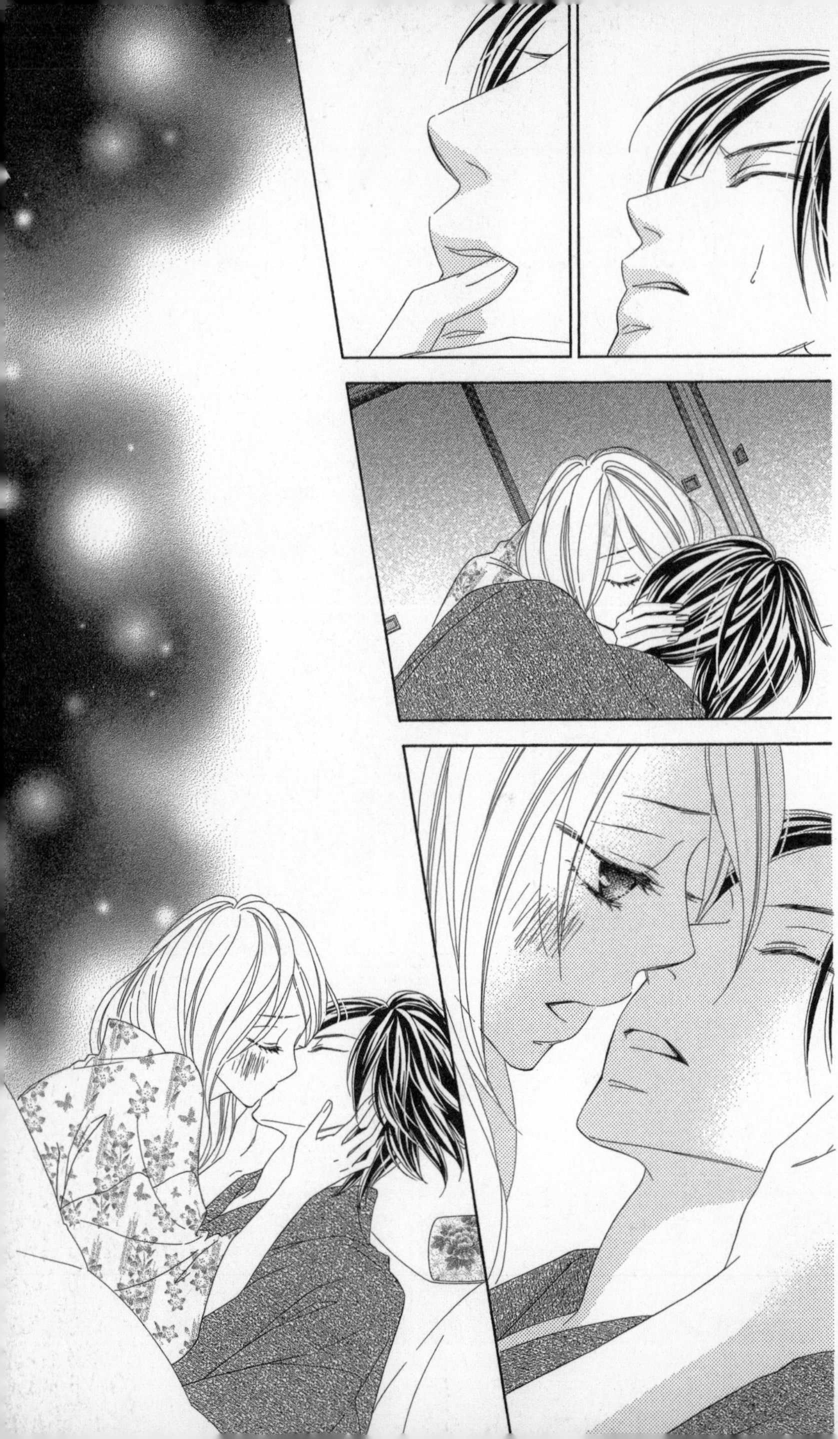

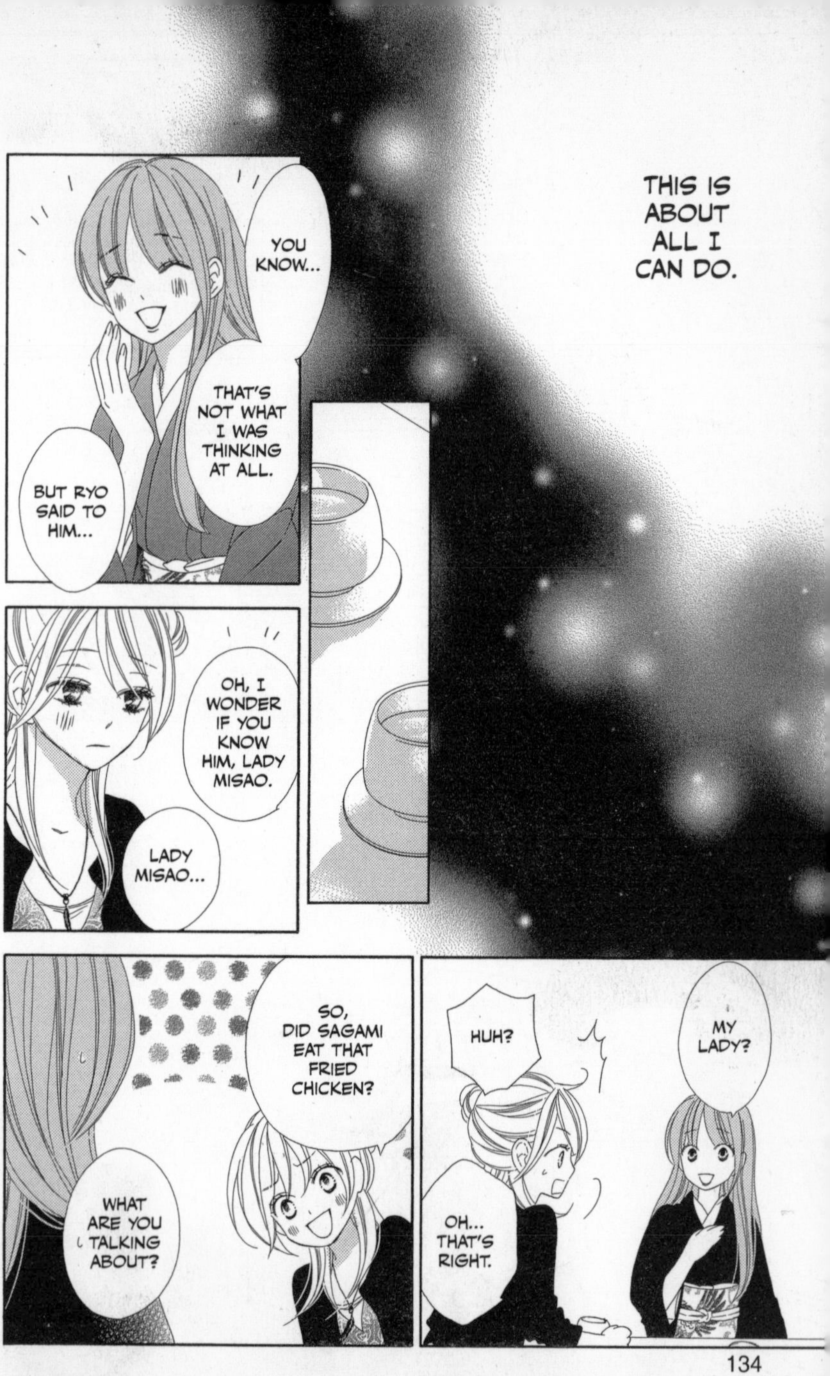
THIS IS ABOUT ALL I CAN DO.
YOU KNOW...
THAT'S NOT WHAT I WAS THINKING AT ALL.
BUT RYO SAID TO HIM...
OH, I WONDER IF YOU KNOW HIM, LADY MISAO.
LADY MISAO...
MY LADY?
HUH?
OH... THAT'S RIGHT.
SO, DID SAGAMI EAT THAT FRIED CHICKEN?
WHAT ARE YOU TALKING ABOUT?

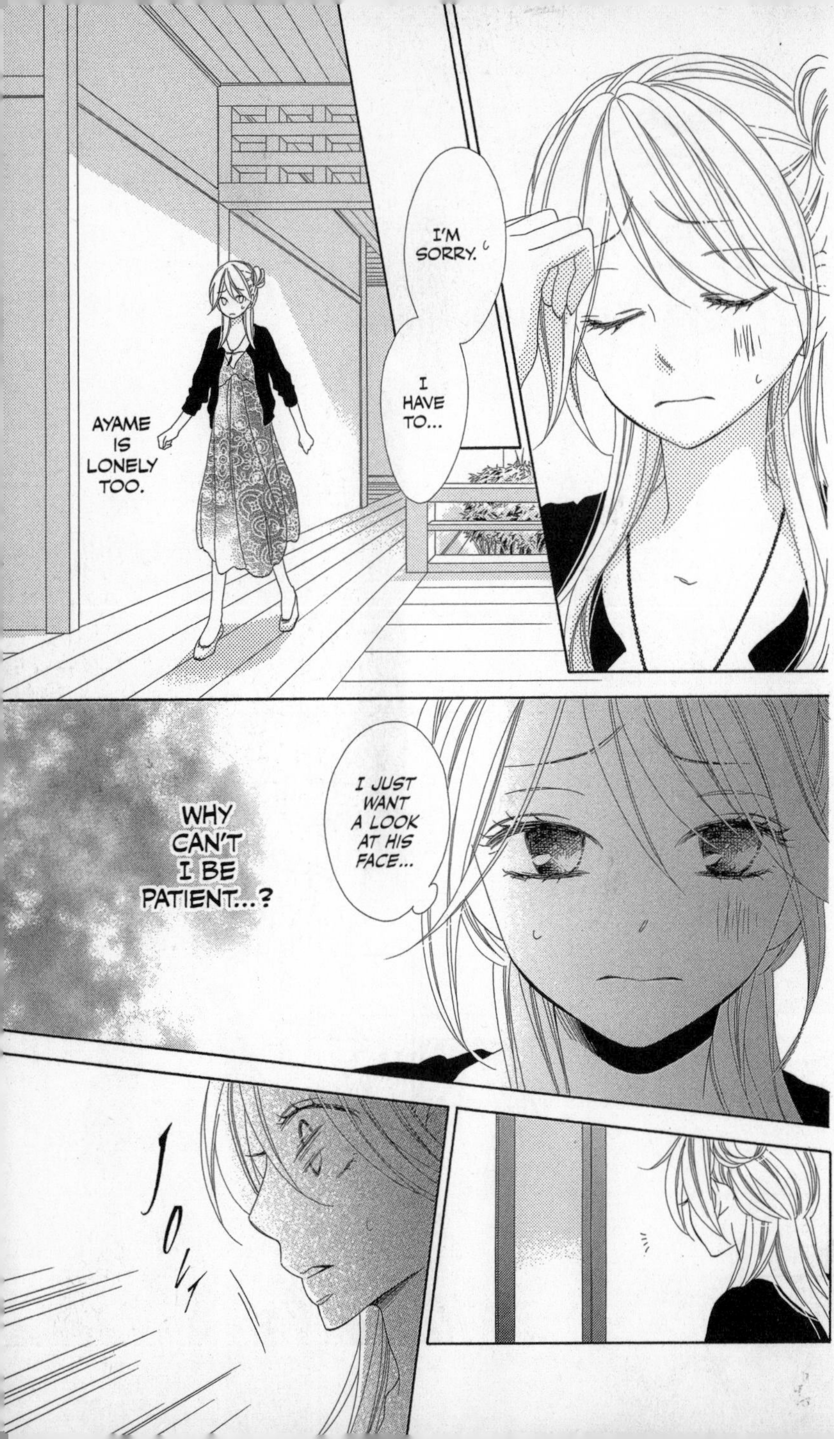
I'M SORRY.
I HAVE TO...
AYAME IS LONELY TOO.
I JUST WANT A LOOK AT HIS FACE...
WHY CAN'T I BE PATIENT...?

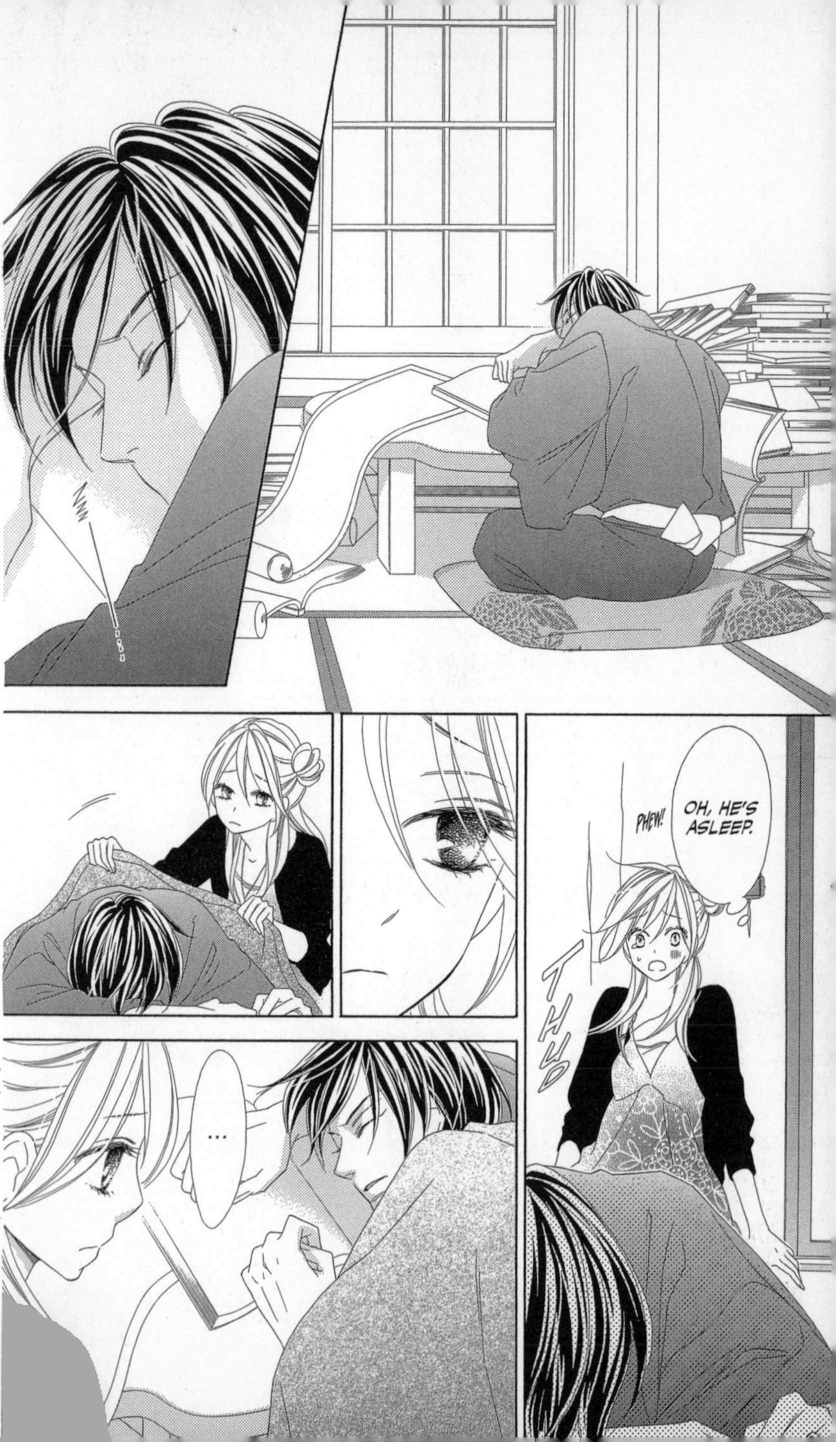
OH, HE'S ASLEEP.
PHEW!
THUD
...

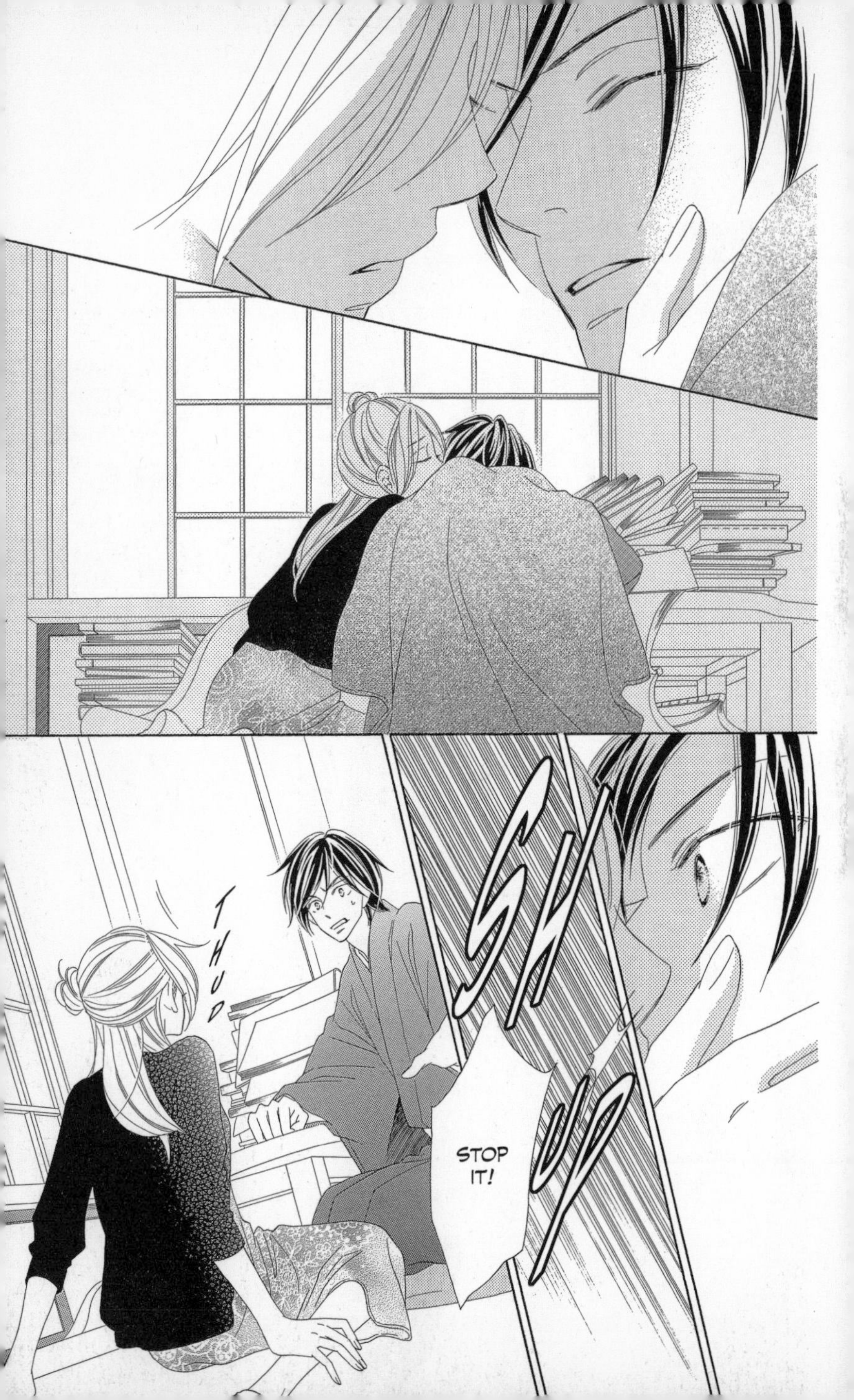
STOP IT!
THUD

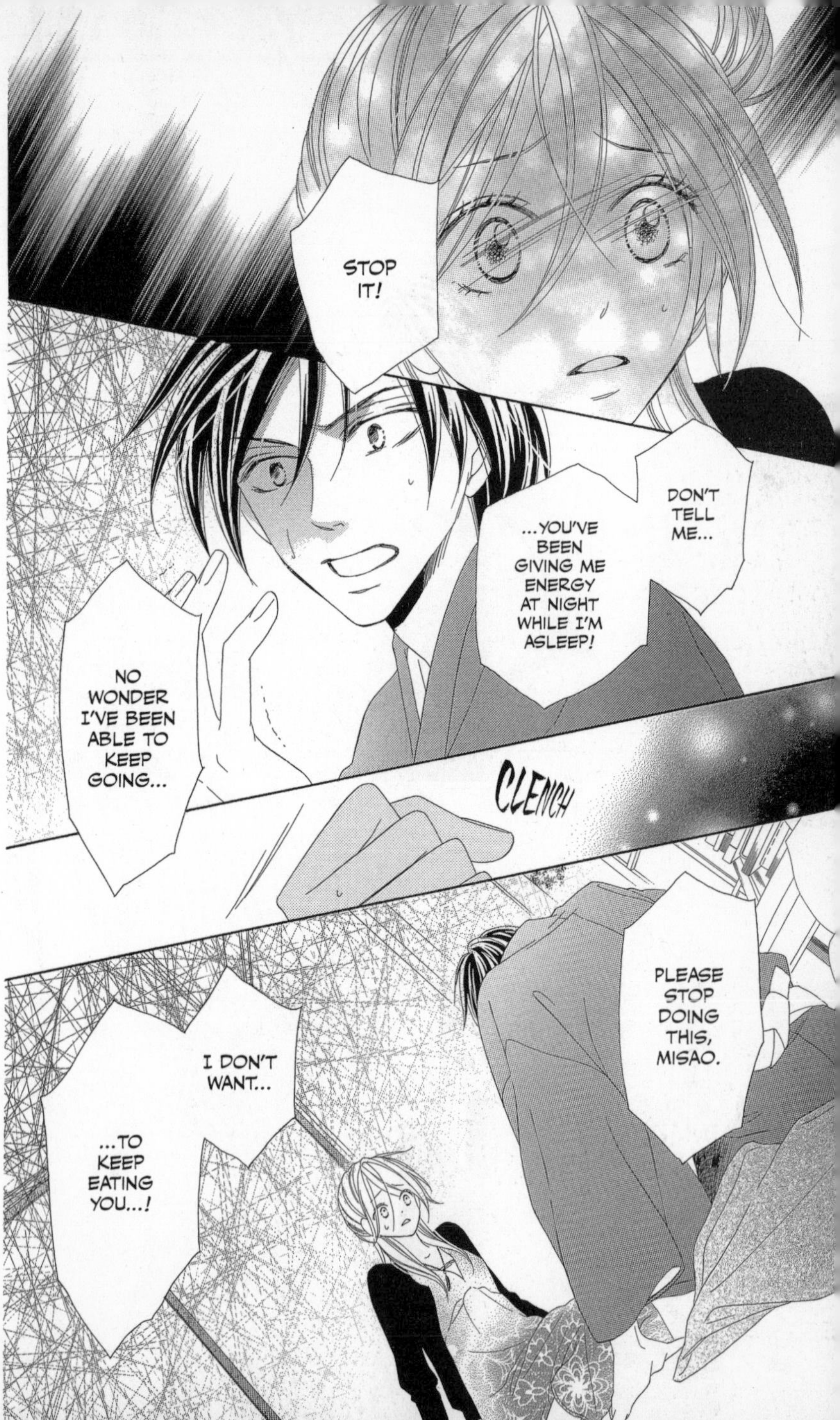
STOP IT!
DON'T TELL ME...
...YOU'VE BEEN GIVING ME ENERGY AT NIGHT WHILE I'M ASLEEP!
NO WONDER I'VE BEEN ABLE TO KEEP GOING...
CLENCH
PLEASE STOP DOING THIS, MISAO.
I DON'T WANT...
...TO KEEP EATING YOU...!

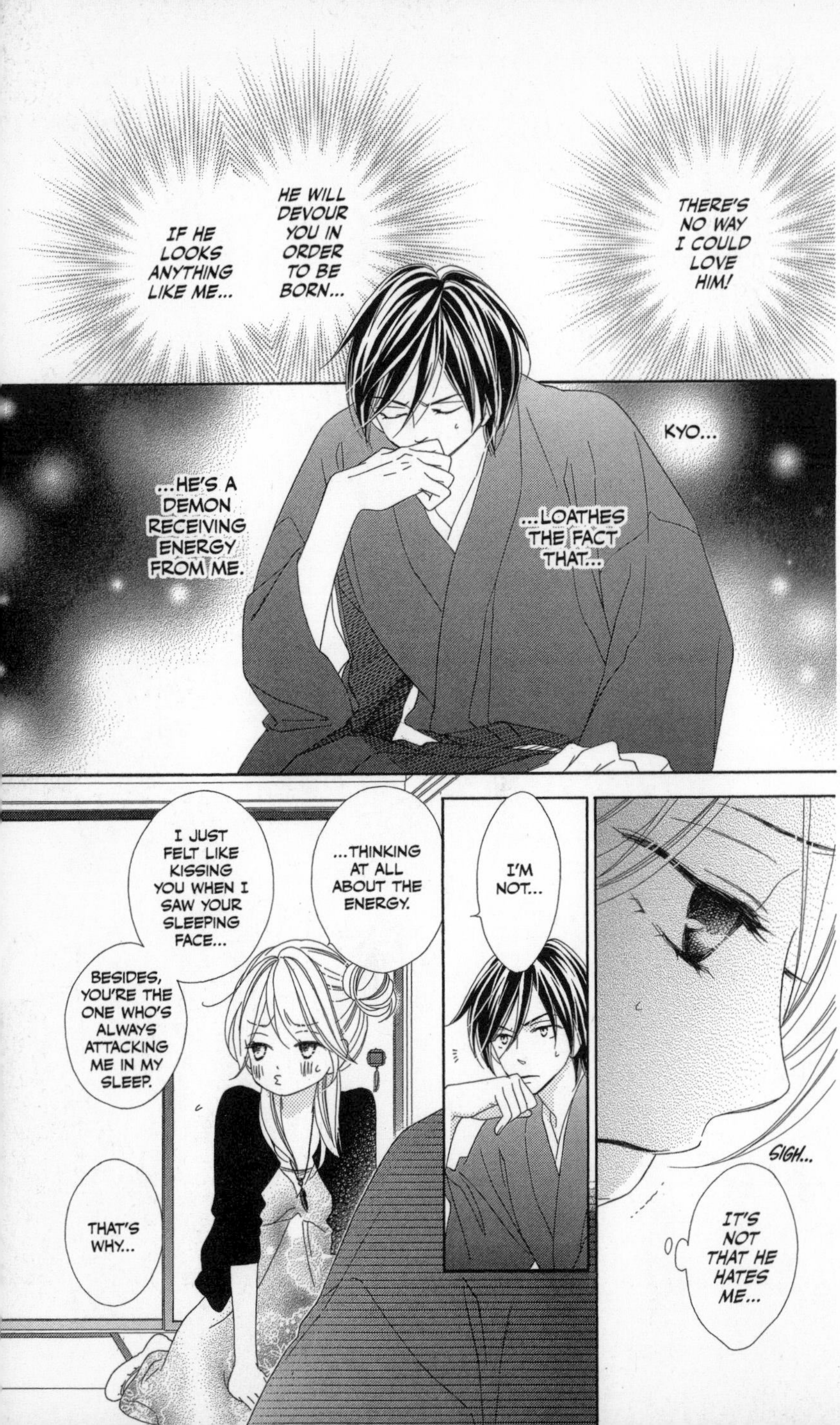
THERE'S NO WAY I COULD LOVE HIM!
HE WILL DEVOUR YOU IN ORDER TO BE BORN...
IF HE LOOKS ANYTHING LIKE ME...
KYO...
...LOATHES THE FACT THAT...
...HE'S A DEMON RECEIVING ENERGY FROM ME.
SIGH...
IT'S NOT THAT HE HATES ME...
I'M NOT...
...THINKING AT ALL ABOUT THE ENERGY.
I JUST FELT LIKE KISSING YOU WHEN I SAW YOUR SLEEPING FACE...
BESIDES, YOU'RE THE ONE WHO'S ALWAYS ATTACKING ME IN MY SLEEP.
THAT'S WHY...

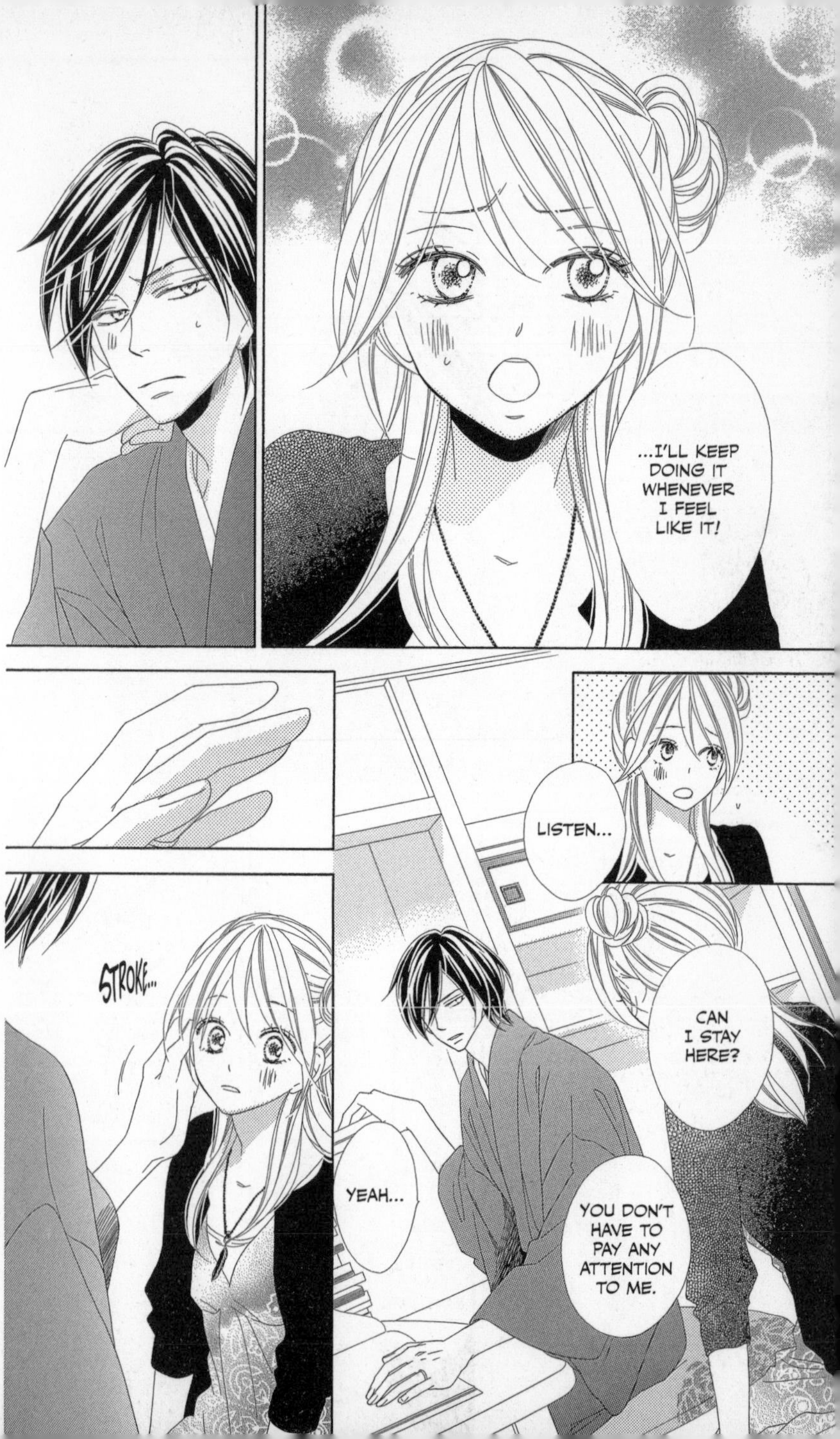
...I'LL KEEP DOING IT WHENEVER I FEEL LIKE IT!
LISTEN...
CAN I STAY HERE?
YOU DON'T HAVE TO PAY ANY ATTENTION TO ME.
YEAH...
STROKE...

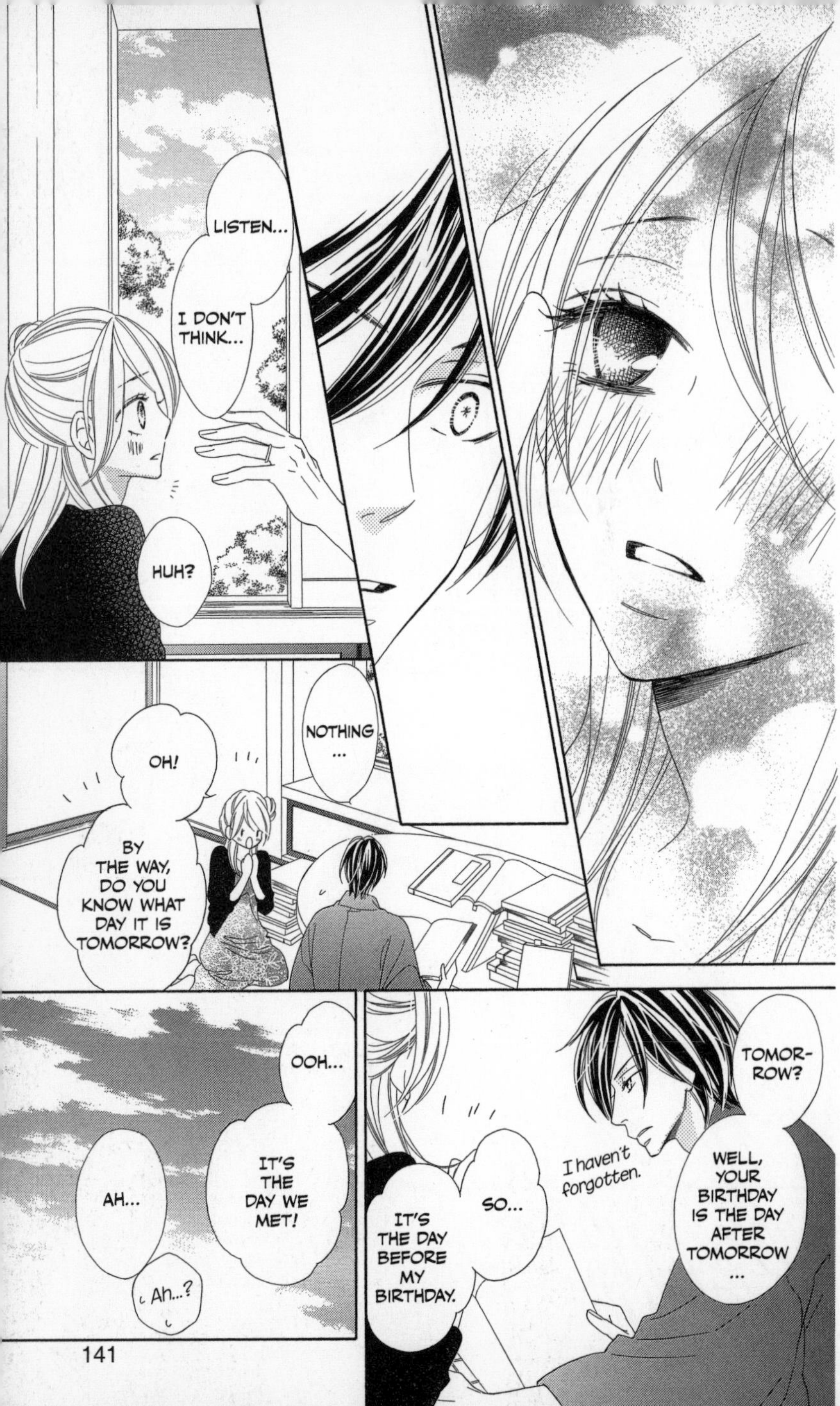
LISTEN...
I DON'T THINK...
HUH?
NOTHING ...
OH!
BY THE WAY, DO YOU KNOW WHAT DAY IT IS TOMORROW?
TOMOR-ROW?
WELL, YOUR BIRTHDAY IS THE DAY AFTER TOMORROW ...
I haven't forgotten.
SO...
IT'S THE DAY BEFORE MY BIRTHDAY.
OOH...
IT'S THE DAY WE MET!
AH...
Ah...?

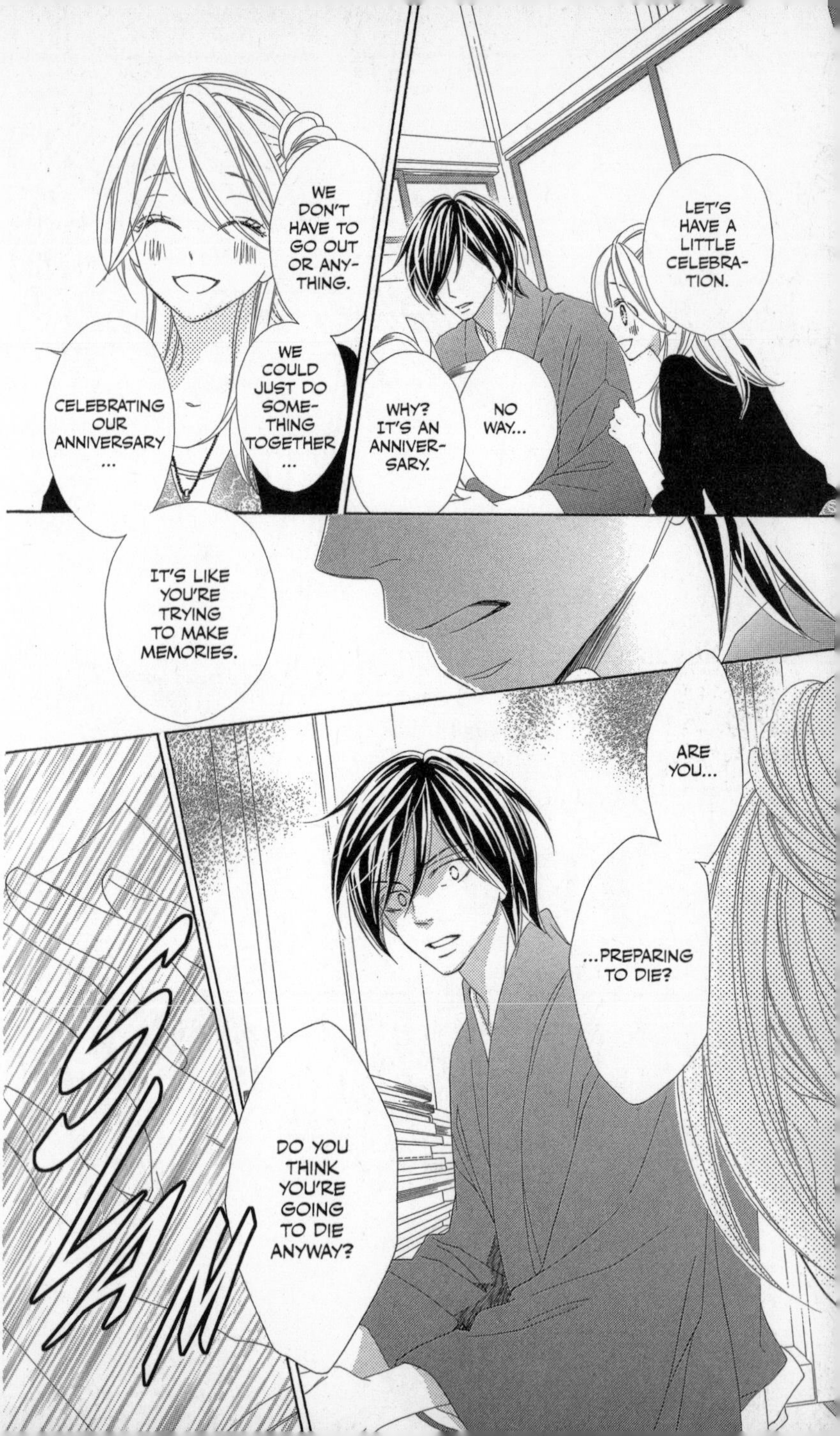
LET'S HAVE A LITTLE CELEBRATION.
NO WAY...
WHY? IT'S AN ANNIVERSARY.
WE DON'T HAVE TO GO OUT OR ANYTHING.
WE COULD JUST DO SOMETHING TOGETHER...
CELEBRATING OUR ANNIVERSARY...
IT'S LIKE YOU'RE TRYING TO MAKE MEMORIES.
ARE YOU...
...PREPARING TO DIE?
DO YOU THINK YOU'RE GOING TO DIE ANYWAY?

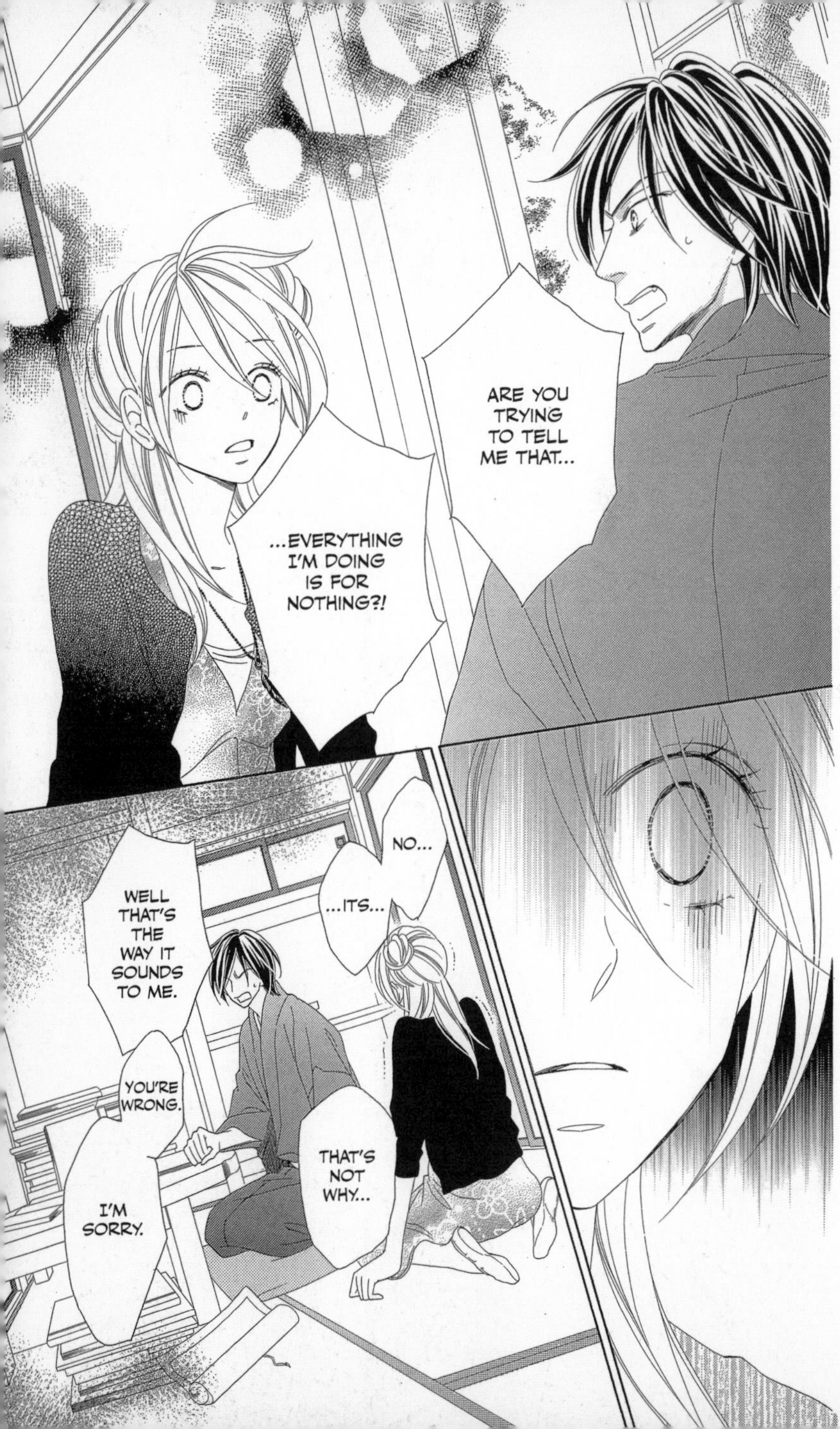
ARE YOU TRYING TO TELL ME THAT...
...EVERYTHING I'M DOING IS FOR NOTHING?!
NO...
...ITS...
WELL THAT'S THE WAY IT SOUNDS TO ME.
THAT'S NOT WHY...
YOU'RE WRONG.
I'M SORRY.

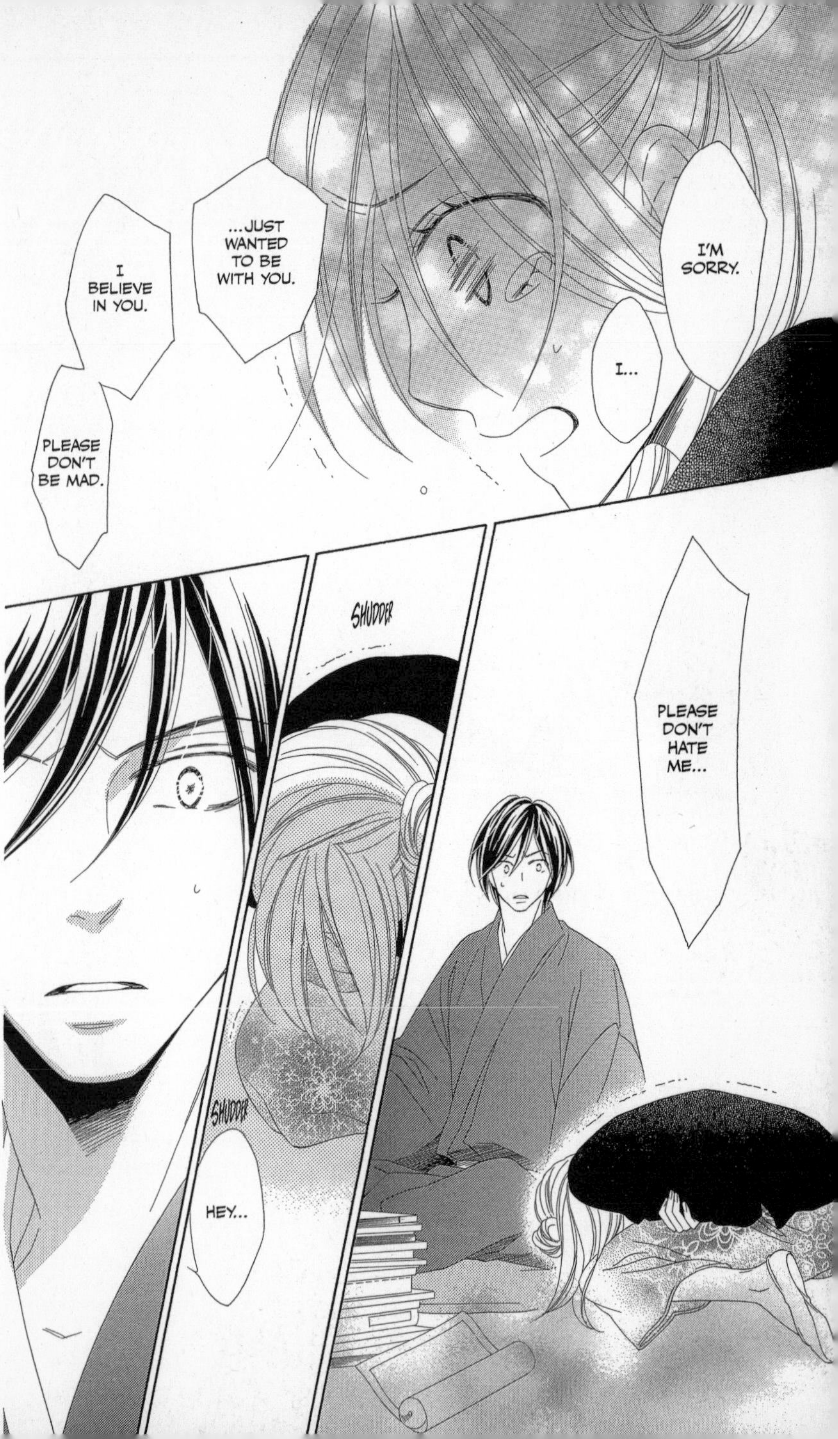
I'M SORRY.
I...
...JUST WANTED TO BE WITH YOU.
I BELIEVE IN YOU.
PLEASE DON'T BE MAD.
PLEASE DON'T HATE ME...
SHUDDER
SHUDDER
HEY...

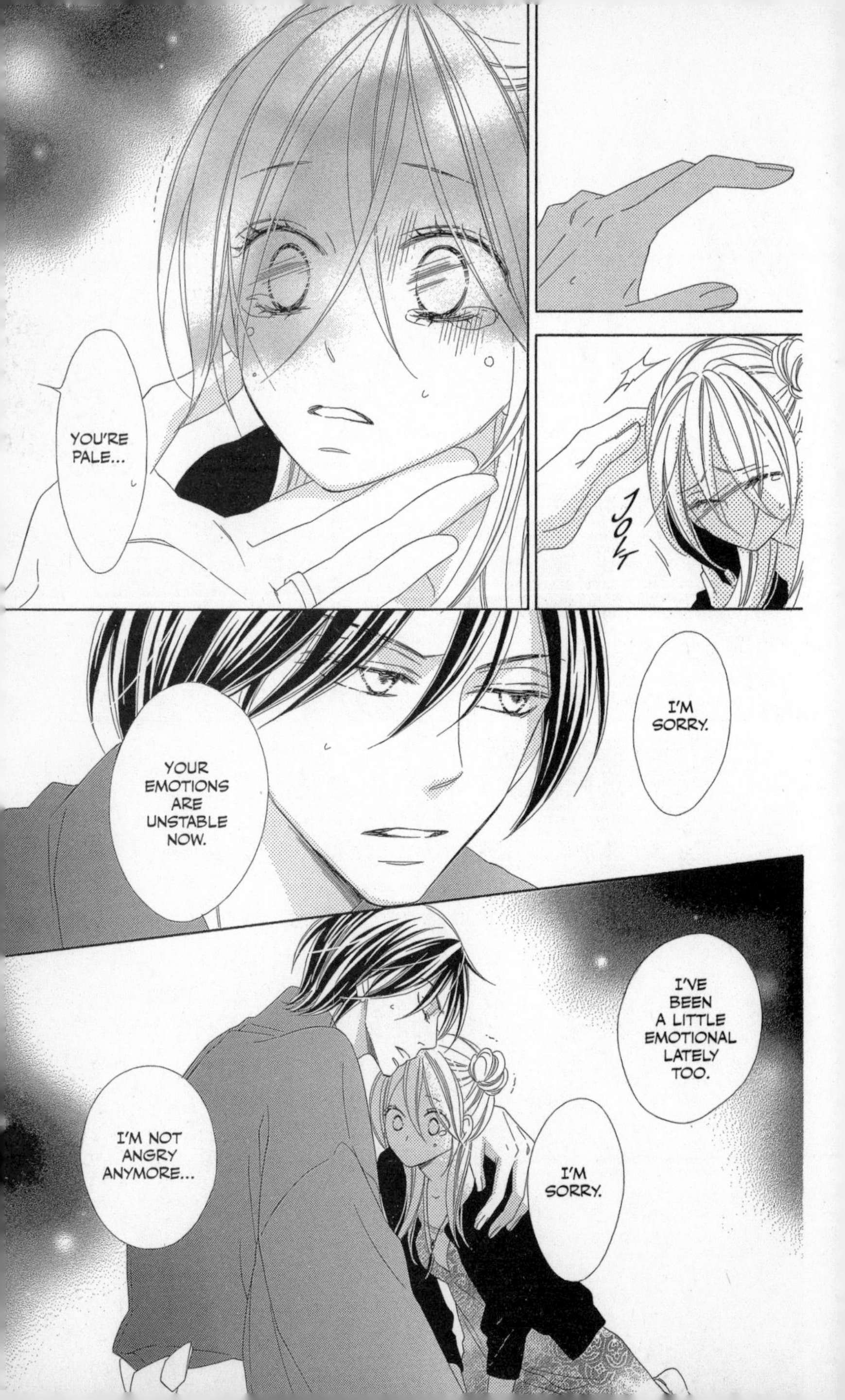
JOLT
YOU'RE PALE...
I'M SORRY.
YOUR EMOTIONS ARE UNSTABLE NOW.
I'VE BEEN A LITTLE EMOTIONAL LATELY TOO.
I'M SORRY.
I'M NOT ANGRY ANYMORE...

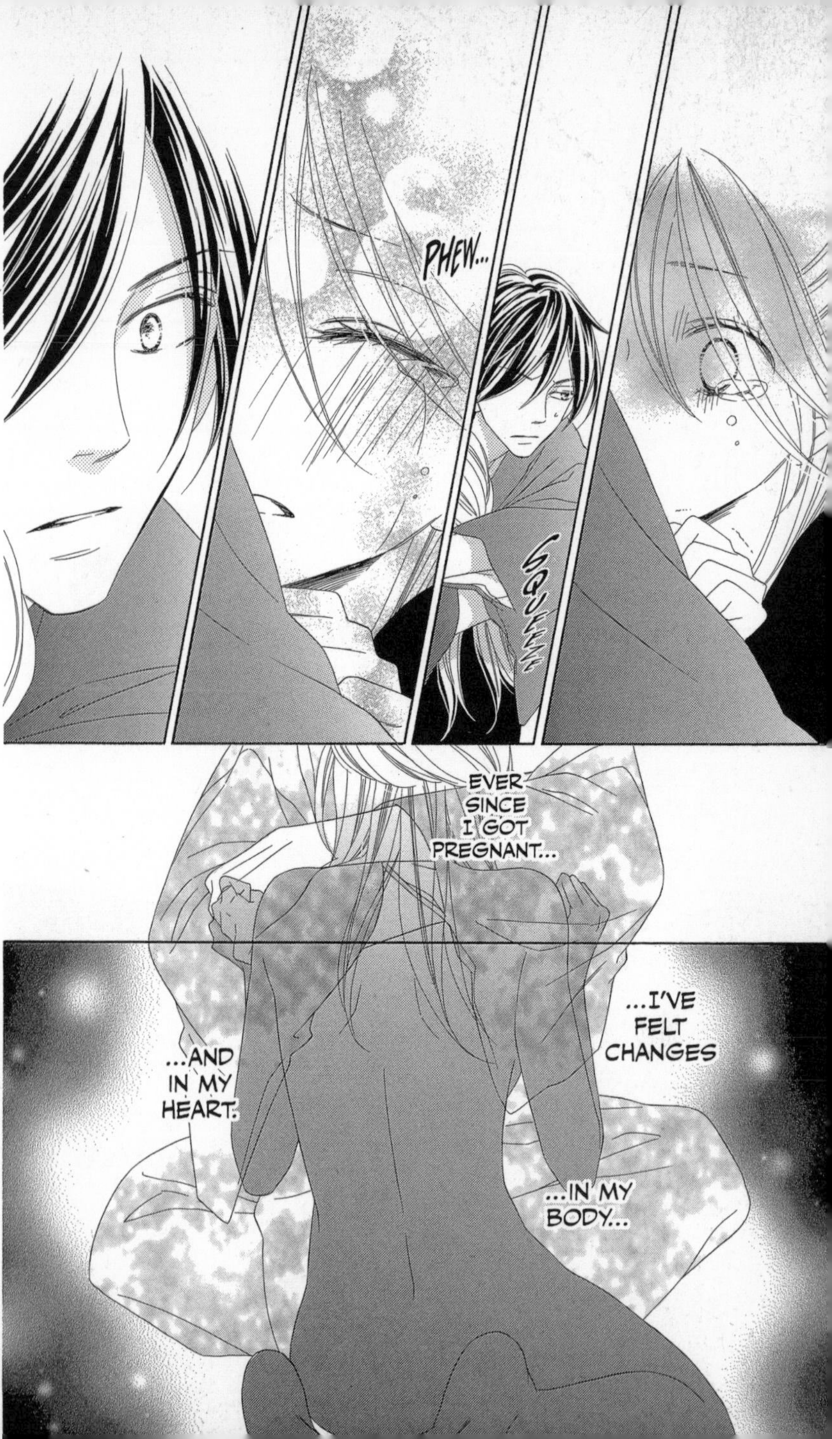
PHEW...
SQUEEZE
EVER SINCE I GOT PREGNANT...
...I'VE FELT CHANGES
...IN MY BODY...
...AND IN MY HEART.

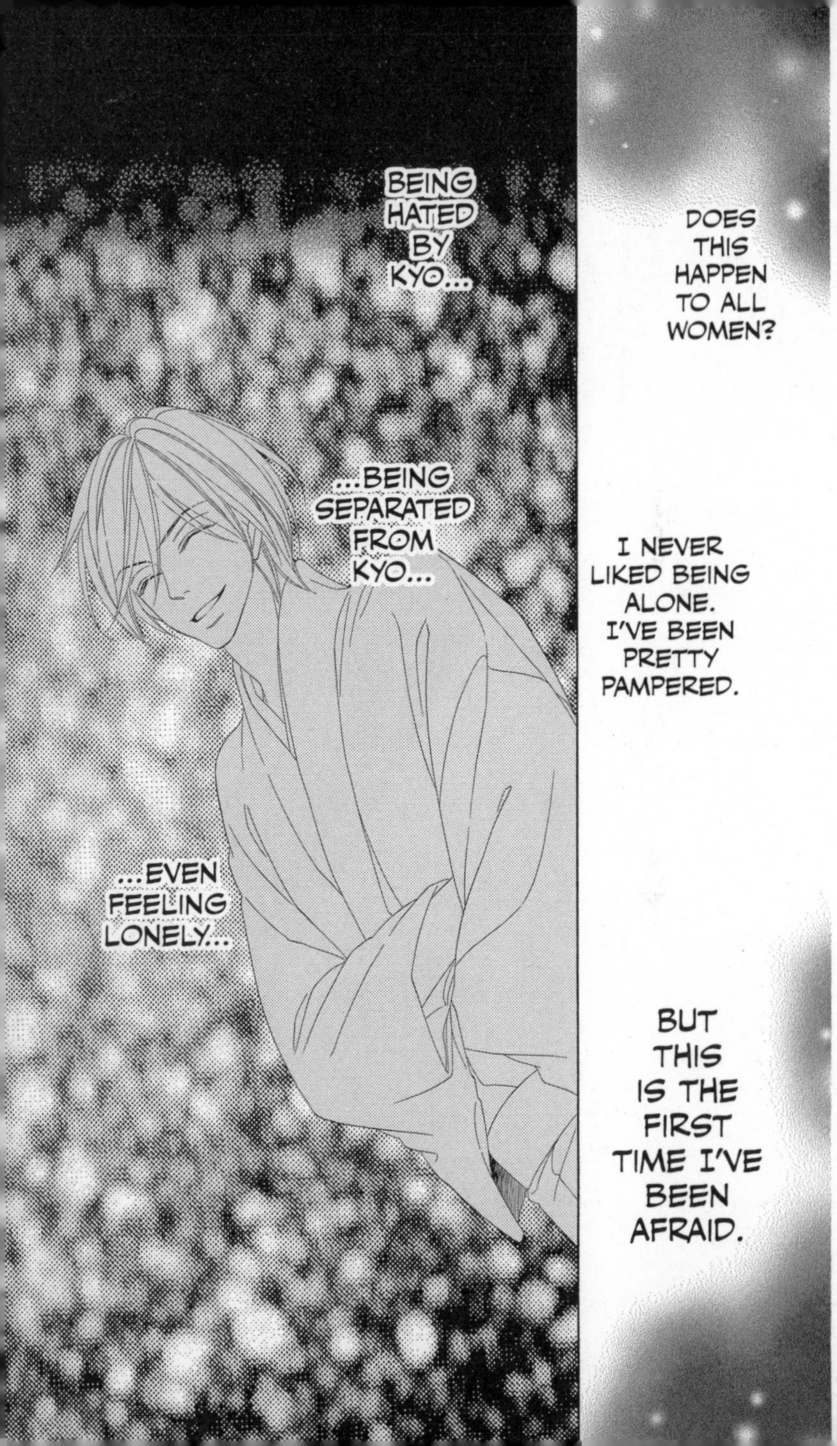
DOES THIS HAPPEN TO ALL WOMEN?
I NEVER LIKED BEING ALONE. I'VE BEEN PRETTY PAMPERED.
BUT THIS IS THE FIRST TIME I'VE BEEN AFRAID.
BEING HATED BY KYO...
...BEING SEPARATED FROM KYO...
...EVEN FEELING LONELY...

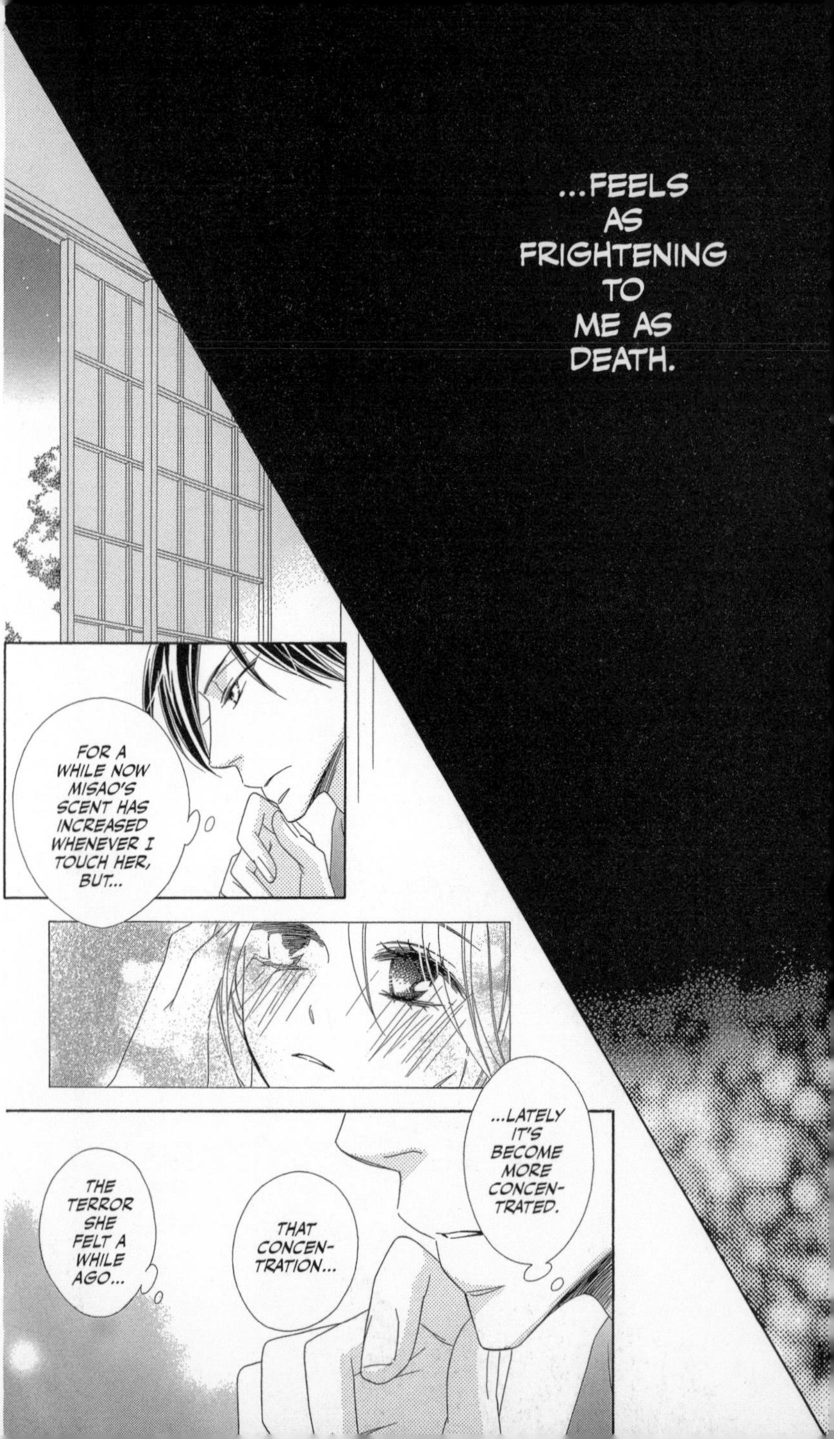
...FEELS AS FRIGHTENING TO ME AS DEATH.
FOR A WHILE NOW MISAO'S SCENT HAS INCREASED WHENEVER I TOUCH HER, BUT...
...LATELY IT'S BECOME MORE CONCEN-TRATED.
THAT CONCEN-TRATION...
THE TERROR SHE FELT A WHILE AGO...

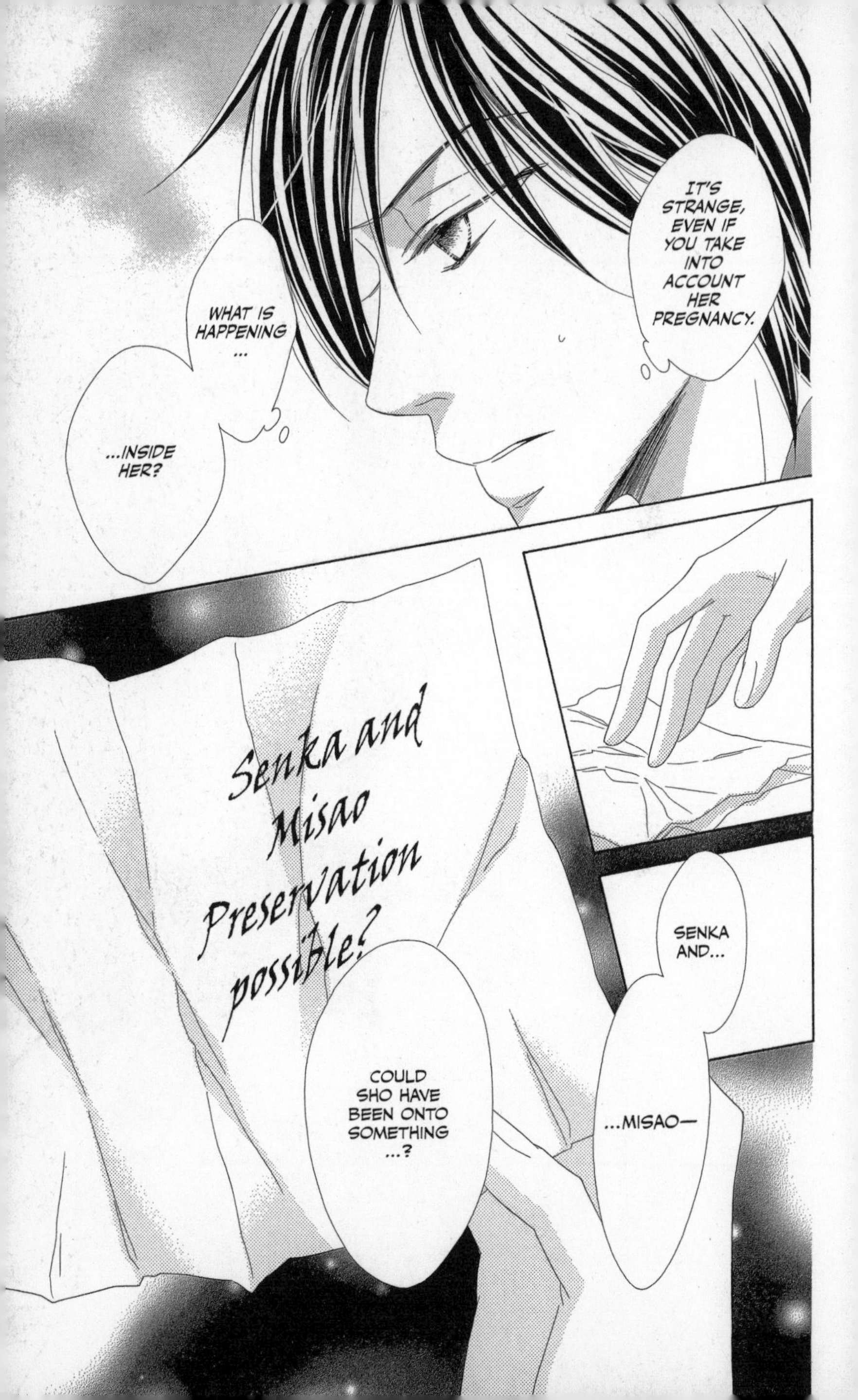
IT'S STRANGE, EVEN IF YOU TAKE INTO ACCOUNT HER PREGNANCY.
WHAT IS HAPPENING ...
...INSIDE HER?
SENKA AND...
...MISAO—
Senka and Misao Preservation possible?
COULD SHO HAVE BEEN ONTO SOMETHING ...?

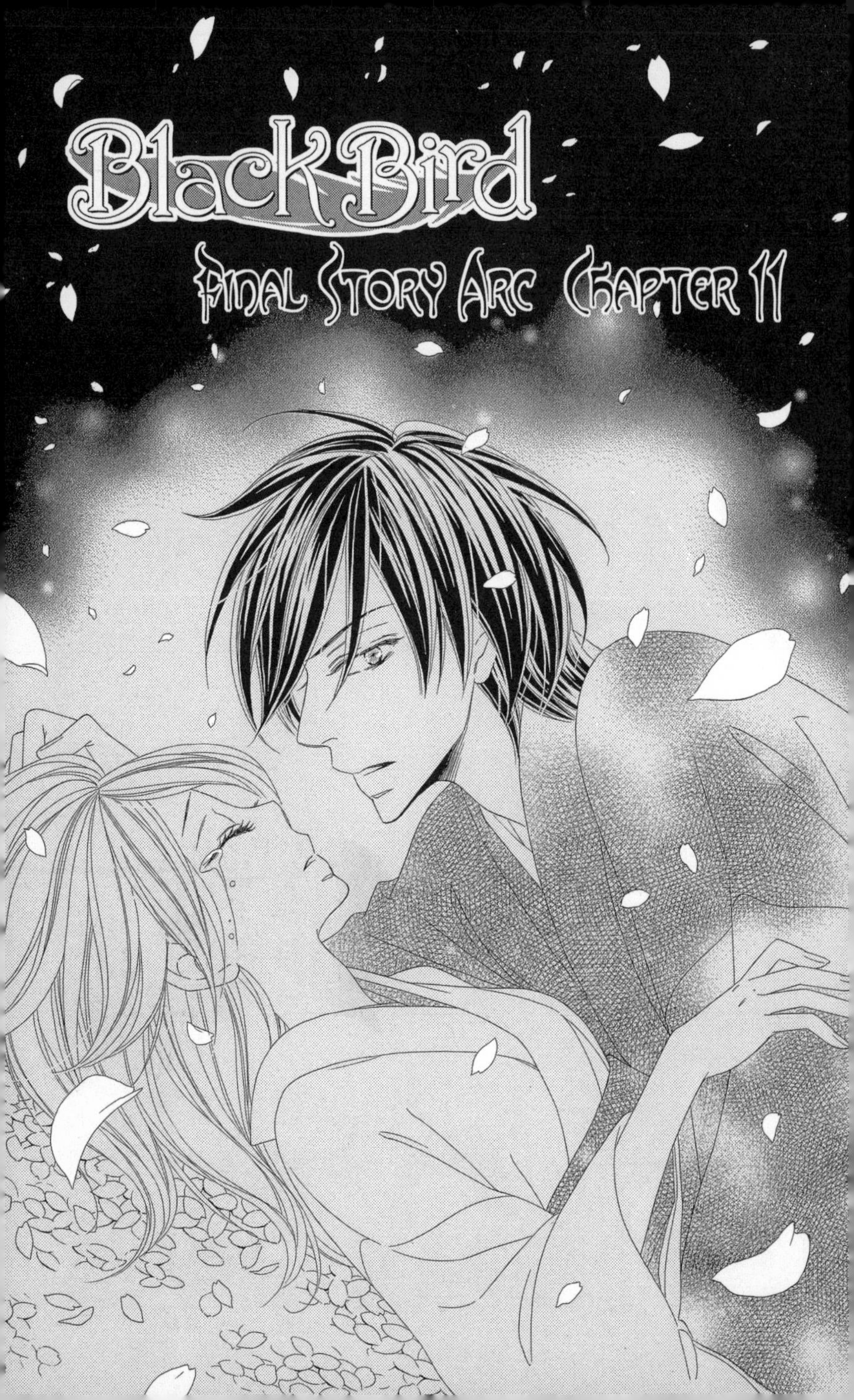
Black Bird
Final Story Arc Chapter 11

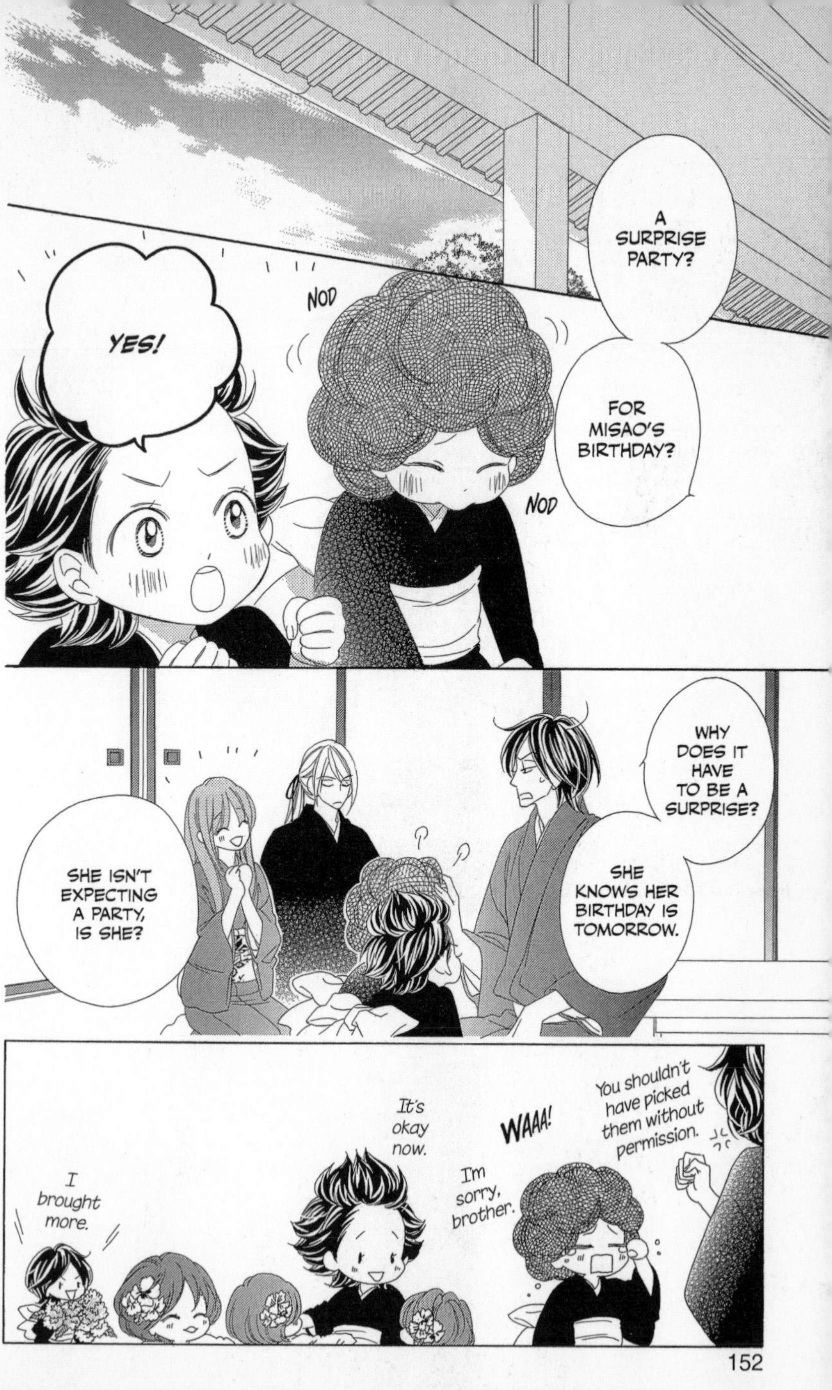
A SURPRISE PARTY?
FOR MISAO'S BIRTHDAY?
NOD
NOD
YES!
WHY DOES IT HAVE TO BE A SURPRISE?
SHE KNOWS HER BIRTHDAY IS TOMORROW.
SHE ISN'T EXPECTING A PARTY, IS SHE?
You shouldn't have picked them without permission.
WAAA!
I'm sorry, brother.
It's okay now.
I brought more.

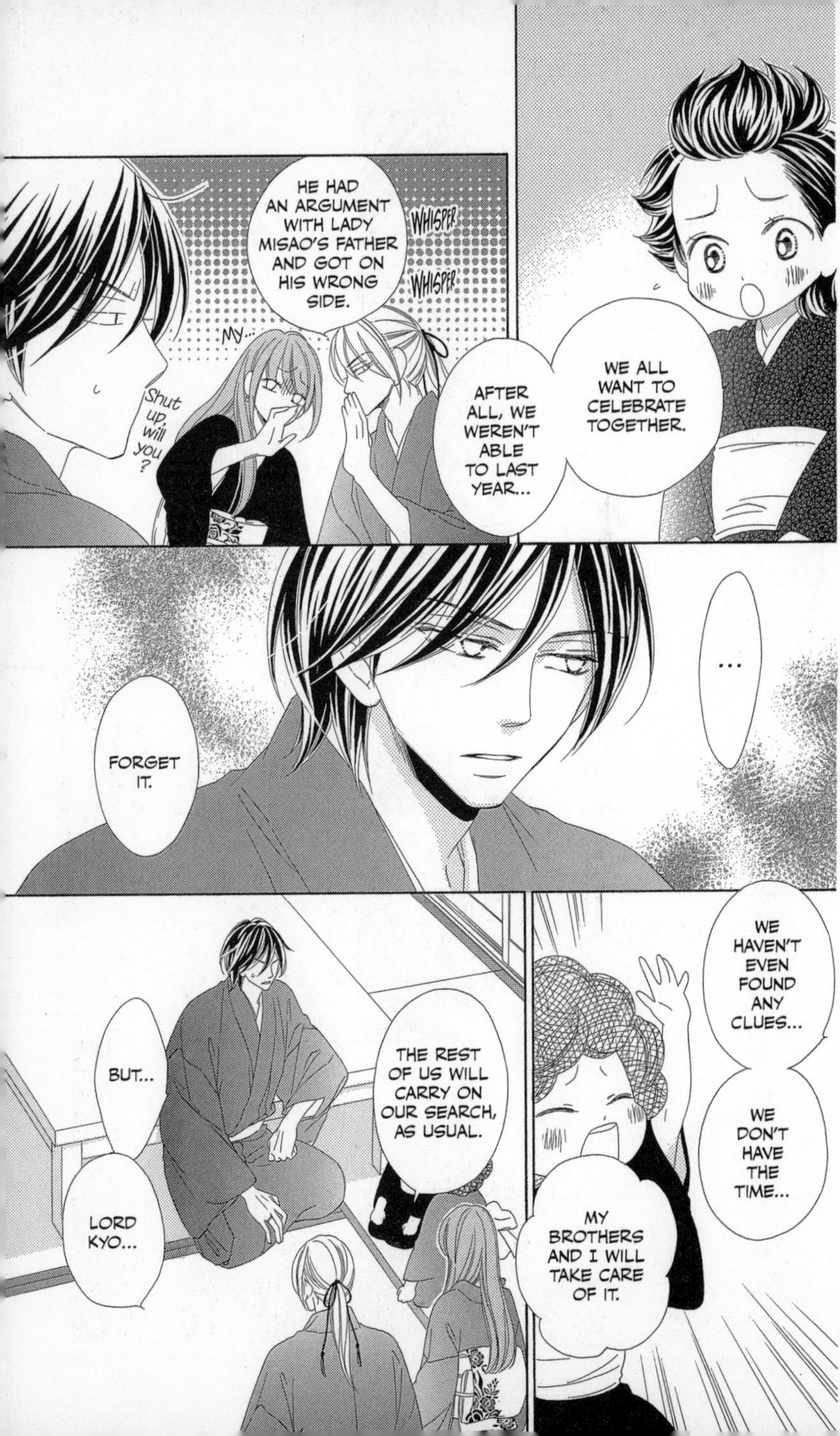
WE ALL WANT TO CELEBRATE TOGETHER.
AFTER ALL, WE WEREN'T ABLE TO LAST YEAR...
HE HAD AN ARGUMENT WITH LADY MISAO'S FATHER AND GOT ON HIS WRONG SIDE.
WHISPER
WHISPER
My...
Shut up, will you?
...
FORGET IT.
WE HAVEN'T EVEN FOUND ANY CLUES...
WE DON'T HAVE THE TIME...
MY BROTHERS AND I WILL TAKE CARE OF IT.
THE REST OF US WILL CARRY ON OUR SEARCH, AS USUAL.
BUT...
LORD KYO...

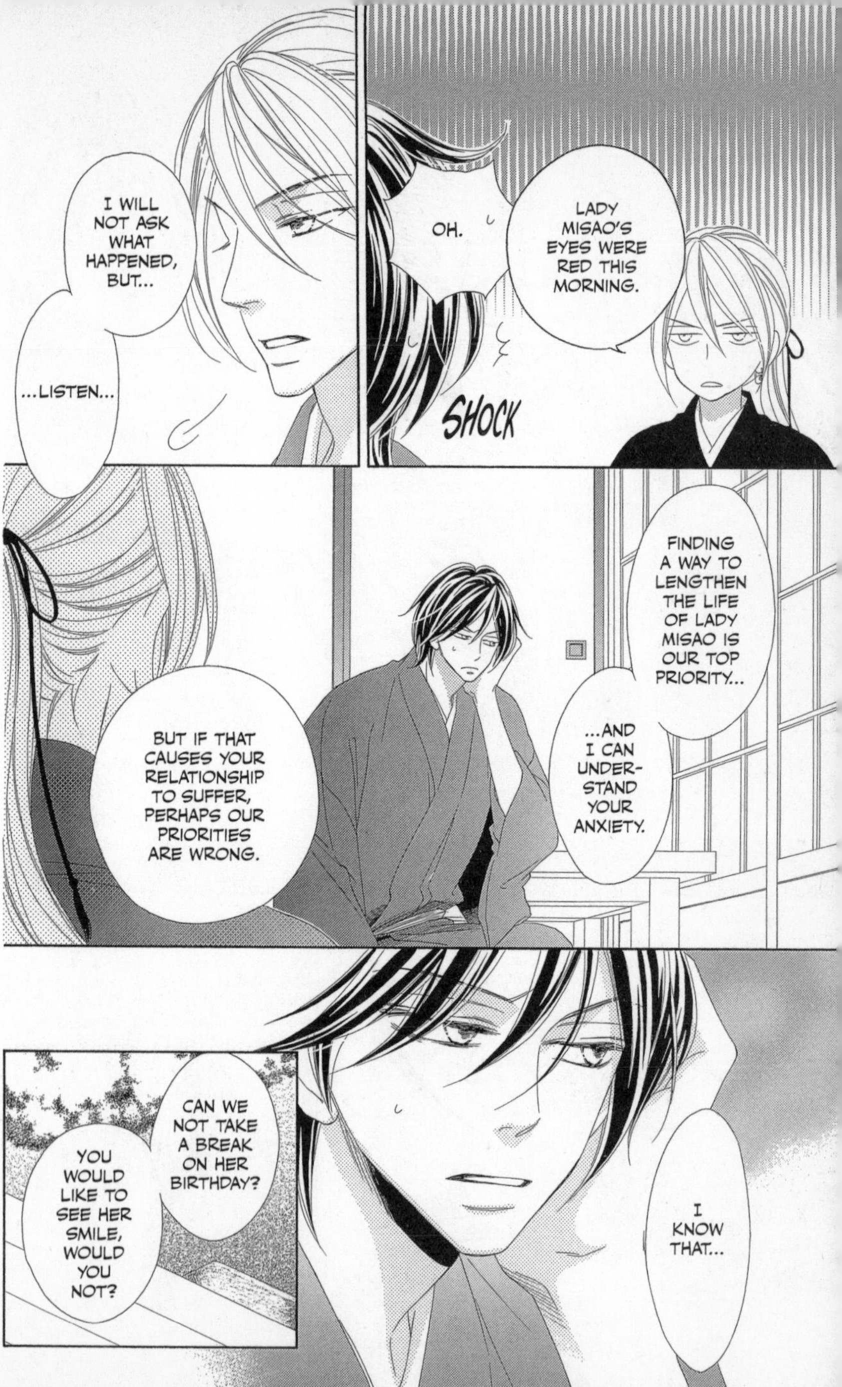
LADY MISAO'S EYES WERE RED THIS MORNING.
OH.
SHOCK
I WILL NOT ASK WHAT HAPPENED, BUT...
...LISTEN...
FINDING A WAY TO LENGTHEN THE LIFE OF LADY MISAO IS OUR TOP PRIORITY...
...AND I CAN UNDER-STAND YOUR ANXIETY.
BUT IF THAT CAUSES YOUR RELATIONSHIP TO SUFFER, PERHAPS OUR PRIORITIES ARE WRONG.
I KNOW THAT...
CAN WE NOT TAKE A BREAK ON HER BIRTHDAY?
YOU WOULD LIKE TO SEE HER SMILE, WOULD YOU NOT?

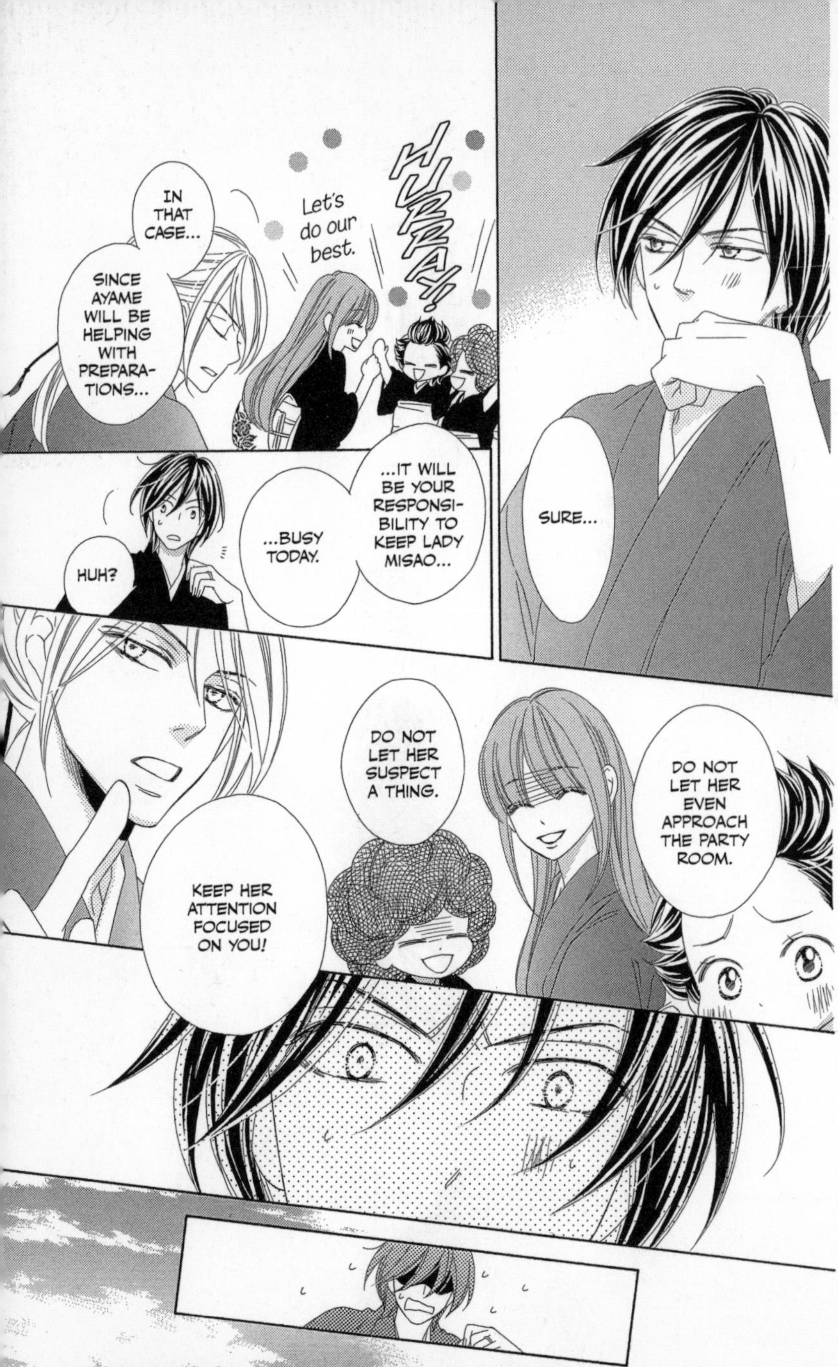
SURE...
HURRAH!
Let's do our best.
IN THAT CASE...
SINCE AYAME WILL BE HELPING WITH PREPARATIONS...
...IT WILL BE YOUR RESPONSIBILITY TO KEEP LADY MISAO...
...BUSY TODAY.
HUH?
DO NOT LET HER EVEN APPROACH THE PARTY ROOM.
DO NOT LET HER SUSPECT A THING.
KEEP HER ATTENTION FOCUSED ON YOU!

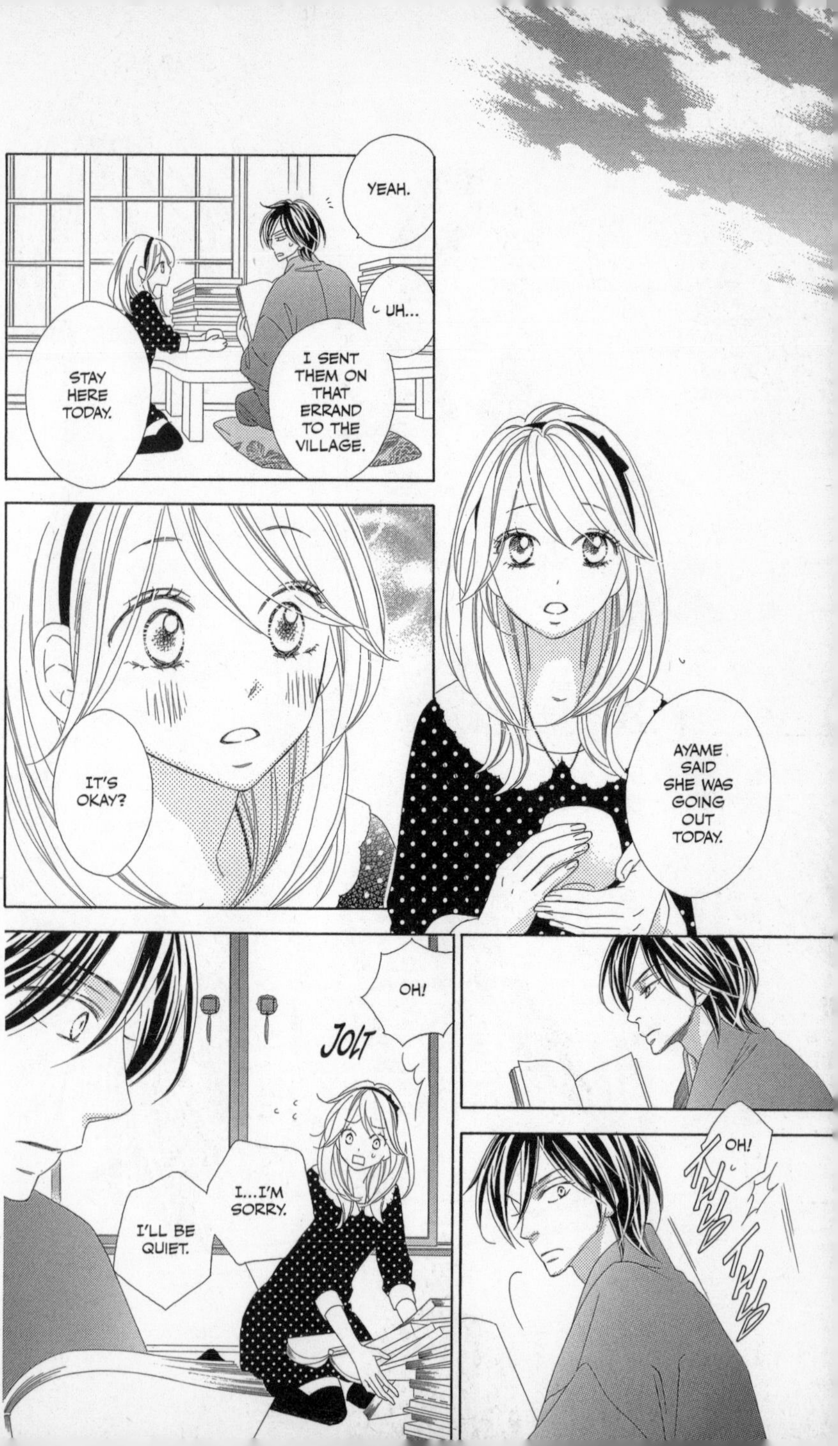
AYAME SAID SHE WAS GOING OUT TODAY.
YEAH.
UH...
I SENT THEM ON THAT ERRAND TO THE VILLAGE.
STAY HERE TODAY.
IT'S OKAY?
OH!
OH!
JOLT
I...I'M SORRY.
I'LL BE QUIET.

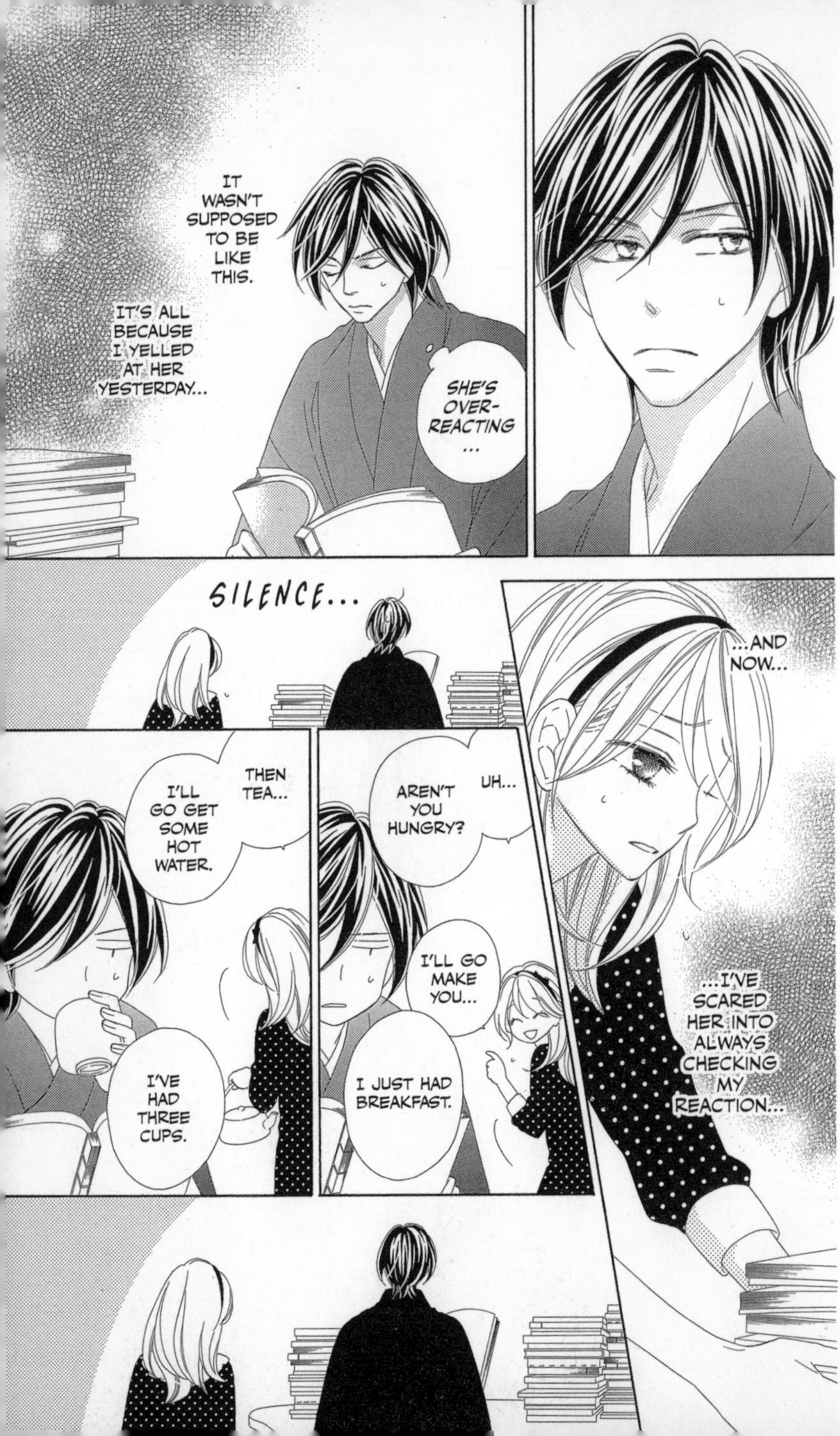
SHE'S OVER-REACTING...
IT WASN'T SUPPOSED TO BE LIKE THIS.
IT'S ALL BECAUSE I YELLED AT HER YESTERDAY...
...AND NOW...
...I'VE SCARED HER INTO ALWAYS CHECKING MY REACTION...
SILENCE...
AREN'T YOU HUNGRY?
UH...
I'LL GO MAKE YOU...
I JUST HAD BREAKFAST.
THEN TEA...
I'LL GO GET SOME HOT WATER.
I'VE HAD THREE CUPS.

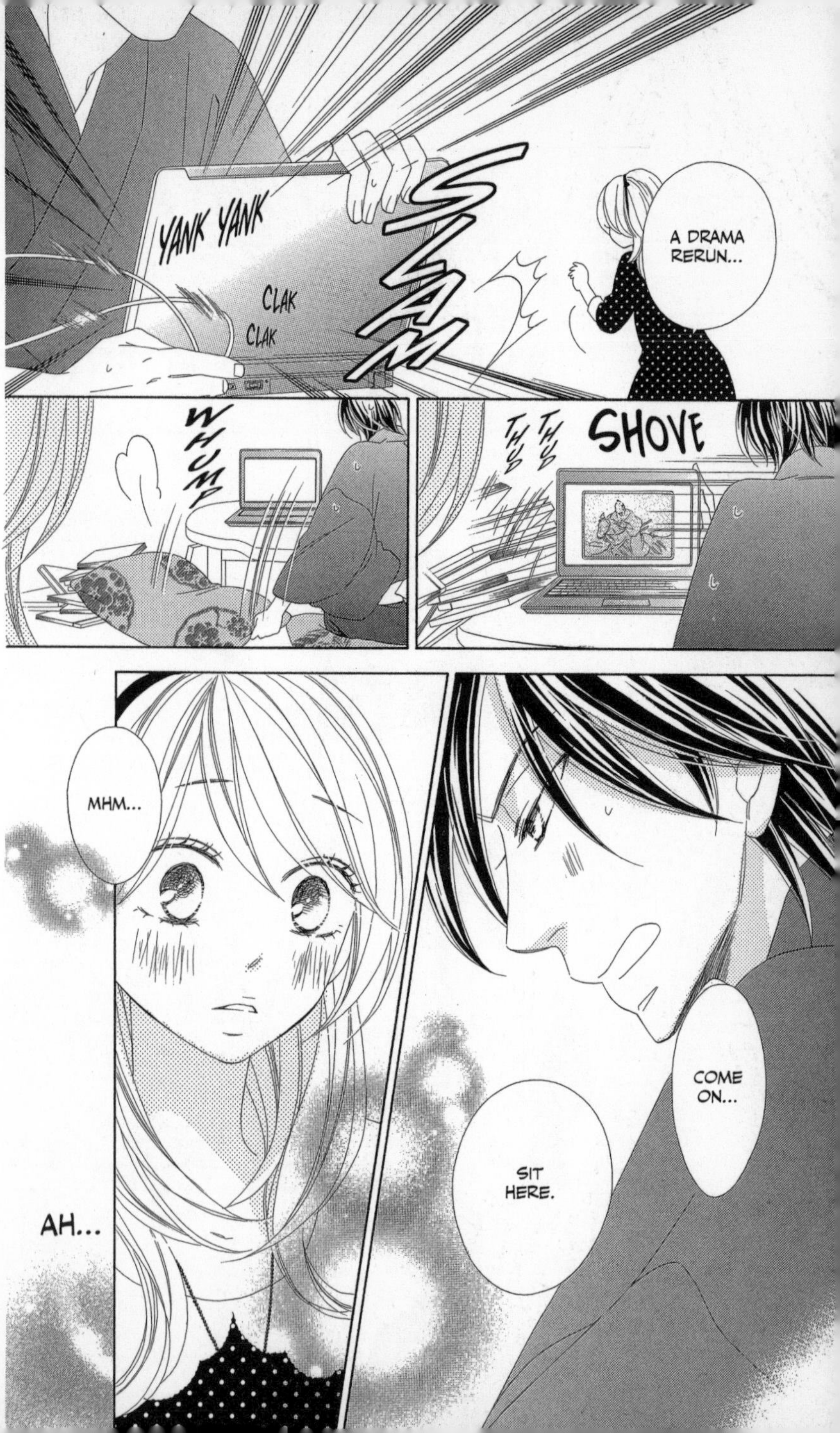
A DRAMA RERUN...
SLAM
YANK YANK
CLAK
CLAK
SHOVE
THUD THUD
WHUMP
COME ON...
SIT HERE.
MHM...
AH...

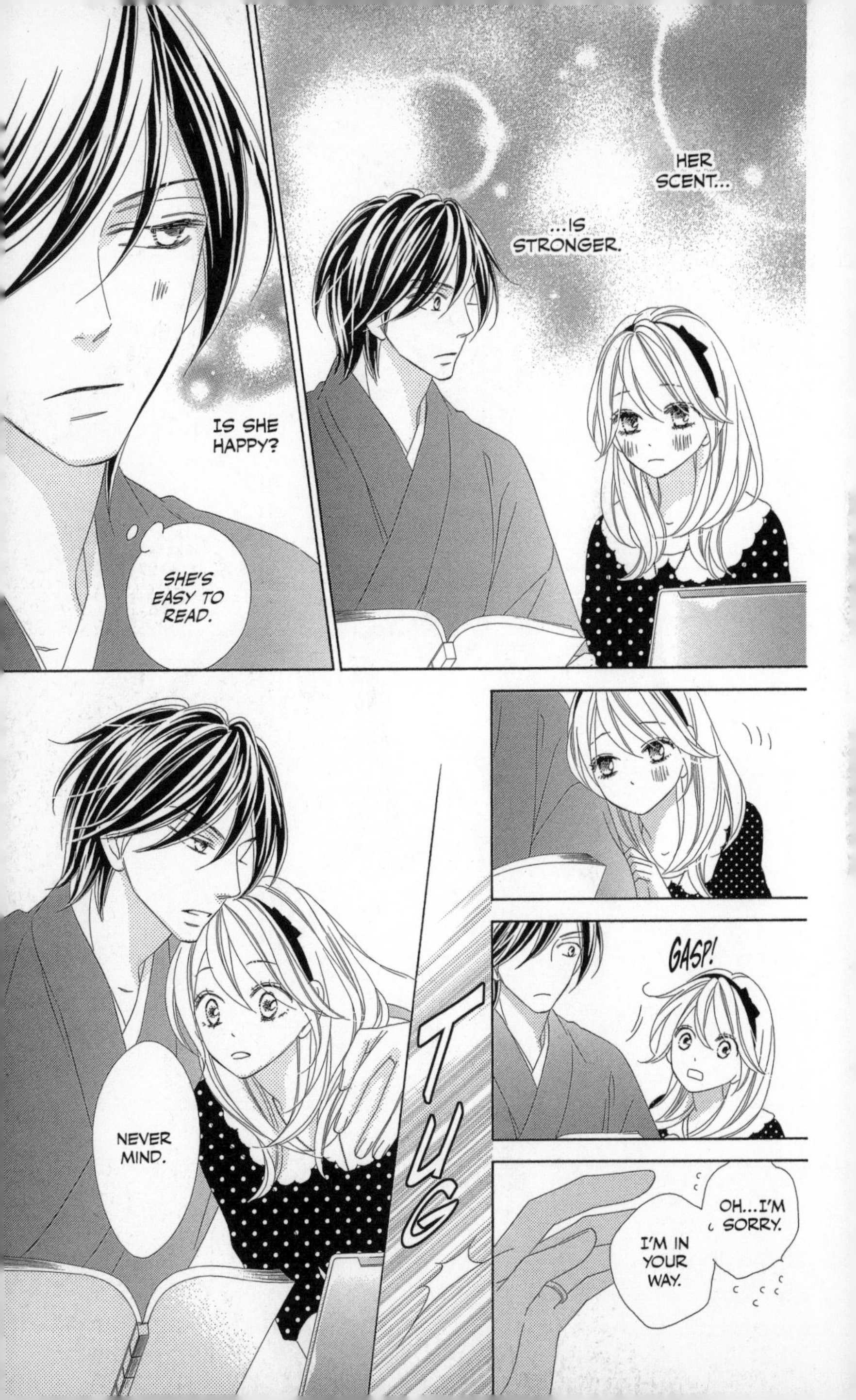
HER SCENT...
...IS STRONGER.
IS SHE HAPPY?
SHE'S EASY TO READ.
GASP!
OH...I'M SORRY.
I'M IN YOUR WAY.
TUG
NEVER MIND.

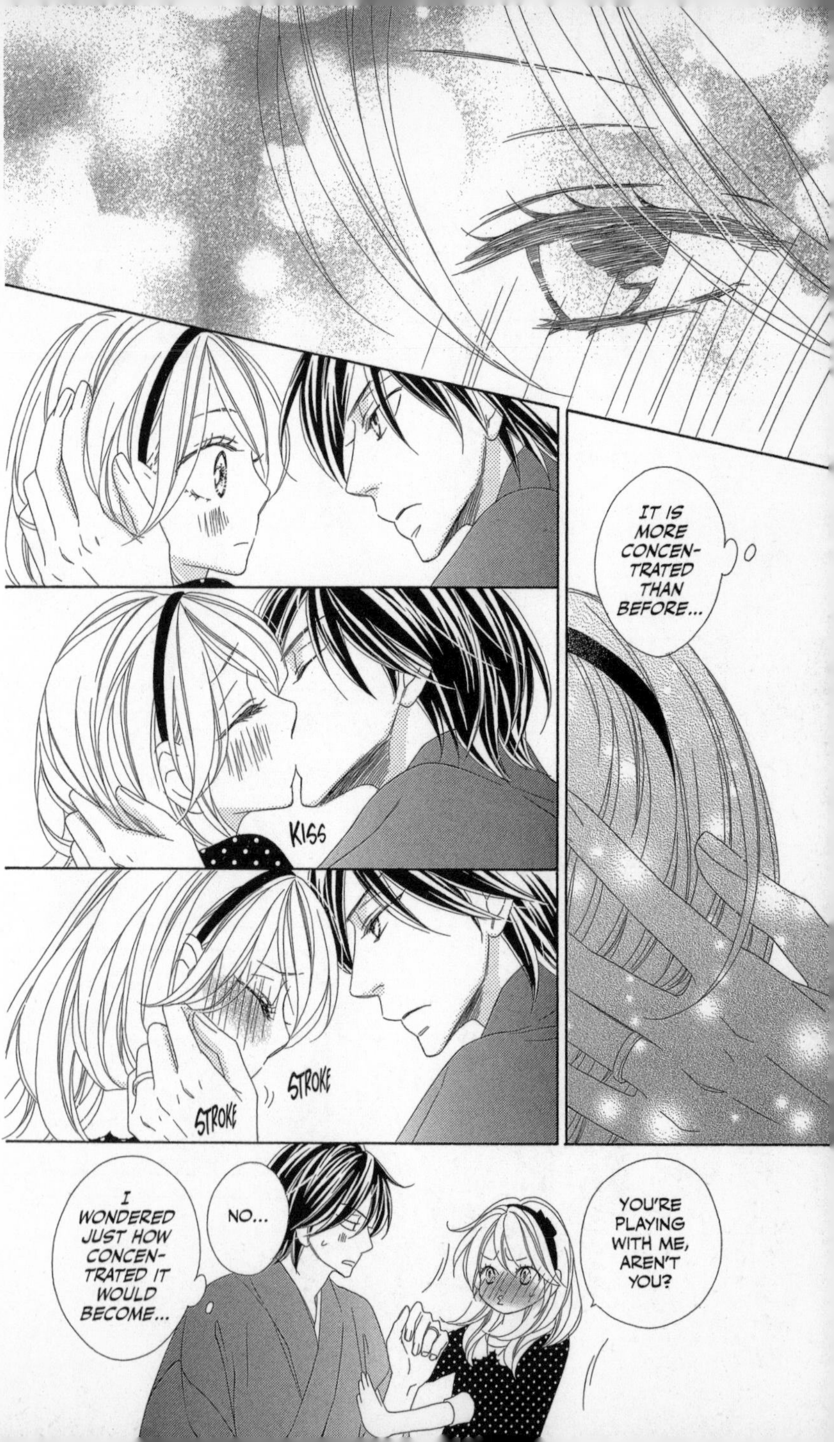
IT IS MORE CONCEN-TRATED THAN BEFORE...
KISS
STROKE
STROKE
YOU'RE PLAYING WITH ME, AREN'T YOU?
NO...
I WONDERED JUST HOW CONCEN-TRATED IT WOULD BECOME...

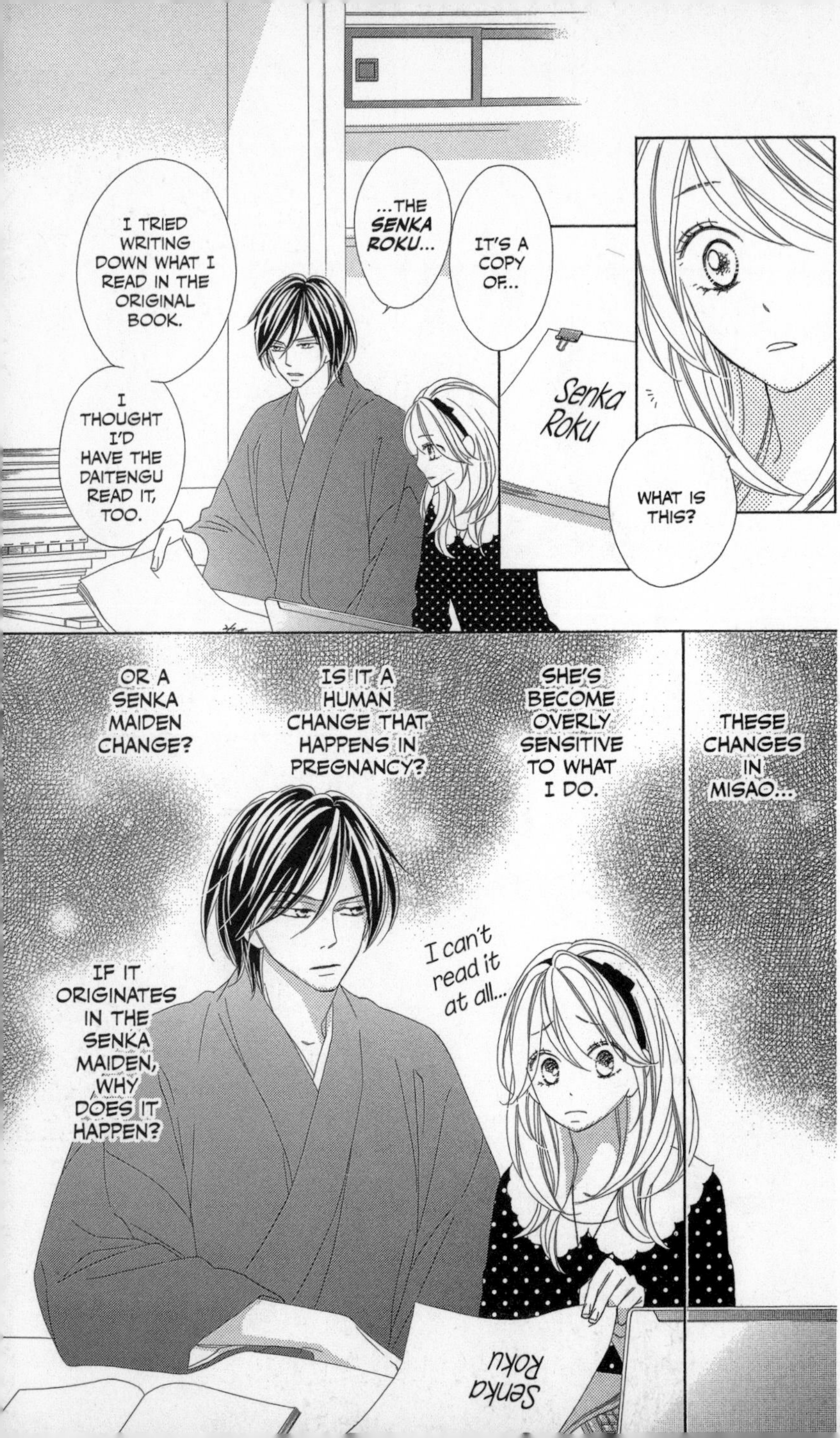
WHAT IS THIS?
Senka Roku
IT'S A COPY OF...
...THE SENKA ROKU...
I TRIED WRITING DOWN WHAT I READ IN THE ORIGINAL BOOK.
I THOUGHT I'D HAVE THE DAITENGU READ IT, TOO.
THESE CHANGES IN MISAO...
SHE'S BECOME OVERLY SENSITIVE TO WHAT I DO.
IS IT A HUMAN CHANGE THAT HAPPENS IN PREGNANCY?
OR A SENKA MAIDEN CHANGE?
I can't read it at all...
IF IT ORIGINATES IN THE SENKA MAIDEN, WHY DOES IT HAPPEN?
Senka Roku

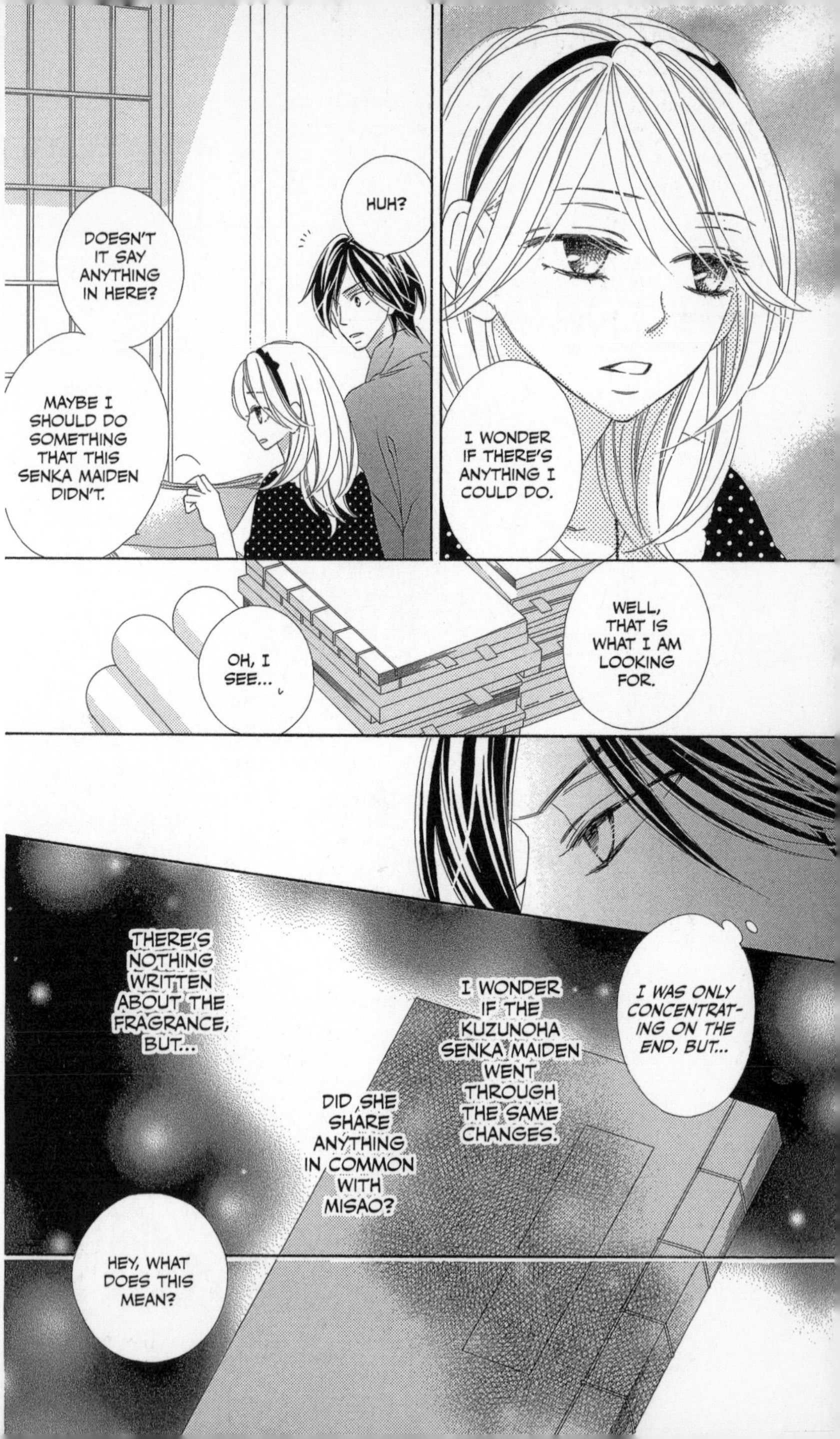
I WONDER IF THERE'S ANYTHING I COULD DO.
HUH?
DOESN'T IT SAY ANYTHING IN HERE?
MAYBE I SHOULD DO SOMETHING THAT THIS SENKA MAIDEN DIDN'T.
WELL, THAT IS WHAT I AM LOOKING FOR.
OH, I SEE...
I WAS ONLY CONCENTRAT-ING ON THE END, BUT...
I WONDER IF THE KUZUNOHA SENKA MAIDEN WENT THROUGH THE SAME CHANGES.
THERE'S NOTHING WRITTEN ABOUT THE FRAGRANCE, BUT...
DID SHE SHARE ANYTHING IN COMMON WITH MISAO?
HEY, WHAT DOES THIS MEAN?

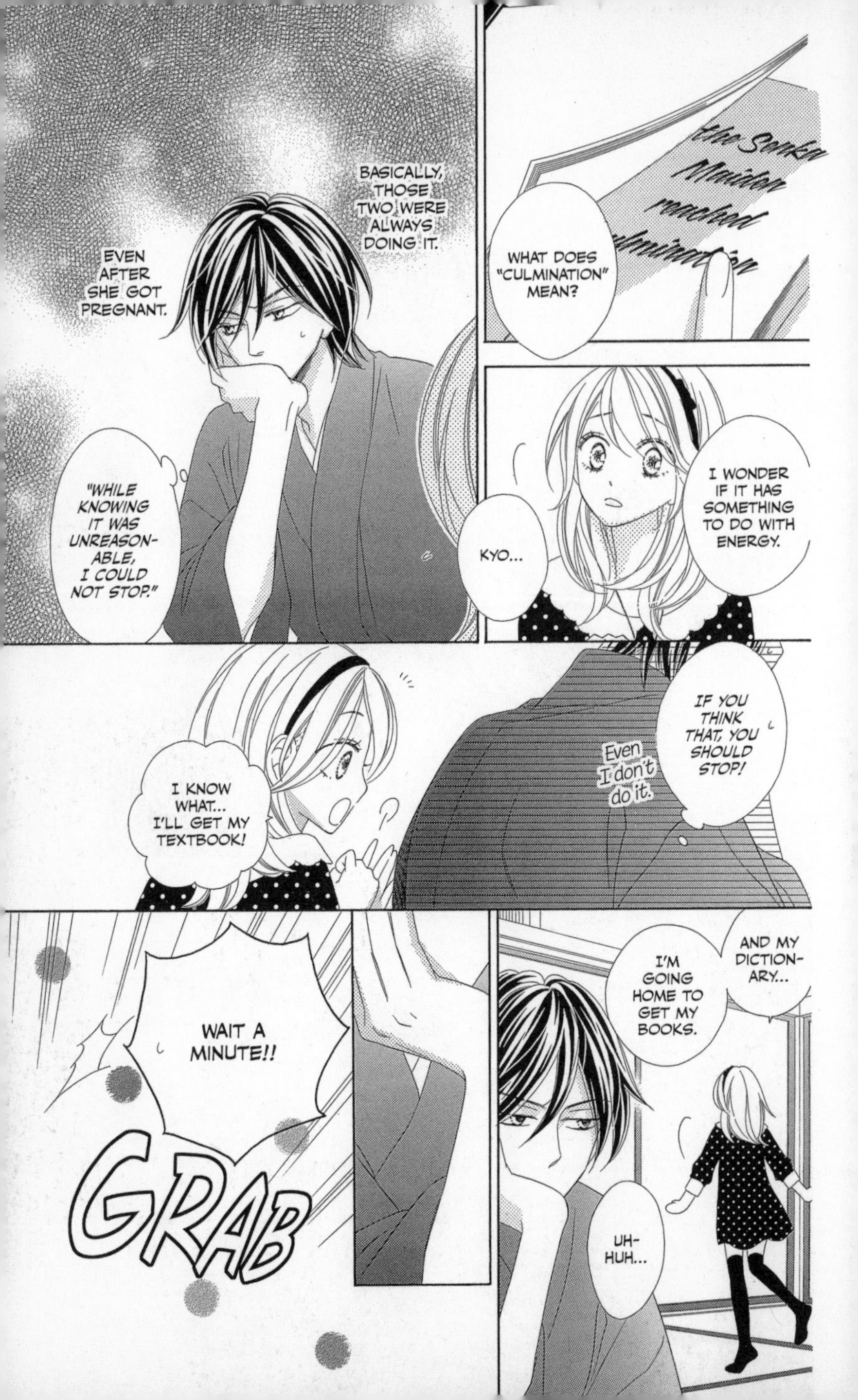
WHAT DOES "CULMINATION" MEAN?
I WONDER IF IT HAS SOMETHING TO DO WITH ENERGY.
KYO...
BASICALLY, THOSE TWO WERE ALWAYS DOING IT.
EVEN AFTER SHE GOT PREGNANT.
"WHILE KNOWING IT WAS UNREASON-ABLE, I COULD NOT STOP."
IF YOU THINK THAT, YOU SHOULD STOP!
Even I don't do it.
I KNOW WHAT... I'LL GET MY TEXTBOOK!
AND MY DICTION-ARY...
I'M GOING HOME TO GET MY BOOKS.
UH-HUH...
WAIT A MINUTE!!
GRAB

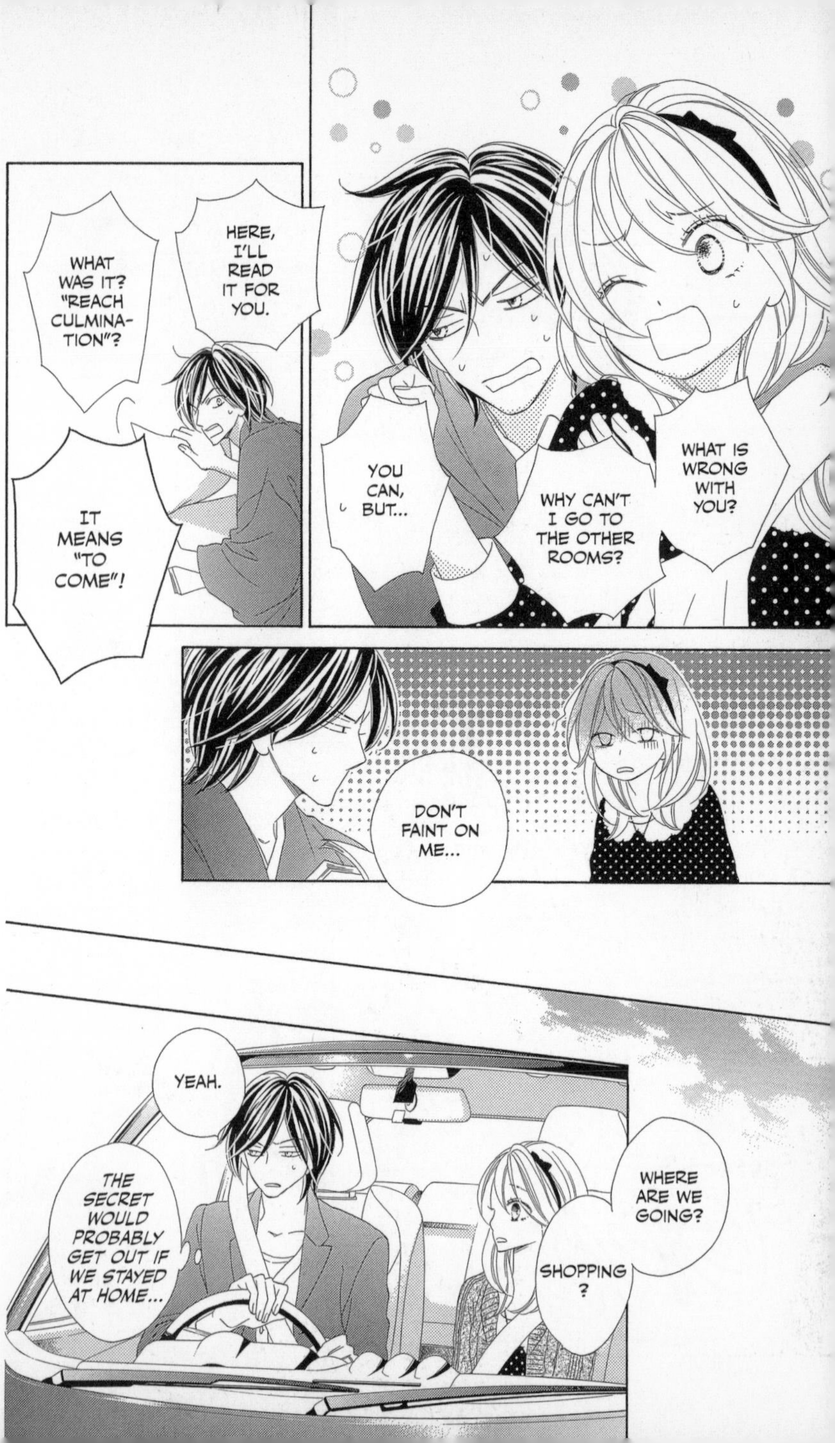
WHAT IS WRONG WITH YOU?
WHY CAN'T I GO TO THE OTHER ROOMS?
YOU CAN, BUT...
HERE, I'LL READ IT FOR YOU.
WHAT WAS IT? "REACH CULMINATION"?
IT MEANS "TO COME"!
DON'T FAINT ON ME...
WHERE ARE WE GOING?
SHOPPING?
YEAH.
THE SECRET WOULD PROBABLY GET OUT IF WE STAYED AT HOME...

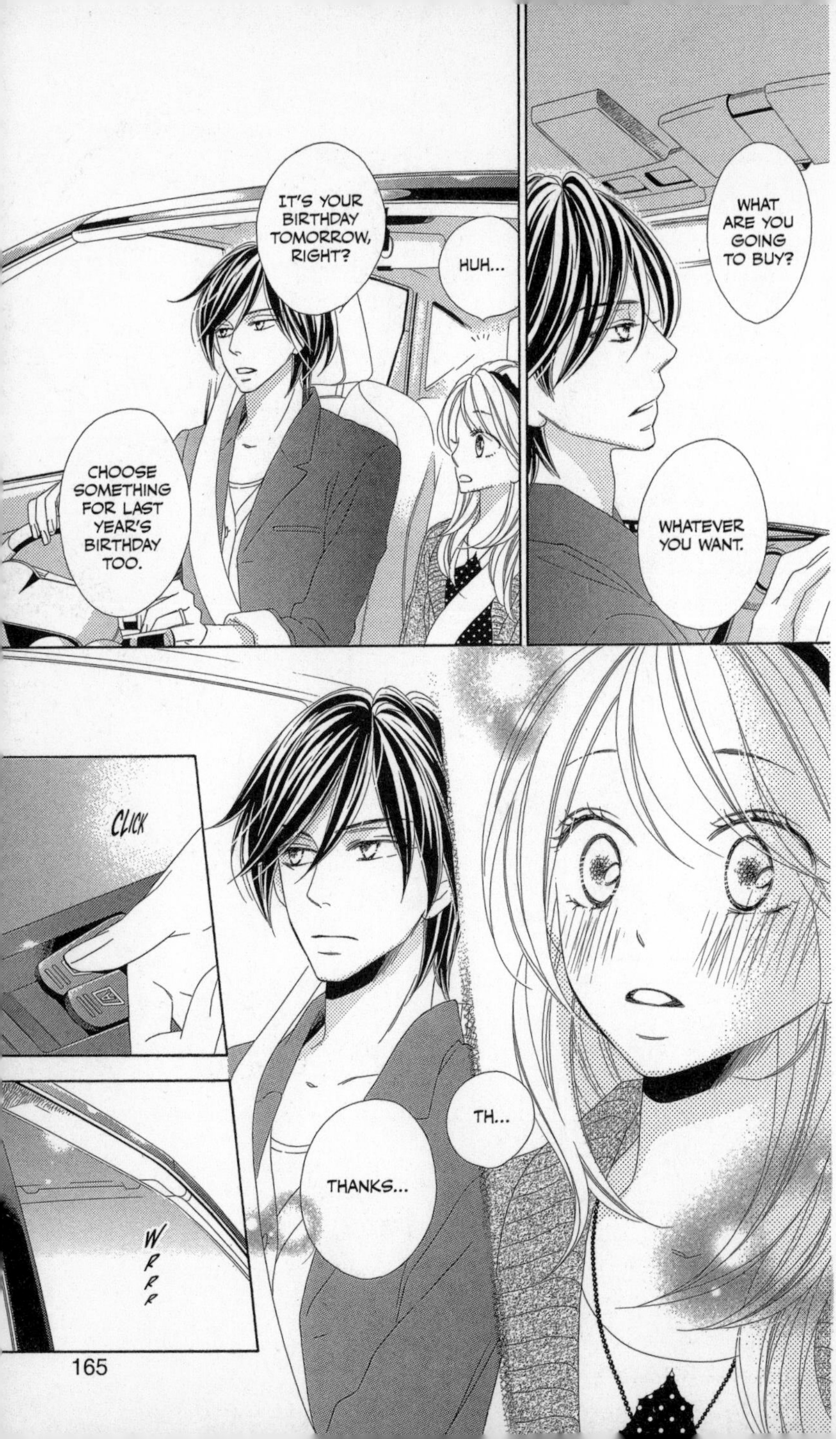
WHAT ARE YOU GOING TO BUY?
WHATEVER YOU WANT.
IT'S YOUR BIRTHDAY TOMORROW, RIGHT?
HUH...
CHOOSE SOMETHING FOR LAST YEAR'S BIRTHDAY TOO.
TH...
THANKS...
CLICK
WRRR

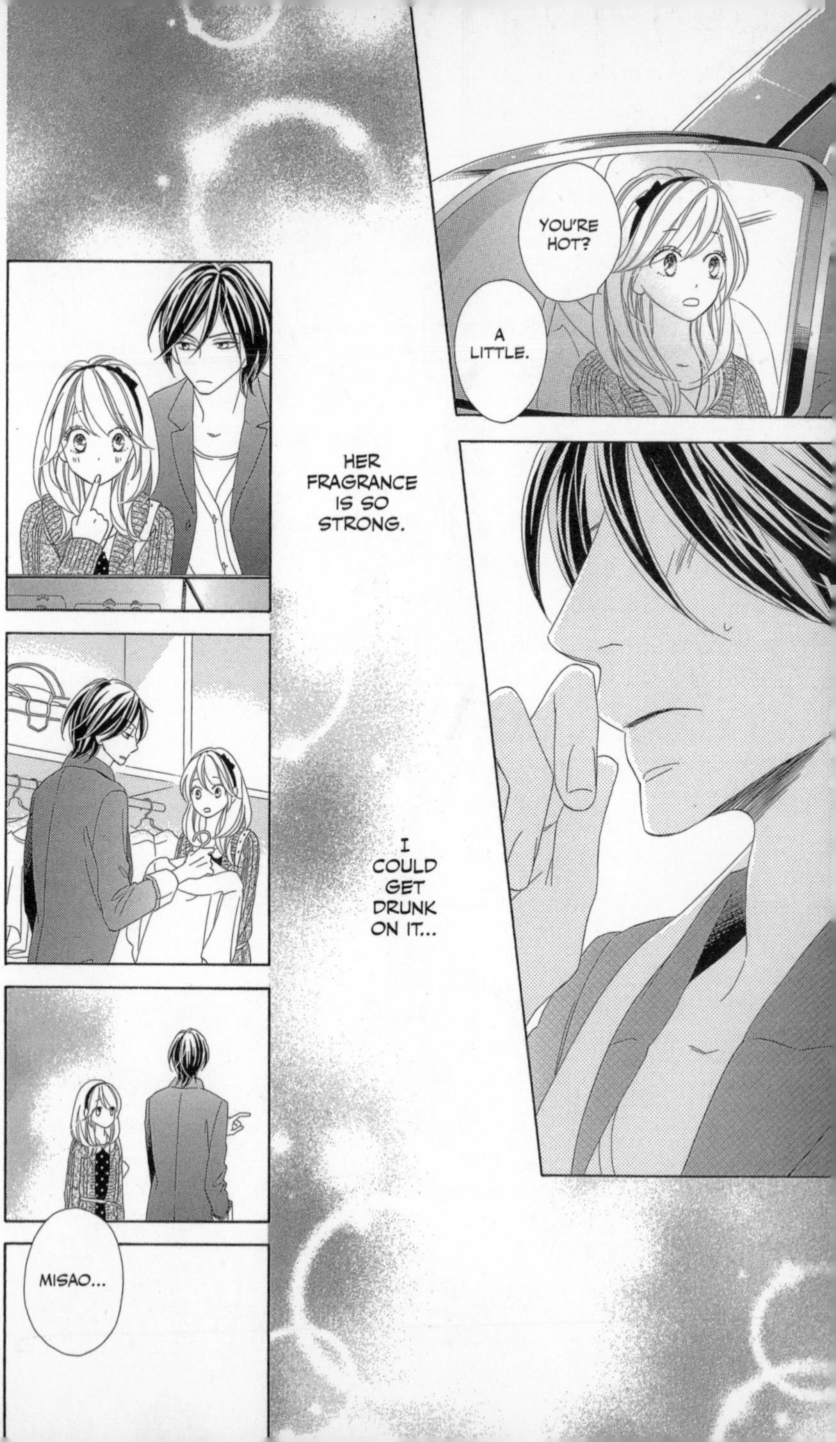
YOU'RE HOT?
A LITTLE.
HER FRAGRANCE IS SO STRONG.
I COULD GET DRUNK ON IT...
MISAO...

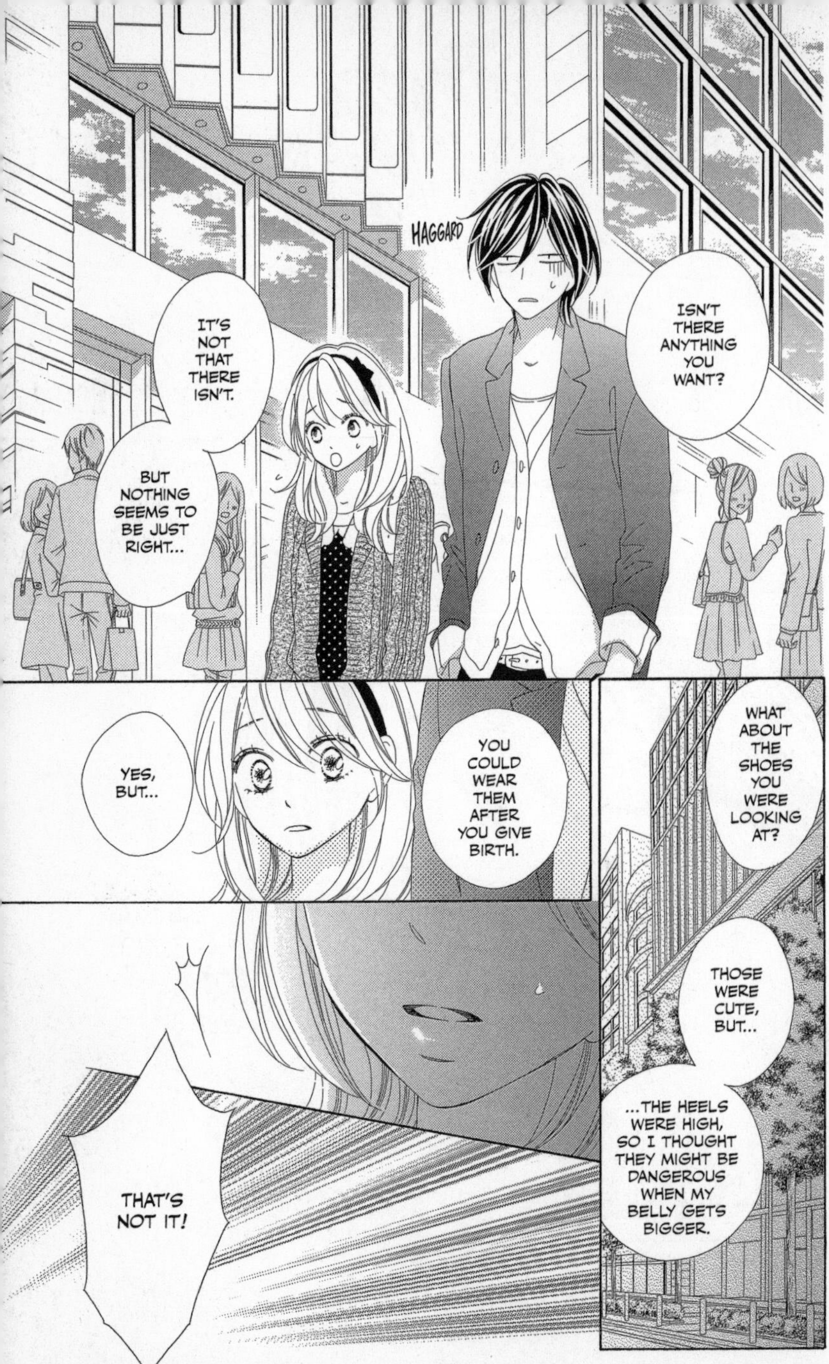
ISN'T THERE ANYTHING YOU WANT?
HAGGARD
IT'S NOT THAT THERE ISN'T.
BUT NOTHING SEEMS TO BE JUST RIGHT...
WHAT ABOUT THE SHOES YOU WERE LOOKING AT?
THOSE WERE CUTE, BUT...
...THE HEELS WERE HIGH, SO I THOUGHT THEY MIGHT BE DANGEROUS WHEN MY BELLY GETS BIGGER.
YOU COULD WEAR THEM AFTER YOU GIVE BIRTH.
YES, BUT...
THAT'S NOT IT!

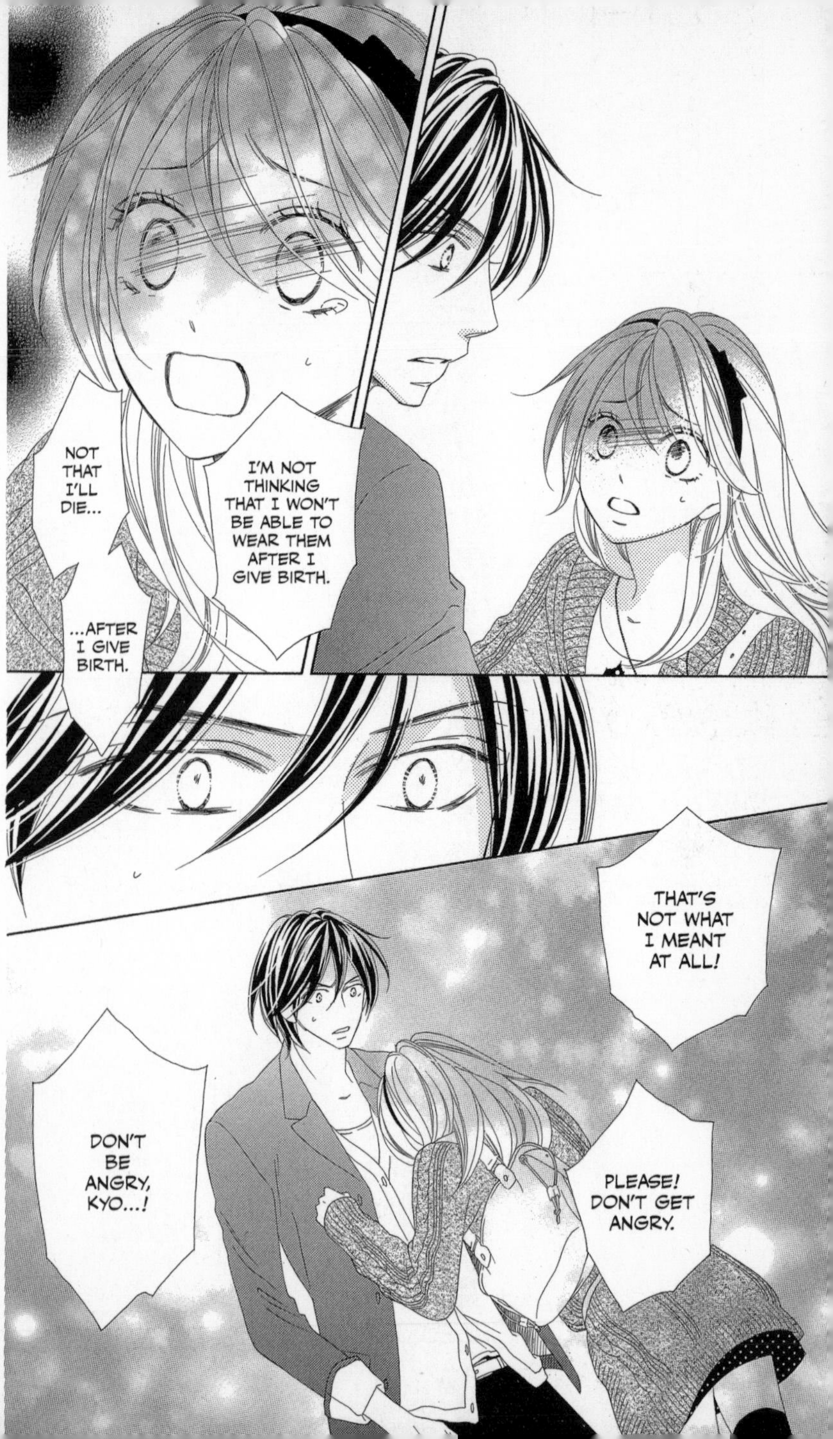
I'M NOT THINKING THAT I WON'T BE ABLE TO WEAR THEM AFTER I GIVE BIRTH.
NOT THAT I'LL DIE...
...AFTER I GIVE BIRTH.
THAT'S NOT WHAT I MEANT AT ALL!
PLEASE! DON'T GET ANGRY.
DON'T BE ANGRY, KYO...!

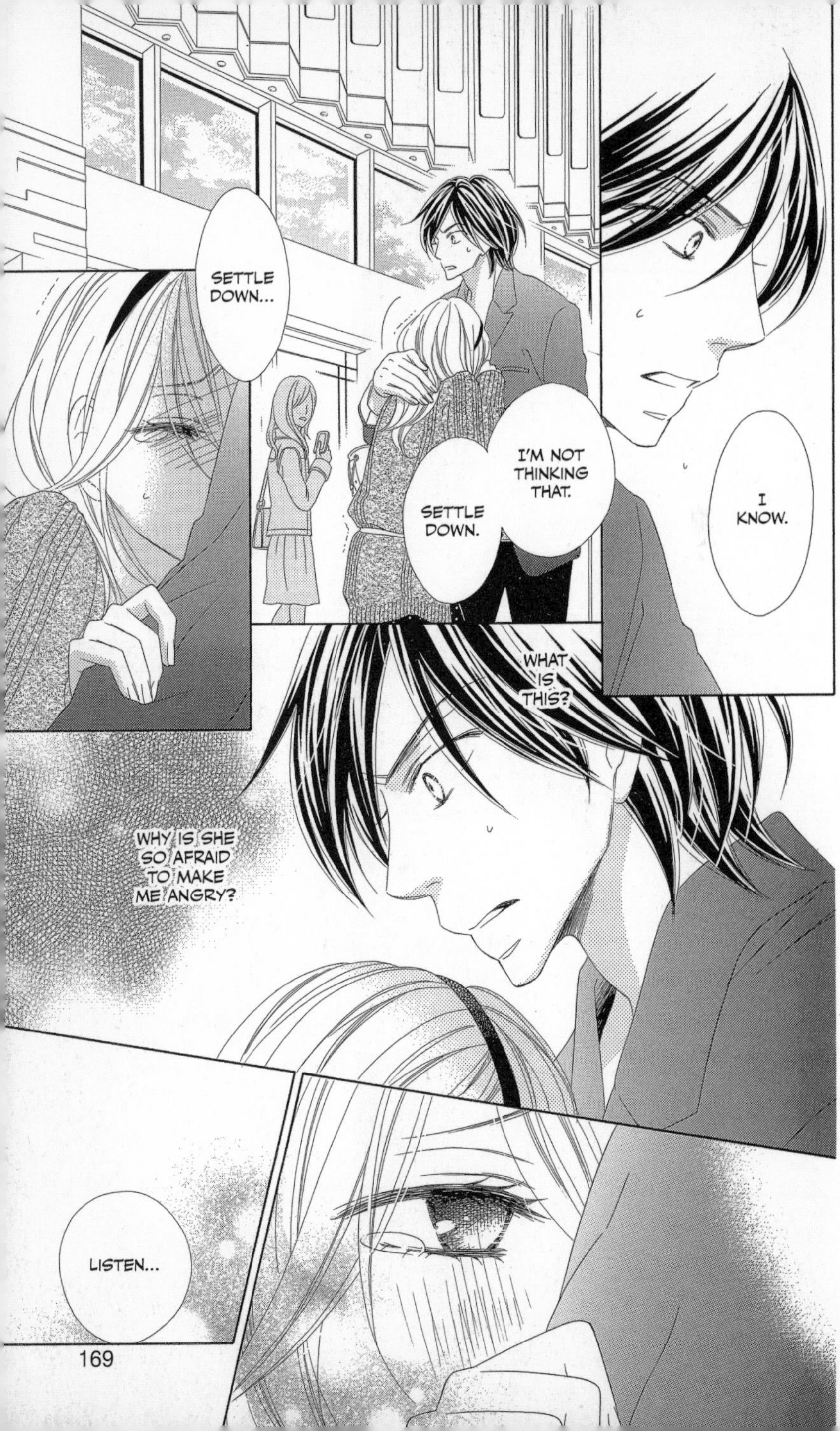
I KNOW.
I'M NOT THINKING THAT.
SETTLE DOWN.
SETTLE DOWN...
WHAT IS THIS?
WHY IS SHE SO AFRAID TO MAKE ME ANGRY?
LISTEN...

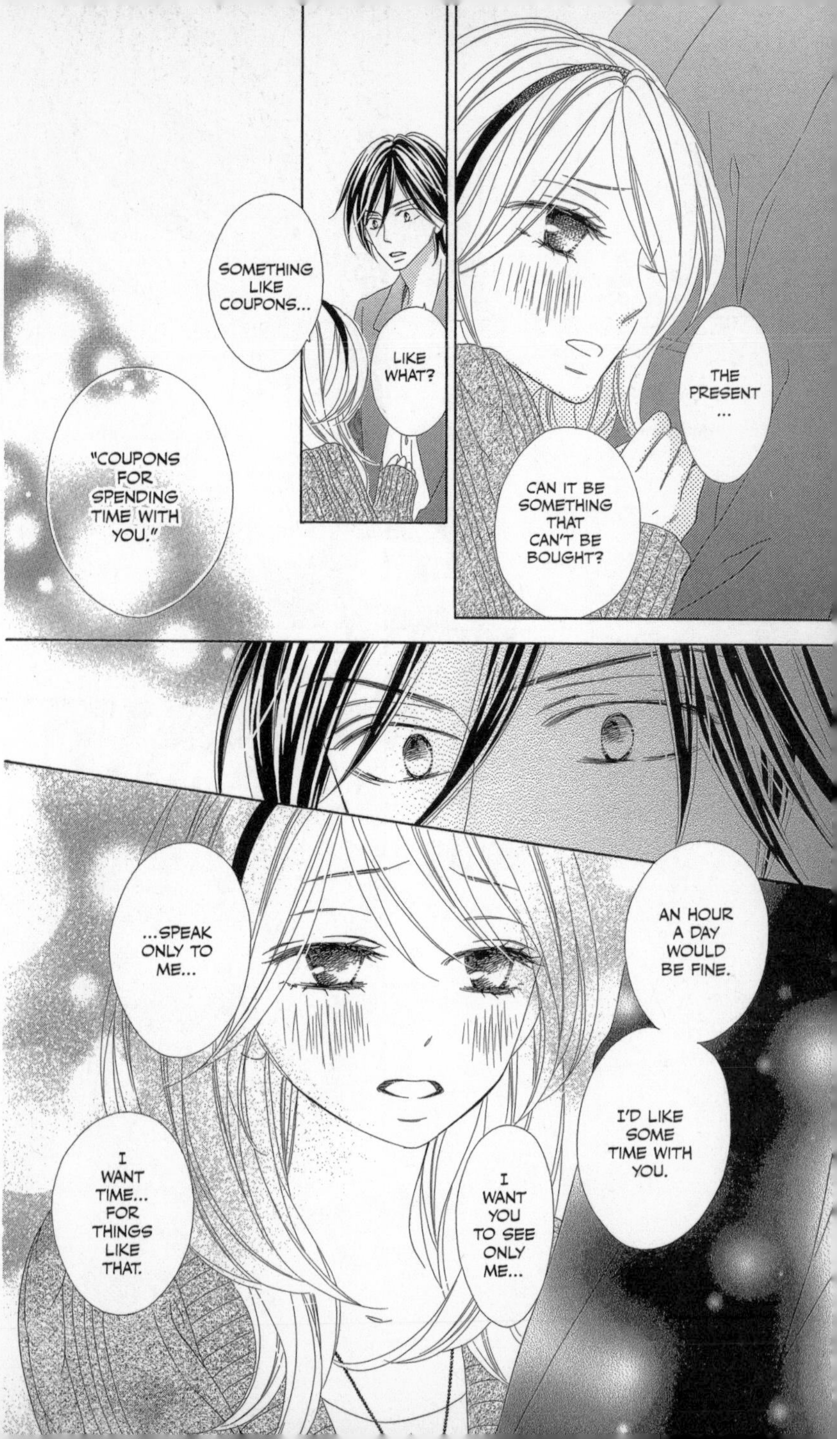
THE PRESENT...
CAN IT BE SOMETHING THAT CAN'T BE BOUGHT?
LIKE WHAT?
SOMETHING LIKE COUPONS...
"COUPONS FOR SPENDING TIME WITH YOU."
AN HOUR A DAY WOULD BE FINE.
I'D LIKE SOME TIME WITH YOU.
I WANT YOU TO SEE ONLY ME...
...SPEAK ONLY TO ME...
I WANT TIME... FOR THINGS LIKE THAT.

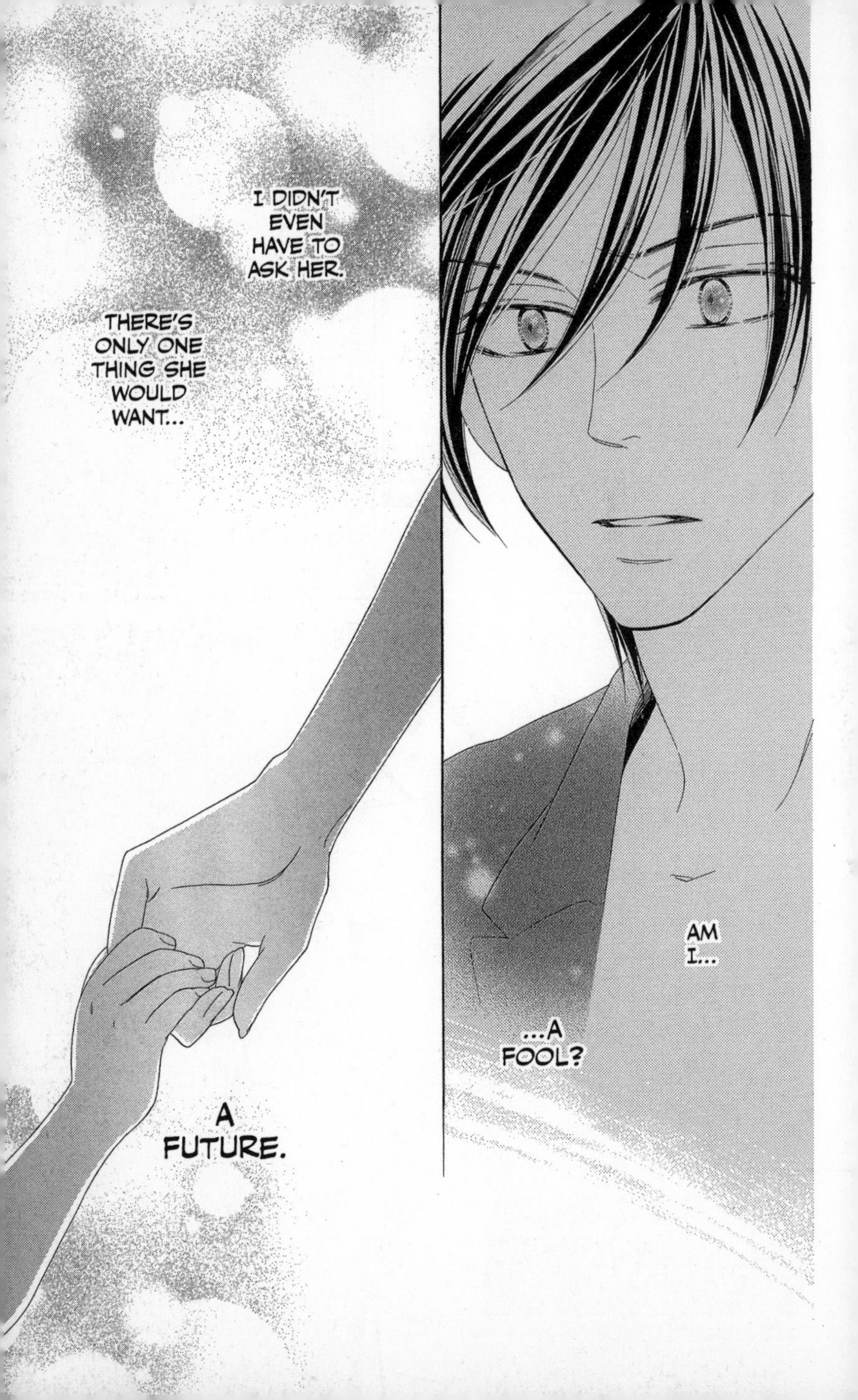
AM I...
...A FOOL?
I DIDN'T EVEN HAVE TO ASK HER.
THERE'S ONLY ONE THING SHE WOULD WANT...
A FUTURE.

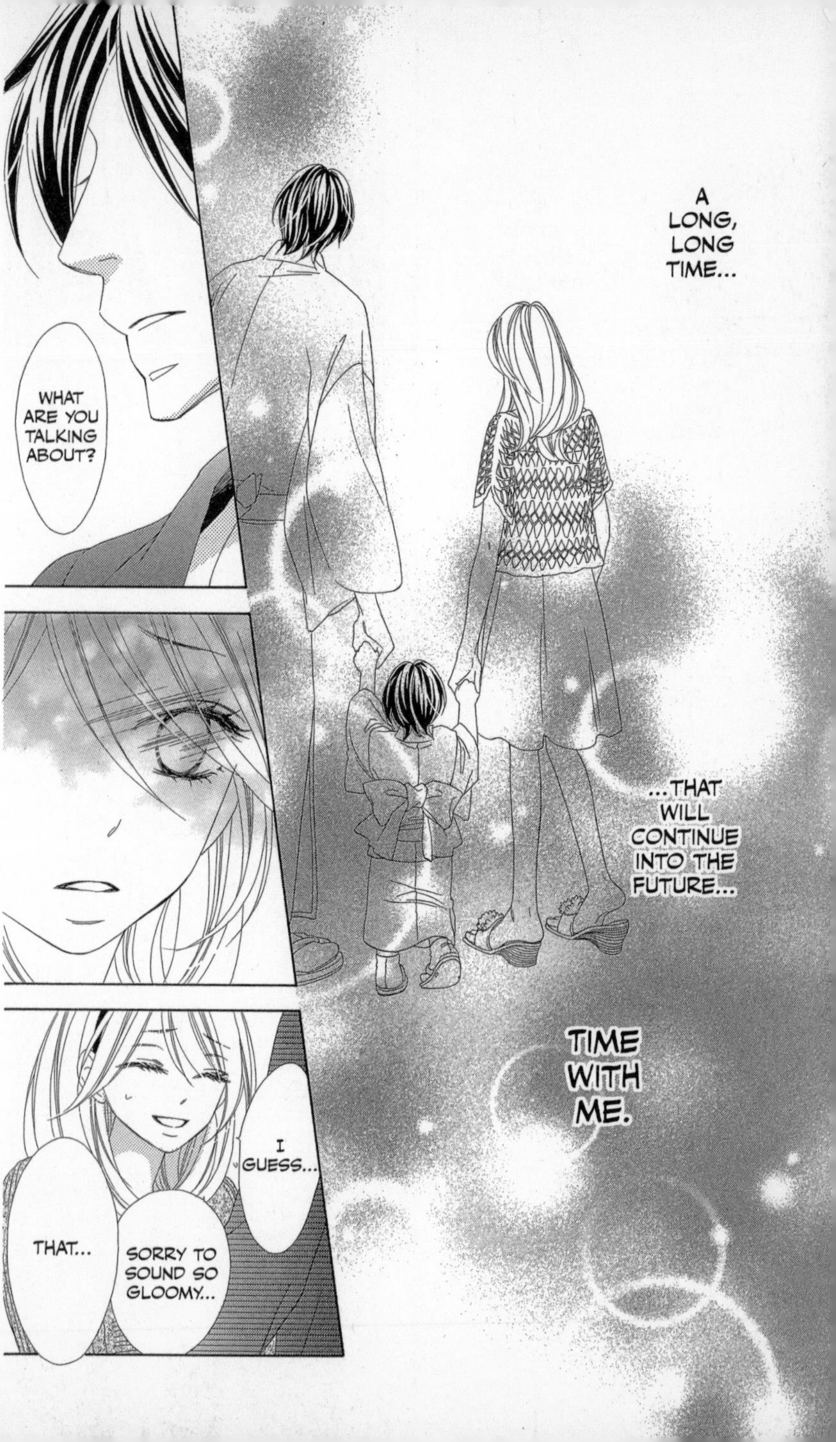
A LONG, LONG TIME...
...THAT WILL CONTINUE INTO THE FUTURE...
TIME WITH ME.
WHAT ARE YOU TALKING ABOUT?
I GUESS...
SORRY TO SOUND SO GLOOMY...
THAT...

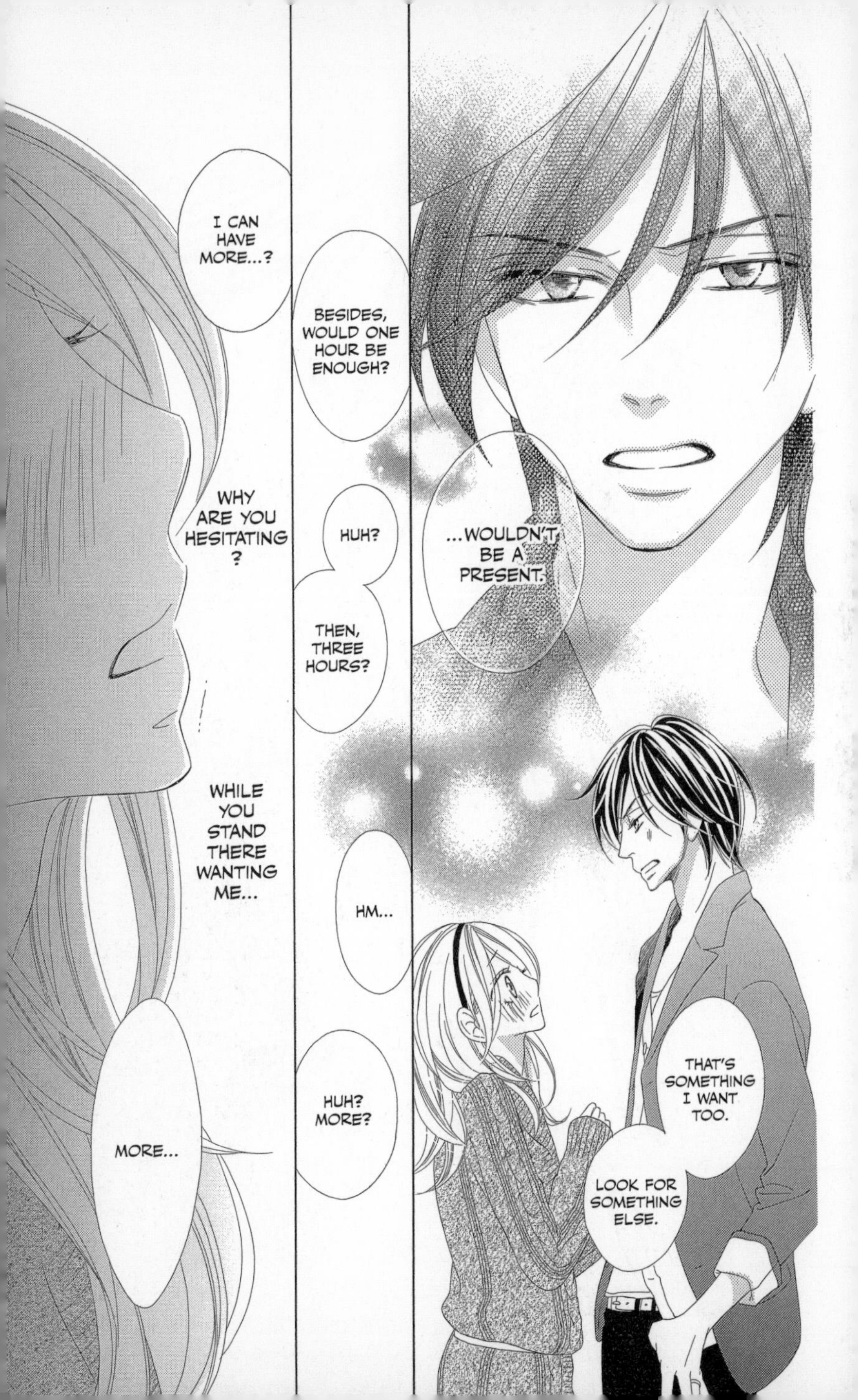
...WOULDN'T BE A PRESENT.
THAT'S SOMETHING I WANT TOO.
LOOK FOR SOMETHING ELSE.
BESIDES, WOULD ONE HOUR BE ENOUGH?
HUH?
THEN, THREE HOURS?
HM...
HUH? MORE?
I CAN HAVE MORE...?
WHY ARE YOU HESITATING?
WHILE YOU STAND THERE WANTING ME...
MORE...

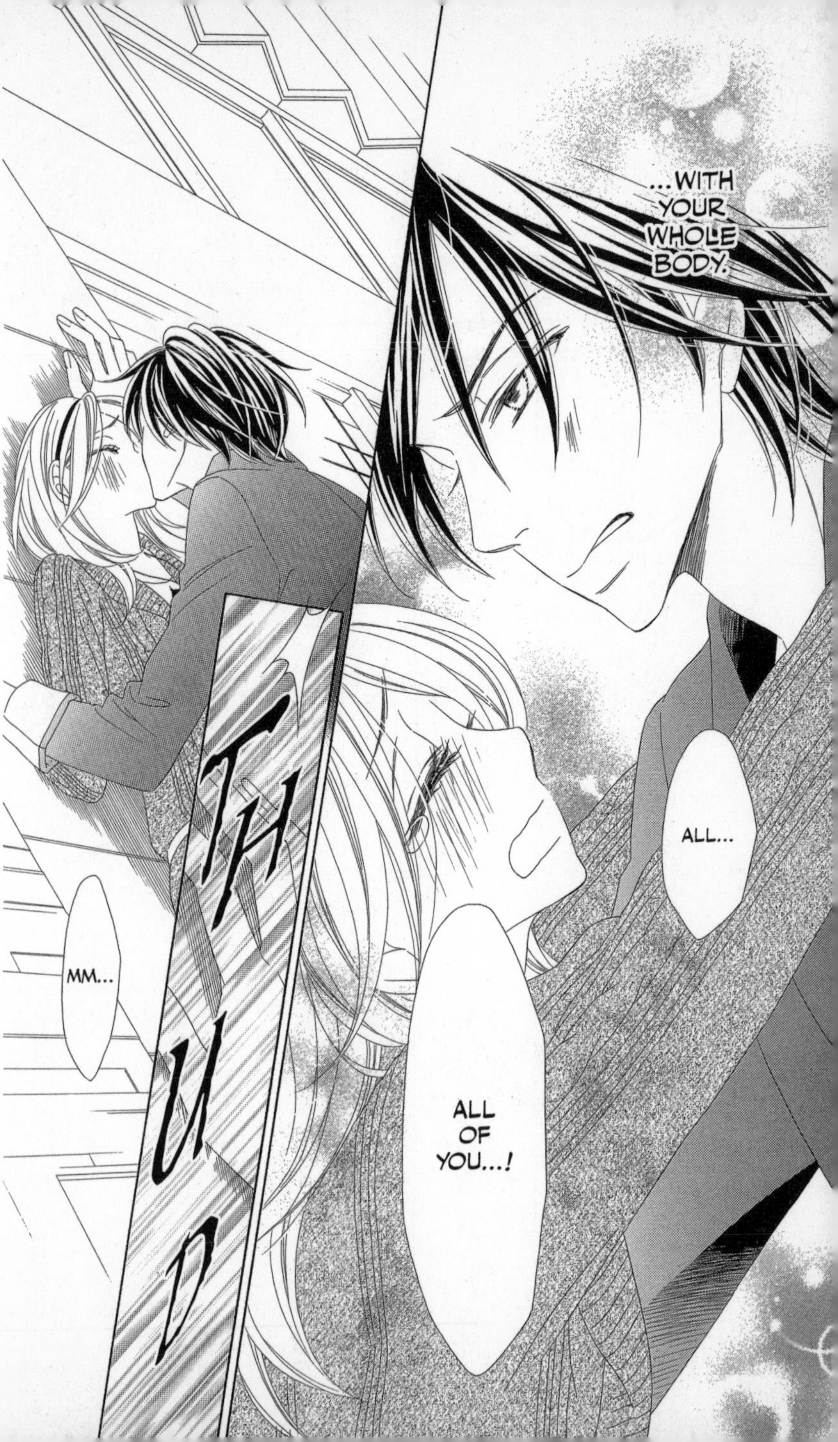
...WITH YOUR WHOLE BODY.
ALL...
ALL OF YOU...!
THUD
MM...

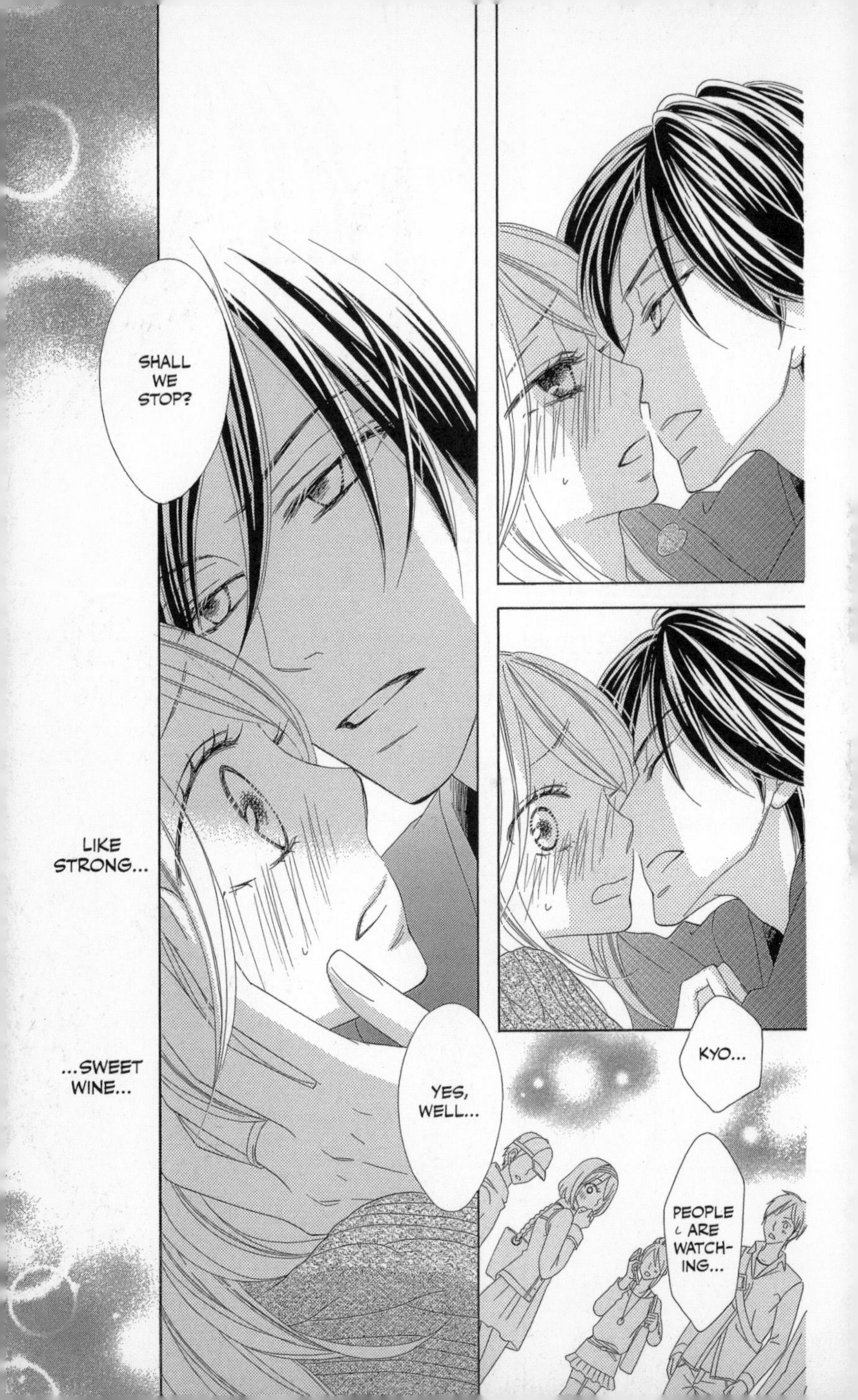
KYO...
PEOPLE ARE WATCH-ING...
SHALL WE STOP?
YES, WELL...
LIKE STRONG...
...SWEET WINE...

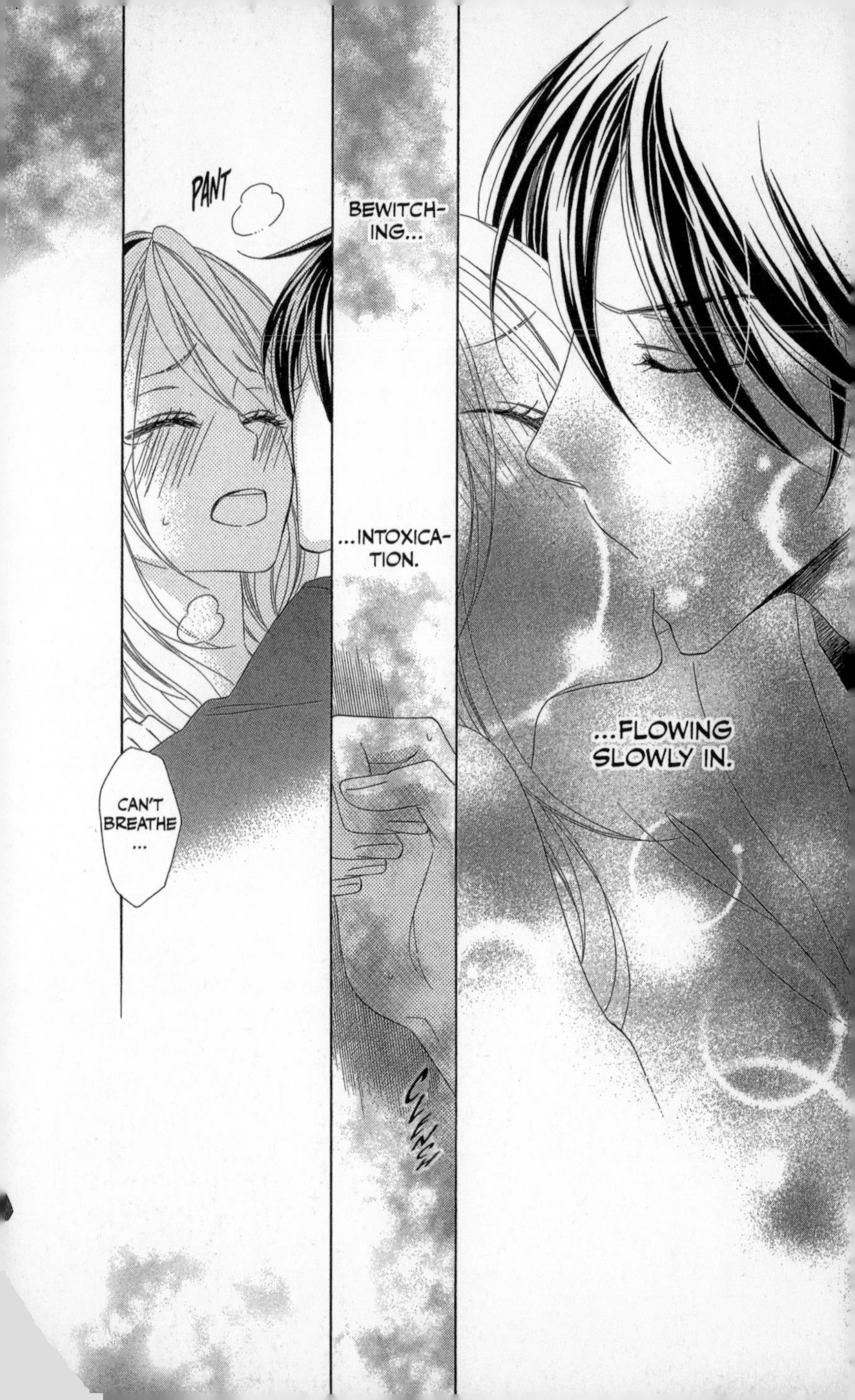
...FLOWING SLOWLY IN.
BEWITCHING...
...INTOXICATION.
PANT
CAN'T BREATHE...

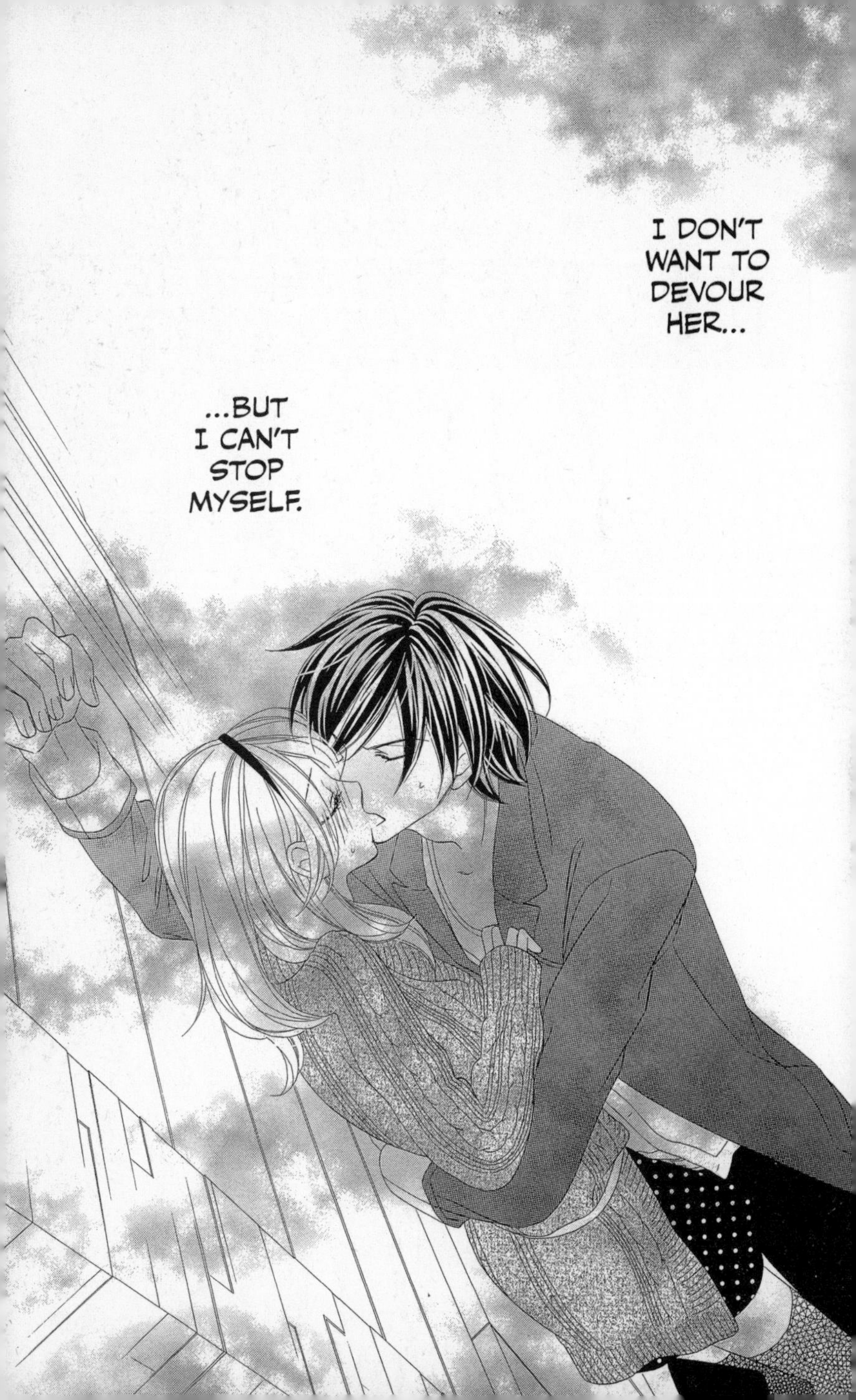
I DON'T WANT TO DEVOUR HER...
...BUT I CAN'T STOP MYSELF.

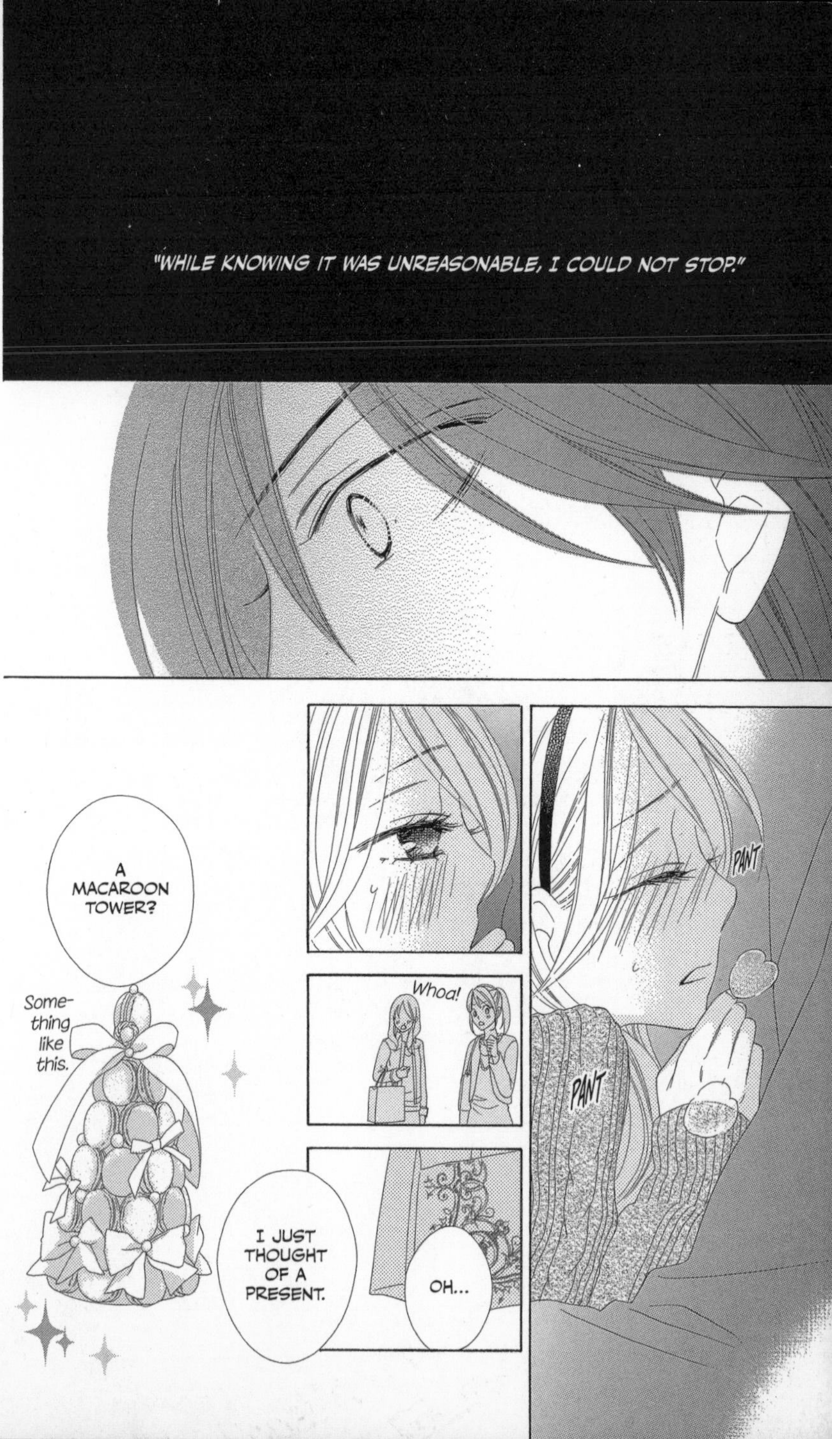
"WHILE KNOWING IT WAS UNREASONABLE, I COULD NOT STOP."
PANT
PANT
Whoa!
OH...
I JUST THOUGHT OF A PRESENT.
A MACAROON TOWER?
Something like this.

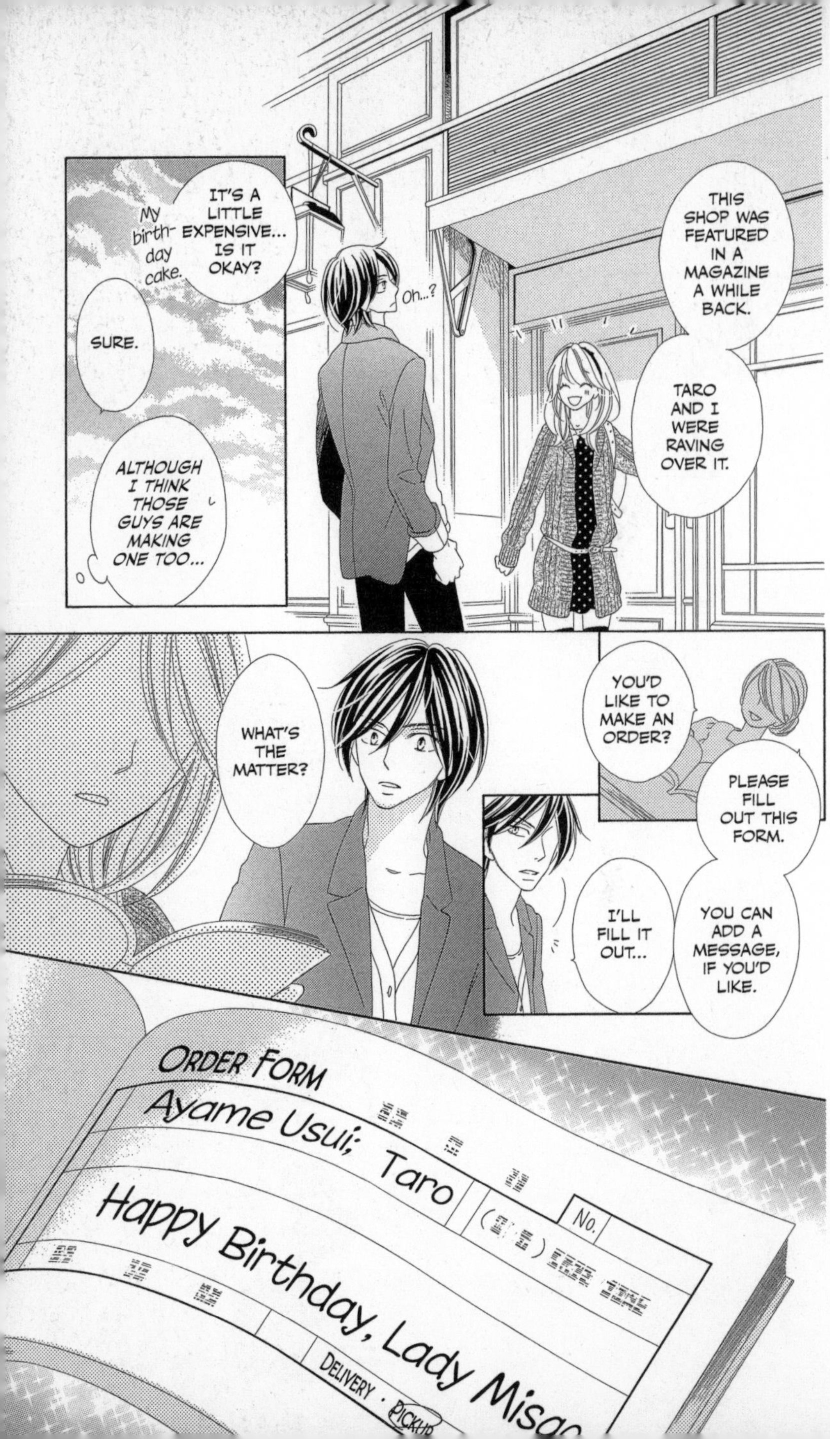
THIS SHOP WAS FEATURED IN A MAGAZINE A WHILE BACK.
TARO AND I WERE RAVING OVER IT.
Oh...?
IT'S A LITTLE EXPENSIVE... IS IT OKAY?
My birthday cake.
SURE.
ALTHOUGH I THINK THOSE GUYS ARE MAKING ONE TOO...
YOU'D LIKE TO MAKE AN ORDER?
PLEASE FILL OUT THIS FORM.
YOU CAN ADD A MESSAGE, IF YOU'D LIKE.
I'LL FILL IT OUT...
WHAT'S THE MATTER?
ORDER FORM
Ayame Usui; Taro
No.
Happy Birthday, Lady Misa
DELIVERY · PICKUP

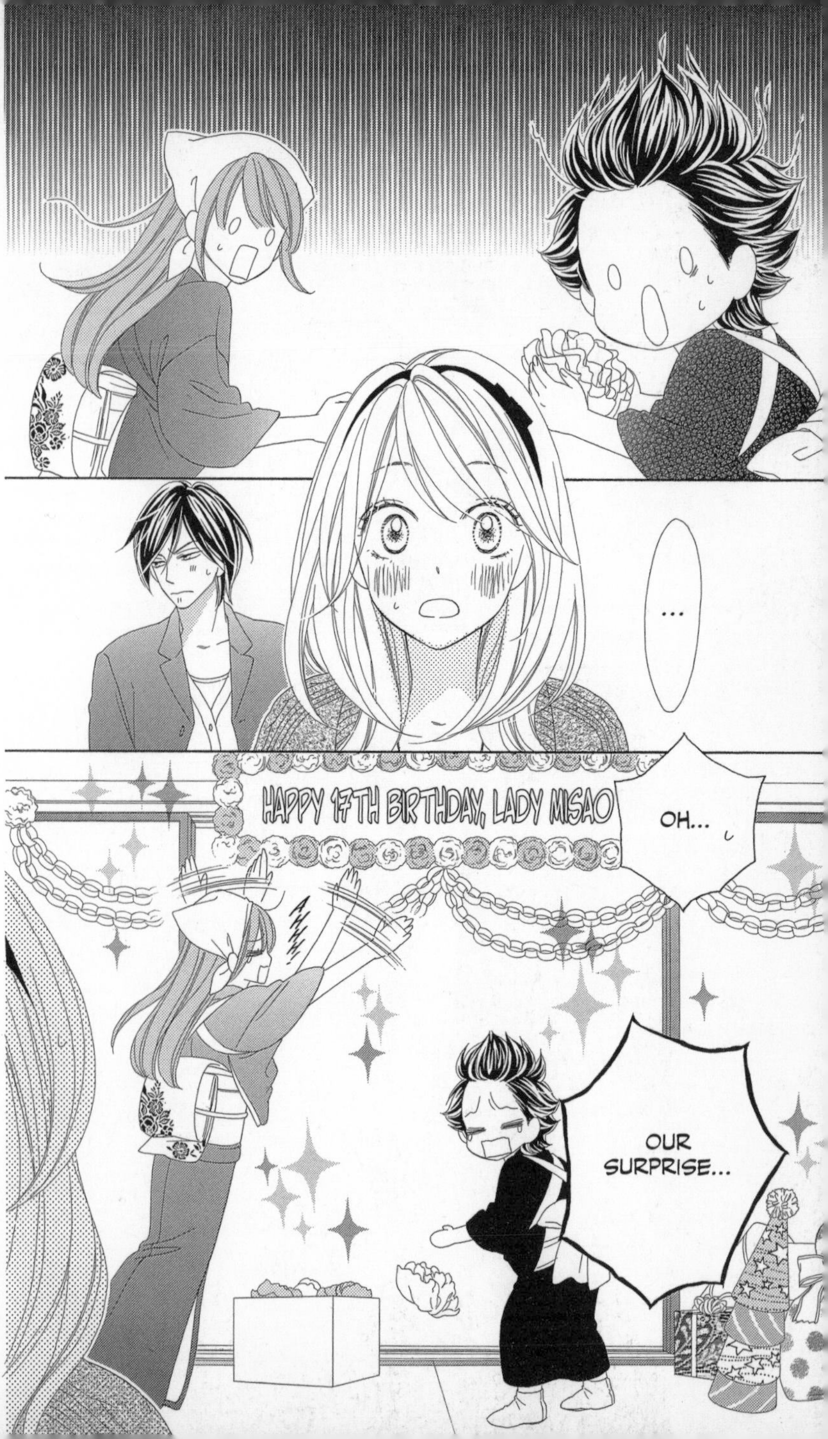
...
OH...
HAPPY 17TH BIRTHDAY, LADY MISAO
AHHH!
OUR SURPRISE...

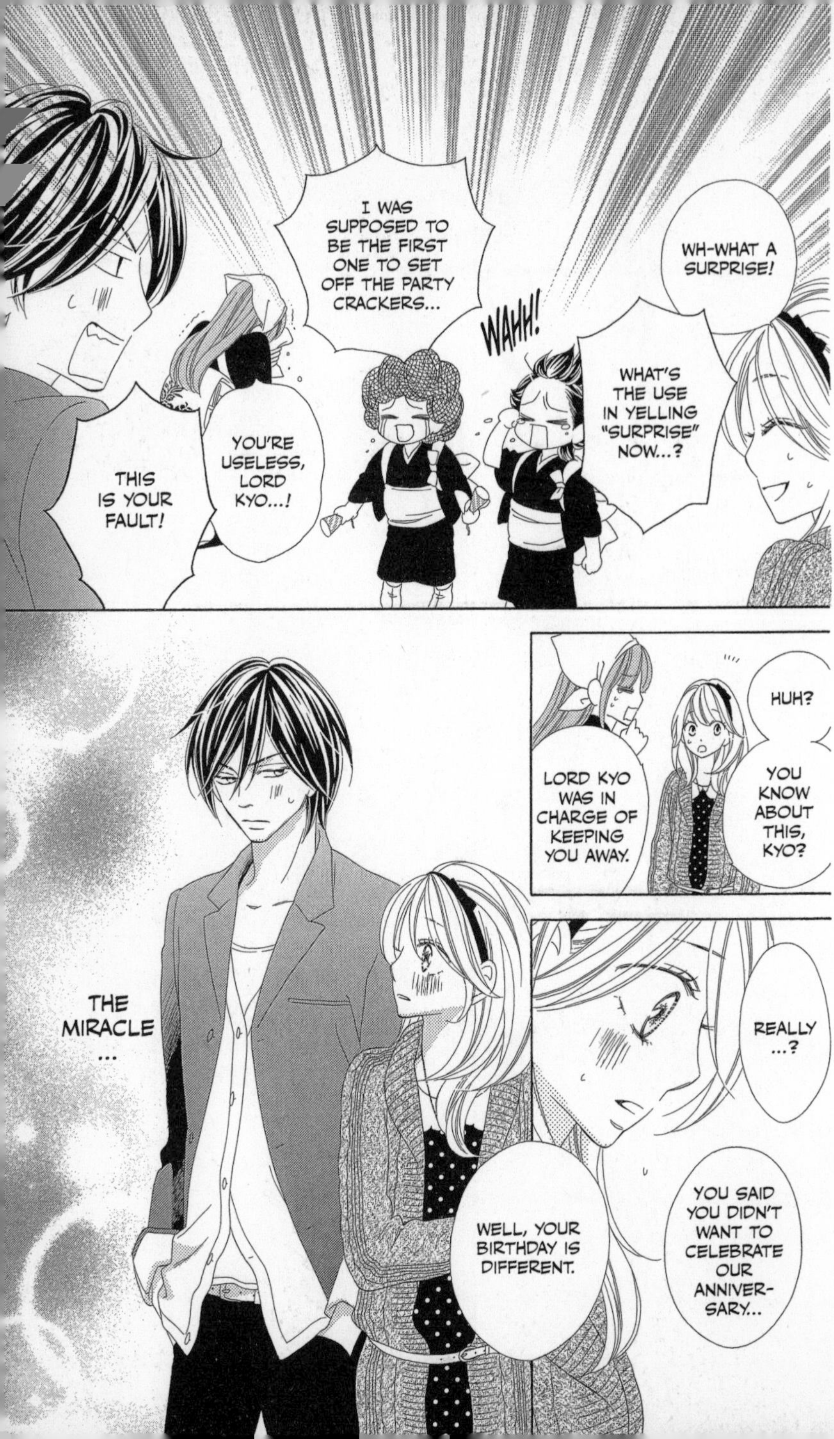
WH-WHAT A SURPRISE!
WHAT'S THE USE IN YELLING "SURPRISE" NOW...?
WAHH!
I WAS SUPPOSED TO BE THE FIRST ONE TO SET OFF THE PARTY CRACKERS...
YOU'RE USELESS, LORD KYO...!
THIS IS YOUR FAULT!
HUH?
YOU KNOW ABOUT THIS, KYO?
LORD KYO WAS IN CHARGE OF KEEPING YOU AWAY.
REALLY...?
YOU SAID YOU DIDN'T WANT TO CELEBRATE OUR ANNIVERSARY...
WELL, YOUR BIRTHDAY IS DIFFERENT.
THE MIRACLE ...

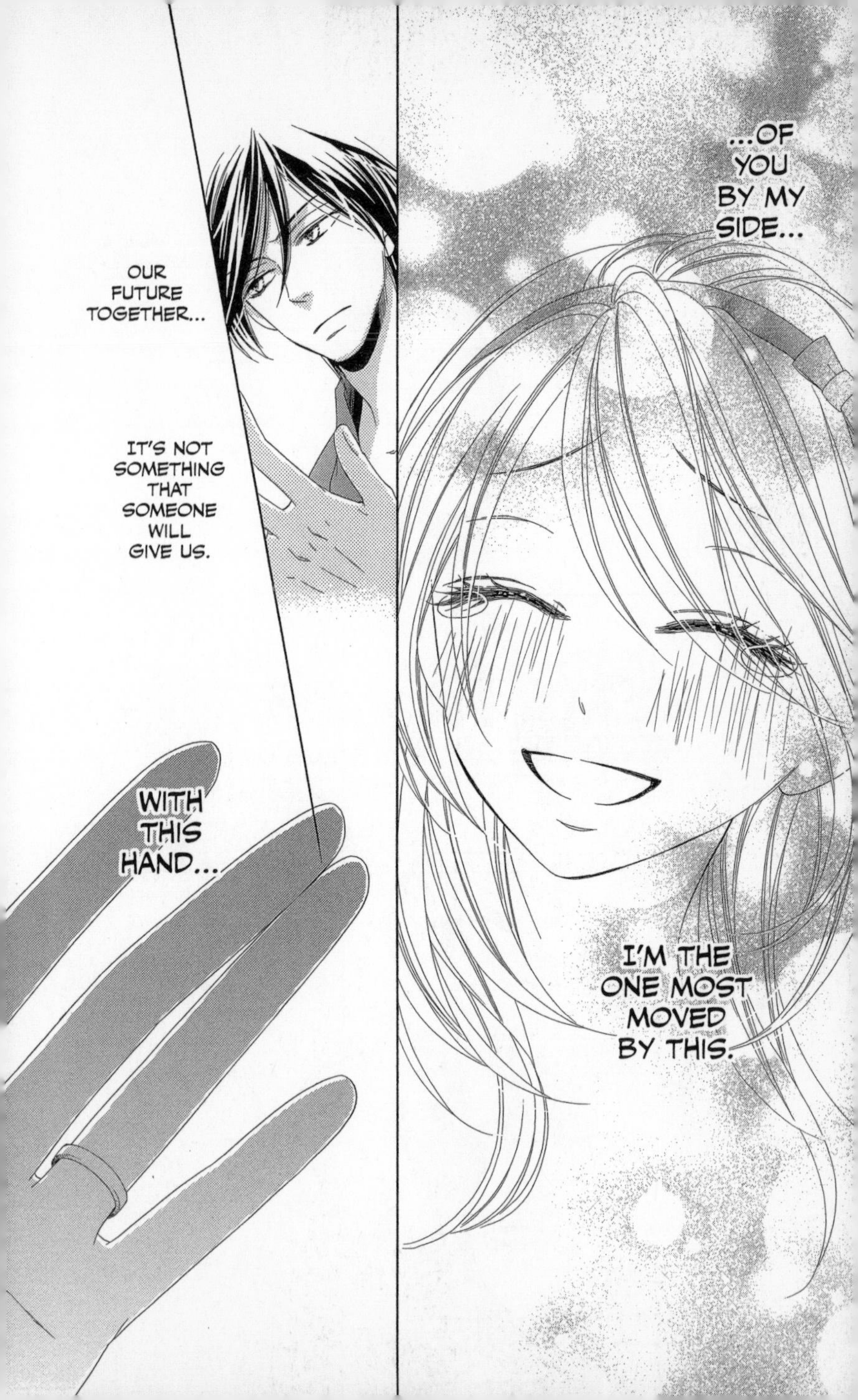
...OF YOU BY MY SIDE...
I'M THE ONE MOST MOVED BY THIS.
OUR FUTURE TOGETHER...
IT'S NOT SOMETHING THAT SOMEONE WILL GIVE US.
WITH THIS HAND...

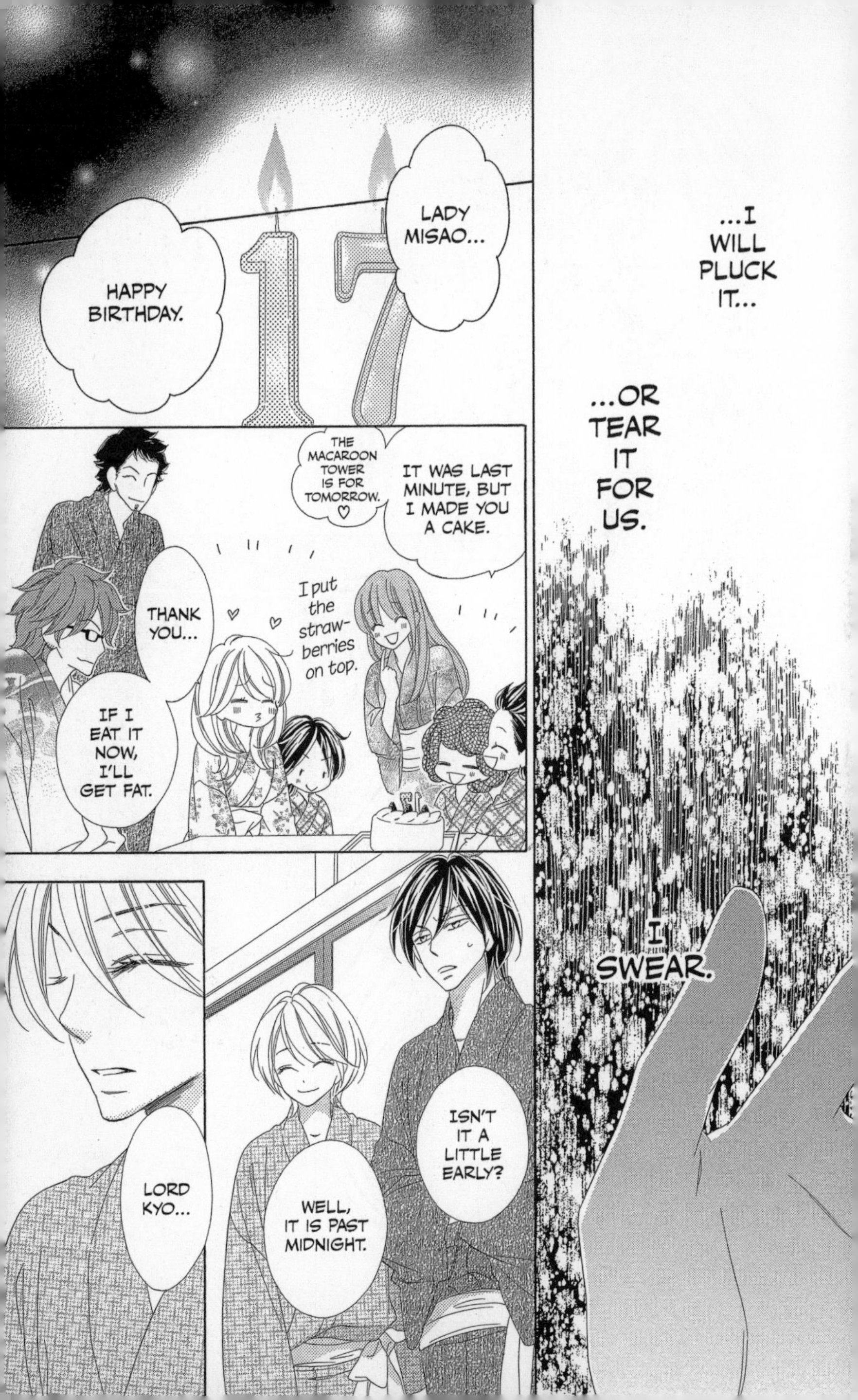
...I WILL PLUCK IT...
...OR TEAR IT FOR US.
I SWEAR.
LADY MISAO...
HAPPY BIRTHDAY.
IT WAS LAST MINUTE, BUT I MADE YOU A CAKE.
THE MACAROON TOWER IS FOR TOMORROW. ♡
I put the straw-berries on top.
THANK YOU...
IF I EAT IT NOW, I'LL GET FAT.
ISN'T IT A LITTLE EARLY?
WELL, IT IS PAST MIDNIGHT.
LORD KYO...

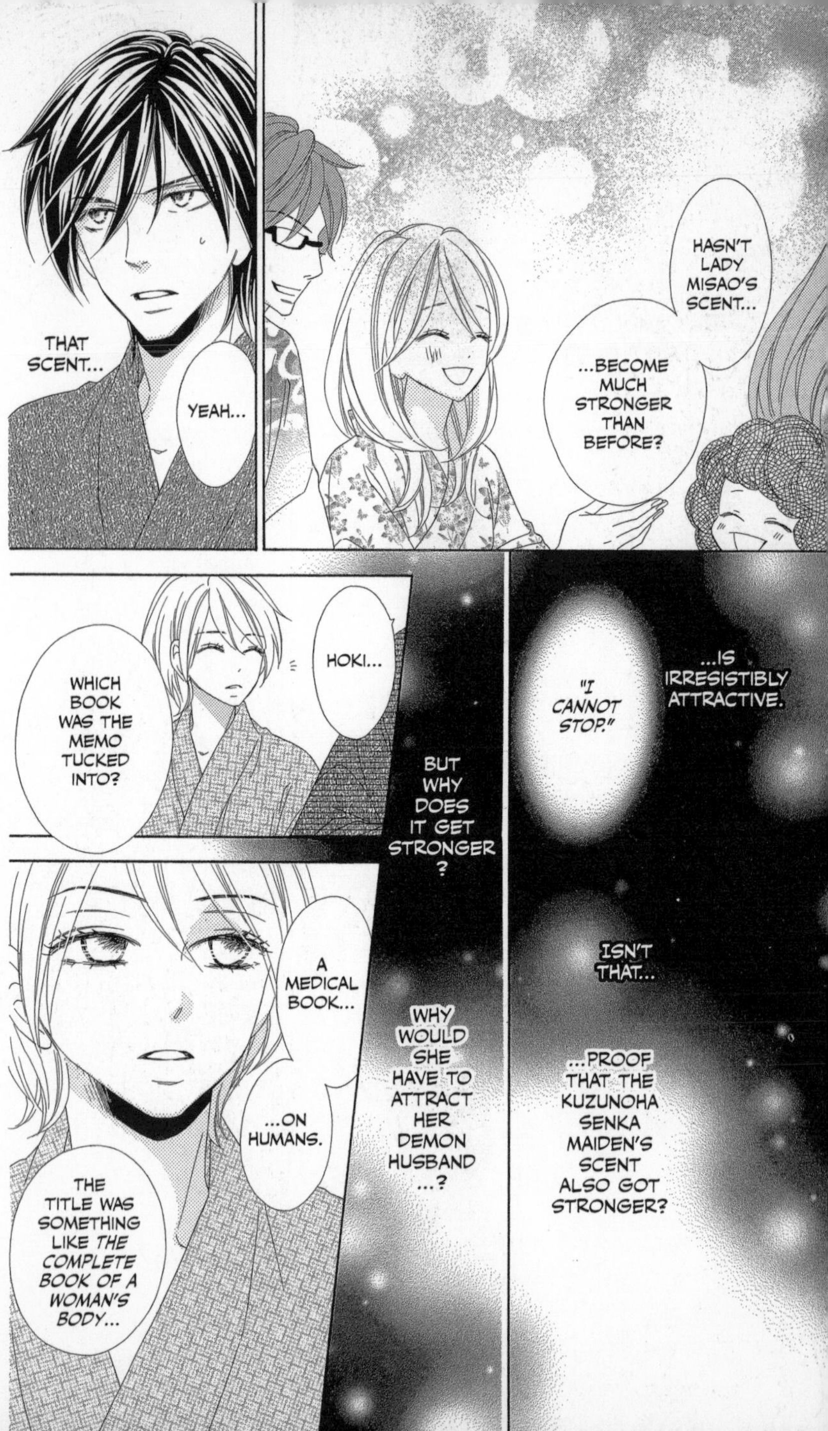
HASN'T LADY MISAO'S SCENT...
...BECOME MUCH STRONGER THAN BEFORE?
THAT SCENT...
YEAH...
...IS IRRESISTIBLY ATTRACTIVE.
"I CANNOT STOP."
ISN'T THAT...
...PROOF THAT THE KUZUNOHA SENKA MAIDEN'S SCENT ALSO GOT STRONGER?
BUT WHY DOES IT GET STRONGER?
WHY WOULD SHE HAVE TO ATTRACT HER DEMON HUSBAND ...?
HOKI...
WHICH BOOK WAS THE MEMO TUCKED INTO?
A MEDICAL BOOK...
...ON HUMANS.
THE TITLE WAS SOMETHING LIKE *THE COMPLETE BOOK OF A WOMAN'S BODY*...

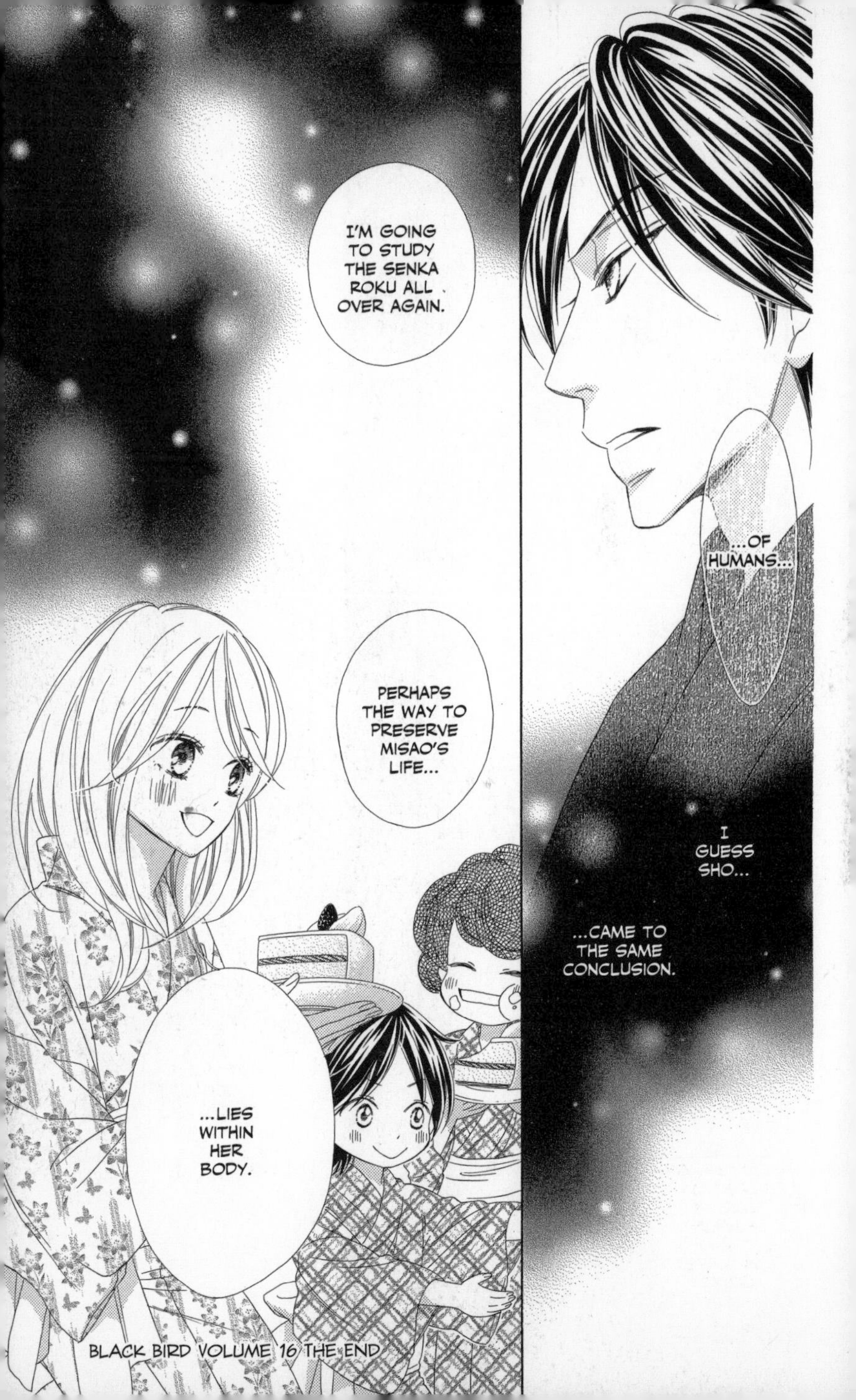
...OF HUMANS...
I GUESS SHO...
...CAME TO THE SAME CONCLUSION.
I'M GOING TO STUDY THE SENKA ROKU ALL OVER AGAIN.
PERHAPS THE WAY TO PRESERVE MISAO'S LIFE...
...LIES WITHIN HER BODY.
BLACK BIRD VOLUME 16 THE END

THE LADY'S BIRTHDAY LAST YEAR.

WELCOME HOME, LORD KYO!

IT'S JUST A SMALL ONE, BUT I HAVE PREPARED A BIRTHDAY PARTY FOR YOU, LADY MISAO. ♡♡

I BAKED A CAKE, TOO.

DO YOU LIKE IT?

OH, WHERE'S...?

WHERE IS LADY MISAO?

Oh.

I GUESS SHE'S GONE HOME TO FRESHEN UP. ♡

SHUT UP...

WHAT'S WITH THIS?!

Lord Kyo and I

Welcome home.

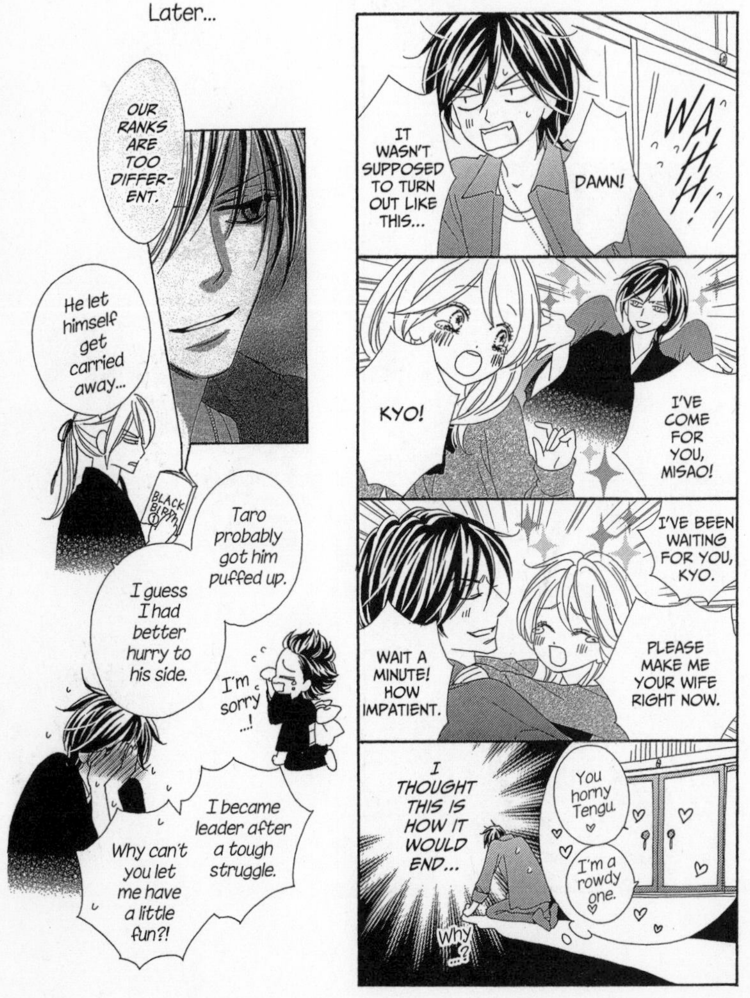
WAHHH!
DAMN!
IT WASN'T SUPPOSED TO TURN OUT LIKE THIS...
I'VE COME FOR YOU, MISAO!
KYO!
I'VE BEEN WAITING FOR YOU, KYO.
PLEASE MAKE ME YOUR WIFE RIGHT NOW.
WAIT A MINUTE! HOW IMPATIENT.
You horny Tengu.
I'm a rowdy one.
I THOUGHT THIS IS HOW IT WOULD END...
Why...?
Later...
OUR RANKS ARE TOO DIFFER-ENT.
He let himself get carried away...
BLACK BIRD 1
Taro probably got him puffed up.
I guess I had better hurry to his side.
I'm sorry...!
I became leader after a tough struggle.
Why can't you let me have a little fun?!

Still,
Taro loves
Lord Kyo.

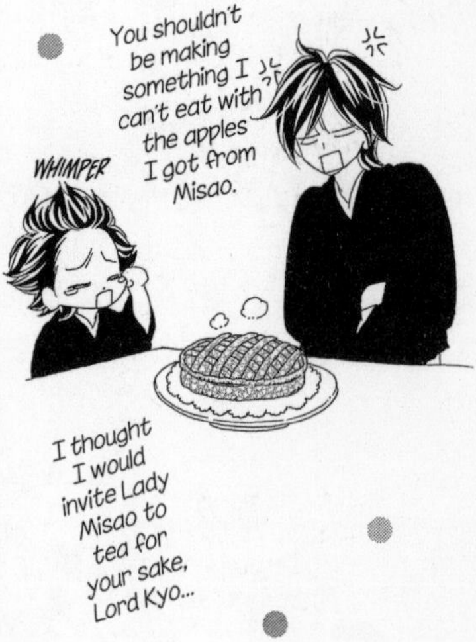
You shouldn't be making something I can't eat with the apples I got from Misao.
WHIMPER
I thought I would invite Lady Misao to tea for your sake, Lord Kyo...

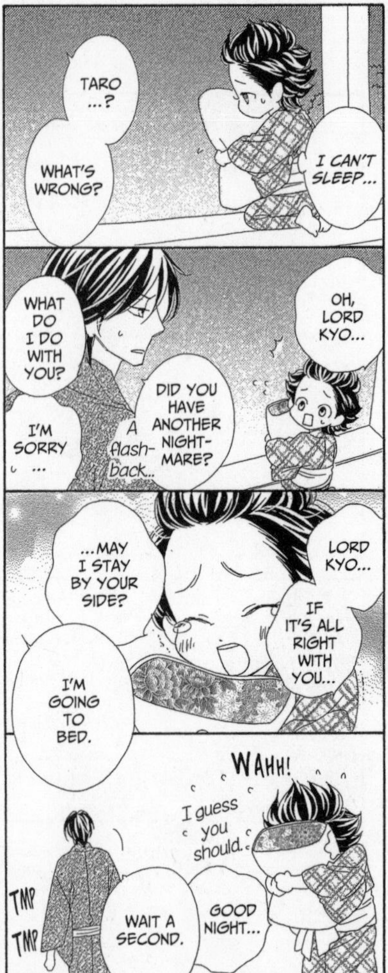
TARO ...?
WHAT'S WRONG?
I CAN'T SLEEP...
OH, LORD KYO...
WHAT DO I DO WITH YOU?
DID YOU HAVE ANOTHER NIGHT-MARE?
A flash-back...
I'M SORRY ...
LORD KYO...
...MAY I STAY BY YOUR SIDE?
IF IT'S ALL RIGHT WITH YOU...
I'M GOING TO BED.
WAHH!
I guess you should.
GOOD NIGHT...
WAIT A SECOND.
TMP
TMP

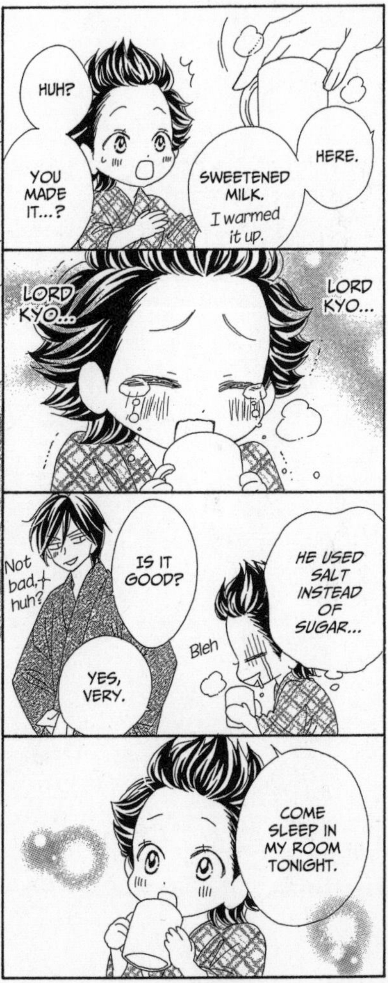
HERE.
SWEETENED MILK. I warmed it up.
HUH?
YOU MADE IT...?
LORD KYO...
LORD KYO...
HE USED SALT INSTEAD OF SUGAR...
IS IT GOOD?
Not bad, huh?
Bleh
YES, VERY.
COME SLEEP IN MY ROOM TONIGHT.

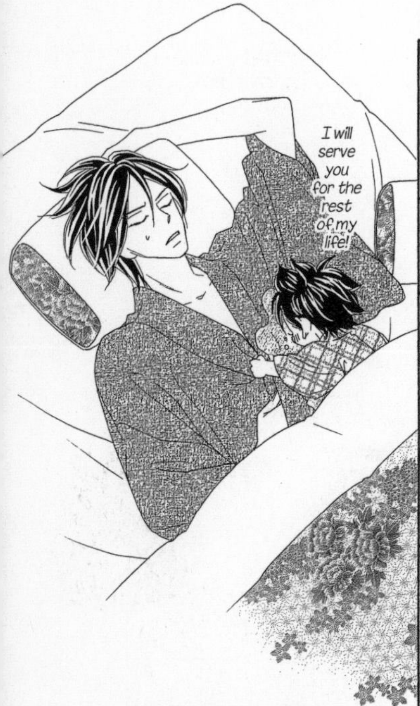
I will serve you for the rest of my life!

Well, I hope we will be able to meet again!
An auspicious day,
May 2012

Kanoko Sakurakouji
桜小路かのこ♥

Kanoko Sakurakouji was born in downtown
Tokyo, and her hobbies include reading,
watching plays, traveling and shopping. Her
debut title, *Raibu ga Hanetara*, ran in *Bessatsu
Shojo Comic* (currently called *Bestucomi)* in
2000, and her 2004 *Bestucomi* title *Backstage
Prince* was serialized in VIZ Media's
Shojo Beat magazine. She won the 54th
Shogakukan Manga Award for *Black Bird*.

BLACK BIRD

VOL. 16
Shojo Beat Edition

Story and Art by KANOKO SAKURAKOUJI

© 2007 Kanoko SAKURAKOUJI/Shogakukan
All rights reserved.
Original Japanese edition "BLACK BIRD" published by SHOGAKUKAN Inc.

TRANSLATION JN Productions
TOUCH-UP ART & LETTERING Gia Cam Luc
DESIGN Amy Martin
EDITOR Pancha Diaz

The rights of the author(s) of the work(s) in this publication
to be so identified have been asserted in accordance with
the Copyright, Designs and Patents Act 1988. A CIP catalogue
record for this book is available from the British Library.

Printed in the U.S.A.

Published by VIZ Media, LLC
P.O. Box 77010
San Francisco, CA 94107

10 9 8 7 6 5 4 3 2 1
First printing, May 2013

www.shojobeat.com   www.viz.com

SURPRISE

You may be reading the wrong way!

It's true: In keeping with the original Japanese comic format, this book reads from right to left—so action, sound effects, and word balloons are completely reversed. This preserves the orientation of the original artwork—plus, it's fun! Check out the diagram shown here to get the hang of things, and then turn to the other side of the book to get started!

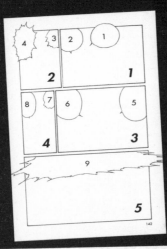